On Competition

The Harvard Business Review Book Series

Designing and Managing Your Career, Edited by Harry Levinson

Ethics in Practice, Edited with an Introduction by Kenneth R. Andrews

Managing Projects and Programs, With a Preface by Norman R. Augustine

Manage People, Not Personnel, With a Preface by Victor H. Vroom

Revolution in Real Time, With a Preface by William G. McGowan

Strategy, Edited with an Introduction by Cynthia A. Montgomery and Michael E. Porter

Leaders on Leadership, Edited with a Preface by Warren Bennis

Seeking Customers, Edited with an Introduction by Benson P. Shapiro and John J. Sviokla

Keeping Customers, Edited with an Introduction by John J. Sviokla and Benson P. Shapiro

The Learning Imperative, Edited with an Introduction by Robert Howard

The Articulate Executive, With a Preface by Fernando Bartolomé

Differences That Work, Edited with an Introduction by Mary C. Gentile

Reach for the Top, Edited with an Introduction by Nancy A. Nichols

Global Strategies, With a Preface by Percy Barnevik

Command Performance, With a Preface by John E. Martin

Manufacturing Renaissance, Edited with an Introduction by Gary P. Pisano and Robert H. Hayes

The Product Development Challenge, Edited with an Introduction by Kim B. Clark and Steven C. Wheelwright

The Evolving Global Economy, Edited with a Preface by Kenichi Ohmae

Managerial Excellence: McKinsey Award Winners from the *Harvard Business Review*, 1980–1994, Foreword by Rajat Gupta, Preface by Nan Stone

Fast Forward, Edited with an Introduction and Epilogue by James Champy and Nitin Nohria

First Person, Edited with an Introduction by Thomas Teal

The Quest for Loyalty, Edited with an Introduction by Frederick F. Reichheld, Foreword by Scott D. Cook

Seeing Differently, Edited with an Introduction by John Seely Brown

Rosabeth Moss Kanter on the Frontiers of Management, by Rosabeth Moss Kanter

Ultimate Rewards, Edited with an Introduction by Stephen Kerr

Peter Drucker on the Profession of Management, by Peter F. Drucker

On Competition, by Michael E. Porter

On Competition

Michael E. Porter

A Harvard Business Review Book

The *Harvard Business Review* articles in this collection are available as individual reprints. Discounts apply to quantity purchases. For information and ordering contact Customer Service, Harvard Business School Publishing, Boston, MA 02163. Telephone: (617) 495-6192, 9 a.m. to 5 p.m. Eastern Time, Monday through Friday. Fax: (617) 495-6985, 24 hours a day.

Library of Congress Cataloging-in-Publication Data

Porter, Michael E., 1947–
    On competition / Michael E. Porter
      p.   cm. — (The Harvard business review book series)
    Includes bibliographical references and index.
    ISBN 0-87584-795-1 (alk. paper)
      1. Competition, International.   2. Comparative advantage (International trade)   3. Industrial policy.   4. Environmental policy.   5. Social policy.   I. Title.   II. Series.
    HF1414.P67   1998
    382'.1042—dc21   98-7643
                                                                            CIP

The paper used in this publication meets the requirements of the American National Standard for Permanence of Paper for Printed Library Materials Z39.48-1984.

Contents

Introduction

COMPETITION HAS INTENSIFIED dramatically over the last decades, in virtually all parts of the world. It was not long ago that competition was all but absent in many countries, and in many industries. Markets were protected, and dominant market positions were the rule. Even where competitors were present rivalry was anything but intense. Stifling government intervention blunted competition, as did outright cartels.

While we now associate the absence of competition with developing economies, it is easy to forget how much change has also taken place in advanced nations. The breakup of cartels and powerful business groups and the intensification of competition had much to do with the remarkable post-World War II economic progress of Germany and Japan. The most competitive Japanese industries today developed under intense internal competition, such as in consumer electronics and cars. Yet the development of large parts of the Japanese economy remains stunted by restraints to competition, in fields such as financial services, chemicals, and retailing.

Even in the United States, the nation with perhaps the strongest commitment to competition during the twentieth century, huge sectors of the economy have until recently been extensively regulated. Telecommunications, transportation, energy, and other sectors all provide vivid examples of the power of competition to unleash innovation and drive unheard of rates of progress.

Very few industries remain in which competition has not intruded on stability and market dominance. No company, and no country, can afford to ignore the need to compete. Every company, and every country, must try to understand and master competition.

The study of competition, in its full richness, has preoccupied me for two decades. While trained as an economist and steeped in the discipline of economic reasoning, I have sought to capture the complexity of what

I

actually happens in companies and industries in a way that both advances theory and brings that theory to life for practitioners. My goal has been to develop both rigorous and useful frameworks for understanding competition that effectively bridge the gap between theory and practice. Striking this balance is challenging, and success sometimes eludes me. My secret weapons: using my ideas in actual practice to expose fuzziness in my thinking, raise new questions, and inform subsequent work.

This book draws together, for the first time in one place, more than a dozen existing and new articles I have written on competition. The articles address competition at multiple levels and in different settings, but a common perspective and set of frameworks unite them.

Most of the articles here first appeared in the *Harvard Business Review*. While I have also published extensively elsewhere, the *Review* has seemed to me the best forum from which to try to influence practitioners. The editors of the *Review* have also provided extraordinary help in making my ideas clearer and more accessible.

I could not resist the opportunity, however, to include two new articles written especially for this collection. One addresses clusters, an important idea introduced in my work on the competitive advantage of nations; the second covers global strategy and reflects my most recent thinking.

The book has three parts. Part I addresses competition and strategy for companies, first at the level of a single industry and then for multibusiness or diversified companies. The structure and evolution of industries, and the ways in which companies gain and sustain competitive advantage in them, lie at the core of competition. A sophisticated understanding of these issues provides the foundation on which all else is built. Diversification, for example, cannot be approached sensibly without linking it directly to competition in individual businesses.

Part II addresses the role of location in competition. Interest in the competitiveness of nations, states, and cities has grown rapidly as competition has spread and intensified. Traditionally, competitiveness has been seen primarily as an issue for governments. Moreover, many theorists claimed that location diminishes in importance as the mobility of capital and technology rises and companies become more global in their activities. The articles in Part II challenge both of these notions. In them, I seek to show how prosperity for both companies and countries depends on the nature of the local environment in which competition takes place. A framework for understanding the influence of location on competition reveals new roles for companies in shaping their competitive context; the need for a new type of relationship between business, government, and other local institutions; and new ways of thinking about government policy. Understanding the influence of location on competition, together with the ideas in Part I, is essential to setting a global strategy.

Part III draws on the frameworks in Parts I and II to address some important societal issues. The environment, urban poverty, health care, and income inequality are normally seen as social problems. As the articles in Part III illustrate, however, each of them is inextricably bound up with economics and, more specifically, with competition. Bringing a sophisticated understanding of competition to bear is not only revealing but offers concrete, workable approaches to solutions.

Competition and Strategy: Core Concepts

The collection begins with "How Competitive Forces Shape Strategy" (1979), the oldest article and my initial effort to influence practitioners. This article, applying the perspectives of industrial economics to strategy, introduces a systematic framework for understanding the structure of industries and how they change.[1] The performance of any company in a business can be divided into two parts: the first attributable to the average performance of all competitors in its industry and the second to whether the company is an above- or below-average performer in its industry. This article concentrates on the first part, that is, on the large and sustained differences in the average profitability of industries. Using the "five-forces framework," consisting of the bargaining power of buyers, the bargaining power of suppliers, the threat of new entry, the threat of substitutes, and the intensity of rivalry, I describe the determinants of long-term industry profitability and ways that companies can influence them.

"What Is Strategy?" addresses the second part of the profitability equation: the profitability differences among competitors. I had tackled the subject of positioning, or the creation of an advantaged approach to competing in an industry previously,[2] but "What Is Strategy?," first published in 1996, contains my latest thinking. In this article, I argue that a firm achieves superior profitability in its industry by attaining either higher prices or lower costs than rivals. The sources of these price or cost differences among competitors can in turn be divided into two types: those due to differences in operational effectiveness, or attainment of best practice, and those due to differences in strategic positioning. Both operational effectiveness and strategy can best be understood by dividing the firms into activities, the discrete economic processes firms perform in competing in any business. Activities are defined more narrowly than are traditional functions. I introduced a framework for systematically examining activities and their connection to competitive advantage, called the value chain, in my book *Competitive Advantage.*

All companies must continually improve operational effectiveness in their activities, but sustainable performance differences will most often depend on having a distinctive strategic position. Strategy differences rest on differences in activities, such as the way companies go about order processing, assembly, product design, training, and so on. Strategies are sustainable because of tradeoffs, or choices that firms make to offer certain types of value but sacrifice others. Both competitive advantage and tradeoffs depend not only on individual activities but on the fit among numerous activities.

The first two articles in Part I provide the core analytical frameworks for developing strategy at the level of an individual business: industry structure and competitive advantage/activities. The next two articles in Part I—"How Information Gives You Competitive Advantage" and "End-Game Strategies for Declining Industries"—apply and extend these core frameworks to address important competitive strategy questions. "How Information Gives You Competitive Advantage" (1985) addresses the role of information technology in affecting competition. In it, Victor Millar and I suggest that information technology plays a role in both industry structure and competitive advantage. The five-forces framework provides the structure for analyzing the industry effect, while activities and the value chain provide the structure for examining the competitive advantage effect. Although this article was written more than ten years ago, the issues are still current. Today's concerns include the role of the Internet, new computer-aided design and manufacturing technologies, and enterprisewide information systems. The tools in this article provide an approach to understanding the competitive significance of the latest generation of information systems and software.

In "End-Game Strategies in Declining Industries" (1983), Kathryn Harrigan and I apply industry structure thinking and competitive advantage thinking to industries undergoing sustained decline due to the emergence of a superior substitute product, a shrinking customer group, or for other reasons. While industry decline is by no means inevitable, this article tackles the question of how to think strategically about competing in an industry facing decline. The tools of industry structure help firms to predict whether an industry can remain profitable as it gets smaller and whether continued participation is desirable. The logic of competitive advantage helps firms to think about what profitable position they can occupy in the shrinking industry. In any economy, a significant number of industries will always be declining, just as some will always be emerging. My observation has been that too often companies, to their detriment, suspend strategic thinking when they find themselves in declining businesses.

The first four articles in Part I address strategy in a single business, or what I call *competitive strategy*. The individual industry is the core level of strategy, because it is at this level that industry profitability is determined and competitive advantage is either won or lost. The article "From Competitive Advantage to Corporate Strategy" (1987) addresses strategy at the other important level—the overall strategy of a corporation diversified into more than one business. I call this *corporate strategy*. Many accounts treat diversification as a distinct question, separate from competitive strategy. This false dichotomy, however, starts to explain the dismal performance of most companies in diversifying over the last three decades, a result vividly illustrated by the data presented in my article. Bad things often happen to companies that attempt to separate their thinking about diversification from their strategies for competing in their various businesses.

"From Competitive Advantage to Corporate Strategy" takes a different approach. It argues that while corporate strategy differs from competitive strategy, the two must be intimately connected. Corporate strategy, like competitive strategy, involves questions both of industry and competitive advantage. At the level of the corporation, however, the questions become somewhat different. From an industry perspective, corporate strategy is concerned with the choice of industries in which a company should compete and how it should enter them. From a competitive advantage perspective, the central question at the corporate level becomes how being part of the overall corporation enhances (rather than undermines) the competitive advantage of individual business units. "From Competitive Advantage to Corporate Strategy" explores these issues, making use of the concepts of industry structure and the value chain. It shows how the notion of activities can be used to understand the strategic logic of diversification, and how corporate strategy must be linked to organization and management practices.

Companies have not lost their taste for diversification since this article was first published, and the diversification track record in the 1990s remains problematic. Notions of core competencies and critical resources have replaced discredited portfolio models in guiding much diversification, but too often the results differ little. These new ideas are imprecise and disconnected from relative cost and differentiation. Experience has shown that diversification not closely tied to sustainable competitive advantage at the business unit level often destroys economic value.

The Competitiveness of Locations

The core concepts of competitive and corporate strategy provide the foundation for examining any competitive situation. With ever increasing frequency, however, competition crosses borders. Firms compete across geographic locations with national, regional, and global strategies. Developing international (or cross locational) strategy requires two new sets of ideas. The first concerns the role of location in competition. As firms begin to compete across borders, they gain the ability to locate activities anywhere. International strategy, then, must involve an understanding of how location affects competitive advantage. The second new issue raised by international competition is the opportunity for firms to gain competitive advantage through coordinating activities across borders in regional or global networks.

Part II begins with the issue of location. In "The Competitive Advantage of Nations" (1990), I develop a new theory of the competitiveness of nations, states, and other geographic areas. Most treatments of competitiveness have concentrated either on macroeconomic policies (government budget deficits, monetary policy, opening of markets, or privatization) or on comparative advantages due to endowments of inputs such as labor, natural resources, and capital. My article takes a very different approach, arguing that the competitiveness of locations is primarily rooted in the nature of the business environment they offer firms. Access to labor, capital, and natural resources does not determine prosperity, because these have become widely accessible. Rather, competitiveness arises from the productivity with which firms in a location can use inputs to produce valuable goods and services. Moreover, the productivity and prosperity possible in a given location depend not on what industries its firms compete in, but on how they compete. Traditional distinctions between high tech and low tech, or between manufacturing and services, have little relevance in an economy in which virtually all industries can employ advanced technologies and high skill levels to achieve high levels of productivity.

The roots of productivity lie in the national and regional environment for competition. In "The Competitive Advantage of Nations," I capture the effect of location on competition in a framework graphically depicted as a diamond made up of four primary facets: factor conditions, demand conditions, the context for strategy and rivalry, and related and supporting industries. The diamond metaphor has become common in referring to my theory. Government policies can influence all four parts of the diamond positively or negatively. "The Competitive Advantage of Nations" explores these sources of competitiveness, how they change, and the implications for governments and companies. Diamond theory is not only a tool for managers but also a microeconomic-based approach to economic development for governments that is closely tied to actual competition.

"Clusters and Competition: New Agendas for Companies, Governments, and Institutions," one of the two articles written especially for this collection, explores one of the most important ideas in my overall competitiveness theory—the concept of clusters. Clusters are geographic concentrations of firms, suppliers, related industries, and specialized institutions that occur in a particular field in a nation, state, or city. This new article pulls together what I have learned about clusters both from research and in practice, in terms of cluster theory, the role of clusters in competition, and their implications for government policy, company and institutional behavior. Clusters are a prominent feature on the landscape of every advanced economy, and cluster formation is an essential ingredient of economic development. Clusters offer a new way to think about economies and economic development; new roles for business, government, and institutions; and new ways to structure the business-government or business-institution relationship. Dozens of cluster initiatives have sprung up in many parts of the world, and this article summarizes some of the learning gleaned from both advanced and developing economies.

"How Global Companies Win Out" (1982) moves from the influence of location to the role of corporate global networks. In it, Thomas Hout, Eileen Rudden, and I describe some of the basic characteristics of a global company and why a truly global company is more than just a company operating in many nations. The article outlines a number of ways in which coordination across nations enhances competitive advantage, illustrated with three case studies of prominent global competitors.

The final article in Part II, "Competing Across Locations: Enhancing Competitive Advantage through a Global Strategy," is the second article newly written for this collection. It brings together the two dimensions of international strategy—location and global networks. The concept of activities, so important to understanding competitive advantage in general terms, provides the basic framework for international strategy as well. When competing across borders, firms can spread activities to multiple locations to harness their locational advantages, while coordinating among dispersed activities in a variety of ways to harness network advantages.

"Competing Across Locations" develops the implications of this framework for global strategy in a particular business. Global strategy taps the innovation advantages of locating headquarters or "home-base" activities in cluster locations while spreading other activities to other locations to source low cost inputs and gain access to foreign markets. Coordination transforms this array of dispersed activities into a global network. Earlier thinking about global strategy, which focused only on globalness and networks, was clearly too simple. This new article aims to take global-strategy thinking to the next level. It also makes clear that global strategy is just a special case of the more general issue of competing across geography. The same framework can be applied to a local producer striving to become national.

Competitive Solutions to Societal Problems

A deep understanding of domestic and international competition offers powerful insights into a wide variety of societal problems. Part III begins with an article on the environment, "Green and Competitive: Ending the Stalemate" (1995), written with Claas van der Linde. Environmental improvement is often seen as at odds with economic competitiveness because environmental standards can impose costs on business. This view, however, derives from a static and oversimplified view of competition. Drawing on my work on competitiveness, "Green and Competitive" suggests that "environment versus competitiveness" is a false dichotomy.

In the new thinking, competitiveness arises from increasing productivity in the use of resources. Productivity improvements must be neverending. Seen in this light, virtually all forms of corporate pollution are manifestations of economic waste; for example, resources used inefficiently or valuable raw materials discarded. Improving environmental performance through better technology and methods, then, will often increase productivity and offset or partially offset the cost of the improvements. This implies that environmental regulation should focus on reducing the transactions cost of the regulation itself, which adds neither environmental nor economic value, while facilitating product and process innovation. Corporations should see environmental improvement not as a regulatory matter but as an essential part of improving productivity and competitiveness.

"The Competitive Advantage of the Inner City" (1995) addresses the economic distress of America's urban cores. Urban poverty has been seen primarily as a social problem, and proposed solutions have focused on meeting the pressing human needs of inner-city residents. But the problem is equally an economic one. Without accessible jobs and opportunities for creating wealth, social investment will be insufficient to achieve lasting benefits. Moreover, while there have been efforts at inner-city economic development, too many have tried to defy the laws of the marketplace. Based on the presumption that inner cities face many competitive disadvantages as business locations, "economic" development has often consisted largely of creating non-profits and relocating government buildings. Alternatively, large subsidies have been used in attempts to influence companies' location choices.

Rather than concentrate on competitive disadvantages, "The Competitive Advantage of the Inner City" turns received wisdom on its head. In it, I argue that only by focusing on the competitive advantages of inner-city locations will economic development be sustainable. Applying my broader work on competitiveness to inner cities, I outline the advantages of inner cities, which are manifested in the many hundreds and even thousands of successful inner-city–based companies in major cities all across the country. An approach that builds on these advantages while tackling frontally the competitive disadvantages of inner cities as a business location offers a new model for addressing our most distressed communities. There is nothing inevitable about the decline of cities if we shift our focus from reducing poverty to creating jobs, income, and wealth.

Health care is another pressing social concern facing the nation, where high costs and the large number of people without health insurance have triggered a national debate on how best to restructure the system. In "Making Competition in Health Care Work" (1994), Elizabeth Teisberg, Gregory Brown, and I argue that cost cutting and managed care will not provide a sustainable solution. Only through continued innovation in medical treatment and service delivery methods can the cost of health care be controlled without rationing care or eroding its quality.

The article explores how faulty incentives produced a form of competition that improved quality but drove up cost. The recent revolution in managed care and the move to capitation has skewed incentives in the other direction, toward rationing care and undermining quality. Further, this new structure has also created barriers to innovation. In "Making Competition in Health Care Work," we outline a new strategy, calling for modified incentives, widely available information on treatment outcomes, and a renewed orientation toward innovation.

The final article in Part III, "Capital Disadvantage: America's Failing Capital Investment System" (1992), takes on the controversial issue of how American capital markets and corporate governance practices affect the long-run prosperity of our economy. At first glance, this may seem obvious: America's capital markets, the most efficient in the world, contribute greatly to the productivity of American industry. A deeper look, however, reveals a more complex relationship. Clearly, the American system fosters efficient use of capital, as the relentless pressures for profit improvement attest. These pressures have created a near-term advantage for American industry, especially given the barriers and impediments to efficiency improvement in Europe and Japan.

The question remains, however, whether the American system as currently structured fosters the appropriate rate of investment in the long term, in such things, for example, as advanced capital goods, R&D, market development, and skills training. Without high rates of investment in capital per worker and in training, not only may companies be unable to sustain their competitive advantages but less-skilled workers will face stagnant prospects and increasing inequality.

Rapid stock trading, a preoccupation with near-term stock-price appreciation, along with a lack of incentives for investors to monitor long-term company prospects raise questions about the alignment between stock-market valuation and the sources of companies' competitive advantage. Interestingly, the legendary American venture-capital system has a very different structure than that of the mainstream capital markets, with patient investors, active monitoring, and long-term ownership of large, controlling equity stakes.

In "Capital Disadvantage," I draw on research by other scholars and lay out the case for why the American capital-allocation system may outperform those of other countries in some respects, while still falling well short of the ideal in other respects. The problems now afflicting Europe and Asia make it tempting to declare the American system the winner. Anemic economic growth in the United States, coupled with rising inequality, however, suggest that the need remains for serious scrutiny of our system.[3]

The articles in Part III represent the beginnings of a new integration of economic and social policy. Traditionally, economic and social policy have been seen as distinct and often competing. Economic policy concerns itself with creating wealth by providing incentives, encouraging savings and investment, and minimizing government intervention. Social policy has concentrated on providing for public education and other human needs, aiding disadvantaged groups, protecting citizens through various forms of regulation, and, recently, preserving the environment. Social policy has relied heavily on market intervention, subsidies, and redistribution.

Social policymakers tend to see the market as the problem and consequently attempt to modify its outcomes. Economic policymakers tend to see government intervention as the problem. Social advocacy groups often view business as the problem. Businesses see social goals as outside their realm of interest and view a strong economy, unshackled by counterproductive intrusions, as the best social program.

These old dichotomies are false ones and represent an increasingly obsolete perspective. Social and economic goals are not inherently conflicting in the long run. A productive and growing economy requires educated, safe, healthy, decently housed workers who are motivated by a sense of opportunity. Economic competitiveness need not be traded away to preserve the environment, because corporate pollution results from unproductive use of resources. The only real conflict lies in means. Efforts to advance social goals via redistribution, subsidies, and market distortion usually fail and inflict in the process steep economic costs, as illustrated in my articles on the environment and the inner city. Similarly, efforts to boost profits at the expense of worker training, motivation, and a sense of well being will fail in the long run.

Instead of such flawed approaches, we need a new one based on harmonizing and pursuing simultaneously economic and social goals. This can be done through a central focus on innovation and competition—working through the market rather than against it. Social programs must prepare individuals to enter and succeed in the market system, not insulate them from it. Efforts to address social issues, such as pollution and the high costs of health care, must harness innovation and competition to address underlying causes, rather than attempt to shift the costs onto some other group within society.

The articles in Part III illustrate these principles, using as illustrations health care, the environment, and urban poverty. The same principles, however, can be applied to many social issues, including social security, education, or housing. Fannie Mae, for example, has done as much as any other social program to bring affordable housing to people with low incomes while still itself making a profit. By reducing the cost of financing and by finding creative ways to assess creditworthiness without resorting to traditional metrics (such as income level and large required down payments), Fannie Mae has expanded home ownership in a sustainable way, which encourages other low-income people who aspire to home ownership to better manage their finances.

"Capital Disadvantage" connects closely to these issues, as well. It shows how artificial short-term profit pressures can lead companies to make choices that compromise their own and society's long-term interests. Hence, scrutiny of our capital-market system has an important role in the creation of a context for bringing together social and economic goals.

Expanding Frontiers

As I hope is evident, my work rests on a core set of ideas about competition and contains a consistent perspective. Yet my ideas continually evolve and have broadened over time to encompass new dimensions. Industry structure, an activity-based view of competitive advantage, and my more recent theory of the role of location in competition represent the three core frameworks that cut across all my work. My understanding of each one and of the connections among them is continually being deepened and extended.

Exploration of one question concerning competition and strategy has suggested the next question, and that one the next. Thinking about competition and strategy in a single industry, for example, led me to an interest in the influence of diversification on industry competition. Early work on positioning provided the impetus for the activity-based view of the firm. Thinking about activities led me to puzzle over the influence of globalization, which in turn raised the question of how location mattered. A focus on location forced me to confront the role of government in competition, not just companies. My work on location also triggered an interest in economic development, urban poverty, and environmental policy.

Over time, I have been led to explore new units of analysis. My initial work stressed *industry* at a time when the firm as the unit of analysis was dominant. Building on thinking about the firm as a whole, my subsequent work stressed the *activity*. Building on the focus on industry, my later work added consideration of the *cluster* and the *geographic location*.

As each new question arose and each new set of ideas developed, I have been led to re-examine what came before. The activity-based view of the firm caused me to refine and extend my earlier thinking about generic strategies. My recent work on distinguishing operational effectiveness and strategy ("What Is Strategy?") both builds on earlier work and informs it. The new theory has deepened my understanding of positioning, and linked it more tightly to activities. Through this new work, I have also extended activity theory through the concepts of tradeoffs and fit.

The distinction between operational effectiveness and positioning also sheds new light on a wide variety of other issues. Financial market pressures, for example, can be desirable motivators of operational improvement, but often lead companies to compromise their unique strategic positions by pursuing growth in segments where they lack any real advantage. Another example of the distinction is in evaluating the role of information technology in competition. Much of the new information technology is being directed at improving best practice—operational effectiveness—rather than enabling unique positioning. The lurking danger with the new generation of IT tools, however, is that too many companies will apply them in the same way. This will have the unwitting effect of homogenizing competition, undermining customer choice, and triggering mutually destructive rivalry.

The research on location has opened up important new connections as well. The most obvious one is in an enriched conception of global strategy. Location, however, clearly plays a role in industry structure and competitive advantage, including helping to define feasible forms of competing. The state of the diamond and the extent of the cluster can raise or lower barriers to entry into an industry, the power of customers and suppliers, and the mix and threat of substitutes. Locational factors also influence the forms of rivalry that are feasible in a nation or state, ranging from imitation and price competition in developing economies to innovation and differentiation in advanced ones. In developing economies, for example, locational deficiencies mean that local firms face great difficulties in attempting to enter attractive industries and in avoiding destructive price rivalry. At the same time, government intervention and a shortage of capital often suspend competitive forces and preserve monopolies.

Location also strongly influences competitive advantage and the types of strategies firms can choose and successfully implement. The state of local infrastructure, the skills of local employees, and other diamond conditions directly influence operational effectiveness. Diamond conditions, such as local demand sophistication, unique skill pools, and the local presence of related industries, can also shape the types and variety of strategic positions chosen, in terms of customer segments selected or product varieties stressed. The business environment at locations not only influences the choice of strategy, but also the ability to carry out strategies. At the level of activities, it is also evident that access to many of the resources, capabilities, and skills that contribute significantly to a firm's uniqueness depends on the nature of the local environment.

Location also bears on corporate strategy. Diamond conditions influence the types of corporate value added that truly affect competitive advantage. In developing countries, value is created by a corporate parent's ability to provide capital access and to introduce professional management. This helps explain the prevalence of conglomerate groups in many emerging economies.[4] In more advanced economies, portfolio management adds little value, and other approaches to diversification are needed; here, diamond conditions affect the kinds of synergies that are feasible.

One connection between location and my earlier ideas creates an apparent puzzle. The industry-structure framework shows how powerful buyers and suppliers and intense rivalry can depress profitability, while diamond theory suggests that local rivalry, demanding customers, and sophisticated local suppliers foster competitiveness by stimulating and supporting high productivity and rapid innovation. How can these be reconciled? First, we must distinguish between the industry in a single location and the industry globally. The presence of a favorable diamond in one location, including intense local rivalry, allows firms based there to achieve collectively a higher level of productivity and also to progress faster than firms based in other locations. Profitability in the local market may be lower, but the global profitability of firms based there will be superior. Another way of making the same point is to recognize that diamond conditions will affect the ability of firms based in a location, on average, to gain a competitive advantage over firms based elsewhere. Average industry profitability globally will be dependent on average industry structure globally.

The work on location illuminates the importance of dynamic improvement to competitive advantage. It shows how rapid upgrading and innovation is needed to create and sustain advantage in advanced economies. In contrast, the industry-structure and activity frameworks did not focus on change; rather, they apply at any point in time. My early investigations were heavily cross-sectional (for example, answering such questions as why some industries are more profitable than others at a given time or why one rival is more profitable than another). These were the logical first questions. My recent work on operational effectiveness and positioning, however, begins to bridge positioning, location, and dynamic improvement. It stresses the necessity of continual improvement in operational effectiveness but emphasizes the need for continuity in strategy, along with the concomitant need for relentless improvement in the means for carrying out strategy. Both operational effectiveness and strategy, however, are influenced by location.

Finally, a deeper understanding of competition, enriched by work on location, has opened up a whole new frontier for exploring the connection between competition and social issues. I am earlier in this process, which is continuing.

New connections remain to be discovered, and my learning about competition is unlikely to stop anytime soon. One unchanging certainty, however, is that competition will continue to be both evolving, unsettling, and the source of much of our prosperity. If this collection could convey only one message, I would want it to be a sense of the staggering power of competition to make things better—both for companies and for society.

NOTES

1. This article became the lead chapter of my book *Competitive Strategy: Techniques for Analyzing Industries and Competitors* (New York: Free Press, 1980).

2. For my earlier work on positioning, see *Competitive Strategy,* Chapter 2, and *Competitive Advantage: Creating and Sustaining Superior Performance* (New York: Free Press, 1985).

3. In 1995, I co-chaired a bipartisan group of business, financial, and government leaders that further explored some of these issues. Its report, "Lifting All Boats," is a good companion piece to my article. See "Lifting All Boats: Increasing the Payoff from Private Investment in the U.S. Economy," a report of the Capital Allocation Subcouncil (Robert Denham and Michael Porter, co-chairmen) to the Competitiveness Policy Council, September 1995.

4. These and other aspects of corporate groups in developing economies are explored in T. Khanna and K. Palepu, "Why Focused Strategies May Be Wrong for Emerging Markets," *Harvard Business Review* 75, no. 4 (1997): 41–51.

Part I   Competition and Strategy: Core Concepts

CHAPTER 1

How Competitive
Forces Shape
Strategy

Michael E. Porter

─────────────

THE ESSENCE OF STRATEGY FORMULATION
is coping with competition. Yet it is easy to view competition too
narrowly and too pessimistically. While one sometimes hears executives
complaining to the contrary, intense competition in an industry is neither coincidence nor bad luck.

Moreover, in the fight for market share, competition is not manifested
only in the other players. Rather, competition in an industry is rooted
in its underlying economics, and competitive forces exist that go well
beyond the established combatants in a particular industry. Customers,
suppliers, potential entrants, and substitute products are all competitors that may be more or less prominent or active depending on the
industry.

The state of competition in an industry depends on five basic forces,
which are diagrammed in Figure 1.1. The collective strength of these
forces determines the ultimate profit potential of an industry. It ranges
from *intense* in industries like tires, metal cans, and steel, where no
company earns spectacular returns on investment, to *mild* in industries
like oil field services and equipment, soft drinks, and toiletries, where
there is room for quite high returns.

In the economists' "perfectly competitive" industry, jockeying for
position is unbridled and entry to the industry very easy. This kind

March–April 1979

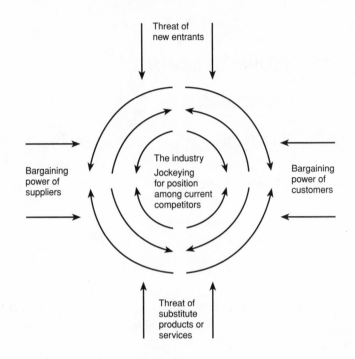

Figure 1.1   Forces Governing Competition in an Industry

of industry structure, of course, offers the worst prospect for longrun profitability. The weaker the forces collectively, however, the greater the opportunity for superior performance.

Whatever their collective strength, the corporate strategist's goal is to find a position in the industry where his or her company can best defend itself against these forces or can influence them in its favor. The collective strength of the forces may be painfully apparent to all the antagonists; but to cope with them, the strategist must delve below the surface and analyze the sources of each. For example, what makes the industry vulnerable to entry? What determines the bargaining power of suppliers?

Knowledge of these underlying sources of competitive pressure provides the groundwork for a strategic agenda of action. They highlight the critical strengths and weaknesses of the company, animate the positioning of the company in its industry, clarify the areas where strategic changes may yield the greatest payoff, and highlight the places where industry trends promise to hold the greatest significance as either opportunities or threats. Understanding these sources also proves to be of help in considering areas for diversification.

Contending Forces

The strongest competitive force or forces determine the profitability of an industry and so are of greatest importance in strategy formulation. For example, even a company with a strong position in an industry unthreatened by potential entrants will earn low returns if it faces a superior or a lower-cost substitute product—as the leading manufacturers of vacuum tubes and coffee percolators have learned to their sorrow. In such a situation, coping with the substitute product becomes the number one strategic priority.

Different forces take on prominence, of course, in shaping competition in each industry. In the ocean-going tanker industry the key force is probably the buyers (the major oil companies), while in tires it is powerful OEM buyers coupled with tough competitors. In the steel industry the key forces are foreign competitors and substitute materials.

Every industry has an underlying structure, or a set of fundamental economic and technical characteristics, that gives rise to these competitive forces. The strategist, wanting to position his or her company to cope best with its industry environment or to influence that environment in the company's favor, must learn what makes the environment tick.

This view of competition pertains equally to industries dealing in services and to those selling products. To avoid monotony in this article, I refer to both products and services as "products." The same general principles apply to all types of business.

A few characteristics are critical to the strength of each competitive force. I shall discuss them in this section.

THREAT OF ENTRY

New entrants to an industry bring new capacity, the desire to gain market share, and often substantial resources. Companies diversifying through acquisition into the industry from other markets often leverage their resources to cause a shake-up, as Philip Morris did with Miller beer.

The seriousness of the threat of entry depends on the barriers present and on the reaction from existing competitors that entrants can expect. If barriers to entry are high and newcomers can expect sharp retaliation from the entrenched competitors, obviously the newcomers will not pose a serious threat of entering.

There are six major sources of barriers to entry:

1. *Economies of scale.* These economies deter entry by forcing the aspirant either to come in on a large scale or to accept a cost disadvantage. Scale economies in production, research, marketing, and service are probably the key barriers to entry in the mainframe computer industry, as Xerox and GE sadly discovered. Economies of scale can also act as hurdles in distribution, utilization of the sales force, financing, and nearly any other part of a business.

2. *Product differentiation.* Brand identification creates a barrier by forcing entrants to spend heavily to overcome customer loyalty. Advertising, customer service, being first in the industry, and product differences are among the factors fostering brand identification. It is perhaps the most important entry barrier in soft drinks, over-the-counter drugs, cosmetics, investment banking, and public accounting. To create high fences around their businesses, brewers couple brand identification with economies of scale in production, distribution, and marketing.

3. *Capital requirements.* The need to invest large financial resources in order to compete creates a barrier to entry, particularly if the capital is required for unrecoverable expenditures in up-front advertising or R&D. Capital is necessary not only for fixed facilities but also for customer credit, inventories, and absorbing start-up losses. While major corporations have the financial resources to invade almost any industry, the huge capital requirements in certain fields, such as computer manufacturing and mineral extraction, limit the pool of likely entrants.

4. *Cost disadvantages independent of size.* Entrenched companies may have cost advantages not available to potential rivals, no matter what their size and attainable economies of scale. These advantages can stem from the effects of the learning curve (and of its first cousin, the experi-

ence curve), proprietary technology, access to the best raw materials sources, assets purchased at preinflation prices, government subsidies, or favorable locations. Sometimes cost advantages are legally enforceable, as they are through patents. (For an analysis of the much-discussed experience curve as a barrier to entry, see the insert, "The Experience Curve as an Entry Barrier.")

5. *Access to distribution channels.* The newcomer on the block must, of course, secure distribution of its product or service. A new food product, for example, must displace others from the supermarket shelf via price breaks, promotions, intense selling efforts, or some other means. The more limited the wholesale or retail channels are and the more that existing competitors have these tied up, obviously the tougher that entry into the industry will be. Sometimes this barrier is so high that, to surmount it, a new contestant must create its own distribution channels, as Timex did in the watch industry in the 1950s.

6. *Government policy.* The government can limit or even foreclose entry to industries with such controls as license requirements and limits on access to raw materials. Regulated industries like trucking, liquor retailing, and freight forwarding are noticeable examples; more subtle government restrictions operate in fields like ski-area development and coal mining. The government also can play a major indirect role by affecting entry barriers through controls such as air and water pollution standards and safety regulations.

The potential rival's expectations about the reaction of existing competitors also will influence its decision on whether to enter. The company is likely to have second thoughts if incumbents have previously lashed out at new entrants or if:

- The incumbents possess substantial resources to fight back, including excess cash and unused borrowing power, productive capacity, or clout with distribution channels and customers.

- The incumbents seem likely to cut prices because of a desire to keep market shares or because of industrywide excess capacity.

• Industry growth is slow, affecting its ability to absorb the new arrival and probably causing the financial performance of all the parties involved to decline.

Changing Conditions. From a strategic standpoint there are two important additional points to note about the threat of entry.

The Experience Curve as an Entry Barrier

In recent years, the experience curve has become widely discussed as a key element of industry structure. According to this concept, unit costs in many manufacturing industries (some dogmatic adherents say in all manufacturing industries) as well as in some service industries decline with "experience," or a particular company's cumulative volume of production. (The experience curve, which encompasses many factors, is a broader concept than the better-known learning curve, which refers to the efficiency achieved over a period of time by workers through much repetition.)

The causes of the decline in unit costs are a combination of elements, including economies of scale, the learning curve for labor, and capital-labor substitution. The cost decline creates a barrier to entry because new competitors with no "experience" face higher costs than established ones, particularly the producer with the largest market share, and have difficulty catching up with the entrenched competitors.

Adherents of the experience curve concept stress the importance of achieving market leadership to maximize this barrier to entry, and they recommend aggressive action to achieve it, such as price cutting in anticipation of falling costs in order to build volume. For the combatant that cannot achieve a healthy market share, the prescription is usually, "Get out."

Is the experience curve an entry barrier on which strategies should be built? The answer is: not in every industry. In fact, in some industries, building a strategy on the experience curve can be potentially disastrous. That costs decline with experience in some industries is not news to corporate executives. The significance of the experience curve for strategy depends on what factors are causing the decline.

If costs are falling because a growing company can reap economies of scale through more efficient, automated facilities and vertical integration, then the cumulative volume of production is unimportant to its relative cost position. Here the lowest-cost producer is the one with the largest, most efficient facilities.

A new entrant may well be more efficient than the more experienced competitors; if it has built the newest plant, it will face no disadvantage in having to catch up. The strategic prescription, "You must have the largest, most efficient plant," is a lot different from, "You must produce the greatest cumulative output of the item to get your costs down."

Whether a drop in costs with cumulative (not absolute) volume erects an entry barrier also depends on the sources of the decline. If costs go down because of technical advances known generally in the industry or because of the development of improved equipment that can be copied or purchased from equipment suppliers, the experience curve is no entry barrier at all—in fact, new or less experienced competitors may actually enjoy a cost *advantage over* the leaders. Free of the legacy of heavy past investments, the newcomer or less experienced competitor can purchase or copy the newest and lowest-cost equipment and technology.

If, however, experience can be kept proprietary, the leaders will maintain a cost advantage. But new entrants may require less experience to reduce their costs than the leaders

needed. All this suggests that the experience curve can be a shaky entry barrier on which to build a strategy.

While space does not permit a complete treatment here, I want to mention a few other crucial elements in determining the appropriateness of a strategy built on the entry barrier provided by the experience curve:

- The height of the barrier depends on how important costs are to competition compared with other areas like marketing, selling, and innovation.

- The barrier can be nullified by product or process innovations leading to a substantially new technology and thereby creating an entirely new experience curve.* New entrants can leapfrog the industry leaders and alight on the new experience curve, to which those leaders may be poorly positioned to jump.

- If more than one strong company is building its strategy on the experience curve, the consequences can be nearly fatal. By the time only one rival is left pursuing such a strategy, industry growth may have stopped and the prospects of reaping the spoils of victory long since evaporated.

*For an example drawn from the history of the automobile industry, see William J. Abernathy and Kenneth Wayne, "The Limits of the Learning Curve," Harvard Business Review 52, no. 5 (1974): 109.

First, it changes, of course, as these conditions change. The expiration of Polaroid's basic patents on instant photography, for instance, greatly reduced its absolute cost entry barrier built by proprietary technology. It is not surprising that Kodak plunged into the market. Product differentiation in printing has all but disappeared. Conversely, in the auto industry economics of scale increased enormously with post-World War II automation and vertical integration—virtually stopping successful new entry.

Second, strategic decisions involving a large segment of an industry can have a major impact on the conditions determining the threat of entry. For example, the actions of many U.S. wine producers in the 1960s to step up product introductions, raise advertising levels, and expand distribution nationally surely strengthened the entry roadblocks by raising economics of scale and making access to distribution channels more difficult. Similarly, decisions by members of the recreational vehicle industry to vertically integrate in order to lower costs have greatly increased the economics of scale and raised the capital cost barriers.

POWERFUL SUPPLIERS & BUYERS

Suppliers can exert bargaining power on participants in an industry by raising prices or reducing the quality of purchased goods and services. Powerful suppliers can thereby squeeze profitability out of an industry unable to recover cost increases in its own prices. By raising their prices, soft drink concentrate producers have contributed to the erosion of profitability of bottling companies because the bottlers, facing intense competition from powdered mixes, fruit drinks, and other beverages, have limited freedom to raise *their* prices accordingly. Customers likewise can force down prices, demand higher quality or more service, and play competitors off against each other—all at the expense of industry profits.

The power of each important supplier or buyer group depends on a number of characteristics of its market situation and on the relative importance of its sales or purchases to the industry compared with its overall business.

A *supplier* group is powerful if:

- It is dominated by a few companies and is more concentrated than the industry it sells to.

- Its product is unique or at least differentiated, or if it has built up switching costs. Switching costs are fixed costs buyers face in changing suppliers. These arise because, among other things, a buyer's product specifications tic it to particular suppliers, it has invested heavily in specialized ancillary equipment or in learning how to operate a supplier's equipment (as in computer software), or its production lines are connected to the supplier's manufacturing facilities (as in some manufacture of beverage containers).

- It is not obliged to contend with other products for sale to the industry. For instance, the competition between the steel companies and the aluminum companies to sell to the can industry checks the power of each supplier.

- It poses a credible threat of integrating forward into the industry's business. This provides a check against the industry's ability to improve the terms on which it purchases.

- The industry is not an important customer of the supplier group. if the industry is an important customer, suppliers' fortunes will be closely tied to the industry, and they will want to protect the industry through reasonable pricing and assistance in activities like R&D and lobbying.

A *buyer* group is powerful if:

- It is concentrated or purchases in large volumes. Large-volume buyers are particularly potent forces if heavy fixed costs characterize the industry—as they do in metal containers, corn refining, and bulk chemicals, for example—which raise the stakes to keep capacity filled.

- The products it purchases from the industry are standard or undifferentiated. The buyers, sure that they can always find alternative suppliers, may play one company against another, as they do in aluminum extrusion.

- The products it purchases from the industry form a component of its product and represent a significant fraction of its cost. The buyers are likely to shop for a favorable price and purchase selectively. Where the product sold by the industry in question is a small fraction of buyers' costs, buyers arc usually much less price sensitive.

- It earns low profits, which create great incentive to lower its purchasing costs. Highly profitable buyers, however, are generally less price sensitive (that is, of course, if the item does not represent a large fraction of their costs).

- The industry's product is unimportant to the quality of the buyers' products or services. Where the quality of the buyers' products is very much affected by the industry's product, buyers are generally less price sensitive. Industries in which this situation obtains include oil field equipment, where a malfunction can lead to large losses, and enclosures for electronic medical and test instruments, where the quality of the enclosure can influence the user's impression about the quality of the equipment inside.

- The industry's product does not save the buyer money. Where the industry's product or service can pay for itself many times over, the buyer is rarely price sensitive; rather, he is interested in quality. This is true in services like investment banking and public accounting, where errors in judgment can be costly and embarrassing, and in businesses like the logging of oil wells, where an accurate survey can save thousands of dollars in drilling costs.

- The buyers pose a credible threat of integrating backward to make the industry's product. The Big Three auto producers and major buyers of cars have often used the threat of self-manufacture as a bargaining lever. But sometimes an industry engenders a threat to buyers that its members may integrate forward.

Most of these sources of buyer power can be attributed to consumers as a group as well as to industrial and commercial buyers; only a modification of the frame of reference is necessary. Consumers tend to be more price sensitive if they are purchasing products that are undifferentiated, expensive relative to their incomes, and of a sort where quality is not particularly important.

The buying power of retailers is determined by the same rules, with one important addition. Retailers can gain significant bargaining power over manufacturers when they can influence consumers' purchasing decisions, as they do in audio components, jewelry, appliances, sporting goods, and other goods.

Strategic Action. A company's choice of suppliers to buy from or buyer groups to sell to should be viewed as a crucial strategic decision. A company can improve its strategic posture by finding suppliers or buyers who possess the least power to influence it adversely.

Most common is the situation of a company being able to choose whom it will sell to—in other words, buyer selection. Rarely do all the buyer groups a company sells to enjoy equal power. Even if a company sells to a single industry, segments usually exist within that industry that exercise less power (and that are therefore less price sensitive) than others. For example, the replacement market for most products is less price sensitive than the overall market.

As a rule, a company can sell to powerful buyers and still come away with above-average profitability only if it is a low-cost producer in its industry or if its product enjoys some unusual, if not unique, features. In supplying large customers with electric motors, Emerson Electric earns high returns because its low cost position permits the company to meet or undercut competitors' prices.

If the company lacks a low cost position or a unique product, selling to everyone is self-defeating because the more sales it achieves, the more vulnerable it becomes. The company may have to muster the courage to turn away business and sell only to less potent customers.

Buyer selection has been a key to the success of National Can and Crown Cork & Seal. They focus on the segments of the can industry where they can create product differentiation, minimize the threat of backward integration, and otherwise mitigate the awesome power of their customers. Of course, some industries do not enjoy the luxury of selecting "good" buyers.

As the factors creating supplier and buyer power change with time or as a result of a company's strategic decisions, naturally the power of these groups rises or declines. In the ready-to-wear clothing industry, as the buyers (department stores and clothing stores) have become more concentrated and control has passed to large chains, the industry has come under increasing pressure and suffered falling margins. The industry has been unable to differentiate its product or engender switching costs that lock in its buyers enough to neutralize these trends.

SUBSTITUTE PRODUCTS

By placing a ceiling on prices it can charge, substitute products or services limit the potential of an industry. Unless it can upgrade the quality of the product or differentiate it somehow (as via marketing), the industry will suffer in earnings and possibly in growth.

Manifestly, the more attractive the price-performance trade-off offered by substitute products, the firmer the lid placed on the industry's profit potential. Sugar producers confronted with the large-scale commercialization of high-fructose corn syrup, a sugar substitute, are learning this lesson today.

Substitutes not only limit profits in normal times; they also reduce the bonanza an industry can reap in boom times. In 1978 the producers of fiberglass insulation enjoyed unprecedented demand as a result of high energy costs and severe winter weather. But the industry's ability to raise prices was tempered by the plethora of insulation substitutes, including cellulose, rock wool, and styrofoam. These substitutes are bound to become an even stronger force once the current round of plant additions by fiberglass insulation producers has boosted capacity enough to meet demand (and then some).

Substitute products that deserve the most attention strategically are those that (a) are subject to trends improving their price-performance trade-off with the industry's product, or (b) are produced by industries earning high profits. Substitutes often come rapidly into play if some development increases competition in their industries and causes price reduction or performance improvement.

JOCKEYING FOR POSITION

Rivalry among existing competitors takes the familiar form of jockeying for position—using tactics like price competition, product introduction, and advertising slugfests. Intense rivalry is related to the presence of a number of factors:

- Competitors are numerous or are roughly equal in size and power. In many U.S. industries in recent years foreign contenders, of course, have become part of the competitive picture.

- Industry growth is slow, precipitating fights for market share that involve expansion-minded members.

- The product or service lacks differentiation or switching costs, which lock in buyers and protect one combatant from raids on its customers by another.

- Fixed costs are high or the product is perishable, creating strong temptation to cut prices. Many basic materials businesses, like paper and aluminum, suffer from this problem when demand slackens.

- Capacity is normally augmented in large increments. Such additions, as in the chlorine and vinyl chloride businesses, disrupt the industry's supply-demand balance and often lead to periods of over-capacity and price cutting.

- Exit barriers are high. Exit barriers, like very specialized assets or management's loyalty to a particular business, keep companies competing even though they may be earning low or even negative returns on investment. Excess capacity remains functioning, and the profitability of the healthy competitors suffers as the sick ones hang on.[1] If the entire industry suffers from overcapacity, it may seek government help—particularly if foreign competition is present.

- The rivals are diverse in strategies, origins, and "personalities." They have different ideas about how to compete and continually run head-on into each other in the process.

As an industry matures, its growth rate changes, resulting in declining profits and (often) a shakeout. In the booming recreational vehicle industry of the early 1970s, nearly every producer did well; but slow growth since then has eliminated the high returns, except for the strongest members, not to mention many of the weaker companies. The same profit story has been played out in industry after industry—snowmobiles, aerosol packaging, and sports equipment are just a few examples.

An acquisition can introduce a very different personality to an industry, as has been the case with Black & Decker's takeover of McCullough, the producer of chain saws. Technological innovation can boost the level of fixed costs in the production process, as it did in the shift from batch to continuous-line photo finishing in the 1960s.

While a company must live with many of these factors—because they are built into industry economics—it may have some latitude for improving matters through strategic shifts. For example, it may try to raise buyers' switching costs or increase product differentiation. A focus on selling efforts in the fastest-growing segments of the industry or on market areas with the lowest fixed costs can reduce the impact of industry rivalry. if it is feasible, a company can try to avoid confrontation with competitors having high exit barriers and can thus sidestep involvement in bitter price cutting.

Formulation of Strategy

Once having assessed the forces affecting competition in an industry and their underlying causes, the corporate strategist can identify the company's strengths and weaknesses. The crucial strengths and weaknesses from a strategic standpoint are the company's posture vis-à-vis the underlying causes of each force. Where does it stand against substitutes? Against the sources of entry barriers?

Then the strategist can devise a plan of action that may include (1) positioning the company so that its capabilities provide the best defense against the competitive force; and/or (2) influencing the balance of the forces through strategic moves, thereby improving the company's position; and/or (3) anticipating shifts in the factors underlying the forces and responding to them, with the hope of exploiting change by choosing a strategy appropriate for the new competitive balance before opponents recognize it. I shall consider each strategic approach in turn.

POSITIONING THE COMPANY

The first approach takes the structure of the industry as given and matches the company's strengths and weaknesses to it. Strategy can be viewed as building defenses against the competitive forces or as finding positions in the industry where the forces are weakest.

Knowledge of the company's capabilities and of the causes of the competitive forces will highlight the areas where the company should confront competition and where avoid it. If the company is a low-cost producer, it may choose to confront powerful buyers while it takes care to sell them only products not vulnerable to competition from substitutes.

The success of Dr Pepper in the soft drink industry illustrates the coupling of realistic knowledge of corporate strengths with sound industry analysis to yield a superior strategy. Coca-Cola and PepsiCola dominate Dr Pepper's industry, where many small concentrate producers compete for a piece of the action. Dr Pepper chose a strategy of avoiding the largest-selling drink segment, maintaining a narrow flavor line, forgoing the development of a captive bottler network, and marketing heavily. The company positioned itself so as to be least vulnerable to its competitive forces while it exploited its small size.

In the $11.5 billion soft drink industry, barriers to entry in the form of brand identification, large-scale marketing, and access to a bottler network are enormous. Rather than accept the formidable costs and scale economies in having its own bottler network—that is, following the lead of the Big Two and of Seven-Up—Dr Pepper took advantage of the different flavor of its drink to "piggyback" on Coke and Pepsi bottlers who wanted a full line to sell to customers. Dr Pepper coped with the power of these buyers through extraordinary service and other efforts to distinguish its treatment of them from that of Coke and Pepsi.

Many small companies in the soft drink business offer cola drinks that thrust them into head-to-head competition against the majors. Dr

Pepper, however, maximized product differentiation by maintaining a narrow line of beverages built around an unusual flavor.

Finally, Dr Pepper met Coke and Pepsi with an advertising onslaught emphasizing the alleged uniqueness of its single flavor. This campaign built strong brand identification and great customer loyalty. Helping its efforts was the fact that Dr Pepper's formula involved lower raw materials cost, which gave the company an absolute cost advantage over its major competitors.

There are no economies of scale in soft drink concentrate production, so Dr Pepper could prosper despite its small share of the business (6 percent). Thus Dr Pepper confronted competition in marketing but avoided it in product line and in distribution. This artful positioning combined with good implementation has led to an enviable record in earnings and in the stock market.

INFLUENCING THE BALANCE

When dealing with the forces that drive industry competition, a company can devise a strategy that takes the offensive. This posture is designed to do more than merely cope with the forces themselves; it is meant to alter their causes.

Innovations in marketing can raise brand identification or otherwise differentiate the product. Capital investments in large-scale facilities or vertical integration affect entry barriers. The balance of forces is partly a result of external factors and partly in the company's control.

EXPLOITING INDUSTRY CHANGE

Industry evolution is important strategically because evolution, of course, brings with it changes in the sources of competition I have identified. In the familiar product life-cycle pattern, for example, growth rates change, product differentiation is said to decline as the business becomes more mature, and the companies tend to integrate vertically.

These trends are not so important in themselves; what is critical is whether they affect the sources of competition. Consider vertical integration. In the maturing minicomputer industry, extensive vertical integration, both in manufacturing and in software development, is taking place. This very significant trend is greatly raising economies of scale as well as the amount of capital necessary to compete in the industry. This in turn is raising barriers to entry and may drive some smaller competitors out of the industry once growth levels off.

Obviously, the trends carrying the highest priority from a strategic standpoint are those that affect the most important sources of competition in the industry and those that elevate new causes to the forefront. In contract aerosol packaging, for example, the trend toward less product differentiation is now dominant. It has increased buyers' power, lowered the barriers to entry, and intensified competition.

The framework for analyzing competition that I have described can also be used to predict the eventual profitability of an industry. In long-range planning the task is to examine each competitive force, forecast the magnitude of each underlying cause, and then construct a composite picture of the likely profit potential of the industry.

The outcome of such an exercise may differ a great deal from the existing industry structure. Today, for example, the solar heating business is populated by dozens and perhaps hundreds of companies, none with a major market position. Entry is easy, and competitors are battling to establish solar heating as a superior substitute for conventional methods.

The potential of this industry will depend largely on the shape of future barriers to entry, the improvement of the industry's position relative to substitutes, the ultimate intensity of competition, and the power captured by buyers and suppliers. These characteristics will in turn be influenced by such factors as the establishment of brand identities, significant economics of scale or experience curves in equipment manufacture wrought by technological change, the ultimate capital costs to compete, and the extent of overhead in production facilities.

The framework for analyzing industry competition has direct benefits in setting diversification strategy. It provides a road map for answering the extremely difficult question inherent in diversification decisions: "What is the potential of this business?" Combining the framework with judgment in its application, a company may be able to spot an industry with a good future before this good future is reflected in the prices of acquisition candidates.

Multifaceted Rivalry

Corporate managers have directed a great deal of attention to defining their businesses as a crucial step in strategy formulation. Theodore Levitt, in his classic 1960 article in the *Harvard Business Review*, argued strongly for avoiding the myopia of narrow, product-oriented industry definition.[2] Numerous other authorities have also stressed the need to look beyond product to function in defining a business, beyond national boundaries to potential international competition, and beyond the ranks of one's competitors today to those that may become competitors tomorrow. As a result of these urgings, the proper definition of a company's industry or industries has become an endlessly debated subject.

One motive behind this debate is the desire to exploit new markets. Another, perhaps more important motive is the fear of overlooking latent sources of competition that someday may threaten the industry. Many managers concentrate so single-mindedly on their direct antagonists in the fight for market share that they fail to realize that they are also competing with their customers and their suppliers for bargaining power. Meanwhile, they also neglect to keep a wary eye out for new entrants to the contest or fail to recognize the subtle threat of substitute products.

The key to growth—even survival—is to stake out a position that is less vulnerable to attack from head-to-head opponents, whether established or new, and less vulnerable to erosion from the direction of buyers, suppliers, and substitute goods. Establishing such a position can take many forms—solidifying relationships with favorable customers, differentiating the product either substantively or psychologically through marketing, integrating forward or backward, establishing technological leadership.

NOTES

1. For a more complete discussion of exit barriers and their implications for strategy, see my article, "Please Note Location of Nearest Exit," *California Management Review* 19, no. 2 (Winter 1976): 21.

2. Theodore Levitt, "Marketing Myopia," *Harvard Business Review* 53, no. 5 (1975): 26.

CHAPTER 2

What Is Strategy?

Michael E. Porter

Operational Effectiveness Is Not Strategy

For almost two decades, managers have been learning to play by a new set of rules. Companies must be flexible to respond rapidly to competitive and market changes. They must benchmark continuously to achieve best practice. They must outsource aggressively to gain efficiencies. And they must nurture a few core competencies in the race to stay ahead of rivals.

Positioning—once the heart of strategy—is rejected as too static for today's dynamic markets and changing technologies. According to the new dogma, rivals can quickly copy any market position, and competitive advantage is, at best, temporary.

But those beliefs are dangerous half-truths, and they are leading more and more companies down the path of mutually destructive competition. True, some barriers to competition are falling as regulation eases and markets become global. True, companies have properly invested energy in becoming leaner and more nimble. In many industries, however, what some call *hypercompetition* is a self-inflicted wound, not the inevitable outcome of a changing paradigm of competition.

The root of the problem is the failure to distinguish between operational effectiveness and strategy. The quest for productivity, quality, and speed has spawned a remarkable number of management tools and

This article has benefited greatly from the assistance of many individuals and companies. The author gives special thanks to Jan Rivkin, the coauthor of a related paper. Substantial research contributions have been made by Nicolaj Siggelkow, Dawn Sylvester, and Lucia Marshall. Tarun Khanna, Roger Martin, and Anita McGahan have provided especially extensive comments.

November–December 1996

techniques: total quality management, benchmarking, time-based com-petition, outsourcing, partnering, reengineering, change management. Although the resulting operational improvements have often been dra-matic, many companies have been frustrated by their inability to trans-late those gains into sustainable profitability. And bit by bit, almost imperceptibly, management tools have taken the place of strategy. As managers push to improve on all fronts, they move farther away from viable competitive positions.

OPERATIONAL EFFECTIVENESS: NECESSARY BUT NOT SUFFICIENT

Operational effectiveness and strategy are both essential to superior performance, which, after all, is the primary goal of any enterprise. But they work in very different ways.

A company can outperform rivals only if it can establish a difference that it can preserve. It must deliver greater value to customers or create comparable value at a lower cost, or do both. The arithmetic of superior profitability then follows: delivering greater value allows a company to charge higher average unit prices; greater efficiency results in lower average unit costs.

Ultimately, all differences between companies in cost or price derive from the hundreds of activities required to create, produce, sell, and deliver their products or services, such as calling on customers, assem-bling final products, and training employees. Cost is generated by per-forming activities, and cost advantage arises from performing particular activities more efficiently than competitors. Similarly, differentiation arises from both the choice of activities and how they are performed. Activities, then, are the basic units of competitive advantage. Overall advantage or disadvantage results from all a company's activities, not only a few.[1]

Operational effectiveness (OE) means performing similar activities *better* than rivals perform them. Operational effectiveness includes but is not limited to efficiency. It refers to any number of practices that allow a company to better utilize its inputs by, for example, reducing defects in products or developing better products faster. In contrast, strategic positioning means performing *different* activities from rivals' or performing similar activities in *different ways*. (See Figure 2.1.)

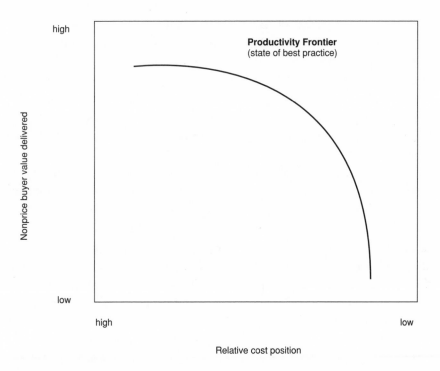

Figure 2.1   Operational Effectiveness Versus Strategic Positioning

Differences in operational effectiveness among companies are pervasive. Some companies are able to get more out of their inputs than others because they eliminate wasted effort, employ more advanced technology, motivate employees better, or have greater insight into managing particular activities or sets of activities. Such differences in operational effectiveness are an important source of differences in profitability among competitors because they directly affect relative cost positions and levels of differentiation.

Differences in operational effectiveness were at the heart of the Japanese challenge to Western companies in the 1980s. The Japanese were so far ahead of rivals in operational effectiveness that they could offer lower cost and superior quality at the same time. It is worth dwelling on this point, because so much recent thinking about competition depends on it. Imagine for a moment a *productivity frontier* that constitutes the sum of all existing best practices at any given time. Think of it as the maximum value that a company delivering a particular product or service can create at a given cost, using the best available technologies, skills, management techniques, and purchased inputs. The productivity frontier can apply to individual activities, to groups of linked activities such as order processing and manufacturing, and to an entire company's activities. When a company improves its operational effectiveness, it moves toward the frontier. Doing so may require capital investment, different personnel, or simply new ways of managing.

The productivity frontier is constantly shifting outward as new technologies and management approaches are developed and as new inputs become available. Laptop computers, mobile communications, the Internet, and software such as Lotus Notes, for example, have redefined the productivity frontier for sales-force operations and created rich possibilities for linking sales with such activities as order processing and after-sales support. Similarly, lean production, which involves a family of activities, has allowed substantial improvements in manufacturing productivity and asset utilization.

For at least the past decade, managers have been preoccupied with improving operational effectiveness. Through programs such as TQM, time-based competition, and benchmarking, they have changed how they perform activities in order to eliminate inefficiencies, improve customer satisfaction, and achieve best practice. Hoping to keep up with shifts in the productivity frontier, managers have embraced continuous improvement, empowerment, change management, and the so-called learning organization. The popularity of outsourcing and the virtual corporation reflect the growing recognition that it is difficult to perform all activities as productively as specialists.

As companies move to the frontier, they can often improve on multiple dimensions of performance at the same time. For example, manufacturers that adopted the Japanese practice of rapid changeovers in the 1980s were able to lower cost and improve differentiation simultaneously. What were once believed to be real trade-offs— between defects and costs, for example—turned out to be illusions created by poor operational effectiveness. Managers have learned to reject such false trade-offs.

Constant improvement in operational effectiveness is necessary to achieve superior profitability. However, it is not usually sufficient. Few companies have competed successfully on the basis of operational effectiveness over an extended period, and staying ahead of rivals gets harder every day. The most obvious reason for that is the rapid diffusion of best practices. Competitors can quickly imitate management techniques, new technologies, input improvements, and superior ways of meeting customers' needs. The most generic solutions—those that can be used in multiple settings—diffuse the fastest. Witness the proliferation of OE techniques accelerated by support from consultants.

OE competition shifts the productivity frontier outward, effectively raising the bar for everyone. But although such competition produces absolute improvement in operational effectiveness, it leads to relative improvement for no one. Consider the $5 billion-plus U.S. commercial-printing industry. The major players—R.R. Donnelley & Sons Company, Quebecor, World Color Press, and Big Flower Press—are competing head to head, serving all types of customers, offering the same array of printing technologies (gravure and web offset), investing heavily in the same new equipment, running their presses faster, and reducing crew sizes. But the resulting major productivity gains are being captured by customers and equipment suppliers, not retained in superior profitability. Even industry-leader Donnelley's profit margin, consistently higher than 7 percent in the 1980s, fell to less than 4.6 percent in 1995. This pattern is playing itself out in industry after industry. Even the Japanese, pioneers of the new competition, suffer from persistently low profits. (See the insert "Japanese Companies Rarely Have Strategies.")

Japanese Companies Rarely Have Strategies

The Japanese triggered a global revolution in operational effectiveness in the 1970s and 1980s, pioneering practices such as total quality management and continuous improvement. As a result, Japanese manufacturers enjoyed substantial cost and quality advantages for many years.

But Japanese companies rarely developed distinct strategic positions of the kind discussed in this article. Those that did—Sony, Canon, and Sega, for example—were the exception rather than the rule. Most Japanese companies imitate and emulate one another. All rivals offer most if not all product varieties, features, and services; they employ all channels and match one anothers' plant configurations.

The dangers of Japanese-style competition are now becoming easier to recognize. In the 1980s, with rivals operating far from the productivity frontier, it seemed possible to win on both cost and quality indefinitely. Japanese companies were all able to grow in an expanding domestic economy and by penetrating global markets. They appeared unstoppable. But as the gap in operational effectiveness narrows, Japanese companies are increasingly caught in a trap of their own making. If they are to escape the mutually destructive battles now ravaging their performance, Japanese companies will have to learn strategy.

To do so, they may have to overcome strong cultural barriers. Japan is notoriously consensus oriented, and companies have a strong tendency to mediate differences among individuals rather than accentuate them. Strategy, on the other hand, requires hard choices. The Japanese also have a deeply ingrained service tradition that predisposes them to go to great lengths to satisfy any need a customer expresses. Companies that compete in that way end up blurring their distinct positioning, becoming all things to all customers.

This discussion of Japan is drawn from the author's research with Hirotaka Takeuchi, with help from Mariko Sakakibara.

The second reason that improved operational effectiveness is insufficient—competitive convergence—is more subtle and insidious. The more benchmarking companies do, the more they look alike. The more that rivals outsource activities to efficient third parties, often the same ones, the more generic those activities become. As rivals imitate one another's improvements in quality, cycle times, or supplier partnerships, strategies converge and competition becomes a series of races down identical paths that no one can win. Competition based on operational effectiveness alone is mutually destructive, leading to wars of attrition that can be arrested only by limiting competition.

The recent wave of industry consolidation through mergers makes sense in the context of OE competition. Driven by performance pressures but lacking strategic vision, company after company has had no better idea than to buy up its rivals. The competitors left standing are often those that outlasted others, not companies with real advantage.

After a decade of impressive gains in operational effectiveness, many companies are facing diminishing returns. Continuous improvement has been etched on managers' brains. But its tools unwittingly draw companies toward imitation and homogeneity. Gradually, managers have let operational effectiveness supplant strategy. The result is zero-sum competition, static or declining prices, and pressures on costs that compromise companies' ability to invest in the business for the long term.

Strategy Rests on Unique Activities

Competitive strategy is about being different. It means deliberately choosing a different set of activities to deliver a unique mix of value. (See the insert "Finding New Positions: The Entrepreneurial Edge.")

Southwest Airlines Company, for example, offers short-haul, low-cost, point-to-point service between midsize cities and secondary airports in large cities. Southwest avoids large airports and does not fly great distances. Its customers include business travelers, families, and students. Southwest's frequent departures and low fares attract price-sensitive customers who otherwise would travel by bus or car, and convenience-oriented travelers who would choose a full-service airline on other routes.

Most managers describe strategic positioning in terms of their customers: "Southwest Airlines serves price- and convenience-sensitive travelers," for example. But the essence of strategy is in the activities—choosing to perform activities differently or to perform different activities than rivals. Otherwise, a strategy is nothing more than a marketing slogan that will not withstand competition.

A full-service airline is configured to get passengers from almost any point A to any point B. To reach a large number of destinations and serve passengers with connecting flights, full-service airlines employ a hub-and-spoke system centered on major airports. To attract passengers who desire more comfort, they offer first-class or business-class service. To accommodate passengers who must change planes, they coordinate schedules and check and transfer baggage. Because some passengers will be traveling for many hours, full-service airlines serve meals.

Southwest, in contrast, tailors all its activities to deliver low-cost, convenient service on its particular type of route. Through fast turn-arounds at the gate of only fifteen minutes, Southwest is able to keep planes flying longer hours than rivals and provide frequent departures with fewer aircraft. Southwest does not offer meals, assigned seats, interline baggage checking, or premium classes of service. Automated ticketing at the gate encourages customers to bypass travel agents, allowing Southwest to avoid their commissions. A standardized fleet of 737 aircraft boosts the efficiency of maintenance.

Southwest has staked out a unique and valuable strategic position based on a tailored set of activities. On the routes served by Southwest, a full service airline could never be as convenient or as low cost. (See Figure 2.2.)

Ikea, the global furniture retailer based in Sweden, also has a clear strategic positioning. Ikea targets young furniture buyers who want

---

Finding New Positions: The Entrepreneurial Edge

Strategic competition can be thought of as the process of perceiving new positions that woo customers from established positions or draw new customers into the market. For example, superstores offering depth of merchandise in a single product category take market share from broad-line department stores offering a more limited selection in many categories. Mail-order catalogs pick off customers who crave convenience. In principle, incumbents and entrepreneurs face the same challenges in finding new strategic positions. In practice, new entrants often have the edge.

Strategic positionings are often not obvious, and finding them requires creativity and insight. New entrants often discover unique positions that have been available but simply overlooked by established competitors. Ikea, for example, recognized a customer group that had been ignored or served poorly. Circuit City Stores' entry into used cars, CarMax, is based on a new way of performing activities—extensive refurbishing of cars, product guarantees, no-haggle pricing, sophisticated use of in-house customer financing—that has long been open to incumbents.

New entrants can prosper by occupying a position that a competitor once held but has ceded through years of imitation and straddling. And entrants coming from other industries can create new positions because of distinctive activities drawn from their other businesses. CarMax borrows heavily from Circuit City's expertise in inventory management, credit, and other activities in consumer electronics retailing.

Most commonly, however, new positions open up because of change.

New customer groups or purchase occasions arise; new needs emerge as societies evolve; new distribution channels appear; new technologies are developed; new machinery or information systems become available. When such changes happen, new entrants, unencumbered by a long history in the industry, can often more easily perceive the potential for a new way of competing. Unlike incumbents, newcomers can be more flexible because they face no trade-offs with their existing activities.

style at low cost. What turns this marketing concept into a strategic positioning is the tailored set of activities that make it work. Like Southwest, Ikea has chosen to perform activities differently from its rivals.

Consider the typical furniture store. Showrooms display samples of the merchandise. One area might contain twenty-five sofas; another will display five dining tables. But those items represent only a fraction of the choices available to customers. Dozens of books displaying fabric swatches or wood samples or alternate styles offer customers thousands of product varieties to choose from. Salespeople often escort customers through the store, answering questions and helping them navigate this maze of choices. Once a customer makes a selection, the order is relayed to a third-party manufacturer. With luck, the furniture will be delivered to the customer's home within six to eight weeks. This is a value chain that maximizes customization and service but does so at high cost.

In contrast, Ikea serves customers who are happy to trade off service for cost. Instead of having a sales associate trail customers around the store, Ikea uses a self-service model based on clear, in-store displays. Rather than rely solely on third party manufacturers, Ikea designs its own low-cost, modular, ready-to-assemble furniture to fit its positioning. In huge stores, Ikea displays every product it sells in room-like

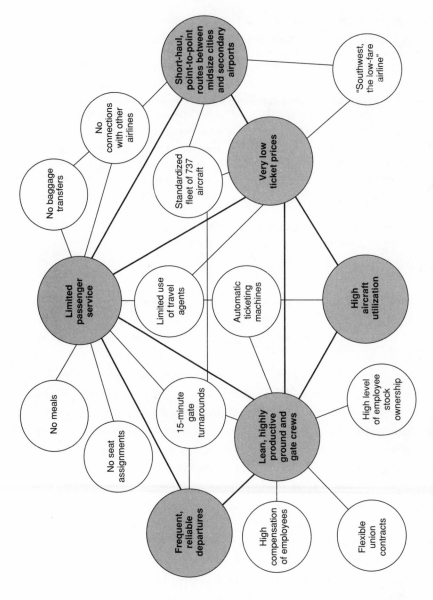

Figure 2.2 Southwest Airlines' Activity System

settings, so customers don't need a decorator to help them imagine how to put the pieces together. Adjacent to the furnished showrooms is a warehouse section with the products in boxes on pallets. Customers are expected to do their own pickup and delivery, and Ikea will even sell you a roof rack for your car that you can return for a refund on your next visit.

Although much of its low-cost position comes from having customers "do it themselves," Ikea offers a number of extra services that its competitors do not. In-store child care is one. Extended hours are another. Those services are uniquely aligned with the needs of its customers, who are young, not wealthy, likely to have children (but no nanny), and, because they work for a living, have a need to shop at odd hours. (See Figure 2.3.)

THE ORIGINS OF STRATEGIC POSITIONS

Strategic positions emerge from three distinct sources, which are not mutually exclusive and often overlap. First, positioning can be based on producing a subset of an industry's products or services. I call this *variety-based positioning* because it is based on the choice of product or service varieties rather than customer segments. Variety-based positioning makes economic sense when a company can best produce particular products or services using distinctive sets of activities.

Jiffy Lube International, for instance, specializes in automotive lubricants and does not offer other car repair or maintenance services. Its value chain produces faster service at a lower cost than broader line repair shops, a combination so attractive that many customers subdivide their purchases, buying oil changes from the focused competitor, Jiffy Lube, and going to rivals for other services.

The Vanguard Group, a leader in the mutual fund industry, is another example of variety-based positioning. Vanguard provides an array of common stock, bond, and money market funds that offer predictable performance and rock-bottom expenses. The company's investment approach deliberately sacrifices the possibility of extraordinary performance in any one year for good relative performance in every year. Vanguard is known, for example, for its index funds. It avoids making

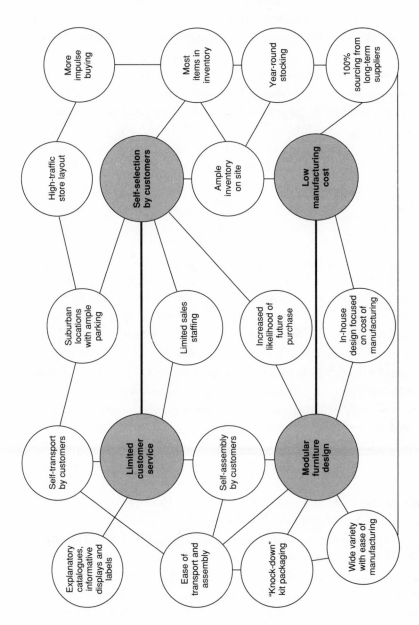

Figure 2.3 Mapping Activity Systems

Activity-system maps, such as this one for Ikea, show how a company's strategic position is contained in a set of tailored activities designed to deliver it. In companies with a clear strategic position, a number of higher-order strategic themes (in shaded circles) can be identified and implemented through clusters of tightly linked activities (in white circles).

Circles (shaded):
- Self-selection by customers
- Low manufacturing cost
- Limited customer service
- Modular furniture design

Circles (white):
- More impulse buying
- Most items in inventory
- Year-round stocking
- 100% sourcing from long-term suppliers
- High-traffic store layout
- Ample inventory on site
- Suburban locations with ample parking
- Limited sales staffing
- Increased likelihood of future purchase
- In-house design focused on cost of manufacturing
- Self-transport by customers
- Self-assembly by customers
- Explanatory catalogues, informative displays and labels
- Ease of transport and assembly
- "Knock-down" kit packaging
- Wide variety with ease of manufacturing

bets on interest rates and steers clear of narrow stock groups. Fund managers keep trading levels low, which holds expenses down; in addition, the company discourages customers from rapid buying and selling because doing so drives up costs and can force a fund manager to trade in order to deploy new capital and raise cash for redemptions. Vanguard also takes a consistent low-cost approach to managing distribution, customer service, and marketing. Many investors include one or more Vanguard funds in their portfolio, while buying aggressively managed or specialized funds from competitors.

The people who use Vanguard or Jiffy Lube are responding to a superior value chain for a particular type of service. A variety-based positioning can serve a wide array of customers, but for most it will meet only a subset of their needs. (See Figure 2.4.)

A second basis for positioning is that of serving most or all the needs of a particular group of customers. I call this *needs-based positioning*, which comes closer to traditional thinking about targeting a segment of customers. It arises when there are groups of customers with differing needs, and when a tailored set of activities can serve those needs best. Some groups of customers are more price sensitive than others, demand different product features, and need varying amounts of information, support, and services. Ikea's customers are a good example of such a group. Ikea seeks to meet all the home furnishing needs of its target customers, not just a subset of them.

A variant of needs-based positioning arises when the same customer has different needs on different occasions or for different types of transactions. The same person, for example, may have different needs when traveling on business than when traveling for pleasure with the family. Buyers of cans—beverage companies, for example—will likely have different needs from their primary supplier than from their secondary source.

It is intuitive for most managers to conceive of their business in terms of the customers' needs they are meeting. But a critical element of needs-based positioning is not at all intuitive and is often overlooked. Differences in needs will not translate into meaningful positions unless the best set of activities to satisfy them *also* differs. If that were not the case, every competitor could meet those same needs, and there would be nothing unique or valuable about the positioning.

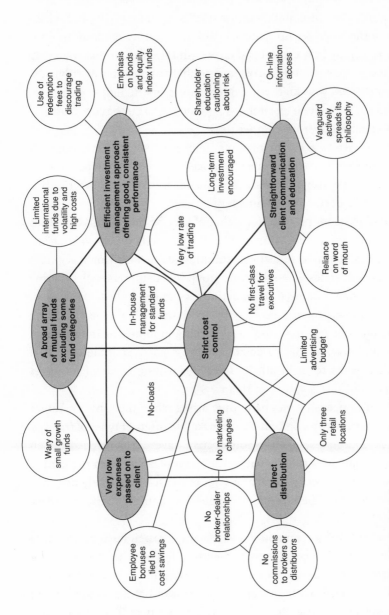

Figure 2.4 Vanguard's Activity System

Activity-system maps can be useful for examining and strengthening strategic fit. A set of basic questions should guide the process. First, is each activity consistent with the overall positioning—the varieties produced, the needs served, and the type of customers accessed? Ask those responsible for each activity to identify how other activities within the company improve or detract from their performance. Second, are there ways to strengthen how activities and groups of activities reinforce one another? Finally, could changes in one activity eliminate the need to perform others?

In private banking, for example, Bessemer Trust Company targets families with a minimum of $5 million in investable assets who want capital preservation combined with wealth accumulation. By assigning one sophisticated account officer for every 14 families, Bessemer has configured its activities for personalized service. Meetings, for example, are more likely to be held at a client's ranch or yacht than in the office. Bessemer offers a wide array of customized services, including investment management and estate administration, oversight of oil and gas investments, and accounting for racehorses and aircraft. Loans, a staple of most private banks, are rarely needed by Bessemer's clients and make up a tiny fraction of its client balances and income. Despite the most generous compensation of account officers and the highest personnel cost as a percentage of operating expenses, Bessemer's differentiation with its target families produces a return on equity estimated to be the highest of any private banking competitor.

Citibank's private bank, on the other hand, serves clients with minimum assets of about $250,000 who, in contrast to Bessemer's clients, want convenient access to loans—from jumbo mortgages to deal financing. Citibank's account managers are primarily lenders. When clients need other services, their account manager refers them to other Citibank specialists, each of whom handles prepackaged products. Citibank's system is less customized than Bessemer's and allows it to have a lower manager-to-client ratio of 1:125. Biannual office meetings are offered only for the largest clients. Both Bessemer and Citibank have tailored their activities to meet the needs of a different group of private banking customers. The same value chain cannot profitably meet the needs of both groups.

The third basis for positioning is that of segmenting customers who are accessible in different ways. Although their needs are similar to those of other customers, the best configuration of activities to reach them is different. I call this *access-based positioning*. Access can be a function of customer geography or customer scale—or of anything that requires a different set of activities to reach customers in the best way.

Segmenting by access is less common and less well understood than the other two bases. Carmike Cinemas, for example, operates movie theaters exclusively in cities and towns with populations under 200,000.

How does Carmike make money in markets that are not only small but also won't support big-city ticket prices? It does so through a set of activities that result in a lean cost structure. Carmike's small-town customers can be served through standardized, low-cost theater complexes requiring fewer screens and less sophisticated projection technology than big-city theaters. The company's proprietary information system and management process eliminate the need for local administrative staff beyond a single theater manager. Carmike also reaps advantages from centralized purchasing, lower rent and payroll costs (because of its locations), and rock-bottom corporate overhead of 2 percent (the industry average is 5 percent). Operating in small communities also allows Carmike to practice a highly personal form of marketing in which the theater manager knows patrons and promotes attendance through personal contacts. By being the dominant if not the only theater in its markets—the main competition is often the high school football team—Carmike is also able to get its pick of films and negotiate better terms with distributors.

Rural versus urban-based customers are one example of access driving differences in activities. Serving small rather than large customers or densely rather than sparsely situated customers are other examples in which the best way to configure marketing, order processing, logistics, and after-sale service activities to meet the similar needs of distinct groups will often differ.

Positioning is not only about carving out a niche. A position emerging from any of the sources can be broad or narrow. A focused competitor, such as Ikea, targets the special needs of a subset of customers and designs its activities accordingly. Focused competitors thrive on groups of customers who are overserved (and hence overpriced) by more broadly targeted competitors, or underserved (and hence underpriced). A broadly targeted competitor—for example, Vanguard or Delta Air Lines—serves a wide array of customers, performing a set of activities designed to meet their common needs. It ignores or meets only partially the more idiosyncratic needs of particular customer groups. (See the insert "The Connection with Generic Strategies.")

Whatever the basis—variety, needs, access, or some combination of the three—positioning requires a tailored set of activities because it is

The Connection with Generic Strategies

In *Competitive Strategy* (The Free Press, 1985), I introduced the concept of generic strategies—cost leadership, differentiation, and focus—to represent the alternative strategic positions in an industry. The generic strategies remain useful to characterize strategic positions at the simplest and broadest level. Vanguard, for instance, is an example of a cost leadership strategy, whereas Ikea, with its narrow customer group, is an example of cost-based focus. Neutrogena is a focused differentiator. The bases for positioning—varieties, needs, and access—carry the understanding of those generic strategies to a greater level of specificity. Ikea and Southwest are both cost-based focusers, for example, but Ikea's focus is based on the needs of a customer group, and Southwest's is based on offering a particular service variety.

The generic strategies framework introduced the need to choose in order to avoid becoming caught between what I then described as the inherent contradictions of different strategies. Trade-offs between the activities of incompatible positions explain those contradictions. Witness Continental Lite, which tried and failed to compete in two ways at once.

always a function of differences on the supply side; that is, of differences in activities. However, positioning is not always a function of differences on the demand, or customer, side. Variety and access positionings, in particular, do not rely on *any* customer differences. In practice, however, variety or access differences often accompany needs differences. The tastes—that is, the needs—of Carmike's small-town customers, for instance, run more toward comedies, Westerns, action films, and family entertainment. Carmike does not run any films rated NC-17.

Having defined positioning, we can now begin to answer the question, "What is strategy?" Strategy is the creation of a unique and valuable position, involving a different set of activities. If there were only one ideal position, there would be no need for strategy. Companies would face a simple imperative—win the race to discover and preempt it. The essence of strategic positioning is to choose activities that are different from rivals'. If the same set of activities were best to produce all varieties, meet all needs, and access all customers, companies could easily shift among them and operational effectiveness would determine performance.

A Sustainable Strategic Position Requires Trade-offs

Choosing a unique position, however, is not enough to guarantee a sustainable advantage. A valuable position will attract imitation by incumbents, who are likely to copy it in one of two ways.

First, a competitor can reposition itself to match the superior performer. J.C. Penney, for instance, has been repositioning itself from a Sears clone to a more upscale, fashion-oriented, soft-goods retailer. A second and far more common type of imitation is straddling. The straddler seeks to match the benefits of a successful position while maintaining its existing position. It grafts new features, services, or technologies onto the activities it already performs.

For those who argue that competitors can copy any market position, the airline industry is a perfect test case. It would seem that nearly any competitor could imitate any other airline's activities. Any airline can buy the same planes, lease the gates, and match the menus and ticketing and baggage handling services offered by other airlines.

Continental Airlines saw how well Southwest was doing and decided to straddle. While maintaining its position as a full-service airline, Continental also set out to match Southwest on a number of point-to-point routes. The airline dubbed the new service Continental Lite. It eliminated meals and first-class service, increased departure frequency, lowered fares, and shortened turnaround time at the gate. Because Continental remained a full-service airline on other routes, it continued to use travel agents and its mixed fleet of planes and to provide baggage checking and seat assignments.

But a strategic position is not sustainable unless there are trade-offs with other positions. Trade-offs occur when activities are incompatible. Simply put, a trade-off means that more of one thing necessitates less of another. An airline can choose to serve meals—adding cost and slowing turnaround time at the gate—or it can choose not to, but it cannot do both without bearing major inefficiencies.

Trade-offs create the need for choice and protect against repositioners and straddlers. Consider Neutrogena soap. Neutrogena Corporation's variety-based positioning is built on a "kind to the skin," residue-free soap formulated for pH balance. With a large detail force calling on dermatologists, Neutrogena's marketing strategy looks more like a drug company's than a soap maker's. It advertises in medical journals, sends direct mail to doctors, attends medical conferences, and performs research at its own Skincare Institute. To reinforce its positioning, Neutrogena originally focused its distribution on drugstores and avoided price promotions. Neutrogena uses a slow, more expensive manufacturing process to mold its fragile soap.

In choosing this position, Neutrogena said no to the deodorants and skin softeners that many customers desire in their soap. It gave up the large volume potential of selling through supermarkets and using price promotions. It sacrificed manufacturing efficiencies to achieve the soap's desired attributes. In its original positioning, Neutrogena made a whole raft of trade-offs like those, trade-offs that protected the company from imitators.

Trade-offs arise for three reasons. The first is inconsistencies in image or reputation. A company known for delivering one kind of value may lack credibility and confuse customers—or even undermine its reputation—if it delivers another kind of value or attempts to deliver two inconsistent things at the same time. For example, Ivory soap, with its position as a basic, inexpensive everyday soap would have a hard time reshaping its image to match Neutrogena's premium "medical" reputation. Efforts to create a new image typically cost tens or even hundreds of millions of dollars in a major industry—a powerful barrier to imitation.

Second, and more important, trade-offs arise from activities themselves. Different positions (with their tailored activities) require different product configurations, different equipment, different employee behavior, different skills, and different management systems. Many trade-offs reflect inflexibilities in machinery, people, or systems. The more Ikea has configured its activities to lower costs by having its customers do their own assembly and delivery, the less able it is to satisfy customers who require higher levels of service.

However, trade-offs can be even more basic. In general, value is destroyed if an activity is overdesigned or underdesigned for its use. For example, even if a given salesperson were capable of providing a high level of assistance to one customer and none to another, the salesperson's talent (and some of his or her cost) would be wasted on the second customer. Moreover, productivity can improve when variation of an activity is limited. By providing a high level of assistance all the time, the salesperson and the entire sales activity can often achieve efficiencies of learning and scale.

Finally, trade-offs arise from limits on internal coordination and control. By clearly choosing to compete in one way and not another, senior management makes organizational priorities clear. Companies that try to be all things to all customers, in contrast, risk confusion in the trenches as employees attempt to make day-to-day operating decisions without a clear framework.

Positioning trade-offs are pervasive in competition and essential to strategy. They create the need for choice and purposefully limit what a company offers. They deter straddling or repositioning, because competitors that engage in those approaches undermine their strategies and degrade the value of their existing activities.

Trade-offs ultimately grounded Continental Lite. The airline lost hundreds of millions of dollars, and the CEO lost his job. Its planes were delayed leaving congested hub cities or slowed at the gate by baggage transfers. Late flights and cancellations generated a thousand complaints a day. Continental Lite could not afford to compete on price and still pay standard travel-agent commissions, but neither could it do without agents for its full-service business. The airline compromised by cutting commissions for all Continental flights across the board. Similarly, it could not afford to offer the same frequent-flier benefits to travelers paying the much lower ticket prices for Lite service. It compromised again by lowering the rewards of Continental's entire frequent-flier program. The results: angry travel agents and full-service customers.

Continental tried to compete in two ways at once. In trying to be low cost on some routes and full service on others, Continental paid an enormous straddling penalty. If there were no trade-offs between the two positions, Continental could have succeeded. But the absence of trade-offs is a dangerous half-truth that managers must unlearn. Quality is not always free. Southwest's convenience, one kind of high quality, happens to be consistent with low costs because its frequent departures are facilitated by a number of low-cost practices—fast gate turnarounds and automated ticketing, for example. However, other dimensions of airline quality—an assigned seat, a meal, or baggage transfer—require costs to provide.

In general, false trade-offs between cost and quality occur primarily when there is redundant or wasted effort, poor control or accuracy, or weak coordination. Simultaneous improvement of cost and differentiation is possible only when a company begins far behind the productivity frontier or when the frontier shifts outward. At the frontier, where companies have achieved current best practice, the trade-off between cost and differentiation is very real indeed.

After a decade of enjoying productivity advantages, Honda Motor Company and Toyota Motor Corporation recently bumped up against the frontier. In 1995, faced with increasing customer resistance to higher automobile prices, Honda found that the only way to produce a less-expensive car was to skimp on features. In the United States, it replaced the rear disk brakes on the Civic with lower-cost drum brakes and used cheaper fabric for the back seat, hoping customers would not notice. Toyota tried to sell a version of its best-selling Corolla in Japan with unpainted bumpers and cheaper seats. In Toyota's case, customers rebelled, and the company quickly dropped the new model.

For the past decade, as managers have improved operational effectiveness greatly, they have internalized the idea that eliminating trade-offs is a good thing. But if there are no trade-offs companies will never achieve a sustainable advantage. They will have to run faster and faster just to stay in place.

As we return to the question, What is strategy? we see that trade-offs add a new dimension to the answer. Strategy is making trade-offs in competing. The essence of strategy is choosing what not to do. Without trade-offs, there would be no need for choice and thus no need for strategy. Any good idea could and would be quickly imitated. Again, performance would once again depend wholly on operational effectiveness.

Fit Drives Both Competitive Advantage and Sustainability

Positioning choices determine not only which activities a company will perform and how it will configure individual activities but also how activities relate to one another. While operational effectiveness is about achieving excellence in individual activities, or functions, strategy is about *combining* activities.

Southwest's rapid gate turnaround, which allows frequent departures and greater use of aircraft, is essential to its high-convenience, low-cost positioning. But how does Southwest achieve it? Part of the answer lies in the company's well-paid gate and ground crews, whose productivity in turn-arounds is enhanced by flexible union rules. But the bigger part of the answer lies in how Southwest performs other activities. With no meals, no seat assignment, and no interline baggage transfers, Southwest avoids having to perform activities that slow down other airlines. It selects airports and routes to avoid congestion that introduces delays. Southwest's strict limits on the type and length of routes make standardized aircraft possible: every aircraft Southwest turns is a Boeing 737.

What is Southwest's core competence? Its key success factors? The correct answer is that everything matters. Southwest's strategy involves a whole system of activities, not a collection of parts. Its competitive advantage comes from the way its activities fit and reinforce one another.

Fit locks out imitators by creating a chain that is as strong as its *strongest* link. As in most companies with good strategies, Southwest's activities complement one another in ways that create real economic value. One activity's cost, for example, is lowered because of the way other activities are performed. Similarly, one activity's value to customers can be enhanced by a company's other activities. That is the way strategic fit creates competitive advantage and superior profitability.

TYPES OF FIT

The importance of fit among functional policies is one of the oldest ideas in strategy. Gradually, however, it has been supplanted on the management agenda. Rather than seeing the company as a whole, managers have turned to "core" competencies, "critical" resources, and "key" success factors. In fact, fit is a far more central component of competitive advantage than most realize.

Fit is important because discrete activities often affect one another. A sophisticated sales force, for example, confers a greater advantage when the company's product embodies premium technology and its marketing approach emphasizes customer assistance and support. A production line with high levels of model variety is more valuable when combined with an inventory and order processing system that minimizes the need for stocking finished goods, a sales process equipped to explain and encourage customization, and an advertising theme that stresses the benefits of product variations that meet a customer's special needs. Such complementarities are pervasive in strategy. Although some fit among activities is generic and applies to many companies, the most valuable fit is strategy-specific because it enhances a position's uniqueness and amplifies trade-offs.[2]

There are three types of fit, although they are not mutually exclusive. First-order fit is *simple consistency* between each activity (function) and the overall strategy. Vanguard, for example, aligns all activities with its low-cost strategy. It minimizes portfolio turnover and does not need highly compensated money managers. The company distributes its funds directly, avoiding commissions to brokers. It also limits advertising, relying instead on public relations and word-of-mouth recommendations. Vanguard ties its employees' bonuses to cost savings.

Consistency ensures that the competitive advantages of activities cumulate and do not erode or cancel themselves out. It makes the strategy easier to communicate to customers, employees, and shareholders, and improves implementation through single-mindedness in the corporation.

Second-order fit occurs when *activities are reinforcing.* Neutrogena, for example, markets to upscale hotels eager to offer their guests a soap recommended by dermatologists. Hotels grant Neutrogena the privilege of using its customary packaging while requiring other soaps to feature the hotel's name. Once guests have tried Neutrogena in a luxury hotel, they are more likely to purchase it at the drugstore or ask their doctor about it. Thus Neutrogena's medical and hotel marketing activities reinforce one another, lowering total marketing costs.

In another example, Bic Corporation sells a narrow line of standard, low-priced pens to virtually all major customer markets (retail, commercial, promotional, and giveaway) through virtually all available channels. As with any variety-based positioning serving a broad group of customers, Bic emphasizes a common need (low price for an acceptable pen) and uses marketing approaches with a broad reach (a large sales force and heavy television advertising). Bic gains the benefits of consistency across nearly all activities, including product design that emphasizes ease of manufacturing, plants configured for low cost, aggressive purchasing to minimize material costs, and in-house parts production whenever the economics dictate.

Yet Bic goes beyond simple consistency because its activities are reinforcing. For example, the company uses point-of-sale displays and frequent packaging changes to stimulate impulse buying. To handle point-of-sale tasks, a company needs a large sales force. Bic's is the largest in its industry, and it handles point-of-sale activities better than its rivals do. Moreover, the combination of point-of-sale activity, heavy television advertising, and packaging changes yields far more impulse buying than any activity in isolation could.

Third-order fit goes beyond activity reinforcement to what I call *optimization of effort*. The Gap, a retailer of casual clothes, considers product availability in its stores a critical element of its strategy. The Gap could keep products either by holding store inventory or by restocking from warehouses. The Gap has optimized its effort across these activities by restocking its selection of basic clothing almost daily out of three warehouses, thereby minimizing the need to carry large in-store inventories. The emphasis is on restocking because the Gap's merchandising strategy sticks to basic items in relatively few colors. While comparable retailers achieve turns of three to four times per year, the Gap turns its inventory seven and a half times per year. Rapid restocking, moreover, reduces the cost of implementing the Gap's short model cycle, which is six to eight weeks long.[3]

Coordination and information exchange across activities to eliminate redundancy and minimize wasted effort are the most basic types of effort optimization. But there are higher levels as well. Product design choices, for example, can eliminate the need for after-sale service or make it possible for customers to perform service activities themselves. Similarly, coordination with suppliers or distribution channels can eliminate the need for some in-house activities, such as end-user training.

In all three types of fit, the whole matters more than any individual part. Competitive advantage grows out of the *entire system* of activities. The fit among activities substantially reduces cost or increases differentiation. Beyond that, the competitive value of individual activities—or the associated skills, competencies, or resources—cannot be decoupled from the system or the strategy. Thus in competitive companies it can be misleading to explain success by specifying individual strengths, core competencies, or critical resources. The list of strengths cuts across many functions, and one strength blends into others. It is more useful to think in terms of themes that pervade many activities, such as low cost, a particular notion of customer service, or a particular conception of the value delivered. These themes are embodied in nests of tightly linked activities.

FIT AND SUSTAINABILITY

Strategic fit among many activities is fundamental not only to competitive advantage but also to the sustainability of that advantage. It is harder for a rival to match an array of interlocked activities than it is merely to imitate a particular sales-force approach, match a process technology, or replicate a set of product features. Positions built on systems of activities are far more sustainable than those built on individual activities. (See Table 2.1.)

Consider this simple exercise. The probability that competitors can match any activity is often less than one. The probabilities then quickly compound to make matching the entire system highly unlikely ($.9 \times .9 = .81$; $.9 \times .9 \times .9 \times .9 = .66$, and so on). Existing companies that try to reposition or straddle will be forced to reconfigure many activities. And even new entrants, though they do not confront the trade-offs facing established rivals, still face formidable barriers to imitation.

The more a company's positioning rests on activity systems with second- and third-order fit, the more sustainable its advantage will be. Such systems, by their very nature, are usually difficult to untangle from outside the company and therefore hard to imitate. And even if rivals can identify the relevant interconnections, they will have difficulty replicating them. Achieving fit is difficult because it requires the integration of decisions and actions across many independent subunits.

A competitor seeking to match an activity system gains little by imitating only some activities and not matching the whole. Performance does not improve; it can decline. Recall Continental Lite's disastrous attempt to imitate Southwest.

Finally, fit among a company's activities creates pressures and incentives to improve operational effectiveness, which makes imitation even harder. Fit means that poor performance in one activity will degrade the performance in others, so that weaknesses are exposed and more prone to get attention. Conversely, improvements in one activity will pay dividends in others. Companies with strong fit among their activities are rarely inviting targets. Their superiority in strategy and in execution only compounds their advantages and raises the hurdle for imitators.

When activities complement one another, rivals will get little benefit from imitation unless they successfully match the whole system. Such situations tend to promote winner-take-all competition. The company that builds the best activity system—Toys R Us, for instance—wins, while rivals with similar strategies—Child World and Lionel Leisure—fall behind. Thus finding a new strategic position is often preferable to being the second or third imitator of an occupied position.

The most viable positions are those whose activity systems are incompatible because of trade-offs. Strategic positioning sets the trade-off rules that define how individual activities will be configured and integrated. Seeing strategy in terms of activity systems only makes it clearer why organizational structure, systems, and processes need to be strategy-specific. Tailoring organization to strategy, in turn, makes complementarities more achievable and contributes to sustainability.

One implication is that strategic positions should have a horizon of a decade or more, not of a single planning cycle. Continuity fosters improvements in individual activities and the fit across activities, allowing an organization to build unique capabilities and skills tailored to its strategy. Continuity also reinforces a company's identity.

Conversely, frequent shifts in positioning are costly. Not only must a company reconfigure individual activities, but it must also realign entire systems. Some activities may never catch up to the vacillating strategy. The inevitable result of frequent shifts in strategy, or of failure to choose a distinct position in the first place, is "me-too" or hedged activity configurations, inconsistencies across functions, and organizational dissonance.

What is strategy? We can now complete the answer to this question. Strategy is creating fit among a company's activities. The success of a strategy depends on doing many things well—not just a few—and integrating among them. If there is no fit among activities, there is no distinctive strategy and little sustainability. Management reverts to the simpler task of overseeing independent functions, and operational effectiveness determines an organization's relative performance.

Rediscovering Strategy

Why do so many companies fail to have a strategy? Why do managers avoid making strategic choices? Or, having made them in the past, why do managers so often let strategies decay and blur? (See the insert "Reconnecting with Strategy.")

Commonly, the threats to strategy are seen to emanate from outside a company because of changes in technology or the behavior of competitors. Although external changes can be the problem, the greater threat to strategy often comes from within. A sound strategy is undermined by a misguided view of competition, by organizational failures, and, especially, by the desire to grow.

THE FAILURE TO CHOOSE

Managers have become confused about the necessity of making choices. When many companies operate far from the productivity frontier, trade-offs appear unnecessary. It can seem that a well-run company should be able to beat its ineffective rivals on all dimensions simultaneously. Taught by popular management thinkers that they do not have to make trade-offs, managers have acquired a macho sense that to do so is a sign of weakness.

Unnerved by forecasts of hypercompetition, managers increase its likelihood by imitating everything about their competitors. Exhorted to think in terms of revolution, managers chase every new technology for its own sake.

The pursuit of operational effectiveness is seductive because it is concrete and actionable. Over the past decade, managers have been under increasing pressure to deliver tangible, measurable performance improvements. Programs in operational effectiveness produce reassuring progress, although superior profitability may remain elusive. Business

Reconnecting with Strategy

Most companies owe their initial success to a unique strategic position involving clear trade-offs. Activities once were aligned with that position. The passage of time and the pressures of growth, however, led to compromises that were, at first, almost imperceptible. Through a succession of incremental changes that each seemed sensible at the time, many established companies have compromised their way to homogeneity with their rivals.

The issue here is not with the companies whose historical position is no longer viable; their challenge is to start over, just as a new entrant would. At issue is a far more common phenomenon: the established company achieving mediocre returns and lacking a clear strategy. Through incremental additions of product varieties, incremental efforts to serve new customer groups, and emulation of rivals' activities, the existing company loses its clear competitive position. Typically, the company has matched many of its competitors' offerings and practices and attempts to sell to most customer groups.

A number of approaches can help a company reconnect with strategy. The first is a careful look at what it already does. Within most well-established companies is a core of uniqueness. It is identified by answering questions such as the following:

- Which of our product or service varieties are the most distinctive?
- Which of our product or service varieties are the most profitable?
- Which of our customers are the most satisfied?
- Which customers, channels, or purchase occasions are the most profitable?
- Which of the activities in our value chain are the most different and effective?

Around this core of uniqueness are encrustations added incrementally over time. Like barnacles, they must be removed to reveal the underlying strategic positioning. A small percentage of varieties or customers may well account for most of a company's sales and especially its profits. The challenge, then, is to refocus on the unique core and realign the company's activities with it. Customers and product varieties at the periphery can be sold or allowed through inattention or price increases to fade away.

A company's history can also be instructive. What was the vision of the founder? What were the products and customers that made the company? Looking backward, one can reexamine the original strategy to see if it is still valid. Can the historical positioning be implemented in a modern way, one consistent with today's technologies and practices? This sort of thinking may lead to a commitment to renew the strategy and may challenge the organization to recover its distinctiveness. Such a challenge can be galvanizing and can instill the confidence to make the needed trade-offs.

Table 2.1 Alternative Views of Strategy

The Implicit Strategy Model of the Past Decade	Sustainable Competitive Advantage
One ideal competitive position in the industry	Unique competitive position for the company
Benchmarking of all activities and achieving best practice	Activities tailored to stratgy
Aggressive outsourcing and partnering to gain efficiencies	Clear trade-offs and choices vis-à-vis competitors
Advantages rest on a few key success factors, critical resources, core competencies	Competitive advantage arises from fit across activities
Flexibility and rapid responses to all competitive and market changes	Sustainability comes from the activity system, not the parts
	Operational effectiveness a given

---

publications and consultants flood the market with information about what other companies are doing, reinforcing the best-practice mentality. Caught up in the race for operational effectiveness, many managers simply do not understand the need to have a strategy.

Companies avoid or blur strategic choices for other reasons as well. Conventional wisdom within an industry is often strong, homogenizing competition. Some managers mistake "customer focus" to mean they must serve all customer needs or respond to every request from distribution channels. Others cite the desire to preserve flexibility.

Organizational realities also work against strategy. Trade-offs are frightening, and making no choice is sometimes preferred to risking blame for a bad choice. Companies imitate one another in a type of herd behavior, each assuming rivals know something they do not. Newly empowered employees, who are urged to seek every possible source of improvement, often lack a vision of the whole and the perspective to recognize trade-offs. The failure to choose sometimes comes down to the reluctance to disappoint valued managers or employees.

THE GROWTH TRAP

Among all other influences, the desire to grow has perhaps the most perverse effect on strategy. Trade-offs and limits appear to constrain growth. Serving one group of customers and excluding others, for instance, places a real or imagined limit on revenue growth. Broadly targeted strategies emphasizing low price result in lost sales with customers sensitive to features or service. Differentiators lose sales to price-sensitive customers.

Managers are constantly tempted to take incremental steps that surpass those limits but blur a company's strategic position. Eventually, pressures to grow or apparent saturation of the target market lead managers to broaden the position by extending product lines, adding new features, imitating competitors' popular services, matching processes, and even making acquisitions. For years, Maytag Corporation's success was based on its focus on reliable, durable washers and dryers, later extended to include dishwashers. However, conventional wisdom emerging within the industry supported the notion of selling a full line of products. Concerned with slow industry growth and competition from broad-line appliance makers, Maytag was pressured by dealers and encouraged by customers to extend its line. Maytag expanded into refrigerators and cooking products under the Maytag brand and acquired other brands—Jenn-Air, Hardwick Stove, Hoover, Admiral, and Magic Chef—with disparate positions. Maytag has grown substantially from $684 million in 1985 to a peak of $3.4 billion in 1994, but return on sales has declined from 8 percent to 12 percent in the 1970s and 1980s to an average of less than 1% between 1989 and 1995. Cost cutting will improve this performance, but laundry and dishwasher products still anchor Maytag's profitability.

Neutrogena may have fallen into the same trap. In the early 1990s, its U.S. distribution broadened to include mass merchandisers such as Wal-Mart Stores. Under the Neutrogena name, the company expanded into a wide variety of products—eye-makeup remover and shampoo, for example—in which it was not unique and which diluted its image, and it began turning to price promotions.

Compromises and inconsistencies in the pursuit of growth will erode the competitive advantage a company had with its original varieties or target customers. Attempts to compete in several ways at once create confusion and undermine organizational motivation and focus. Profits fall, but more revenue is seen as the answer. Managers are unable to make choices, so the company embarks on a new round of broadening and compromises. Often, rivals continue to match each other until desperation breaks the cycle, resulting in a merger or downsizing to the original positioning.

PROFITABLE GROWTH

Many companies, after a decade of restructuring and cost-cutting, are turning their attention to growth. Too often, efforts to grow blur uniqueness, create compromises, reduce fit, and ultimately undermine competitive advantage. In fact, the growth imperative is hazardous to strategy.

What approaches to growth preserve and reinforce strategy? Broadly, the prescription is to concentrate on deepening a strategic position rather than broadening and compromising it. One approach is to look for extensions of the strategy that leverage the existing activity system by offering features or services that rivals would find impossible or costly to match on a stand-alone basis. In other words, managers can ask themselves which activities, features, or forms of competition are feasible or less costly to them because of complementary activities that their company performs.

Deepening a position involves making the company's activities more distinctive, strengthening fit, and communicating the strategy better to those customers who should value it. But many companies succumb to the temptation to chase "easy" growth by adding hot features, products, or services without screening them or adapting them to their strategy. Or they target new customers or markets in which the company has little special to offer. A company can often grow faster—and far more profitably—by better penetrating needs and varieties where it is distinctive than by slugging it out in potentially higher growth arenas in which the company lacks uniqueness. Carmike, now the largest theater chain in the United States, owes its rapid growth to its disciplined concentration on small markets. The company quickly sells any big-city theaters that come to it as part of an acquisition.

Globalization often allows growth that is consistent with strategy, opening up larger markets for a focused strategy. Unlike broadening domestically, expanding globally is likely to leverage and reinforce a company's unique position and identity.

Companies seeking growth through broadening within their industry can best contain the risks to strategy by creating stand-alone units, each with its own brand name and tailored activities. Maytag has clearly struggled with this issue. On the one hand, it has organized its premium and value brands into separate units with different strategic positions. On the other, it has created an umbrella appliance company for all its brands to gain critical mass. With shared design, manufacturing, distribution, and customer service, it will be hard to avoid homogenization. If a given business unit attempts to compete with different positions for different products or customers, avoiding compromise is nearly impossible.

THE ROLE OF LEADERSHIP

The challenge of developing or reestablishing a clear strategy is often primarily an organizational one and depends on leadership. With so many forces at work against making choices and trade-offs in organizations, a clear intellectual framework to guide strategy is a necessary counterweight. Moreover, strong leaders willing to make choices are essential.

In many companies, leadership has degenerated into orchestrating operational improvements and making deals. But the leader's role is broader and far more important. General management is more than the stewardship of individual functions. Its core is strategy: defining and communicating the company's unique position, making trade-offs, and forging fit among activities. The leader must provide the discipline to decide which industry changes and customer needs the company will respond to, while avoiding organizational distractions and maintaining the company's distinctiveness. Managers at lower levels lack the perspective and the confidence to maintain a strategy. There will be constant pressures to compromise, relax trade-offs, and emulate rivals. One of the leader's jobs is to teach others in the organization about strategy—and to say no.

Strategy renders choices about what not to do as important as choices about what to do. Indeed, setting limits is another function of leadership. Deciding which target group of customers, varieties, and needs the company should serve is fundamental to developing a strategy. But so is deciding not to serve other customers or needs and not to offer certain features or services. Thus strategy requires constant discipline and clear communication. Indeed, one of the most important functions of an explicit, communicated strategy is to guide employees in making choices that arise because of trade-offs in their individual activities and in day-to-day decisions.

Improving operational effectiveness is a necessary part of management, but it is *not* strategy. In confusing the two, managers have unintentionally backed into a way of thinking about competition that is driving many industries toward competitive convergence, which is in no one's best interest and is not inevitable.

Managers must clearly distinguish operational effectiveness from strategy. Both are essential, but the two agendas are different.

The operational agenda involves continual improvement everywhere there are no trade-offs. Failure to do this creates vulnerability even for companies with a good strategy. The operational agenda is the proper place for constant change, flexibility, and relentless efforts to achieve best practice. In contrast, the strategic agenda is the right place for defining a unique position, making clear trade-offs, and tightening fit. It involves the continual search for ways to reinforce and extend the company's position. The strategic agenda demands discipline and continuity; its enemies are distraction and compromise.

Strategic continuity does not imply a static view of competition. A company must continually improve its operational effectiveness and actively try to shift the productivity frontier; at the same time, there needs to be ongoing effort to extend its uniqueness while strengthening the fit among its activities. Strategic continuity, in fact, should make an organization's continual improvement more effective.

A company may have to change its strategy if there are major structural changes in its industry. In fact, new strategic positions often arise because of industry changes, and new entrants unencumbered by history often can exploit them more easily. However, a company's choice of a

---

Emerging Industries and Technologies

Developing a strategy in a newly emerging industry or in a business undergoing revolutionary technological changes is a daunting proposition. In such cases, managers face a high level of uncertainty about the needs of customers, the products and services that will prove to be the most desired, and the best configuration of activities and technologies to deliver them. Because of all this uncertainty, imitation and hedging are rampant: unable to risk being wrong or left behind, companies match all features, offer all new services, and explore all technologies.

During such periods in an industry's development, its basic productivity frontier is being established or reestablished. Explosive growth can make such times profitable for many companies, but profits will be temporary because imitation and strategic convergence will ultimately destroy industry profitability. The companies that are enduringly successful will be those that begin as early as possible to define and embody in their activities a unique

competitive position. A period of imitation may be inevitable in emerging industries, but that period reflects the level of uncertainty rather than a desired state of affairs.

In high-tech industries, this imitation phase often continues much longer than it should. Enraptured by technological change itself, companies pack more features—most of which are never used—into their products while slashing prices across the board. Rarely are trade-offs even considered. The drive for growth to satisfy market pressures leads companies into every product area. Although a few companies with fundamental advantages prosper, the majority are doomed to a rat race no one can win.

Ironically, the popular business press, focused on hot, emerging industries, is prone to presenting these special cases as proof that we have entered a new era of competition in which none of the old rules are valid. In fact, the opposite is true.

new position must be driven by the ability to find new trade-offs and leverage a new system of complementary activities into a sustainable advantage. (See the insert "Emerging Industries and Technologies.")

NOTES

1. I first described the concept of activities and its use in understanding competitive advantage in *Competitive Advantage* (New York: The Free Press, 1985). The ideas in this article build on and extend that thinking.

2. Paul Milgrom and John Roberts have begun to explore the economics of systems of complementary functions, activities, and functions. Their focus is on the emergence of "modern manufacturing" as a new set of complementary activities, on the tendency of companies to react to external changes with coherent bundles of internal responses, and on the need for central coordination—a strategy—to align functional managers. In the latter case, they model what has long been a bedrock principle of strategy. See Paul Milgrom and John Roberts, "The Economics of Modern Manufacturing: Technology, Strategy, and Organization," *American Economic Review* 80 (1990): 511-528; Paul Milgrom, Yingyi Qian, and John Roberts, "Complementarities, Momentum, and Evolution of Modern Manufacturing," *American Economic Review* 81 (1991) 84-88; and Paul Milgrom and John Roberts, "Complementarities and Fit: Strategy, Structure, and Organizational Changes in Manufacturing," *Journal of Accounting and Economics,* vol. 19 (March-May 1995): 179-208.

3. Material on retail strategies is drawn in part from Jan Rivkin, "The Rise of Retail Category Killers," unpublished working paper, January 1995. Nicolaj Siggelkow prepared the case study on the Gap.

CHAPTER 3

How Information Gives You Competitive Advantage

Michael E. Porter

Victor E. Millar

THE INFORMATION REVOLUTION IS sweeping through our economy. No company can escape its effects. Dramatic reductions in the cost of obtaining, processing, and transmitting information are changing the way we do business.

Most general managers know that the revolution is under way, and few dispute its importance. As more and more of their time and investment capital is absorbed in information technology and its effects, executives have a growing awareness that the technology can no longer be the exclusive territory of EDP or IS departments. As they see their rivals use information for competitive advantage, these executives recognize the need to become directly involved in the management of the new technology. In the face of rapid change, however, they don't know how.

This chapter aims to help general managers respond to the challenges of the information revolution. How will advances in information technology affect competition and the sources of competitive advantage? What strategies should a company pursue to exploit the technology?

Author's note: We wish to thank Monitor Company and Arthur Andersen for their assistance in preparing this article. F. Warren McFarlan also provided valuable comments.

July–August 1985

What are the implications of actions that competitors may already have taken? Of the many opportunities for investment in information technology, which are the most urgent?

To answer these questions, managers must first understand that information technology is more than just computers. Today, information technology must be conceived of broadly to encompass the information that businesses create and use as well as a wide spectrum of increasingly convergent and linked technologies that process the information. In addition to computers, then, data recognition equipment, communications technologies, factory automation, and other hardware and services are involved.

The information revolution is affecting competition in three vital ways:

- It changes industry structure and, in so doing, alters the rules of competition.

- It creates competitive advantage by giving companies new ways to outperform their rivals.

- It spawns whole new businesses, often from within a company's existing operations.

We discuss the reasons why information technology has acquired strategic significance and how it is affecting all businesses. We then describe how the new technology changes the nature of competition and how astute companies have exploited this. Finally, we outline a procedure managers can use to assess the role of information technology in their business and to help define investment priorities to turn the technology to their competitive advantage.

Strategic Significance

Information technology is changing the way companies operate. It is affecting the entire process by which companies create their products. Furthermore, it is reshaping the product itself: the entire package of physical goods, services, and information companies provide to create value for their buyers.

An important concept that highlights the role of information technology in competition is the "value chain."[1] This concept divides a company's activities into the technologically and economically distinct activities it performs to do business. We call these "value activities." The value a company creates is measured by the amount that buyers are willing to pay for a product or service. A business is profitable if the value it creates exceeds the cost of performing the value activities. To gain competitive advantage over its rivals, a company must either perform these activities at a lower cost or perform them in a way that leads to differentiation and a premium price (more value).[2]

A company's value activities fall into nine generic categories (see Figure 3.1). Primary activities are those involved in the physical creation of the product, its marketing and delivery to buyers, and its support and servicing after sale. Support activities provide the inputs and infrastructure that allow the primary activities to take place. Every activity employs purchased inputs, human resources, and a combination of technologies. Firm infrastructure, including such functions as general management, legal work, and accounting, supports the entire chain. Within each of these generic categories, a company will perform a number of discrete activities, depending on the particular business. Service, for example, frequently includes activities such as installation, repair, adjustment, upgrading, and parts inventory management.

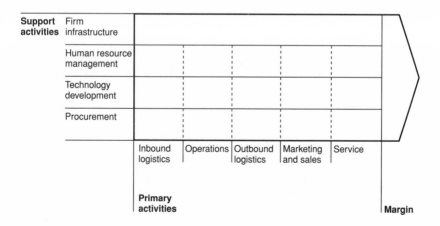

Figure 3.1   The Value Chain

A company's value chain is a system of interdependent activities, which are connected by linkages. Linkages exist when the way in which one activity is performed affects the cost or effectiveness of other activities. Linkages often create trade-offs in performing different activities that should be optimized. This optimization may require trade-offs. For example, a more costly product design and more expensive raw materials can reduce after-sale service costs. A company must resolve such trade-offs, in accordance with its strategy, to achieve competitive advantage.

Linkages also require activities to be coordinated. On-time delivery requires that operations, outbound logistics, and service activities (installation, for example) should function smoothly together. Good coordination allows on-time delivery without the need for costly inventory. Careful management of linkages is often a powerful source of competitive advantage because of the difficulty rivals have in perceiving them and in resolving trade-offs across organizational lines.

The value chain for a company in a particular industry is embedded in a larger stream of activities that we term the "value system" (see Figure 3.2). The value system includes the value chains of suppliers, who provide inputs (such as raw materials, components, and purchased services) to the company's value chain. The company's product often passes through its channels' value chains on its way to the ultimate buyer. Finally, the product becomes a purchased input to the value chains of its buyers, who use it to perform one or more buyer activities.

Linkages not only connect value activities inside a company but also create interdependencies between its value chain and those of its suppliers and channels. A company can create competitive advantage by optimizing or coordinating these links to the outside. For example, a candy manufacturer may save processing steps by persuading its suppliers to deliver chocolate in liquid form rather than in molded bars. Just-in-time

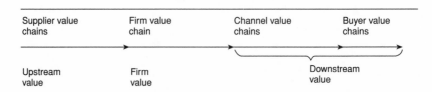

Figure 3.2   The Value System

deliveries by the supplier may have the same effect. But the opportunities for savings through coordinating with suppliers and channels go far beyond logistics and order processing. The company, suppliers, and channels can all benefit through better recognition and exploitation of such linkages.

Competitive advantage in either cost or differentiation is a function of a company's value chain. A company's cost position reflects the collective cost of performing all its value activities relative to rivals. Each value activity has cost drivers that determine the potential sources of a cost advantage. Similarly, a company's ability to differentiate itself reflects the contribution of each value activity toward fulfillment of buyer needs. Many of a company's activities—not just its physical product or service—contribute to differentiation. Buyer needs, in turn, depend not only on the impact of the company's product on the buyer but also on the company's other activities (for example, logistics or after-sale services).

In the search for competitive advantage, companies often differ in competitive scope—or the breadth of their activities. Competitive scope has four key dimensions: segment scope, vertical scope (degree of vertical integration), geographic scope, and industry scope (or the range of related industries in which the company competes).

Competitive scope is a powerful tool for creating competitive advantage. Broad scope can allow the company to exploit interrelationships between the value chains serving different industry segments, geographic areas, or related industries. For example, two business units may share one sales force to sell their products, or the units may coordinate the procurement of common components. Competing nationally or globally with a coordinated strategy can yield a competitive advantage over local or domestic rivals. By employing a broad vertical scope, a company can exploit the potential benefits of performing more activities internally rather than use outside suppliers.

By selecting a narrow scope, on the other hand, a company may be able to tailor the value chain to a particular target segment to achieve lower cost or differentiation. The competitive advantage of a narrow scope comes from customizing the value chain to best serve particular product varieties, buyers, or geographic regions. If the target segment has unusual needs, broad-scope competitors will not serve it well.

TRANSFORMING THE VALUE CHAIN

Information technology is permeating the value chain at every point, transforming the way value activities are performed and the nature of the linkages among them. It also is affecting competitive scope and reshaping the way products meet buyer needs. These basic effects explain why information technology has acquired strategic significance and is different from the many other technologies businesses use.

Every value activity has both a physical and an information-processing component. The physical component includes all the physical tasks required to perform the activity. The information-processing component encompasses the steps required to capture, manipulate, and channel the data necessary to perform the activity.

Every value activity creates and uses information of some kind. A logistics activity, for example, uses information like scheduling promises, transportation rates, and production plans to ensure timely and cost-effective delivery. A service activity uses information about service requests to schedule calls and order parts, and generates information on product failures that a company can use to revise product designs and manufacturing methods.

An activity's physical and information-processing components may be simple or quite complex. Different activities require a different mix of the two components. For instance, metal stamping uses more physical processing than information processing; processing of insurance claims requires just the opposite balance.

For most of industrial history, technological progress principally affected the physical component of what businesses do. During the Industrial Revolution, companies achieved competitive advantage by substituting machines for human labor. Information processing at that time was mostly the result of human effort.

Now the pace of technological change is reversed. Information technology is advancing faster than technologies for physical processing. The costs of information storage, manipulation, and transmittal are falling rapidly and the boundaries of what is feasible in information processing are at the same time expanding. During the Industrial Revolution, the railroad cut the travel time from Boston, Massachusetts, to Concord, New Hampshire, from five days to four hours, a factor of thirty.[3] But the advances in information technology are even greater. The cost of computer power relative to the cost of manual information processing is at least 8,000 times less expensive than the cost thirty years ago. Between 1958 and 1980 the time for one electronic operation fell by a factor of 80 million. Department of Defense studies show that the error rate in recording data through bar coding is 1 in 3,000,000, compared to 1 error in 300 manual data entries.[4]

This technological transformation is expanding the limits of what companies can do faster than managers can explore the opportunities. The information revolution affects all nine categories of value activity, from allowing computer-aided design in technology development to incorporating automation in warehouses (see Figure 3.3). The new technology substitutes machines for human effort in information processing. Paper ledgers and rules of thumb have given way to computers.

Initially, companies used information technology mainly for accounting and record-keeping functions. In these applications, the computers automated repetitive clerical functions such as order processing. Today information technology is spreading throughout the value chain and is performing optimization and control functions as well as more judgmental executive functions. General Electric, for instance, uses a data base that includes the accumulated experience and (often intuitive) knowledge of its appliance service engineers to provide support to customers by phone.

Information technology is generating more data as a company performs its activities and is permitting it to collect or capture information that was not available before. Such technology also makes room for a more comprehensive analysis and use of the expanded data. The number of variables that a company can analyze or control has grown dramatically. Hunt-Wesson, for example, developed a computer model to aid it in studying distribution-center expansion and relocation issues. The model enabled the company to evaluate many more different variables, scenarios, and alternative strategies than had been possible before. Similarly, information technology helped Sulzer Brothers' engineers improve the design of diesel engines in ways that manual calculations could not.

Information technology is also transforming the physical processing component of activities. Computer-controlled machine tools are faster, more accurate, and more flexible in manufacturing than the older, manu-

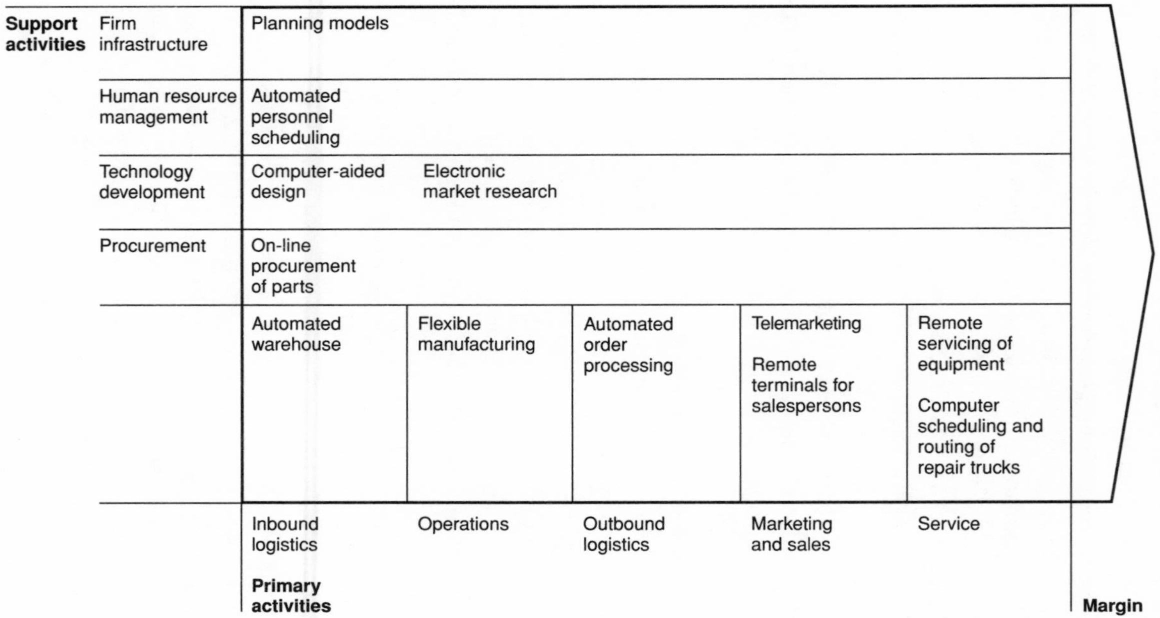

Support activities	Firm infrastructure	Planning models				
	Human resource management	Automated personnel scheduling				
	Technology development	Computer-aided design	Electronic market research			
	Procurement	On-line procurement of parts				
		Automated warehouse	Flexible manufacturing	Automated order processing	Telemarketing Remote terminals for salespersons	Remote servicing of equipment Computer scheduling and routing of repair trucks
		Inbound logistics	Operations	Outbound logistics	Marketing and sales	Service
		Primary activities				

Margin

Figure 3-3 Information Technology Permeates the Value Chain

ally operated machines. Schlumberger has developed an electronic device permitting engineers to measure the angle of a drill bit, the temperature of a rock, and other variables while drilling oil wells. The result: drilling time is reduced and some well-logging steps are eliminated. On the West Coast, some fishermen now use weather satellite data on ocean temperatures to identify promising fishing grounds. This practice greatly reduces the fishermen's steaming time and fuel costs.

Information technology not only affects how individual activities are performed but, through new information flows, it is also greatly enhancing a company's ability to exploit linkages between activities, both within and outside the company. The technology is creating new linkages between activities, and companies can now coordinate their actions more closely with those of their buyers and suppliers. For example, McKesson, the nation's largest drug distributor, provides its drugstore customers with terminals. The company makes it so easy for clients to order, receive, and prepare invoices that the customers, in return, are willing to place larger orders. At the same time, McKesson has streamlined its order processing.

Finally, the new technology has a powerful effect on competitive scope. Information systems allow companies to coordinate value activities in far-flung geographic locations. (For example, Boeing engineers work on designs on-line with foreign suppliers.) Information technology is also creating many new interrelationships among businesses, expanding the scope of industries in which a company must compete to achieve competitive advantage.

So pervasive is the impact of information technology that it confronts executives with a tough problem: too much information. This problem creates new uses of information technology to store and analyze the flood of information available to executives.

TRANSFORMING THE PRODUCT

Most products have always had both a physical and an information component. The latter, broadly defined, is everything that the buyer needs to know to obtain the product and use it to achieve the desired result. That is, a product includes information about its characteristics and how it should be used and supported. For example, convenient, accessible information on maintenance and service procedures is an important buyer criterion in consumer appliances.

Historically, a product's physical component has been more important than its information component. The new technology, however, makes it feasible to supply far more information along with the physical product. For example, General Electric's appliance service data base supports a consumer hotline that helps differentiate GE's service support from its rivals'. Similarly, some railroad and trucking companies offer up-to-the-minute information on the whereabouts of shippers' freight, which improves coordination between shippers and the railroad. The new technology is also making it increasingly possible to offer products with no physical component at all. Compustat's customers have access to corporate financial data filed with the Securities and Exchange Commission, and many companies have sprung up to perform energy use analyses of buildings.

Many products also process information in their normal functioning. A dishwasher, for example, requires a control system that directs the various components of the unit through the washing cycle and displays the process to the user. The new information technology is enhancing product performance and is making it easier to boost a product's information content. Electronic control of the automobile, for example, is becoming more visible in dashboard displays, talking dashboards, diagnostic messages, and the like.

There is an unmistakable trend toward expanding the information content in products. This component, combined with changes in companies' value chains, underscores the increasingly strategic role of information technology. There are no longer mature industries; rather, there are mature ways of doing business.

DIRECTION & PACE OF CHANGE

Although a trend toward information intensity in companies and products is evident, the role and importance of the technology differs in each industry. Banking and insurance, for example, have always been information intensive. Such industries were naturally among the first and most enthusiastic users of data processing. On the other hand, physical processing will continue to dominate in industries that produce, say, cement, despite increased information processing in such businesses.

Figure 3.4, which relates information intensity in the value chain to information content in the product, illuminates the differences in the role and intensity of information among various industries. The banking and newspaper industries have a high information-technology content in both product and process. The oil-refining industry has a high use of information in the refining process but a relatively low information content in the product dimension.

Because of the falling cost and growing capacity of the new technology, many industries seem to be moving toward a higher information content in both product and process. It should be emphasized that technology

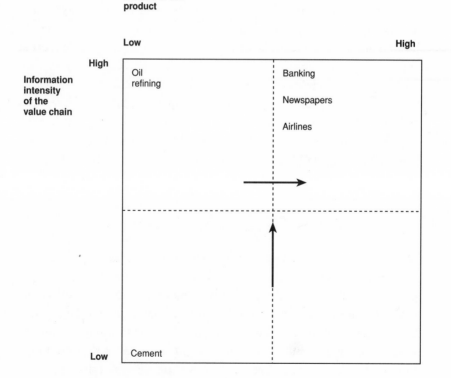

Figure 3.4   Information Intensity Matrix

will continue to improve rapidly. The cost of hardware will continue to drop, and managers will continue to distribute the technology among even the lower levels of the company. The cost of developing software, now a key constraint, will fall as more packages become available that are easily tailored to customers' circumstances. The applications of information technology that companies are using today are only a beginning.

Information technology is not only transforming products and processes but also the nature of competition itself. Despite the growing use of information technology, industries will always differ in their position in Figure 3.4 and their pace of change.

Changing the Nature of Competition

After surveying a wide range of industries, we find that information technology is changing the rules of competition in three ways. First, advances in information technology are changing the industry structure. Second, information technology is an increasingly important lever that companies can use to create competitive advantage. A company's search for competitive advantage through information technology often also spreads to affect industry structure as competitors imitate the leader's strategic innovations. Finally, the information revolution is spawning completely new businesses. These three effects are critical for understanding the impact of information technology on a particular industry and for formulating effective strategic responses.

CHANGING INDUSTRY STRUCTURE

The structure of an industry is embodied in five competitive forces that collectively determine industry profitability: the power of buyers, the power of suppliers, the threat of new entrants, the threat of substitute products, and the rivalry among existing competitors (see Figure 3.5). The collective strength of the five forces varies from industry to industry, as does average profitability. The strength of each of the five forces can also change, either improving or eroding the attractiveness of an industry.[5]

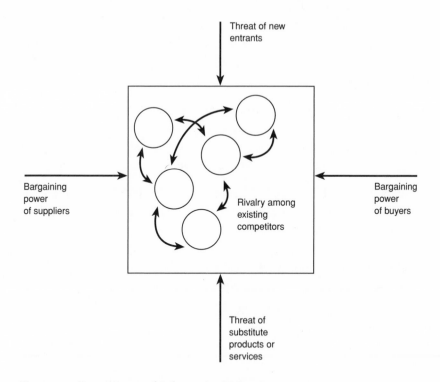

Figure 3.5   Determinants of Industry Attractiveness

Information technology can alter each of the five competitive forces and, hence, industry attractiveness as well. The technology is unfreezing the structure of many industries, creating the need and opportunity for change. For example:

• Information technology increases the power of buyers in industries assembling purchased components. Automated bills for materials and vendor quotation files make it easier for buyers to evaluate sources of materials and make-or-buy decisions.

• Information technologies requiring large investments in complex software have raised the barriers to entry. For example, banks competing in cash management services for corporate clients now need advanced software to give customers on-line account information. These banks may also need to invest in improved computer hardware and other facilities.

- Flexible computer-aided design and manufacturing systems have influenced the threat of substitution in many industries by making it quicker, easier, and cheaper to incorporate enhanced features into products.

- The automation of order processing and customer billing has increased rivalry in many distribution industries. The new technology raises fixed costs at the same time as it displaces people. As a result, distributors must often fight harder for incremental volume.

Industries such as airlines, financial services, distribution, and information suppliers (see the upper right-hand corner of Figure 3.4) have felt these effects so far.[6] (See the insert "Information Technology and Industry Structure" for more examples.)

Information technology has had a particularly strong impact on bargaining relationships between suppliers and buyers since it affects the linkages between companies and their suppliers, channels, and buyers. Information systems that cross company lines are becoming common. In some cases, the boundaries of industries themselves have changed.[7]

Systems that connect buyers and suppliers are spreading. Xerox gives manufacturing data to suppliers electronically to help them deliver materials. To speed up order entry, Westinghouse Electric Supply Company and American Hospital Supply have furnished their customers with terminals. Among other things, many systems raise the costs of switching to a new partner because of the disruption and retraining required. These systems tend to tie companies more closely to their buyers and suppliers.

Information technology is altering the relationship among scale, automation, and flexibility with potentially profound consequences. Large-scale production is no longer essential to achieve automation. As a result, entry barriers in a number of industries are falling.

At the same time, automation no longer necessarily leads to inflexibility. For example, General Electric rebuilt its Erie locomotive facility as a large-scale yet flexible factory using computers to store all design and manufacturing data. Ten types of motor frames can be accommodated without manual adjustments to the machines. After installation of a "smart" manufacturing system, BMW can build customized cars (each with its own tailored gearbox, transmission system, interior, and other

Information Technology and Industry Structure

Buyer Power

Videotex home shopping services, such as Comp-U-Card, increase buyers' information. Buyers use their personal computers to browse through electronic catalogs and compare prices and product specifications. Customers can make purchases at any hour at prices typically 25 percent to 30 percent below suggested retail levels. Comp-U-Card is growing quickly: revenues have quintupled in two years to $9.5 million and membership is now 15,000. According to some projections, by the mid-1990s, 75 percent of U.S. households will have access to such services.

Buyer Power

Shelternet, an electronic information exchange offered by First Boston Corporation, allows real estate brokers to determine quickly and easily what mortgage packages are available and whether the buyer will qualify for financing. This improves the position of both brokers and homebuyers in shopping for mortgages. The parties can make preliminary commitments within thirty minutes.

Substitution

Electronic data bases, such as NEXIS, are substituting for libraray research and consulting firms. NEXIS subscribers can quickly search the full text of any article in 225 periodicals. Users drastically reduce the time spent in literature searches. In addition, the buyer avoids the cost of journal subscriptions and pays only for the information required.

features) on the normal assembly line. Automation and flexibility are achieved simultaneously, a pairing that changes the pattern of rivalry among competitors.

The increasing flexibility in performing many value activities combined with the falling costs of designing products has triggered an avalanche of opportunities to customize and to serve small market niches. Computer-aided design capability not only reduces the cost of designing new products but also dramatically reduces the cost of modifying or adding features to existing products. The cost of tailoring products to market segments is falling, again affecting the pattern of industry rivalry.

While managers can use information technology to improve their industry structure, the technology also has the potential to destroy that structure. For example, information systems now permit the airline industry to alter fares frequently and to charge many different fares between any two points. At the same time, however, the technology makes the flight and fare schedules more readily available and allows travel agents and individuals to shop around quickly for the lowest fare. The result is a lower fare structure than might otherwise exist. Information technology has made a number of professional service industries less attractive by reducing personal interaction and making service more of a commodity. Managers must look carefully at the structural implications of the new technology to realize its advantages or to be prepared for its consequences.

CREATING COMPETITIVE ADVANTAGE

In any company, information technology has a powerful effect on competitive advantage in either cost or differentiation. The technology affects value activities themselves or allows companies to gain competitive advantage by exploiting changes in competitive scope.

Lowering Cost. As we have seen, information technology can alter a company's costs in any part of the value chain.[8] The technology's historical impact on cost was confined to activities in which repetitive information processing played a large part. These limits no longer exist, however. Even activities like assembly that mainly involve physical processing now have a large information-processing component.

Canon, for example, built a low-cost copier assembly process around an automated parts-selection and materials-handling system. Assembly workers have bins containing all the parts needed for the particular copier. Canon's success with this system derives from the software that controls parts inventory and selection. In insurance brokerage, a number of insurance companies usually participate in underwriting a contract. The costs of documenting each company's participation are high. Now a computer model can optimize (and often reduce) the number of insurers per contract, lowering the broker's total cost. In garment production, equipment such as automated pattern drawers, fabric cutters, and systems for delivering cloth to the final sewing station have reduced the labor time for manufacturing by up to 50 percent. (See the insert "Aim: A Competitive Edge" for further examples.)

In addition to playing a direct role in cost, information technology often alters the cost drivers of activities in ways that can improve (or erode) a company's relative cost position. For example, Louisiana Oil & Tire has taken all ten of its salespeople off the road and made them into telemarketers. As a result, sales expenses have fallen by 10 percent and sales volume has doubled. However, the move has made the national scale of operations the key determinant of the cost of selling, rather than regional scale.

Enhancing Differentiation. The impact of information technology on differentiation strategies is equally dramatic. As noted earlier, the role of a company and its product in the buyer's value chain is the key determinant of differentiation. The new information technology makes it possible to customize products. Using automation, for instance, Sulzer Brothers has increased from five to eight the number of cylinder bore sizes of new low-speed marine diesel engines. Shipowners now choose an engine that is more precisely suited to their needs and thereby recoup

---

Aim: A Competitive Edge

Lowering Cost

Casinos spend up to 20% of revenues on complimentary services for high rollers. One assignment for pit bosses has always been to keep an eye out for the big spenders. Now, however, many casinos have developed computer systems to analyze data on customers. Caesar's Palace lowered its complimentary budget more than 20% by developing a player-rating system for more accurate identification of big spenders.

Enhancing Differentiation

American Express has developed differentiated travel services for corporate customers through the use of information technology. The services include arranging travel and close monitoring of individual expenses. Computers search for the lowest airplane fares, track travel expenses for each cardholder, and issue monthly statements.

significant fuel savings. Similarly, Digital Equipment's artificial intelligence system, XCON, uses decision rules to develop custom computer configurations. This dramatically reduces the time required to fill orders and increases accuracy—which enhances Digital's image as a quality provider.

By bundling more information with the physical product package sold to the buyer, the new technology affects a company's ability to differentiate itself. For example, a magazine distributor offers retailers processing credits for unsold items more efficiently than its competitors. Similarly, the embedding of information systems in the physical product itself is an increasingly powerful way to distinguish it from competing goods.

Changing Competitive Scope. Information technology can alter the relationship between competitive scope and competitive advantage. The technology increases a company's ability to coordinate its activities regionally, nationally, and globally. It can unlock the power of broader geographic scope to create competitive advantage. Consider the newspaper industry. Dow Jones, publisher of the *Wall Street Journal*, pioneered the page transmission technology that links its seventeen U.S. printing plants to produce a truly national newspaper. Such advances in communication plants have also made it possible to move toward a global strategy. Dow Jones has started the *Asian Wall Street Journal* and the *Wall Street Journal-European Edition* and shares much of the editorial content while printing the papers in plants all over the world.

The information revolution is creating interrelationships among industries that were previously separate. The merging of computer and telecommunications technologies is an important example. This convergence has profound effects on the structure of both industries. For example, AT&T is using its position in telecommunications as a staging point for entry into the computer industry. IBM, which recently acquired Rolm, the telecommunications equipment manufacturer, is now joining the competition from the other direction. Information technology is also at the core of growing interrelationships in financial services, where the banking, insurance, and brokerage industries are merging, and in office equipment, where once distinct functions such as typing, photocopying, and data and voice communications can now be combined.

Broad-line companies are increasingly able to segment their offerings in ways that were previously feasible only for focused companies. In the trucking industry, Intermodal Transportation Services, Inc. of Cincinnati has completely changed its system for quoting prices. In the past, each local office set prices using manual procedures. Intermodal now uses microcomputers to link its offices to a center that calculates all prices. The new system gives the company the capacity to introduce a new pricing policy to offer discounts to national accounts, which place their orders from all over the country. Intermodal is tailoring its value chain to large national customers in a way that was previously impossible.

As information technology becomes more widespread, the opportunities to take advantage of a new competitive scope will only increase. The benefits of scope (and the achievement of linkages), however, can accrue only when the information technology spread throughout the organization can communicate. Completely decentralized organizational design and application of information technology will thwart these possibilities, because the information technology introduced in various parts of a company will not be compatible.

SPAWNING NEW BUSINESSES

The information revolution is giving birth to completely new industries in three distinct ways. First, it makes new businesses technologically feasible. For example, modern imaging and telecommunications technology blend to support new facsimile services such as Federal Express's Zapmail. Similarly, advances in microelectronics made personal computing possible. Services such as Merrill Lynch's Cash Management Account required new information technology to combine several financial products into one.

Second, information technology can also spawn new businesses by creating derived demand for new products. One example is Western Union's EasyLink service, a sophisticated, high-speed, data-communications network that allows personal computers, word processors, and other electronic devices to send messages to each other and to telex machines throughout the world. This service was not needed before the spread of information technology caused a demand for it.

Third, information technology creates new businesses within old ones. A company with information processing embedded in its value chain may have excess capacity or skills that can be sold outside. Sears took advantage of its skills in processing credit card accounts and of its massive scale to provide similar services to others. It sells credit-authorization and transaction-processing services to Phillips Petroleum and retail remittance-processing services to Mellon Bank. Similarly, a manufacturer of automotive parts, A.O. Smith, developed data-commu-nications expertise to meet the needs of its traditional businesses. When a bank consortium went looking for a contractor to run a network of automated teller machines, A.O. Smith got the job. Eastman Kodak recently began offering long-distance telephone and data-transmission services through its internal telecommunications system. Where the information technology used in a company's value chain is sensitive to scale, a company may improve its overall competitive advantage by increasing the scale of information processing and lowering costs. By selling extra capacity outside, it is at the same time generating new revenue.

Companies also are increasingly able to create and sell to others infor-mation that is a by-product of their operations. National Benefit Life reportedly merged with American Can in part to gain access to data on the nine million customers of American Can's direct-mail retailing subsidiary. The use of bar-code scanners in supermarket retailing has turned grocery stores into market research labs. Retailers can run an ad in the morning newspaper and find out its effect by early afternoon. They can also sell this data to market research companies and to food processors.

Competing in the Age of Information

Senior executives can follow five steps to take advantage of opportunities that the information revolution has created.

1. **Assess information intensity.** A company's first task is to evaluate the existing and potential information intensity of the products and processes of its business units. To help managers accomplish this, we

have developed some measures of the potential importance of information technology.

It is very likely that information technology will play a strategic role in an industry that is characterized by one or more of the following features:

- Potentially high information intensity in the value chain—a large number of suppliers or customers with whom the company deals directly, a product requiring a large quantity of information in selling, a product line with many distinct product varieties, a product composed of many parts, a large number of steps in a company's manufacturing process, a long cycle time from the initial order to the delivered product.

- Potentially high information intensity in the product—a product that mainly provides information, a product whose operation involves substantial information processing, a product whose use requires the buyer to process a lot of information, a product requiring especially high costs for buyer training, a product that has many alternative uses or is sold to a buyer with high information intensity in his or her own business.

These may help identify priority business units for investment in information technology. When selecting priority areas, remember the breadth of information technology—it involves more than simple computing.

2. **Determine the role of information technology in industry structure.** Managers should predict the likely impact of information technology on their industry's structure. They must examine how information technology might affect each of the five competitive forces. Not only is each force likely to change but industry boundaries may change as well. Chances are that a new definition of the industry may be necessary.

Many companies are partly in control of the nature and pace of change in the industry structure. Companies have permanently altered the bases of competition in their favor in many industries through aggressive investments in information technology and have forced other companies to follow. Citibank, with its automated teller machines and transaction processing; American Airlines, with its computerized reservations system; and *USA Today*, with its newspaper page transmission to decentralized printing plants, are pioneers that have used information technology to alter industry structure. A company should understand how structural change is forcing it to respond and look for ways to lead change in the industry.

3. Identify and rank the ways in which information technology might create competitive advantage. The starting assumption must be that the technology is likely to affect every activity in the value chain. Equally important is the possibility that new linkages among activities are being made possible. By taking a careful look, managers can identify the value activities that are likely to be most affected in terms of cost and differentiation. Obviously, activities that represent a large proportion of cost or that are critical to differentiation bear closest scrutiny, particularly if they have a significant information-processing component. Activities with important links to other activities inside and outside the company are also critical. Executives must examine such activities for ways in which information technology can create sustainable competitive advantage.

In addition to taking a hard look at its value chain, a company should consider how information technology might allow a change in competitive scope. Can information technology help the company serve new segments? Will the flexibility of information technology allow broad-line competitors to invade areas that were once the province of niche competitors? Will information technology provide the leverage to expand the business globally? Can managers harness information technology to exploit interrelationships with other industries? Or, can the technology help a company create competitive advantage by narrowing its scope?

A fresh look at the company's product may also be in order:

Can the company bundle more information with the product?

Can the company embed information technology in it?

4. Investigate how information technology might spawn new businesses. Managers should consider opportunities to create new businesses from existing ones. Information technology is an increasingly important avenue for corporate diversification. Lockheed, for example, entered the data base business by perceiving an opportunity to use its spare computer capacity.

Identifying opportunities to spawn new businesses requires answering questions such as:

What information generated (or potentially generated) in the business could the company sell?

What information-processing capacity exists internally to start a new business?

Does information technology make it feasible to produce new items related to the company's product?

5. **Develop a plan for taking advantage of information technology.** The first four steps should lead to an action plan to capitalize on the information revolution. This action plan should rank the strategic investments necessary in hardware and software, and in new product development activities that reflect the increasing information content in products. Organizational changes that reflect the role that the technology plays in linking activities inside and outside the company are likely to be necessary.

The management of information technology can no longer be the sole province of the EDP department. Increasingly, companies must employ information technology with a sophisticated understanding of the requirements for competitive advantage. Organizations need to distribute the responsibility for systems development more widely in the organization. At the same time, general managers must be involved to ensure that cross-functional linkages, more possible to achieve with information technology, are exploited.

These changes do not mean that a central information-technology function should play an insignificant role. Rather than control information technology, however, an information services manager should coordinate the architecture and standards of the many applications throughout the organization, as well as provide assistance and coaching in systems development. Unless the numerous applications of information technology inside a company are compatible with each other, many benefits may be lost.

Information technology can help in the strategy implementation process. Reporting systems can track progress toward milestones and success factors. By using information systems, companies can measure their activities more precisely and help motivate managers to implement strategies successfully.[9]

The importance of the information revolution is not in dispute. The question is not whether information technology will have a significant impact on a company's competitive position; rather the question is when and how this impact will strike. Companies that anticipate the power of information technology will be in control of events. Companies that do not respond will be forced to accept changes that others initiate and will find themselves at a competitive disadvantage.

NOTES

1. For more information on the value chain concept, see Michael E. Porter, *Competitive Advantage* (New York: Free Press, 1985).

2. For a discussion of the two basic types of competitive advantage, see Michael E. Porter, *Competitive Strategy* (New York: Free Press, 1980), Chapter 2.

3. Alfred D. Chandler, Jr., *The Visible Hand* (Cambridge: Belknap Press of Harvard University Press, 1977), p. 86.

4. James L. McKenney and F. Warren McFarlan, "The Information Archipelago—Maps and Bridges," *Harvard Business Review* 60, no. 5 (1982): 109.

5. See Michael E. Porter, "How Competitive Forces Shape Strategy," *Harvard Business Review* 57, no. 2 (1979): 137.

6. See F. Warren McFarlan, "Information Technology Changes the Way You Compete," *Harvard Business Review* 62, no. 3 (1984): 98.

7. James I. Cash, Jr. and Benn R. Konsynski, "IS Redraws Competitive Boundaries," *Harvard Business Review* 63, no. 2 (1985): 134.

8. See Gregory L. Parsons, "Information Technology: A New Competitive Weapon," *Sloan Management Review,* Fall 1983, p. 3.

9. Victor E. Millar, "Decision-Oriented Information," *Datamation,* January 1984, p. 159.

CHAPTER 4

End-Game Strategies
for Declining Industries

Kathryn Rudie Harrigan

Michael E. Porter

END GAME *N;* (1) the last stage (as the last three tricks) in playing a bridge hand; (2) the final phase of a board game; specifically the stage of a chess game following serious reduction of forces.[1]

As early as 1948, when researchers discovered the "transistor effect," it was evident that vacuum tubes in television sets had become technologically obsolete. Within a few years, transistor manufacturers were predicting that by 1961 half the television sets then in use would employ transistors instead of vacuum tubes.

Since the 1950s, manufacturers of vacuum tubes have been engaged in the industry's end game. Like other end games, this one is played in an environment of declining product demand where conditions make it very unlikely that all the plant capacity and competitors put in place during the industry's heyday will ever be needed. In today's world of little or no economic growth and rapid technological change, more and more companies are being faced with the need to cope with an end game.

Because of its musical chair character, the end game can be brutal. Consider the bloodbath in U.S. gasoline marketing today. Between 1973 and 1983, in response to high crude oil prices and conservation efforts by consumers, the output from petroleum refineries declined precipitately. Uncertainty concerning supply and demand for refined products has made predicting the speed and extent of decline difficult, and an industry

---

July–August 1993

consensus has never evolved. Moreover, the competitors in this end game are very diverse in their outlooks and in the tactics they use to cope with the erratic nature of decline.

As in the baby food industry's end game, where a ten-year price war raged until demand plateaued, gasoline marketers and refiners are fighting to hold market shares of a shrinking pie. As industry capacity is painfully rationalized and companies dig in for the lean years ahead in their end game, a long period of low profits is inevitable.

In the vacuum tube industry, however, the end game was starkly different. Commercialization of solid-state devices progressed more slowly than the transistor manufacturers forecast. The last television set containing vacuum tubes was produced in 1974, and a vast population of electronic products requiring replacement tubes guaranteed a sizable market of relatively price-insensitive demand for some years. In 1983, several plants still produce tubes. Where obsolescence was a certainty and the decline rate slow, the six leading vacuum tube manufacturers were able to shut down excess plant capacity while keeping supply in line with demand. Price wars never ruined the profitability of their end game, and the companies that managed well during the decline earned satisfactorily high returns, particularly for declining businesses.

To recoup the maximum return on their investments, managers of some declining businesses are turning with considerable success to strategies that they had used only when demand was growing. In the past, the accepted prescription for a business on the wane has been a "harvest" strategy—eliminate investment, generate maximum cash flow, and eventually divest. The strategic portfolio models managers commonly use for planning yield this advice on declining industries: do not invest in low- or negative-growth markets; pull cash out instead.

Our study of declining industries suggests, however, that the nature of competition during a decline and the strategic alternatives available for coping with it are complex (see the insert "Study of Strategies for Declining Businesses" for a description of the study). The experiences of industries that have suffered an absolute decline in unit sales over a sustained period differ markedly. Some industries, like vacuum receiving tubes, age gracefully, and profitability for remaining competitors has been extremely high. Others, like rayon, decline amid bitter warfare, prolonged excess capacity, and heavy operating losses.

Study of Strategies for Declining Businesses

Compiling twenty-year histories of industry competition and company departures, we studied the strategies of sixty-one companies in eight declining industries.* We interviewed key competitors in the rayon and acetate, cigar, baby food, electric percolator coffee maker, electronic vacuum receiving tube, acetylene, synthetic soda ash, and U.S. leather tanning industries. (Follow-up studies examined the petroleum refining and whiskey distilling industries and attained consistent results.) Leaving their industries, forty-two companies were profitable or did not suffer significant losses, while nineteen were unprofitable or suffered sizable losses. Thirty-nine of the forty-two successful companies followed the prescriptions of the strategy matrix shown in Figure 4.1. Sixteen of the nineteen unsuccessful companies acted contrary to the recommendations of the strategy matrix. In short, if companies followed the matrix recommendations, the chances for success were better than 92 percent, while if they did not follow them, their chances of success were about 15 percent.

---

*See Kathryn Rudie Harrigan's *Strategies for Declining Businesses* (Lexington, Mass.: D.C. Heath, 1980).

The stories of companies that have successfully coped with decline vary just as widely. Some companies, like GTE Sylvania, reaped high returns by making heavy investments in a declining industry that made their businesses better sources of cash later. By selling out before their competitors generally recognized the decline, and not harvesting, other companies, like Raytheon and DuPont, avoided losses that competitors subsequently bore.

In this article we discuss the strategic problems that declining demand poses, where decline is a painful reality and not a function of the business cycle or other short-term discontinuities. Sometimes, of course, innovations, cost reductions, and shifts in other circumstances may reverse a decline.[2] Our focus here, however, is on industries in which available remedies have been exhausted and the strategic problem is coping with decline. When decline is beyond the control of incumbent companies, managers need to develop end-game strategies.

First, we sketch the structural conditions that determine if the environment of a declining industry is hospitable, particularly as these affect competition. Second, we discuss the generic end-game strategy alternatives available to companies in decline. We conclude with some principles for choosing an end-game strategy.

What Determines the Competition?

Shrinking industry sales make the decline phase volatile. The extent to which escalating competitive pressures erode profitability during decline, however, depends on how readily industry participants pull out and how fiercely the companies that remain try to contain their shrinking sales.

CONDITIONS OF DEMAND

Demand in an industry declines for a number of reasons. Technological advances foster substitute products (electronic calculators for slide rules) often at lower cost or higher quality (synthetics for leather). Sometimes the customer group shrinks (baby foods) or buyers slide into trouble (railroads). Changes in life-style, buyers' needs, or tastes can also cause demand to decline (cigars and hatmaking equipment). Finally, the cost of inputs or complementary products may rise and shrink demand (recreational vehicles). The cause of decline helps determine how companies will perceive both future demand and the profitability of serving the diminished market.

Companies' expectations concerning demand will substantially affect the type of competitive environment that develops in an end game. The process by which demand in an industry declines and the characteristics of those market segments that remain also have a great influence on competition during the decline phase.

Uncertainty. Correct or not, competitors' perceptions of demand in a declining industry potently affect how they play out their end-game strategies. If managers in the industry believe that demand will revitalize or level off, they will probably try to hold onto their positions. As the baby food industry example shows, efforts to maintain position despite shrinking sales will probably lead to warfare. On the other hand, if, as was the case of synthetic sodium carbonate (soda ash), managers in different companies are all certain that industry demand will continue to decline, reduction of capacity is more likely to be orderly.

Companies may well differ in their perceptions of future demand, with those that foresee revitalization persevering. A company's perception of the likelihood of decline is influenced by its position in the industry and its difficulty in getting out. The stronger its stake or the higher its exit barriers, the more optimistic a company's forecast of demand is likely to be.

Rate & Pattern of Decline. Rapid and erratic decline greatly exacerbate the volatility of competition. How fast the industry collapses depends partly on the way in which companies withdraw capacity. In industrial businesses (such as the synthesis of soda ash) where the product is very important to customers but where a substitute is available, demand can fall drastically if one or two major producers decide to retire and customers doubt the continued availability of the original product. Announcements of early departure can give great impetus to the decline. Because shrinking volume raises costs and often prices, the decline rate tends to accelerate as time passes.

Structure of Remaining Demand Pockets. In a shrinking market, the nature of the demand pockets that remain plays a major role in determining the remaining competitors' profitability. The remaining pocket in cigars has been premium-quality cigars, for example, while in vacuum tubes it has been replacement and military tubes.

If the remaining pocket has favorable structure, decline can be profitable for well-positioned competitors. For example, demand for premium-quality cigars is price insensitive: customers are immune to substitute products and very brand loyal. Thus, even as the industry declines, companies that offer branded, premium cigars are earning above-average returns. For the same reasons, upholstery leathers are a profitable market segment in the leather industry.

On the other hand, in the acetylene industry, ethylene has already replaced acetylene in some market segments and other substitutes threaten the remaining pockets. In those pockets, acetylene is a commodity product that, because of its high fixed manufacturing costs, is subject to price warfare. The potential for profit for its remaining manufacturers is dismal.

In general, if the buyers in the remaining demand pockets are price insensitive, e.g., buyers of replacement vacuum tubes for television receivers, or have little bargaining power, survivors can profit. Price insensitivity is important because shrinking sales imply that companies must raise prices to maintain profitability in the face of fixed overhead.

The profit potential of remaining demand pockets will also depend on whether companies that serve them have mobility barriers that protect them from attack by companies seeking to replace lost sales.

EXIT BARRIERS

Just as companies have to overcome barriers in entering a market, they meet exit barriers in leaving it. These barriers can be insurmountable even when a company is earning subnormal returns on its investment. The higher the exit barriers, the less hospitable the industry is during the industry's decline. A number of basic aspects of a business can become exit barriers.

Durable & Specialized Assets. If the assets, either fixed or working capital or both, are specialized to the business, company, or location in which they are being used, their diminished liquidation value creates exit barriers. A company with specialized assets such as sole-leather tanneries must either sell them to someone who intends to use them in the same business, usually in the same location, or scrap them. Naturally, few buyers wish to use the assets of a declining business.

Once the acetylene and rayon industries started to contract, for example, potential buyers for plants were few or nonexistent; companies sold plants at enormous discounts from book value to speculators or desperate employee groups. Particularly if it represents a large part of assets and normally turns over very slowly, specialized inventory may also be worth very little in these circumstances. The problem of specialized assets is more acute where a company must make an all-or-nothing exit decision (e.g., continuous process plants) versus a decision to reduce the number of sites or close down lines.

If the liquidation value of the assets is low, it is possible for a company to show a loss on the books but earn discounted cash flows that exceed the value that could be realized if management sold the business. When several companies perform this same analysis and choose to remain in a declining industry, excess capacity grows and profit margins are usually depressed.

By expanding their search for buyers, managers can lower exit barriers arising from specialized assets. Sometimes assets find a market overseas even though they have little value in the home country. But as the industry decline becomes increasingly clear, the value of specialized assets will usually diminish. For example, when Raytheon sold its vacuum tube-making assets in the early 1960s while tube demand was strong for color TV sets, it recovered a much higher liquidation than companies that tried to unload their vacuum tube facilities in the early 1970s, when the industry was clearly in its twilight years.

High Costs of Exit. Large fixed costs—labor settlements, contingent liabilities for land use, or costs of dismantling facilities—associated with leaving a business elevate exit barriers. Sometimes even after a company leaves, it will have to supply spare parts to past customers or resettle employees. A company may also have to break long-term contracts, which, if they can be abrogated at all, may involve severe cancellation penalties. In many cases, the company will have to pay the cost of having another company fulfill such contracts.

On the other hand, companies can sometimes avoid making fixed investments such as for pollution control equipment, alternative fuel systems, or maintenance expenditures by abandoning a business. These requirements promote getting out because they increase investment without raising profits, and improve prospects for decline.

Strategic Considerations. A diversified company may decide to remain in a declining industry for strategic reasons even if the barriers just described are low. These reasons include:

Interrelatedness. A business may be part of a strategy that involves a group of businesses, such as whiskey and other distilled liquors, and dropping it would diminish overall corporate strategy. Or a business may be central to a company's identity or image, as in the case of General Cigar and Allied Leather, and leaving could hurt the company's relationships with key distribution channels and customers or lower the company's purchasing clout. Moreover, depending on the company's ability to transfer assets to new markets, quitting the industry may make shared plants or other assets idle.

Access to financial markets. Leaving an industry may reduce a company's financial credibility and lessen its attractiveness to acquisition candidates or buyers. If the divested business is large relative to the total, divestment may hurt earnings growth or in some way raise the cost of capital, even if the write-off is economically justified. The financial market is likely to ignore small operating losses over a period of years buried among other profitable businesses while it will react strongly to a single large loss. While a diversified company may be able to use the tax loss from a write-off to mitigate the negative cash flow impact of exit decisions, the write-off will typically still have an effect on financial markets. Recently the markets have looked favorably on companies who take their losses on businesses with little future, an encouraging sign.

Vertical integration. When companies are vertically integrated, barriers to exit will depend on whether the cause of decline touches the entire chain or just one link. In the case of acetylene, obsolescence made downstream chemical businesses, using acetylene as a feedstock, redundant; a company's decision whether to stay or go had to encompass the whole chain. In contrast, if a downstream unit depended on a feedstock that a substitute product had made obsolete, it would be strongly motivated to find an outside supplier of the substitute. In this case, the company's forward integration might hasten the decision to abandon the upstream unit because it had become a strategic liability to the whole company. In our study of endgame strategies, we found that most vertically integrated companies "deintegrated" before facing the final go/no go decision.

Information Gaps. The more a business is related to others in the company, and especially when it shares assets or has a buyer-seller relationship, the more difficult it can be for management to get reliable information about its performance. For example, a failing coffee percolator unit may be part of a profit center with other small electrical housewares that sell well, and the company might not see the percolator unit's performance accurately and thus fail to consider abandoning the business.

Managerial Resistance. Although the exit barriers we've described are based on rational calculations, or the inability to make them because of failures in information, the difficulties of leaving a business extend well beyond the purely economic. Managers' emotional attachments and commitments to a business—coupled with pride in their accomplishments and fears about their own futures—create emotional exit barriers. In a single-business company, quitting the business costs managers their jobs and creates personal problems for them such as a blow to their pride, the stigma of having "given up," severance of an identification that may have been longstanding, and a signal of failure that reduces job mobility.

It is difficult for managers of a sick division in a diversified company to propose divestment, so the burden of deciding when to quit usually falls on top management. But loyalty can be strong even at that level, particularly if the sick division is part of the historical core of the company or was started or acquired by the current CEO. For example, General Mills's decision to divest its original business, flour, was an agonizing choice that took management many years to make. And the suggestion that Sunbeam stop producing electric percolator coffee makers and waffle irons met stiff resistance in the boardroom.

In some cases, even though unsatisfactory performance is chronic, managerial exit barriers can be so strong that divestments are not made until top management changes.[3] Divestments are probably the most unpalatable decisions managers have to make.[4]

Personal experience with abandoning businesses, however, can reduce managers' reluctance to get out of an industry. In an industry such as chemicals where technological failure and product substitution are common, in industries where product lives are historically short, or in high-technology companies where new businesses continually replace old ones, executives can become used to distancing themselves from emotional considerations and making sound divestment decisions.

Social Barriers. Because government concern for jobs is high and the price of divestiture may be concessions from other businesses in the company or other prohibitive terms, closing down a business can often be next to impossible, especially in foreign countries. Divestiture often means putting people out of work, and managers understandably feel concern for their employees. Workers who have produced vacuum tubes for thirty years may have little understanding of solid-state manufacturing techniques. Divestiture can also mean crippling a local economy. In the depressed Canadian pulp industry, closing down mills means closing down whole towns.[5]

Asset Disposition. The manner in which companies dispose of assets can strongly influence the profitability of a declining industry and create or destroy exit barriers for competitors. If a company doesn't retire a large plant but sells it to a group of entrepreneurs at a low price, the industry capacity does not change but the competition does. The new entity can make pricing decisions and take other actions that are rational for it but cripple the competition. Thus if the owners of a plant don't retire assets but sell out instead, the remaining competitors can suffer more than if the original owners had stayed on.

VOLATILITY OF END GAME

Because of falling sales and excess capacity, competitors fighting in an end game are likely to resort to fierce price warfare. Aggression is especially likely if the industry has maverick competitors with diverse goals and outlooks and high exit barriers, or if the market is very inhospitable (see Table 4.1).

As an industry declines, it can become less important to suppliers (which raises costs or diminishes service) while the power of distributors increases. In the cigar business, for example, because cigars are an impulse item, shelf positioning is crucial to success, and it's the distributor who deals with the retailer. In the whiskey trade too, distillers hotly compete for the best wholesalers. Decline has led to substantial price pressures from these powerful middlemen that have reduced profitability. On the other hand, if the industry is a key customer, suppliers may attempt to help fight off decline as, for example, pulp producers helped the rayon industry fight cotton.

Perhaps the worst kind of waning-industry environment occurs when one or more weakened companies with significant corporate resources are committed to stay in the business. Their weakness forces them to use desperate actions, such as cutting prices, and their staying power forces other companies to respond likewise.

Strategic Alternatives for Declining Businesses

Discussions of strategy for shrinking industries usually focus on divestment or harvest strategies, but managers should consider two other alternatives as well—leadership and niche. These four strategies for decline vary greatly, not only in their goals but also in their implications for investment, and managers can pursue them individually or, in some cases, sequentially.

Leadership. A company following the marketshare leadership strategy tries to reap above-average profitability by becoming one of the few companies remaining in a declining industry. Once a company attains this position, depending on the subsequent pattern of industry sales, it usually switches to holding position or controlled harvest strategy. The underlying premise is that by achieving leadership the company can be more profitable (taking the investment into account) because it can exert more control over the process of decline and avoid destabilizing price competition. Investing in a slow or diminishing market is risky because capital may be frozen and resistant to retrieval through profits or liquidation. Under this strategy, however, the company's dominant position in the industry should give it cost leadership or differentiation that allows recovery of assets even if it reinvests during the decline period.

Managers can achieve a leadership position via several tactical maneuvers:

• Ensure that other companies rapidly retire from the industry. H.J. Heinz and Gerber Products took aggressive competitive actions in pricing, marketing, and other areas that built market share and dispelled competitors' dreams of battling it out.

• Reduce competitors' exit barriers. GTE Sylvania built market share by acquiring competitors' product lines at prices above the going rate. American Viscose purchased—and retired—competitors' capacity. (Taking this step ensures that others within the industry do not buy the capacity.) General Electric manufactured spare parts for competitors' products. Rohm & Haas took over competitors' long-term contracts in the acetylene industry. Proctor-Silex produced private-label goods for competitors so that they could stop their manufacturing operations.

• Develop and disclose credible market information. Reinforcing other managers' certainty about the inevitability of decline makes it less likely that competitors will overestimate the prospects for the industry and remain in it.

• Raise the stakes. Precipitating the need of other competitors to reinvest in new products or process improvements makes it more costly for them to stay in the business.

Niche. The objective of this focus strategy is to identify a segment of the declining industry that will either maintain stable demand or decay slowly, and that has structural characteristics allowing high returns. A company then moves preemptively to gain a strong position in this segment while disinvesting from other segments. Armira followed a niche strategy in leather tanning, as Courtaulds did in rayon. To reduce either competitors' exit barriers from the chosen segment or their uncertainty about the segment's profitability, management might decide to take some of the actions listed under the leadership strategy.

Harvest. In the harvest strategy, undergoing a controlled disinvestment, management seeks to get the most cash flow it can from the business. DuPont followed this course with its rayon business and BASF Wyandotte did the same in soda ash. To increase cash flow, management eliminates or severely curtails new investment, cuts maintenance of facilities, and reduces advertising and research while reaping the benefits of past goodwill. Other common harvest tactics include reducing the number of models produced; cutting the number of distribution channels; eliminating small customers; and eroding service in terms of delivery time (and thus reducing inventory), speed of repair, or sales assistance.

Companies following a harvest strategy often have difficulty maintaining suppliers' and customers' confidence, however, and thus some businesses cannot be fully harvested. Moreover, harvesting tests managers' skills as administrators because it creates problems in retaining and motivating employees. These considerations make harvest a risky option and far from the universal cure-all that it is sometimes purported to be.

Ultimately, managers following a harvest strategy will sell or liquidate the business.

Quick divestment. Executives employing this strategy assume that the company can recover more of its investment from the business by selling it in the early stages of the decline, as Raytheon did, than by harvesting and selling it later or by following one of the other courses of action. The earlier the business is sold, the greater is potential buyers' uncertainty about a future slide in demand and thus the more likely that management will find buyers either at home or in foreign countries for the assets.

In some situations it may be desirable to divest the business before decline or, as DuPont did with its acetylene business, in the maturity phase. Once it's clear that the industry is waning, buyers for the assets will be in a strong bargaining position. On the other hand, a company that sells early runs the risk that its forecast will prove incorrect, as did RCA's judgment of the future of vacuum tubes.

Divesting quickly will force the company to confront its own exit barriers, such as its customer relationships and corporate interdependencies. Planning for an early departure can help managers mitigate the effect of these factors to some extent, however. For example, a company can arrange for remaining competitors to sell its products if it is necessary to continue to supply replacements, as Westinghouse Electric did for vacuum tubes.

Choosing a Strategy for Decline

With an understanding of the characteristics that shape competition in a declining industry and the different strategies they might use, managers can now ask themselves what their position should be:

> Can the structure of the industry support a hospitable, potentially profitable, decline phase (see Table 4.1)?

> What are the exit barriers that each significant competitor faces? Who will exit quickly and who will remain?

> Do your company's strengths fit the remaining pockets of demand?

> What are your competitors' strengths in these pockets? How can their exit barriers be overcome?

In selecting a strategy, managers need to match the remaining opportunities in the industry with their companies' positions. The strengths and weaknesses that helped and hindered a company during the industry's development are not necessarily those that will count during the end game, where success will depend on the requirements to serve the pockets of demand that persist and the competition for this demand.

Figure 4.1 displays, albeit crudely, the strategic options open to a company in decline. When, because of low uncertainty, low exit barriers, and so forth, the industry structure is likely to go through an orderly decline phase, strong companies can either seek leadership or defend a niche, depending on the value to them of remaining market segments. When a company has no outstanding strengths for the remaining segments, it should either harvest or divest early. The choice depends, of course, on the feasibility of harvesting and the opportunities for selling the business.

When high uncertainty, high exit barriers, or conditions leading to volatile end-game rivalry make the industry environment hostile, investing to achieve leadership is not likely to yield rewards. If the company has strengths in the market segments that will persist, it can try either shrinking into a protected niche, or harvesting, or both. Otherwise, it is well advised to get out as quickly as its exit barriers permit. If it tries to hang on, other companies with high exit barriers and greater strengths will probably attack its position.

Table 4.1 Structural Factors that Influence the Attractiveness of Declining Industry Environments

Structural Factors	Environmental Attractiveness	
	Hospitable	Inhospitable
Conditions of Demand		
Speed of decline	Very slow	Rapid or erratic
Certainty of decline	100% certain predictable patterns	Great uncertainty, erratic patterns
Pockets of enduring demand	Several or major ones	No niches
Product differentiation	Brand loyalty	Commodity-like products
Price stability	Stable, price premiums attainable	Very unstable, pricing below costs
Exit Barriers		
Reinvestment requirements	None	High, often mandatory and involving capital assets
Excess capacity	Little	Substantial
Asset age	Mostly old assets	Sizable new assets and old ones not retired
Resale markets for assets	Easy to convert or sell	No markets available, substantial costs to retire
Shared facilities	Few free-standing plants	Substantial and interconnected with important businesses
Vertical integration	Little	Substantial
"Single product" competitors	None	Several large companies
Rivalry Determinants		
Customer industries	Fragmented, weak	Strong bargaining power
Customer switching costs	High	Minimal
Diseconomies of scale	None	Substantial penalty
Dissimilar strategic groups	Few	Several in same target markets

	Has competitive strengths for remaining demand pockets	Lacks competitive strengths for remaining demand pockets
Favorable industry structure for decline	Leadership or niche	Harvest or divest quickly
Unfavorable industry structure for decline	Niche or harvest	Divest quickly

Figure 4.1   Strategies for Declining Businesses

This simple framework must be supplemented by a third dimension of this problem—that is to say, a company's strategic need to remain in the business. For example, cash flow requirements may skew a decision toward harvest or early sale even though other factors point to leadership, as interrelationships with other units may suggest a more aggressive stance than otherwise. To determine the correct strategy a company should assess its strategic needs vis-á-vis the business and modify its end-game strategy accordingly.

Usually it is advantageous to make an early commitment to one end-game strategy or another. For instance, if a company lets competitors know from the outset that it is bent on a leadership position, it may not only encourage other companies to quit the business but also gain more time to establish its leadership. However, sometimes companies may want to bide their time by harvesting until indecisive competitors make up their minds. Until the situation is clear, a company may want to make preparations to invest should the leader go, and have plans to harvest or divest immediately should the leader stay. In any case, however, successful companies should choose an end-game strategy rather than let one be chosen for them.

The best course, naturally, is anticipation of the decline. If a company can forecast industry conditions, it may be able to improve its end-game position by taking steps during the maturity phase (sometimes such moves cost little in strategic position at the time):

- Minimize investments or other actions that will raise exit barriers unless clearly beneficial to overall corporate strategy.

- Increase the flexibility of assets so that they can accept different raw materials or produce related products.

- Place strategic emphasis on market segments that can be expected to endure when the industry is in a state of decline.

- Create customer-switching costs in these segments.

Avoiding Checkmate

Finding your company's position in Figure 4.1 requires a great deal of subtle analysis that is often shortchanged in the face of severe operating problems during decline. Many managers overlook the need to make strategy in decline consistent with industry structure because decline is viewed as somehow different. Our study of declining industries revealed other factors common to profitable players:

They recognize decline. With hindsight, it is all too easy to admonish companies for being overoptimistic about the prospects for their declining industries' revitalization. Nevertheless, some executives, such as those of U.S. oil refineries, fail to look objectively at the prospects of decline. Either their identification with an industry is too great or their perception of substitute products is too narrow. The presence of high exit barriers may also subtly affect how managers perceive their environment; because bad omens are so painful to recognize, people understandably look for good signs.

Our examination of many declining industries indicates that the companies that are most objective about managing the decline process are also participants in the substitute industry. They have a clearer perception concerning the prospects of the substitute product and the reality of decline.

They avoid wars of attrition. Warfare among competitors that have high exit barriers, such as the leather tanning companies, usually leads to disaster. Competitors are forced to respond vigorously to others' moves and cannot yield position without a big investment loss.

They don't harvest without definite strengths. Unless the industry's structure is very favorable during the decline phase, companies that try to harvest without definite strengths usually collapse. Once marketing or service deteriorates or a company raises its prices, customers quickly take their business elsewhere. In the process of harvesting, the resale value of the business may also dissipate. Because of the competitive and administrative risks of harvesting, managers need a clear justification to choose this strategy.

They view decline as a potential opportunity. Declining industries can sometimes be extraordinarily profitable for the well-positioned players, as GE and Raytheon have discovered in vacuum tubes. Companies that can view an industry's decline as an opportunity rather than just a problem, and make objective decisions, can reap handsome rewards.

NOTES

1. *Webster's Third New International Dictionary* (Springfield, Mass.: G. & C. Merriam, 1976). The term has also been used for an existentialist play by Samuel Beckett.

2. See Michael E. Porter, *Competitive Strategy* (New York: Free Press, 1980), Chapter 8. The book also contains a treatment of exit barriers and other industry and competitor characteristics discussed in this article.

3. See, for example, Stuart C. Gilmour, "The Divestment Decision Process" (DBA diss., Harvard Graduate School of Business Administration, 1973); and Kathryn Rudie Harrigan, *Strategies for Declining Businesses* (Lexington, Mass.: D.C. Heath, 1980).

4. See Michael E. Porter, *Interbrand Choice, Strategy and Bilateral Market Power* (Cambridge: Harvard University Press, 1976).

5. See Nitin T. Mehta, "Policy Formulation in a Declining Industry: The Case of the Canadian Dissolving Pulp Industry" (DBA diss., Harvard Graduate School of Business Administration, 1978).

CHAPTER 5

From Competitive Advantage to Corporate Strategy

Michael E. Porter

CORPORATE STRATEGY, THE OVERALL PLAN for a diversified company, is both the darling and the stepchild of contemporary management practice—the darling because CEOs have been obsessed with diversification since the early 1960s, the stepchild because almost no consensus exists about what corporate strategy is, much less about how a company should formulate it.

A diversified company has two levels of strategy: business unit (or competitive) strategy and corporate (or companywide) strategy. Competitive strategy concerns how to create competitive advantage in each of the businesses in which a company competes. Corporate strategy concerns two different questions: what businesses the corporation should be in and how the corporate office should manage the array of business units.

Corporate strategy is what makes the corporate whole add up to more than the sum of its business unit parts. The track record of corporate strategies has been dismal. I studied the diversification records of thirty-three large, prestigious U.S. companies over the 1950-1986 period and found that most of them had divested many more acquisitions than they had kept. The corporate strategies of most companies have dissipated instead of created shareholder value.

The need to rethink corporate strategy could hardly be more urgent. By taking over companies and breaking them up, corporate raiders thrive

May–June 1987

on failed corporate strategy. Fueled by junk bond financing and growing acceptability, raiders can expose any company to takeover, no matter how large or blue chip.

Recognizing past diversification mistakes, some companies have initiated large-scale restructuring programs. Others have done nothing at all. Whatever the response, the strategic questions persist. Those who have restructured must decide what to do next to avoid repeating the past; those who have done nothing must awake to their vulnerability. To survive, companies must understand what good corporate strategy is.

A Sober Picture

While there is disquiet about the success of corporate strategies, none of the available evidence satisfactorily indicates the success or failure of corporate strategy. Most studies have approached the question by measuring the stock market valuation of mergers, captured in the movement of the stock prices of acquiring companies immediately before and after mergers are announced.

These studies show that the market values mergers as neutral or slightly negative, hardly cause for serious concern.[1] Yet the short-term market reaction is a highly imperfect measure of the long-term success of diversification, and no self-respecting executive would judge a corporate strategy this way.

Studying the diversification programs of a company over a long period of time is a much more telling way to determine whether a corporate strategy has succeeded or failed. My study of thirty-three companies, many of which have reputations for good management, is a unique look at the track record of major corporations. (For an explanation of the

---

Where the Data Come From

We studied the 1950–1986 diversification histories of thirty-three large diversified U.S. companies. They were chosen at random from many broad sectors of the economy.

To eliminate distortions caused by World War II, we chose 1950 as the base year and then identified each business the company was in. We tracked every acquisition, joint venture, and start-up made over this period—3,788 in all. We classified each as an entry into an entirely new sector or field (financial services, for example), a new industry within a field the company was already in (insurance, for example), or a geographic extension of an existing product or service. We also classified each new field as related or unrelated to existing units. Then we tracked whether and when each entry was divested or shut down and the number of years each remained part of the corporation.

Our sources included annual reports, 10K forms, the F&S Index, and Moody's, supplemented by our judgment and general knowledge of the industries involved. In a few cases, we asked the companies specific questions.

It is difficult to determine the success of an entry without knowing the full purchase or start-up price, the profit history, the amount and timing of ongoing investments made in the unit, whether any write-offs or write-downs were taken, and the selling price and terms of sale. Instead, we employed a relatively simple way to gauge success: *whether the entry was divested or shut down.* The underlying assumption is that a company will generally not divest or close down a successful business except in a comparatively few special cases. Companies divested many of the entries in our sample within five years, a reflection of disappointment with performance. Of the compara-

tively few divestments where the company disclosed a loss or gain, the divestment resulted in a reported loss in more than half the cases.

The data in Table 5.1 cover the entire 1950–1986 period. However, the divestment ratios in Table 5.2 and Table 5.3 do not compare entries and divestments over the entire period because doing so would over-state the success of diversification. Companies usually do not shut down or divest new entries immediately but hold them for some time to give them an opportunity to succeed. Our data show that the average holding period is five to slightly more than ten years, though many divestments occur within five years. To accurately gauge the success of diversification, we calculated the percentage of entries made by 1975 and by 1980 that were divested or closed down as of January 1987. If we had included more recent entries, we would have biased upward our assessment of how successful these entries had been.

As compiled, these data probably understate the rate of failure. Companies tend to announce acquisitions and other forms of new entry with a flourish but divestments and shutdowns with a whimper, if at all. We have done our best to root out every such transaction, but we have undoubtedly missed some. There may also be new entries that we did not uncover, but our best impression is that the number is not large.

research, see the insert "Where the Data Come From.") Each company entered an average of eighty new industries and twenty-seven new fields. Just over 70 percent of the new entries were acquisitions, 22 percent were start-ups, and 8 percent were joint ventures. IBM, Exxon, Du Pont, and 3M, for example, focused on start-ups, while ALCO Standard, Beatrice, and Sara Lee diversified almost solely through acquisitions (Table 5.1 has a complete rundown).

My data paint a sobering picture of the success ratio of these moves (see Table 5.2). I found that on average corporations divested more than half their acquisitions in new industries and more than 60 percent of their acquisitions in entirely new fields. Fourteen companies left more than 70 percent of all the acquisitions they had made in new fields. The track record in unrelated acquisitions is even worse—the average divestment rate is a startling 74 percent (see Table 5.3). Even a highly respected company like General Electric divested a very high percentage of its acquisitions, particularly those in new fields. Companies near the top of the list in Table 5.2 achieved a remarkably low rate of divestment. Some bear witness to the success of well-thought-out corporate strategies. Others, however, enjoy a lower rate simply because they have not faced up to their problem units and divested them.

I calculated total shareholder returns (stock price appreciation plus dividends) over the period of the study for each company so that I could compare them with its divestment rate. While companies near the top of the list have above-average shareholder returns, returns are not a reliable measure of diversification success. Shareholder return often depends heavily on the inherent attractiveness of companies' base industries. Companies like CBS and General Mills had extremely profitable base businesses that subsidized poor diversification track records.

I would like to make one comment on the use of shareholder value to judge performance. Linking shareholder value quantitatively to diversification performance only works if you compare the share-holder value that is with the shareholder value that might have been without diversification. Because such a comparison is virtually impossible to make, measuring diversification success—the number of units retained by the company—seems to be as good an indicator as any of the contribution of diversification to corporate performance.

My data give a stark indication of the failure of corporate strategies.[2] Of the thirty-three companies, six had been taken over as my study was being completed (see the note on Table 5.2). Only the lawyers, investment bankers, and original sellers have prospered in most of these acquisitions, not the shareholders.

Premises of Corporate Strategy

Any successful corporate strategy builds on a number of premises. These are facts of life about diversification. They cannot be altered, and when ignored, they explain in part why so many corporate strategies fail.

Competition Occurs at the Business Unit Level. Diversified companies do not compete; only their business units do. Unless a corporate strategy places primary attention on nurturing the success of each unit, the strategy will fail, no matter how elegantly constructed. Successful corporate strategy must grow out of and reinforce competitive strategy.

Diversification Inevitably Adds Costs and Constraints to Business Units. Obvious costs such as the corporate overhead allocated to a unit may not be as important or subtle as the hidden costs and constraints. A business unit must explain its decisions to top management, spend time complying with planning and other corporate systems, live with parent company guidelines and personnel policies, and forgo the opportunity to motivate employees with direct equity ownership. These costs and constraints can be reduced but not entirely eliminated.

Shareholders Can Readily Diversify Themselves. Shareholders can diversify their own portfolios of stocks by selecting those that best match their preferences and risk profiles.[3] Shareholders can often diversify more cheaply than a corporation because they can buy shares at the market price and avoid hefty acquisition premiums. These premises mean that corporate strategy cannot succeed unless it truly adds value—to business units by providing tangible benefits that offset the inherent costs of lost independence and to shareholders by diversifying in a way they could not replicate.

Table 5.1 Diversification Profiles of 33 Leading U.S. Companies, 1950–1986

Company	Number Total Entries	All Entries into New Industries	Percent Acquisitions	Percent Joint Ventures
ALCO Standard	221	165	99%	0%
Allied Corp.	77	49	67	10
Beatrice	382	204	97	1
Borden	170	96	77	4
CBS	148	81	67	16
Continental Group	75	47	77	6
Cummins Engine	30	24	54	17
Du Pont	80	39	33	16
Exxon	79	56	34	5
General Electric	160	108	47	20
General Foods	92	53	91	4
General Mills	110	102	84	7
W.R. Grace	275	202	83	7
Gulf & Western	178	140	91	4
IBM	46	38	18	18
IC Industries	67	41	85	3
ITT	246	178	89	2
Johnson & Johnson	88	77	77	0
Mobil	41	32	53	16
Procter & Gamble	28	23	61	0
Raytheon	70	58	86	9
RCA	53	46	35	15
Rockwell	101	75	73	24
Sara Lee	197	141	96	1
Scovill	52	36	97	0
Signal	53	45	67	4
Tenneco	85	62	81	6
3M	144	125	54	2
TRW	119	82	77	10
United Technologies	62	49	57	18
Westinghouse	129	73	63	11
Wickes	71	47	83	0
Xerox	59	50	66	6
Total	3,788	2,644		
Average	114.8	80.1	70.3	7.9

Notes: Beatrice, Continental Group, General Foods, RCA, Scovill, and Signal were taken over as the study was being completed. Their data cover the period up through takeover but not subsequent divestments. The percentage averages may not add up to 100% because of rounding off.

Percent Start-ups	Entries into New Industries That Represented Entirely New Fields	Percent Acquisitions	Percent Joint Ventures	Percent Start-ups
1%	56	100%	0%	0%
22	17	65	6	29
2	61	97	0	3
19	32	75	3	22
17	28	65	21	14
17	19	79	11	11
29	13	46	23	31
51	19	37	0	63
61	17	29	6	65
33	29	48	14	38
6	22	86	5	9
9	27	74	7	19
10	66	74	5	21
6	48	88	2	10
63	16	19	0	81
12	17	88	6	6
9	50	92	0	8
23	18	56	0	44
31	15	60	7	33
39	14	79	0	21
5	16	81	19	6
50	19	37	21	42
3	27	74	22	4
4	41	95	2	2
3	12	92	0	8
29	20	75	0	25
13	26	73	8	19
45	34	71	3	56
13	28	64	11	25
24	17	23	17	39
26	36	61	3	36
17	22	68	0	32
28	18	50	11	39
	906			
21.8	27.4	67.9	7.0	25.9

Table 5.2 Acquisition Track Records of Leading U.S. Diversifiers Ranked by Percent Divested, 1950–1986

Company	All Acquisitions in New Industries	Percent Made by 1980 and Then Divested	Percent Made by 1975 and Then Divested
Johnson & Johnson	59	17%	12%
Procter & Gamble	14	17	17
Raytheon	50	17	26
United Technologies	28	25	13
3M	67	26	27
TRW	63	27	31
IBM	7	33	0*
Du Pont	13	38	43
Mobil	17	38	57
Borden	74	39	40
IC Industries	35	42	50
Tenneco	50	43	47
Beatrice	198	46	45
ITT	159	52	52
Rockwell	55	56	57
Allied Corp.	33	57	45
Exxon	19	62	20*
Sara Lee	135	62	65
General Foods	48	63	62
Scovill	35	64	77
Signal	30	65	63
ALCO Standard	164	65	70
W.R. Grace	167	65	70
General Electric	51	65	78
Wickes	38	67	72
Westinghouse	46	68	69
Xerox	33	71	79
Continental Group	36	71	72
General Mills	86	75	73
Gulf & Western	127	79	78
Cummins Engine	13	80	80
RCA	16	80	92
CBS	54	87	89
Total	**2,021**		
Average per company†	**61.2**	**53.4%**	**56.5%**

*Companies with three or fewer acquisitions by the cutoff year.

†Companies with three or fewer acquisitions by the cutoff year are excluded from the average to minimize statistical distortions.

Note: Beatrice, Continental Group, General Foods, RCA, Scovill, and Signal were taken over as the study was being completed. Their data cover the period up through takeover but not subsequent divestments.

Acquisitions in New Industries That Represented Entirely New Fields	Percent Made by 1980 and Then Divested	Percent Made by 1975 and Then Divested
10	33%	14%
11	17	17
13	25	33
10	17	0
24	42	45
18	40	38
3	33	0*
7	60	75
9	50	50
24	45	50
15	46	44
19	27	33
59	52	51
46	61	61
20	71	71
11	80	67
5	80	50*
39	80	76
19	93	93
11	64	70
15	70	67
56	72	76
49	71	70
14	100	100
15	73	70
22	61	59
9	100	100
15	60	60
20	65	60
42	75	72
6	83	83
7	86	100
18	88	88
661		
20.0	**61.2%**	**61.1%**

Table 5.3   Diversification Performance in Joint Ventures, Start-ups, and Unrelated Acquisitions, 1950–1986 (Companies in same order as in Exhibit 2)

Company	Joint Ventures as a Percent of New Entries	Percent Made by 1980 and Then Divested	Percent Made by 1975 and Then Divested	Start-Ups as a Percent of New Entries
Johnson & Johnson	0%	†	†	23%
Procter & Gamble	0	†	†	39
Raytheon	9	60%	60%	5
United Technologies	18	50	50	24
3M	2	100*	100*	45
TRW	10	20	25	13
IBM	18	100*	†	63
Du Pont	16	100*	†	51
Mobil	16	33	33	31
Borden	4	33	33	19
IC Industries	3	100*	100*	13
Tenneco	6	67	67	13
Beatrice	1	†	†	2
ITT	2	0*	†	8
Rockwell	24	38	42	3
Allied Corp.	10	100	75	22
Exxon	5	0	0	61
Sara Lee	1	†	†	4
General Foods	4	†	†	6
Scovill	0	†	†	3
Signal	4	†	†	29
ALCO Standard	0	†	†	1
W.R. Grace	7	33	38	10
General Electric	20	20	33	33
Wickes	0	†	†	17
Westinghouse	11	0*	0*	26
Xerox	6	100*	100*	28
Continental Group	6	67	67	17
General Mills	7	71	71	9
Gulf & Western	4	75	50	6
Cummins Engine	17	50	50	29
RCA	15	67	67	50
CBS	16	71	71	17
Average per company‡‡	**7.9%**	**50.3%**	**48.9%**	**21.8%**

*Companies with two or fewer entries.

†No entries in this category.

‡‡Average excludes companies with two or fewer entries to minimize statistical distortions.

Note: Beatrice, Continental Group, General Foods, RCA, Scovill, and Signal were taken over as the study was being completed. Their data cover the period up through takeover, but not subsequent divestments.

Percent Made by 1980 and Then Divested	Percent Made by 1975 and Then Divested	Acquisitions in Unrelated New Fields as a Percent of Total Acquisitions in New Fields	Percent Made by 1980 and Then Divested	Percent Made by 1975 and Then Divested
14%	20%	0%	†	†
0	0	9	†	†
50	50	46	40%	40%
11	20	40	0*	0*
2	3	33	75	86
63	71	39	71	71
20	22	33	100*	100*
61	61	43	0*	0*
50	56	67	60	100
17	13	21	80	80
80	30	33	50	50
67	80	42	33	40
0	0	63	59	53
38	57	61	67	64
0	0	35	100	100
38	29	45	50	0
27	19	100	80	50*
75	100*	41	73	73
67	50	42	86	83
100	100*	45	80	100
20	11	67	50	50
†	†	63	79	81
71	71	39	65	65
33	44	36	100	100
63	57	60	80	75
44	44	36	57	67
50	56	22	100	100
14	0	40	83	100
89	80	65	77	67
100	100	74	77	74
0	0	67	100	100
99	55	36	100	100
86	80	39	100	100
44.0%	**40.9%**	**46.1%**	**74.0%**	**74.4%**

Passing the Essential Tests

To understand how to formulate corporate strategy, it is necessary to specify the conditions under which diversification will truly create shareholder value. These conditions can be summarized in three essential tests:

1. **The attractiveness test.** The industries chosen for diversification must be structurally attractive or capable of being made attractive.
2. **The cost-of-entry test.** The cost of entry must not capitalize all the future profits.
3. **The better-off test.** Either the new unit must gain competitive advantage from its link with the corporation or vice versa.

Of course, most companies will make certain that their proposed strategies pass some of these tests. But my study clearly shows that when companies ignored one or two of them, the strategic results were disastrous.

HOW ATTRACTIVE IS THE INDUSTRY?

In the long run, the rate of return available from competing in an industry is a function of its underlying structure, which I have described in another *Harvard Business Review* article.[4] An attractive industry with a high average return on investment will be difficult to enter because entry barriers are high, suppliers and buyers have only modest bargaining power, substitute products or services are few, and the rivalry among competitors is stable. An unattractive industry like steel will have structural flaws, including a plethora of substitute materials, powerful and price-sensitive buyers, and excessive rivalry caused by high fixed costs and a large group of competitors, many of whom are state supported.

Diversification cannot create shareholder value unless new industries have favorable structures that support returns exceeding the cost of capital. If the industry doesn't have such returns, the company must be able to restructure the industry or gain a sustainable competitive advantage that leads to returns well above the industry average. An industry need not be attractive before diversification. In fact, a company might benefit from entering before the industry shows its full potential. The diversification can then transform the industry's structure.

In my research, I often found companies had suspended the attractiveness test because they had a vague belief that the industry "fit" very closely with their own businesses. In the hope that the corporate "comfort" they felt would lead to a happy outcome, the companies ignored fundamentally poor industry structures. Unless the close fit allows substantial competitive advantage, however, such comfort will turn into pain when diversification results in poor returns. Royal Dutch Shell and other leading oil companies have had this unhappy experience in a number of chemicals businesses, where poor industry structures overcame the benefits of vertical integration and skills in process technology.

Another common reason for ignoring the attractiveness test is a low entry cost. Sometimes the buyer has an inside track or the owner is anxious to sell. Even if the price is actually low, however, a one-shot gain will not offset a perpetually poor business. Almost always, the company finds it must reinvest in the newly acquired unit, if only to replace fixed assets and fund working capital.

Diversifying companies are also prone to use rapid growth or other simple indicators as a proxy for a target industry's attractiveness. Many that rushed into fast-growing industries (personal computers, video games, and robotics, for example) were burned because they mistook early growth for long-term profit potential. Industries are profitable not because they are sexy or high tech; they are profitable only if their structures are attractive.

WHAT IS THE COST OF ENTRY?

Diversification cannot build shareholder value if the cost of entry into a new business eats up its expected returns. Strong market forces, however, are working to do just that. A company can enter new industries by acquisition or start-up. Acquisitions expose it to an increasingly efficient merger market. An acquirer beats the market if it pays a price not fully reflecting the prospects of the new unit. Yet multiple bidders are commonplace, information flows rapidly, and investment bankers and other intermediaries work aggressively to make the market as efficient as possible. In recent years, new financial instruments such as junk bonds have brought new buyers into the market and made even large companies vulnerable to takeover. Acquisition premiums are high and reflect the acquired company's future prospects—sometimes too well. Philip Morris paid more than four times book value for Seven-Up Company, for example. Simple arithmetic meant that profits had to more than quadruple to sustain the preacquisition ROI. Since there proved to be little Philip Morris could add in marketing prowess to the sophisticated marketing wars in the soft-drink industry, the result was the unsatisfactory financial performance of Seven-Up and ultimately the decision to divest.

In a start-up, the company must overcome entry barriers. It's a real catch-22 situation, however, since attractive industries are attractive because their entry barriers are high. Bearing the full cost of the entry barriers might well dissipate any potential profits. Otherwise, other entrants to the industry would have already eroded its profitability.

In the excitement of finding an appealing new business, companies sometimes forget to apply the cost-of-entry test. The more attractive a new industry, the more expensive it is to get into.

WILL THE BUSINESS BE BETTER OFF?

A corporation must bring some significant competitive advantage to the new unit, or the new unit must offer potential for significant advantage to the corporation. Sometimes, the benefits to the new unit accrue only once, near the time of entry, when the parent instigates a major overhaul of its strategy or installs a first-rate management team. Other diversification yields ongoing competitive advantage if the new unit can market its product through the well-developed distribution system of its sister units, for instance. This is one of the important underpinnings of the merger of Baxter Travenol and American Hospital Supply.

When the benefit to the new unit comes only once, the parent company has no rationale for holding the new unit in its portfolio over the long term. Once the results of the one-time improvement are clear, the diversified company no longer adds value to offset the inevitable costs imposed on the unit. It is best to sell the unit and free up corporate resources.

The better-off test does not imply that diversifying corporate risk creates shareholder value in and of itself. Doing something for shareholders that they can do themselves is not a basis for corporate strategy. (Only in the case of a privately held company, in which the company's and the shareholder's risk are the same, is diversification to reduce risk valuable for its own sake.) Diversification of risk should only be a by-product of corporate strategy, not a prime motivator.

Executives ignore the better-off test most of all or deal with it through arm waving or trumped-up logic rather than hard strategic analysis. One reason is that they confuse company size with shareholder value. In the drive to run a bigger company, they lose sight of their real job. They may justify the suspension of the better-off test by pointing to the way they manage diversity. By cutting corporate staff to the bone and giving business units nearly complete autonomy, they believe they avoid the pitfalls. Such thinking misses the whole point of diversification, which is to create shareholder value rather than to avoid destroying it.

Concepts of Corporate Strategy

The three tests for successful diversification set the standards that any corporate strategy must meet; meeting them is so difficult that most diversification fails. Many companies lack a clear concept of corporate strategy to guide their diversification or pursue a concept that does not address the tests. Others fail because they implement a strategy poorly.

My study has helped me identify four concepts of corporate strategy that have been put into practice—portfolio management, restructuring, transferring skills, and sharing activities. While the concepts are not always mutually exclusive, each rests on a different mechanism by which the corporation creates shareholder value and each requires the diversified company to manage and organize itself in a different way. The first two require no connections among business units; the second two depend on them. (See Table 5.4.) While all four concepts of strategy have succeeded under the right circumstances, today some make more sense than others. Ignoring any of the concepts is perhaps the quickest road to failure.

PORTFOLIO MANAGEMENT

The concept of corporate strategy most in use is portfolio management, which is based primarily on diversification through acquisition. The corporation acquires sound, attractive companies with competent man-

Table 5.4 Concepts of Corporate Strategy

	Portfolio Management	Restructuring	Transferring Skills	Sharing Activities
Strategic Prerequisites	Superior insight into identifying and acquiring undervalued companies	Superior insight into identifying restructuring opportunities	Proprietary skills in activities important to competitive advantage in target industries	Activities in existing units that can be shared with new business units to gain competitive advantage
	Willingness to sell off losers quickly or to opportunistically divest good performers when buyers are willing to pay large premiums	Willingness and capability to intervene to transform acquired units	Ability to accomplish the transfer of skills among units on an ongoing basis	Benefits of sharing that outweigh the costs
	Broad guidelines for and constraints on the types of units in the portfolio so that senior management can play the review role effectively	Broad similarities among the units in the portfolio. Willingness to cut losses by selling off units where restructuring proves unfeasible	Acquisitions of beachhead positions in new industries as a base	Both start-ups and acquisitions as entry vehicles
	A private company or undeveloped capital markets	Willingness to sell units when restructuring is complete, the results are clear, and market conditions are favorable		Ability to overcome organizational resistance to business unit collaboration
	Ability to shift away from portfolio management as the capital markets get more efficient or the company gets unwieldy			

	Portfolio Management	Restructuring	Transferring Skills	Sharing Activities
Organizational Prerequisites	Autonomous business units A very small, low-cost, corporate staff Incentives based largely on business unit results	Autonomous business units A corporate organization with the talent and resources to oversee the turnarounds and strategic repositionings of acquired units Incentives based largely on acquired units' results	Largely autonomous but collaborative business units High-level corporate staff members who see their role primarily as integrators Cross-business-unit committees, task forces, and other forms to serve as focal points for capturing and transferring skills Objectives of line managers that include skills transfer Incentives based in part on corporate results	Strategic business units that are encouraged to share activities An active strategic planning role at group, sector, and corporate levels High-level corporate staff members who see their roles primarily as integrators Incentives based heavily on group and corporate results
Common Pitfalls	Pursuing portfolio management in countries with efficient capital marketing and a developed pool of professional management talent Ignoring the fact that industry structure is not attractive	Mistaking rapid growth or a "hot" indsutry as sufficient evidence of a restructuring opportunity Lacking the resolve or resources to take on troubled situations and to intervene in management Ignoring the fact that industry structure is not attractive Paying lip service to restructuring but actually practicing passive portfolio managmement	Mistaking similarity or comfort with new businesses as sufficient basis for diversification Providing no practical way for skills transfer to occur Ignoring the fact that industry structure is not attractive	Sharing for its own sake rather than because it leads to competitive advantage Assuming sharing will occur naturally without senior management playing an active role Ignoring the fact that industry structure is not attractive

agers who agree to stay on. While acquired units do not have to be in the same industries as existing units, the best portfolio managers generally limit their range of businesses in some way, in part to limit the specific expertise needed by top management.

The acquired units are autonomous, and the teams that run them are compensated according to the unit results. The corporation supplies capital and works with each to infuse it with professional management techniques. At the same time, top management provides objective and dispassionate review of business unit results. Portfolio managers categorize units by potential and regularly transfer resources from units that generate cash to those with high potential and cash needs.

In a portfolio strategy, the corporation seeks to create shareholder value in a number of ways. It uses its expertise and analytical resources to spot attractive acquisition candidates that the individual share-holder could not. The company provides capital on favorable terms that reflect corporatewide fundraising ability. It introduces professional management skills and discipline. Finally, it provides high-quality review and coaching, unencumbered by conventional wisdom or emotional attachments to the business.

The logic of the portfolio management concept rests on a number of vital assumptions. If a company's diversification plan is to meet the attractiveness and cost-of-entry test, it must find good but undervalued companies. Acquired companies must be truly undervalued because the parent does little for the new unit once it is acquired. To meet the better-off test, the benefits the corporation provides must yield a significant competitive advantage to acquired units. The style of operating through highly autonomous business units must both develop sound business strategies and motivate managers.

In most countries, the days when portfolio management was a valid concept of corporate strategy are past. In the face of increasingly well-developed capital markets, attractive companies with good managements show up on everyone's computer screen and attract top dollar in terms of acquisition premium. Simply contributing capital isn't contributing much. A sound strategy can easily be funded; small to medium-size companies don't need a munificent parent.

Other benefits have also eroded. Large companies no longer corner the market for professional management skills; in fact, more and more observers believe managers cannot necessarily run anything in the absence of industry-specific knowledge and experience. Another supposed advantage of the portfolio management concept—dispassionate review—rests on similarly shaky ground since the added value of review alone is questionable in a portfolio of sound companies.

The benefit of giving business units complete autonomy is also questionable. Increasingly, a company's business units are interrelated, drawn together by new technology, broadening distribution channels, and changing regulations. Setting strategies of units independently may well undermine unit performance. The companies in my sample that have succeeded in diversification have recognized the value of interrelationships and understood that a strong sense of corporate identity is as important as slavish adherence to parochial business unit financial results.

But it is the sheer complexity of the management task that has ultimately defeated even the best portfolio managers. As the size of the company grows, portfolio managers need to find more and more deals just to maintain growth. Supervising dozens or even hundreds of disparate units and under chain-letter pressures to add more, management begins to make mistakes. At the same time, the inevitable costs of being part of a diversified company take their toll and unit performance slides while the whole company's ROI turns downward. Eventually, a new management team is installed that initiates wholesale divestments and pares down the company to its core businesses. The experiences of Gulf & Western, Consolidated Foods (now Sara Lee), and ITT are just a few comparatively recent examples. Reflecting these realities, the U.S. capital markets today reward companies that follow the portfolio management model with a "conglomerate discount"; they value the whole less than the sum of the parts.

In developing countries, where large companies are few, capital markets are undeveloped, and professional management is scarce, portfolio management still works. But it is no longer a valid model for corporate strategy in advanced economies. Nevertheless, the technique is in the limelight today in the United Kingdom, where it is supported so far by a newly energized stock market eager for excitement. But this enthusiasm will wane—as well it should. Portfolio management is no way to conduct corporate strategy.

RESTRUCTURING

Unlike its passive role as a portfolio manager, when it serves as banker and reviewer, a company that bases its strategy on restructuring becomes an active restructurer of business units. The new businesses are not necessarily related to existing units. All that is necessary is unrealized potential.

The restructuring strategy seeks out undeveloped, sick, or threatened organizations or industries on the threshold of significant change. The parent intervenes, frequently changing the unit management team, shifting strategy, or infusing the company with new technology. Then it may make follow-up acquisitions to build a critical mass and sell off unneeded or unconnected parts and thereby reduce the effective acquisition cost. The result is a strengthened company or a transformed industry. As a coda, the parent sells off the stronger unit once results are clear because the parent is no longer adding value and top management decides that its attention should be directed elsewhere. (See the insert "An Uncanny British Restructurer" for an example of restructuring.)

When well implemented, the restructuring concept is sound, for it passes the three tests of successful diversification. The restructurer meets the cost-of-entry test through the types of company it acquires. It limits acquisition premiums by buying companies with problems and lackluster images or by buying into industries with as yet unforeseen potential. Intervention by the corporation clearly meets the better-off test. Provided that the target industries are structurally attractive, the restructuring model can create enormous shareholder value. Some restructuring companies are Loew's, BTR, and General Cinema. Ironically, many of today's restructurers are profiting from yesterday's portfolio management strategies.

To work, the restructuring strategy requires a corporate management team with the insight to spot undervalued companies or positions in industries ripe for transformation. The same insight is necessary to actually turn the units around even though they are in new and unfamiliar businesses.

These requirements expose the restructurer to considerable risk and usually limit the time in which the company can succeed at the strategy. The most skillful proponents understand this problem, recognize their mistakes, and move decisively to dispose of them. The best companies

An Uncanny British Restructurer

Hanson Trust, on its way to becoming Britain's largest company, is one of several skillful followers of the restructuring concept. A conglomerate with units in many industries, Hanson might seem on the surface a portfolio manager. In fact, Hanson and one or two other conglomerates have a much more effective corporate strategy. Hanson has acquired companies such as London Brick, Ever Ready Batteries, and SCM, which the city of London rather disdainfully calls "low tech."

Although a mature company suffering from low growth, the typical Hanson target is not just in any industry; it has an attractive structure. Its customer and supplier power is low and rivalry with competitors moderate. The target is a market leader, rich in assets but formerly poor in management. Hanson pays little of the present value of future cash flow out in an acquisition premium and reduces purchase price even further by aggressively selling off businesses that it cannot improve. In this way, it recoups just over a third of the cost of a typical acquisition during the first six months of ownership. Imperial Group's plush properties in London lasted barely two months under Hanson ownership, while Hanson's recent sale of Courage Breweries to Elders recouped £1.4 billion of the original £2.1 billion acquisition price of Imperial Group.

Like the best restructurers, Hanson approaches each unit with a modus operandi that it has perfected through repetition.

Hanson emphasizes low costs and tight financial controls. It has cut an average of 25 percent of labor costs out of acquired companies, slashed fixed overheads, and tightened capital expenditures. To reinforce its strategy of keeping costs low, Hanson carves out detailed one-year financial budgets with divisional managers and (through generous use of performance-related bonuses and share option schemes) gives them incentive to deliver the goods.

It's too early to tell whether Hanson will adhere to the last tenet of restructuring-selling turned-around units once the results are clear. If it succumbs to the allure of bigness, Hanson may take the course of the failed U.S. conglomerates.

realize they are not just acquiring companies but restructuring an industry. Unless they can integrate the acquisitions to create a whole new strategic position, they are just portfolio managers in disguise. Another important difficulty surfaces if so many other companies join the action that they deplete the pool of suitable candidates and bid their prices up.

Perhaps the greatest pitfall, however, is that companies find it very hard to dispose of business units once they are restructured and performing well. Human nature fights economic rationale. Size supplants shareholder value as the corporate goal. The company does not sell a unit even though the company no longer adds value to the unit. While the transformed units would be better off in another company that had related businesses, the restructuring company instead retains them. Gradually, it becomes a portfolio manager. The parent company's ROI declines as the need for reinvestment in the units and normal business risks eventually offset restructuring's one-shot gain. The perceived need to keep growing intensifies the pace of acquisition; errors result and standards fall. The restructuring company turns into a conglomerate with returns that only equal the average of all industries at best.

TRANSFERRING SKILLS

The purpose of the first two concepts of corporate strategy is to create value through a company's relationship with each autonomous unit. The corporation's role is to be a selector, a banker, and an intervenor.

The last two concepts exploit the interrelationships between businesses. In articulating them, however, one comes face-to-face with the often ill-defined concept of synergy. If you believe the text of the countless corporate annual reports, just about anything is related to just about anything else! But imagined synergy is much more common than real synergy. GM's purchase of Hughes Aircraft simply because cars were going electronic and Hughes was an electronics concern demonstrates the folly of paper synergy. Such corporate relatedness is an ex post facto rationalization of a diversification undertaken for other reasons.

Even synergy that is clearly defined often fails to materialize. Instead of cooperating, business units often compete. A company that can define the synergies it is pursuing still faces significant organizational impediments in achieving them.

But the need to capture the benefits of relationships between businesses has never been more important. Technological and competitive developments already link many businesses and are creating new possibilities for competitive advantage. In such sectors as financial services, computing, office equipment, entertainment, and health care, interrelationships among previously distinct businesses are perhaps the central concern of strategy.

To understand the role of relatedness in corporate strategy, we must give new meaning to this ill-defined idea. I have identified a good way to start—the value chain.[5] Every business unit is a collection of discrete activities ranging from sales to accounting that allow it to compete. I call them value activities. It is at this level, not in the company as a whole, that the unit achieves competitive advantage. I group these activities in nine categories. *Primary* activities create the product or service, deliver and market it, and provide after-sale support. The categories of primary activities include inbound logistics, operations, outbound logistics, marketing and sales, and service. *Support* activities provide the inputs and infrastructure that allow the primary activities to take place. The categories are company infrastructure, human resource management, technology development, and procurement.

The value chain defines the two types of interrelationships that may create synergy. The first is a company's ability to transfer skills or expertise among similar value chains. The second is the ability to share activities. Two business units, for example, can share the same sales force or logistics network.

The value chain helps expose the last two (and most important) concepts of corporate strategy. The transfer of skills among business units in the diversified company is the basis for one concept. While each business unit has a separate value chain, knowledge about how to perform activities is transferred among the units. For example, a toiletries business unit, expert in the marketing of convenience products, transmits ideas on new positioning concepts, promotional techniques, and packaging possibilities to a newly acquired unit that sells cough syrup. Newly entered industries can benefit from the expertise of existing units and vice versa.

These opportunities arise when business units have similar buyers or channels, similar value activities like government relations or pro-

curement, similarities in the broad configuration of the value chain
(for example, managing a multisite service organization), or the same
strategic concept (for example, low cost). Even though the units operate
separately, such similarities allow the sharing of knowledge.

Of course, some similarities are common; one can imagine them at
some level between almost any pair of businesses. Countless companies
have fallen into the trap of diversifying too readily because of similarities; mere similarity is not enough.

Transferring skills leads to competitive advantage only if the similarities among businesses meet three conditions:

1. The activities involved in the businesses are similar enough that
   sharing expertise is meaningful. Broad similarities (marketing in-
   tensiveness, for example, or a common core process technology
   such as bending metal) are not a sufficient basis for diversification.
   The resulting ability to transfer skills is likely to have little impact
   on competitive advantage.
2. The transfer of skills involves activities important to competitive
   advantage. Transferring skills in peripheral activities such as government relations or real estate in consumer goods units may be
   beneficial but is not a basis for diversification.
3. The skills transferred represent a significant source of competitive
   advantage for the receiving unit. The expertise or skills to be
   transferred are both advanced and proprietary enough to be beyond
   the capabilities of competitors.

The transfer of skills is an active process that significantly changes
the strategy or operations of the receiving unit. The prospect for change
must be specific and identifiable. Almost guaranteeing that no shareholder value will be created, too many companies are satisfied with
vague prospects or faint hopes that skills will transfer. The transfer of
skills does not happen by accident or by osmosis. The company will
have to reassign critical personnel, even on a permanent basis, and the
participation and support of high-level management in skills transfer
is essential. Many companies have been defeated at skills transfer because they have not provided their business units with any incentives
to participate.

Transferring skills meets the tests of diversification if the company truly mobilizes proprietary expertise across units. This makes certain the company can offset the acquisition premium or lower the cost of overcoming entry barriers.

The industries the company chooses for diversification must pass the attractiveness test. Even a close fit that reflects opportunities to transfer skills may not overcome poor industry structure. Opportunities to transfer skills, however, may help the company transform the structures of newly entered industries and send them in favorable directions.

The transfer of skills can be one-time or ongoing. If the company exhausts opportunities to infuse new expertise into a unit after the initial postacquisition period, the unit should ultimately be sold. The corporation is no longer creating shareholder value. Few companies have grasped this point, however, and many gradually suffer mediocre returns. Yet a company diversified into well-chosen businesses can transfer skills eventually in many directions. If corporate management conceives of its role in this way and creates appropriate organizational mechanisms to facilitate cross-unit interchange, the opportunities to share expertise will be meaningful.

By using both acquisitions and internal development, companies can build a transfer-of-skills strategy. The presence of a strong base of skills sometimes creates the possibility for internal entry instead of the acquisition of a going concern. Successful diversifiers that employ the concept of skills transfer may, however, often acquire a company in the target industry as a beachhead and then build on it with their internal expertise. By doing so, they can reduce some of the risks of internal entry and speed up the process. Two companies that have diversified using the transfer-of-skills concept are 3M and Pepsico.

SHARING ACTIVITIES

The fourth concept of corporate strategy is based on sharing activities in the value chains among business units. Procter & Gamble (P & G), for example, employs a common physical distribution system and sales force in both paper towels and disposable diapers. McKesson, a leading distribution company, will handle such diverse lines as pharmaceuticals and liquor through superwarehouses.

The ability to share activities is a potent basis for corporate strategy because sharing often enhances competitive advantage by lowering cost or raising differentiation. But not all sharing leads to competitive advantage, and companies can encounter deep organizational resistance to even beneficial sharing possibilities. These hard truths have led many companies to reject synergy prematurely and retreat to the false simplicity of portfolio management.

A cost-benefit analysis of prospective sharing opportunities can determine whether synergy is possible. Sharing can lower costs if it achieves economies of scale, boosts the efficiency of utilization, or helps a company move more rapidly down the learning curve. The costs of General Electric's advertising, sales, and after-sales service activities in major appliances are low because they are spread over a wide range of appliance products. Sharing can also enhance the potential for differentiation. A shared order-processing system, for instance, may allow new features and services that a buyer will value. Sharing can also reduce the cost of differentiation. A shared service network, for example, may make more advanced, remote servicing technology economically feasible. Often, sharing will allow an activity to be wholly reconfigured in ways that can dramatically raise competitive advantage.

Sharing must involve activities that are significant to competitive advantage, not just any activity. P&G's distribution system is such an instance in the diaper and paper towel business, where products are bulky and costly to ship. Conversely, diversification based on the opportunities to share only corporate overhead is rarely, if ever, appropriate.

Sharing activities inevitably involves costs that the benefits must outweigh. One cost is the greater coordination required to manage a shared activity. More important is the need to compromise the design or performance of an activity so that it can be shared. A salesperson handling the products of two business units, for example, must operate in a way that is usually not what either unit would choose were it independent. And if compromise greatly erodes the unit's effectiveness, then sharing may reduce rather than enhance competitive advantage.

Many companies have only superficially identified their potential for sharing. Companies also merge activities without consideration of whether they are sensitive to economies of scale. When they are not, the coordination costs kill the benefits. Companies compound such errors by not identifying costs of sharing in advance, when steps can be taken to minimize them. Costs of compromise can frequently be mitigated by redesigning the activity for sharing. The shared salesperson, for example, can be provided with a remote computer terminal to boost productivity and provide more customer information. Jamming business units together without such thinking exacerbates the costs of sharing.

Despite such pitfalls, opportunities to gain advantage from sharing activities have proliferated because of momentous developments in technology, deregulation, and competition. The infusion of electronics and information systems into many industries creates new opportunities to link businesses. The corporate strategy of sharing can involve both acquisition and internal development. Internal development is often possible because the corporation can bring to bear clear resources in launching a new unit. Start-ups are less difficult to integrate than acquisitions. Companies using the shared-activities concept can also make acquisitions as beachhead landings into a new industry and then integrate the units through sharing with other units. Prime examples of companies that have diversified via using shared activities include P&G, Du Pont, and IBM. The fields into which each has diversified are a cluster of tightly related units. Marriott illustrates both successes and failures in sharing activities over time. (See the insert "Adding Value with Hospitality.")

Adding Value with Hospitality

Marriott began in the restaurant business in Washington, D.C. Because its customers often ordered takeouts on the way to the national airport, Marriott eventually entered airline catering. From there, it jumped into food service management for institutions. Marriott then began broadening its base of family restaurants and entered the hotel industry. More recently, it has moved into restaurants, snack bars, and merchandise shops in airport terminals and into gourmet restaurants. In addition, Marriott has branched out from its hotel business into cruise ships, theme parks, wholesale travel agencies, budget motels, and retirement centers.

Marriott's diversification has exploited well-developed skills in food service and hospitality. Marriott's kitchens prepare food according to more than 6,000 standardized recipe cards; hotel procedures are also standardized and painstakingly documented in elaborate manuals. Marriott shares a number of important activities across units. A shared procurement and distribution system for food serves all Marriott units through nine regional procurement centers. As a result, Marriott earns 50 percent higher margins on food service than any other hotel company. Marriott also has a fully integrated real estate unit that brings corporatewide power to bear on site acquisitions as well as on the designing and building of all Marriott locations.

Marriott's diversification strategy balances acquisitions and start-ups. Start-ups or small acquisitions are used for initial entry, depending on how close the opportunities for shar-

ing are. To expand its geographic base, Marriott acquires companies and then disposes of the parts that do not fit.

Apart from this success, it is important to note that Marriott has divested 36 percent of both its acquisitions and its start-ups. While this is an above-average record, Marriott's mistakes are quite illuminating. Marriott has largely failed in diversifying into gourmet restaurants, theme parks, cruise ships, and wholesale travel agencies. In the first three businesses, Marriott discovered it could not transfer skills despite apparent similarities. Standardized menus did not work well in gourmet restaurants. Running cruise ships and theme parks was based more on entertainment and pizzazz than the carefully disciplined management of hotels and mid-price restaurants. The wholesale travel agencies were ill fated from the start because Marriott had to compete with an important customer for its hotels and had no proprietary skills or opportunities to share with which to add value.

Following the shared-activities model requires an organizational context in which business unit collaboration is encouraged and reinforced. Highly autonomous business units are inimical to such collaboration. The company must put into place a variety of what I call horizontal mechanisms—a strong sense of corporate identity, a clear corporate mission statement that emphasizes the importance of integrating business unit strategies, an incentive system that rewards more than just business unit results, cross-business-unit task forces, and other methods of integrating.

A corporate strategy based on shared activities clearly meets the better-off test because business units gain ongoing tangible advantages from others within the corporation. It also meets the cost-of-entry test by reducing the expense of surmounting the barriers to internal entry. Other bids for acquisitions that do not share opportunities will have lower reservation prices. Even widespread opportunities for sharing activities do not allow a company to suspend the attractiveness test, however. Many diversifiers have made the critical mistake of equating the close fit of a target industry with attractive diversification. Target industries must pass the strict requirement test of having an attractive structure as well as a close fit in opportunities if diversification is to ultimately succeed.

Choosing a Corporate Strategy

Each concept of corporate strategy allows the diversified company to create shareholder value in a different way. Companies can succeed with any of the concepts if they clearly define the corporation's role and objectives, have the skills necessary for meeting the concept's prerequisites, organize themselves to manage diversity in a way that fits the strategy, and find themselves in an appropriate capital market environment. The caveat is that portfolio management is only sensible in limited circumstances.

A company's choice of corporate strategy is partly a legacy of its past. If its business units are in unattractive industries, the company must start from scratch. If the company has few truly proprietary skills or activities it can share in related diversification, then its initial diversification must rely on other concepts. Yet corporate strategy should not be a once-and-for-all choice but a vision that can evolve. A company should choose its long-term preferred concept and then proceed pragmatically toward it from its initial starting point.

Both the strategic logic and the experience of the companies studied over the last decade suggest that a company will create shareholder value through diversification to a greater and greater extent as its strategy moves from portfolio management toward sharing activities. Because they do not rely on superior insight or other questionable assumptions about the company's capabilities, sharing activities and transferring skills offer the best avenues for value creation.

Each concept of corporate strategy is not mutually exclusive of those that come before, a potent advantage of the third and fourth concepts. A company can employ a restructuring strategy at the same time it transfers skills or shares activities. A strategy based on shared activities becomes more powerful if business units can also exchange skills. As the Marriott case illustrates, a company can often pursue the two strategies together and even incorporate some of the principles of restructuring with them. When it chooses industries in which to transfer skills or share activities, the company can also investigate the possibility of transforming the industry structure. When a company bases its strategy on interrelationships, it has a broader basis on which to create shareholder value than if it rests its entire strategy on transforming companies in unfamiliar industries.

My study supports the soundness of basing a corporate strategy on the transfer of skills or shared activities. The data on the sample companies' diversification programs illustrate some important characteristics of successful diversifiers. They have made a disproportionately low percentage of unrelated acquisitions, *unrelated* being defined as having no clear opportunity to transfer skills or share important activities (see Table 5.3). Even successful diversifiers such as 3M, IBM, and TRW have terrible records when they have strayed into unrelated acquisitions. Successful acquirers diversify into fields, each of which is related to many others. P & G and IBM, for example, operate in eighteen and nineteen interrelated fields respectively and so enjoy numerous opportunities to transfer skills and share activities.

Companies with the best acquisition records tend to make heavier-than-average use of start-ups and joint ventures. Most companies shy away from modes of entry besides acquisition. My results cast doubt on the conventional wisdom regarding start-ups. Table 5.3 demonstrates that while joint ventures are about as risky as acquisitions, start-ups are not. Moreover, successful companies often have very good records with start-up units, as 3M, P&G, Johnson & Johnson, IBM, and United Technologies illustrate. When a company has the internal strength to start up a unit, it can be safer and less costly to launch a company than to rely solely on an acquisition and then have to deal with the problem of integration. Japanese diversification histories support the soundness of start-up as an entry alternative.

My data also illustrate that none of the concepts of corporate strategy works when industry structure is poor or implementation is bad, no matter how related the industries are. Xerox acquired companies in related industries, but the businesses had poor structures and its skills were insufficient to provide enough competitive advantage to offset implementation problems.

AN ACTION PROGRAM

To translate the principles of corporate strategy into successful diversification, a company must first take an objective look at its existing businesses and the value added by the corporation. Only through such an assessment can an understanding of good corporate strategy grow. That understanding should guide future diversification as well as the development of skills and activities with which to select further new businesses. The following action program provides a concrete approach to conducting such a review. A company can choose a corporate strategy by:

1. *Identifying the interrelationships among already existing business units*. A company should begin to develop a corporate strategy by identifying all the opportunities it has to share activities or transfer skills in its existing portfolio of business units. The company will not only find ways to enhance the competitive advantage of existing units but also come upon several possible diversification avenues. The lack of meaningful interrelationships in the portfolio is an equally important finding, suggesting the need to justify the value added by the corporation or, alternately, a fundamental restructuring.

2. *Selecting the core businesses that will be the foundation of the corporate strategy.* Successful diversification starts with an understanding of the core businesses that will serve as the basis for corporate strategy. Core businesses are those that are in an attractive industry, have the potential to achieve sustainable competi-

tive advantage, have important interrelationships with other business units, and provide skills or activities that represent a base from which to diversify.

The company must first make certain its core businesses are on sound footing by upgrading management, internationalizing strategy, or improving technology. The study shows that geographic extensions of existing units, whether by acquisition, joint venture, or start-up, had a substantially lower divestment rate than diversification.

The company must then patiently dispose of the units that are not core businesses. Selling them will free resources that could be better deployed elsewhere. In some cases disposal implies immediate liquidation, while in others the company should dress up the units and wait for a propitious market or a particularly eager buyer.

3. *Creating horizontal organizational mechanisms to facilitate interrelationships among the core businesses and lay the groundwork for future related diversification.* Top management can facilitate interrelationships by emphasizing cross-unit collaboration, grouping units organizationally and modifying incentives, and taking steps to build a strong sense of corporate identity.

4. *Pursuing diversification opportunities that allow shared activities.* This concept of corporate strategy is the most compelling, provided a company's strategy passes all three tests. A company should inventory activities in existing business units that represent the strongest foundation for sharing, such as strong distribution channels or world-class technical facilities. These will in turn lead to potential new business areas. A company can use acquisitions as a beachhead or employ start-ups to exploit internal capabilities and minimize integrating problems.

5. *Pursuing diversification through the transfer of skills if opportunities for sharing activities are limited or exhausted.* Companies can pursue this strategy through acquisition, although they may be able to use start-ups if their existing units have important skills they can readily transfer.

Such diversification is often riskier because of the tough conditions necessary for it to work. Given the uncertainties, a company should avoid diversifying on the basis of skills transfer alone. Rather it should also be viewed as a stepping-stone to subsequent diversification using shared activities. New industries should be chosen that will lead naturally to other businesses. The goal is to build a cluster of related and mutually reinforcing business units. The strategy's logic implies that the company should not set the rate of return standards for the initial foray into a new sector too high.

6. ***Pursuing a strategy of restructuring if this fits the skills of management or no good opportunities exist for forging corporate interrelationships.*** When a company uncovers undermanaged companies and can deploy adequate management talent and resources to the acquired units, then it can use a restructuring strategy. The more developed the capital markets and the more active the market for companies, the more restructuring will require a patient search for that special opportunity rather than a headlong race to acquire as many bad apples as possible. Restructuring can be a permanent strategy, as it is with Loew's, or a way to build a group of businesses that supports a shift to another corporate strategy.

7. ***Paying dividends so that the shareholders can be the portfolio managers.*** Paying dividends is better than destroying shareholder value through diversification based on shaky underpinnings. Tax considerations, which some companies cite to avoid dividends, are hardly legitimate reasons to diversify if a company cannot demonstrate the capacity to do it profitably.

Creating a Corporate Theme

Defining a corporate theme is a good way to ensure that the corporation will create shareholder value. Having the right theme helps unite the efforts of business units and reinforces the ways they interrelate as well as guides the choice of new businesses to enter. NEC Corporation, with its "C&C" theme, provides a good example. NEC integrates its computer, semiconductor, telecommunications, and consumer electronics businesses by merging computers and communication.

It is all too easy to create a shallow corporate theme. CBS wanted to be an "entertainment company," for example, and built a group of businesses related to leisure time. It entered such industries as toys, crafts, musical instruments, sports teams, and hi-fi retailing. While this corporate theme sounded good, close listening revealed its hollow ring. None of these businesses had any significant opportunity to share activities or transfer skills among themselves or with CBS's traditional broadcasting and record businesses. They were all sold, often at significant losses, except for a few of CBS's publishing-related units. Saddled with the worst acquisition record in my study, CBS has eroded the shareholder value created through its strong performance in broadcasting and records.

Moving from competitive strategy to corporate strategy is the business equivalent of passing through the Bermuda Triangle. The failure of corporate strategy reflects the fact that most diversified companies have failed to think in terms of how they really add value. A corporate strategy that truly enhances the competitive advantage of each business unit is the best defense against the corporate raider. With a sharper focus on the tests of diversification and the explicit choice of a clear concept of corporate strategy, companies' diversification track records from now on can look a lot different.

NOTES

1. The studies also show that sellers of companies capture a large fraction of the gains from merger. See Michael C. Jensen and Richard S. Ruback, "The Market for Corporate Control: The Scientific Evidence," *Journal of Financial Economics* (April 1983): 5, and Michael C. Jensen, "Takeovers: Folklore and Science," *Harvard Business Review* 62, no. 5 (1984): 109.

2. Some recent evidence also supports the conclusion that acquired companies often suffer eroding performance after acquisition. See Frederick M. Scherer, "Mergers, Sell-Offs and Managerial Behavior," in *The Economics of Strategic Planning*, ed. Lacy Glenn Thomas (Lexington, Mass.: Lexington Books, 1986), p. 143; and David A. Ravenscraft and Frederick M. Scherer, "Mergers and Managerial Performance," paper presented at the Conference on Takeovers and Contests for Corporate Control, Columbia Law School, 1985.

3. This observation has been made by a number of authors. See, for example, Malcolm S. Salter and Wolf A. Weinhold, *Diversification Through Acquisition* (New York: Free Press, 1979).

4. See Michael E. Porter, "How Competitive Forces Shape Strategy," *Harvard Business Review* 57, no. 2 (1979): 86.

5. See Michael E. Porter, *Competitive Advantage* (New York: Free Press, 1985).

Part II   The Competitiveness of Locations

CHAPTER 6

The Competitive Advantage of Nations

Michael E. Porter

NATIONAL PROSPERITY IS CREATED, not inherited. It does not grow out of a country's natural endowments, its labor pool, its interest rates, or its currency's value, as classical economics insists.

A nation's competitiveness depends on the capacity of its industry to innovate and upgrade. Companies gain advantage against the world's best competitors because of pressure and challenge. They benefit from having strong domestic rivals, aggressive home-based suppliers, and demanding local customers.

In a world of increasingly global competition, nations have become more, not less, important. As the basis of competition has shifted more and more to the creation and assimilation of knowledge, the role of the nation has grown. Competitive advantage is created and sustained through a highly localized process. Differences in national values, culture, economic structures, institutions, and histories all contribute to competitive success. There are striking differences in the patterns of competitiveness in every country; no nation can or will be competitive in every or even most industries. Ultimately, nations succeed in particular industries because their home environment is the most forward-looking, dynamic, and challenging.

Author's note: Michael J. Enright, who served as project coordinator for this study, has contributed valuable suggestions.

March–April 1990

These conclusions, the product of a four-year study of the patterns of competitive success in ten leading trading nations, contradict the conventional wisdom that guides the thinking of many companies and national governments—and that is pervasive today in the United States. (For more about the study, see the insert "Patterns of National Competitive Success.") According to prevailing thinking, labor costs, interest rates, exchange rates, and economies of scale are the most potent determinants of competitiveness. In companies, the words of the day are merger, alliance, strategic partnerships, collaboration, and supranational

---

Patterns of National Competitive Success

To investigate why nations gain competitive advantage in particular industries and the implications for company strategy and national economies, I conducted a four-year study of ten important trading nations: Denmark, Germany, Italy, Japan, Korea, Singapore, Sweden, Switzerland, the United Kingdom, and the United States. I was assisted by a team of more than 30 researchers, most of whom were natives of and based in the nation they studied. The researchers all used the same methodology.

Three nations—the United States, Japan, and Germany—are the world's leading industrial powers. The other nations represent a variety of population sizes, government policies toward industry, social philosophies, geographical sizes, and locations. Together, the ten nations accounted for fully 50 percent of total world exports in 1985, the base year for statistical analysis.

Most previous analyses of national competitiveness have focused on single nation or bilateral comparisons. By studying nations with widely varying characteristics and circumstances, this study sought to separate the fundamental forces underlying national competitive advantage from the idiosyncratic ones.

In each nation, the study consisted of two parts. The first identified all industries in which the nation's companies were internationally successful, using available statistical data, supplementary published sources, and field interviews. We defined a nation's industry as internationally successful if it *possessed competitive advantage relative to the best worldwide competitors.* Many measures of competitive advantage, such as reported profitability, can be misleading. We chose as the best indicators the presence of substantial and sustained exports to a wide array of other nations and/or significant outbound foreign investment based on skills and assets created in the home country. A nation was considered the home base for a company if it was either a locally owned, indigenous enterprise or managed autonomously although owned by a foreign company or investors. We then created a profile of all the industries in which each nation was internationally successful at three points in time: 1971, 1978, and 1985. The pattern of competitive industries in each economy was far from random: the task was to explain it and how it had changed over time. Of particular interest were the connections or relationships among the nation's competitive industries.

In the second part of the study, we examined the history of competition in particular industries to understand how competitive advantage was created. On the basis of national profiles, we selected over 100 industries or industry groups for detailed study; we examined many more in less detail. We went back as far as necessary to understand how and why the industry began in the nation, how it grew, when and why companies from the nation developed international competitive advantage, and the process by which competitive advantage had been either sustained or lost. The resulting case histories fall short of the work of a good historian in their level of detail, but they do provide insight into the development of both the industry and the nation's economy.

We chose a sample of industries for each nation that represented the most important groups of competitive industries in the economy. The industries studied accounted for a large share of total exports in each nation: more than 20 percent of total exports in Japan, Germany, and Switzerland, for example, and more than 40 percent in South Korea. We studied some of the most famous and important international success stories —German high-performance autos and chemicals, Japanese semi-conductors and VCRs, Swiss banking and pharmaceuticals, Italian footwear and textiles, U.S. commercial aircraft and motion pictures—and some relatively obscure but highly competitive industries—South Korean pianos, Italian ski boots, and British biscuits. We also added a few industries because they appeared to be paradoxes: Japanese home demand for Western-character typewriters is nearly nonexistent, for example, but Japan holds a strong export and foreign investment position in the industry. We avoided industries that were highly dependent on natural resources: such industries do not form the backbone of advanced economies, and the capacity to compete in them is more explicable using classical theory. We did, however, include a number of more technologically intensive, natural-resource-related industries such as newsprint and agricultural chemicals.

The sample of nations and industries offers a rich empirical foundation for developing and testing the new theory of how countries gain competitive advantage. The accompanying article concentrates on the determinants of competitive advantage in individual industries and also sketches out some of the study's overall implications for government policy and company strategy. A fuller treat-

ment in my book, *The Competitive Advantage of Nations*, develops the theory and its implications in greater depth and provides many additional examples. It also contains detailed descriptions of the nations we studied and the future prospects for their economies.

globalization. Managers are pressing for more government support for particular industries. Among governments, there is a growing tendency to experiment with various policies intended to promote national competitiveness—from efforts to manage exchange rates to new measures to manage trade to policies to relax antitrust—which usually end up only undermining it. (See the insert "What Is National Competitiveness?")

These approaches, now much in favor in both companies and governments, are flawed. They fundamentally misperceive the true sources of competitive advantage. Pursuing them, with all their short term appeal, will virtually guarantee that the United States—or any other advanced nation—never achieves real and sustainable competitive advantage.

We need a new perspective and new tools—an approach to competitiveness that grows directly out of an analysis of internationally successful industries, without regard for traditional ideology or current intellectual fashion. We need to know, very simply, what works and why. Then we need to apply it.

What Is National Competitiveness?

National competitiveness has become one of the central preoccupations of government and industry in every nation. Yet for all the discussion, debate, and writing on the topic, there is still no persuasive theory to explain national competitiveness. What is more, there is not even an accepted definition of the term

"competitiveness" as applied to a nation. While the notion of a competitive company is clear, the notion of a competitive nation is not.

Some see national competitiveness as a macroeconomic phenomenon, driven by variables such as exchange rates, interest rates, and government deficits. But Japan, Italy, and South Korea have all enjoyed rapidly rising living standards despite budget deficits; Germany and Switzerland despite appreciating currencies; and Italy and Korea despite high interest rates.

Others argue that competitiveness is a function of cheap and abundant labor. But Germany, Switzerland, and Sweden have all prospered even with high wages and labor shortages. Besides, shouldn't a nation seek higher wages for its workers as a goal of competitiveness?

Another view connects competitiveness with bountiful natural resources. But how, then, can one explain the success of Germany, Japan, Switzerland, Italy, and South Korea—countries with limited natural resources?

More recently, the argument has gained favor that competitiveness is driven by government policy: targeting, protection, import promotion, and subsidies have propelled Japanese and South Korean auto, steel, shipbuilding, and semiconductor industries into global preeminence. But a closer look reveals a spotty record. In Italy, government intervention has been ineffectual—but Italy has experienced a boom in world export share second only to Japan. In Germany, direct government intervention in exporting industries is rare. And even in Japan and South Korea, government's role in such important industries as facsimile machines, copiers, robotics,

and advanced materials has been modest; some of the most frequently cited examples, such as sewing machines, steel, and shipbuilding, are now quite dated.

A final popular explanation for national competitiveness is differences in management practices, including management-labor relations. The problem here, however, is that different industries require different approaches to management. The successful management practices governing small, private, and loosely organized Italian family companies in footwear, textiles, and jewelry, for example, would produce a management disaster if applied to German chemical or auto companies, Swiss pharmaceutical makers, or American aircraft producers. Nor is it possible to generalize about management-labor relations. Despite the commonly held view that powerful unions undermine competitive advantage, unions are strong in Germany and Sweden—and both countries boast internationally preeminent companies.

Clearly, none of these explanations is fully satisfactory; none is sufficient by itself to rationalize the competitive position of industries within a national border. Each contains some truth; but a broader, more complex set of forces seems to be at work.

The lack of a clear explanation signals an even more fundamental question. What is a "competitive" nation in the first place? Is a "competitive" nation one where every company or industry is competitive? No nation meets this test. Even Japan has large sectors of its economy that fall far behind the world's best competitors.

Is a "competitive" nation one whose exchange rate makes its goods price competitive in international markets? Both Germany and Japan have enjoyed remarkable gains in their standards of living—and experienced sustained periods of strong currency and rising prices. Is a "competitive" nation one with a large positive balance of trade? Switzerland has roughly balanced trade; Italy has a chronic trade deficit—both nations enjoy strongly rising national income. Is a "competitive" nation one with low labor costs? India and Mexico both have low wages and low labor costs—but neither seems an attractive industrial model.

The only meaningful concept of competitiveness at the national level is *productivity*. The principal goal of a nation is to produce a high and rising standard of living for its citizens. The ability to do so depends on the productivity with which a nation's labor and capital are employed. Productivity is the value of the output produced by a unit of labor or capital. Productivity depends on both the quality and features of products (which determine the prices that they can command) and the ef-

ficiency with which they are produced. Productivity is the prime determinant of a nation's long-run standard of living; it is the root cause of national per capita income. The productivity of human resources determines employee wages; the productivity with which capital is employed determines the return it earns for its holders.

A nation's standard of living depends on the capacity of its companies to achieve high levels of productivity—and to increase productivity over time. Sustained productivity growth requires that an economy continually *upgrade itself*. A nation's companies must relentlessly improve productivity in existing industries by raising product quality, adding desirable features, improving product technology, or boosting production efficiency. They must develop the necessary capabilities to compete in more and more sophisticated industry segments, where productivity is generally high. They must finally develop the capability to compete in entirely new, sophisticated industries.

International trade and foreign investment can both improve a nation's productivity as well as threaten it. They support rising national productivity by allowing a nation to specialize in those industries and segments of industries where its companies are more productive and to import where its companies are less productive. No nation can be competitive in everything. The ideal is to deploy the nation's limited pool of human and other resources into the most productive uses. Even those nations with the highest standards of living have many industries in which local companies are uncompetitive.

Yet international trade and foreign investment also can threaten productivity growth. They expose a nation's industries to the test of international standards of productivity. An industry will lose out if its productivity is not sufficiently higher than foreign rivals' to offset any advantages in local wage rates. If a nation loses the ability to compete in a range of high-productivity/high-wage industries, its standard of living is threatened.

Defining national competitiveness as achieving a trade surplus or balanced trade per se is inappropriate. The expansion of exports because of low wages and a weak currency, at the same time that the nation imports sophisticated goods that its companies cannot produce competitively, may bring trade into balance or surplus but lowers the nation's standard of living. Competitiveness also does not mean jobs. It's the *type* of jobs, not just the ability to employ citizens at low wages, that is decisive for economic prosperity.

Seeking to explain "competitiveness" at the national level, then, is to answer the wrong question. What we must understand instead is the determinants of productivity and the

rate of productivity growth. To find answers, we must focus not on the economy as a whole but on *specific industries and industry segments.* We must understand how and why commercially viable skills and technology are created, which can only be fully understood at the level of particular industries. It is the outcome of the thousands of struggles for competitive advantage against foreign rivals in particular segments and industries, in which products and processes are created and improved, that underpins the process of upgrading national productivity.

When one looks closely at any national economy, there are striking differences among a nation's industries in competitive success. International advantage is often concentrated in particular industry segments. German exports of cars are heavily skewed toward high performance cars, while Korean exports are all compacts and subcompacts. In many industries and segments of industries, the competitors with true international competitive advantage are *based in only a few nations.*

Our search, then, is for the decisive characteristic of a nation that allows its companies to create and sustain competitive advantage in particular fields—the search is for the competitive advantage of nations. We are particularly concerned with the determinants of international success in technology and skill-intensive segments and industries, which underpin high and rising productivity.

Classical theory explains the success of nations in particular industries based on so-called factors of production such as land, labor, and natural resources. Nations gain factor-based comparative advantage in industries that make intensive use of the factors they possess in abundance. Classical theory, however, has been overshadowed in advanced industries and economies by the globalization of competition and the power of technology.

A new theory must recognize that in modern international competition, companies compete with global strategies involving not only trade but also foreign investment. What a new theory must explain is why a nation provides a favorable home base for companies that compete internationally. The home base is the nation in which the essential competitive advantages of the enterprise are created and sustained. It is where a company's strategy is set, where the core product and process technology is created and maintained, and where the most productive jobs and most advanced skills are located. The presence of the home base in a nation has the greatest positive influence on other linked domestic industries and leads to other benefits in the nation's economy. While the ownership of the company is often concentrated at the home base, the nationality of shareholders is secondary.

A new theory must move beyond comparative advantage to the competitive advantage of a nation. It must reflect a rich conception of competition that includes segmented markets, differentiated products, technology differences, and economies of scale. A new theory must go beyond cost and explain why companies from some nations are better than others at creating advantages based on quality, features, and new product innovation. A new theory must begin from the premise that competition is dynamic and evolving; it must answer the questions: Why do some companies based in some nations innovate more than others? Why do some nations provide an environment that enables companies to improve and innovate faster than foreign rivals?

How Companies Succeed in International Markets

Around the world, companies that have achieved international leadership employ strategies that differ from each other in every respect. But while every successful company will employ its own particular strategy, the underlying mode of operation—the character and trajectory of all successful companies—is fundamentally the same.

Companies achieve competitive advantage through acts of innovation. They approach innovation in its broadest sense, including both new technologies and new ways of doing things. They perceive a new basis for competing or find better means for competing in old ways. Innovation can be manifested in a new product design, a new production process, a new marketing approach, or a new way of conducting training. Much innovation is mundane and incremental, depending more on a cumulation of small insights and advances than on a single, major technological breakthrough. It often involves ideas that are not even "new"—ideas that have been around, but never vigorously pursued. It always involves investments in skill and knowledge, as well as in physical assets and brand reputations.

Some innovations create competitive advantage by perceiving an entirely new market opportunity or by serving a market segment that others have ignored. When competitors are slow to respond, such innovation yields competitive advantage. For instance, in industries such as autos and home electronics, Japanese companies gained their initial advantage by emphasizing smaller, more compact, lower capacity models that foreign competitors disdained as less profitable, less important, and less attractive.

In international markets, innovations that yield competitive advantage anticipate both domestic and foreign needs. For example, as international concern for product safety has grown, Swedish companies like Volvo, Atlas Copco, and AGA have succeeded by anticipating the market opportunity in this area. On the other hand, innovations that respond to concerns or circumstances that are peculiar to the home market can actually retard international competitive success. The lure of the huge U.S. defense market, for instance, has diverted the attention of U.S. materials and machine-tool companies from attractive, global commercial markets.

Information plays a large role in the process of innovation and improvement—information that either is not available to competitors or that they do not seek. Sometimes it comes from simple investment in research and development or market research; more often, it comes from effort and from openness and from looking in the right place unencumbered by blinding assumptions or conventional wisdom.

This is why innovators are often outsiders from a different industry or a different country. Innovation may come from a new company, whose founder has a nontraditional background or was simply not appreciated in an older, established company. Or the capacity for innovation may come into an existing company through senior managers who are new to the particular industry and thus more able to perceive opportunities and more likely to pursue them. Or innovation may occur as a company diversifies, bringing new resources, skills, or perspectives to another industry. Or innovations may come from another nation with different circumstances or different ways of competing.

With few exceptions, innovation is the result of unusual effort. The company that successfully implements a new or better way of competing pursues its approach with dogged determination, often in the face of harsh criticism and tough obstacles. In fact, to succeed, innovation usually requires pressure, necessity, and even adversity: the fear of loss often proves more powerful than the hope of gain.

Once a company achieves competitive advantage through an innovation, it can sustain it only through relentless improvement. Almost any advantage can be imitated. Korean companies have already matched the ability of their Japanese rivals to mass-produce standard color televisions and VCRs; Brazilian companies have assembled technology and designs comparable to Italian competitors in casual leather footwear.

Competitors will eventually and inevitably overtake any company that stops improving and innovating. Sometimes early-mover advantages such as customer relationships, scale economies in existing technologies, or the loyalty of distribution channels are enough to permit a stagnant company to retain its entrenched position for years or even decades. But sooner or later, more dynamic rivals will find a way to innovate around these advantages or create a better or cheaper way of doing things. Italian appliance producers, which competed successfully on the basis of cost in selling midsize and compact appliances through large retail chains, rested too long on this initial advantage. By developing more differentiated products and creating strong brand franchises, German competitors have begun to gain ground.

Ultimately, the only way to sustain a competitive advantage is to *upgrade it*—to move to more sophisticated types. This is precisely what Japanese auto-makers have done. They initially penetrated foreign markets with small, inexpensive compact cars of adequate quality and competed on the basis of lower labor costs. Even while their labor-cost advantage persisted, however, the Japanese companies were upgrading. They invested aggressively to build large modern plants to reap economies of scale. Then they became innovators in process technology, pioneering just-in-time production and a host of other quality and productivity practices. These process improvements led to better product quality, better repair records, and better customer-satisfaction ratings than foreign competitors had. Most recently, Japanese auto makers have advanced to the vanguard of product technology and are introducing new, premium brand names to compete with the world's most prestigious passenger cars.

The example of the Japanese automakers also illustrates two additional prerequisites for sustaining competitive advantage. First, a company must adopt a global approach to strategy. It must sell its product worldwide, under its own brand name, through international marketing channels that it controls. A truly global approach may even require the company to locate production or R&D facilities in other nations to take advantage of lower wage rates, to gain or improve market access, or to take advantage of foreign technology. Second, creating more sustainable advantages often means that a company must make its existing advantage obsolete—even while it is still an advantage. Japanese auto companies recognized this; either they would make their advantage obsolete, or a competitor would do it for them.

As this example suggests, innovation and change are inextricably tied together. But change is an unnatural act, particularly in successful companies; powerful forces are at work to avoid and defeat it. Past approaches become institutionalized in standard operating procedures and management controls. Training emphasizes the one correct way to do anything; the construction of specialized, dedicated facilities solidifies past practice into expensive brick and mortar; the existing strategy takes on an aura of invincibility and becomes rooted in the company culture.

Successful companies tend to develop a bias for predictability and stability; they work on defending what they have. Change is tempered by the fear that there is much to lose. The organization at all levels filters out information that would suggest new approaches, modifications, or departures from the norm. The internal environment operates like an immune system to isolate or expel "hostile" individuals who challenge current directions or established thinking. Innovation ceases; the company becomes stagnant; it is only a matter of time before aggressive competitors overtake it.

The Diamond of National Advantage

Why are certain companies based in certain nations capable of consistent innovation? Why do they ruthlessly pursue improvements, seeking an ever more sophisticated source of competitive advantage? Why are they able to overcome the substantial barriers to change and innovation that so often accompany success?

The answer lies in four broad attributes of a nation, attributes that individually and as a system constitute the diamond of national advantage, the playing field that each nation establishes and operates for its industries. These attributes are:

1. *Factor Conditions.* The nation's position in factors of production, such as skilled labor or infrastructure, necessary to compete in a given industry.

2. *Demand Conditions.* The nature of home-market demand for the industry's product or service.

3. *Related and Supporting Industries.* The presence or absence in the nation of supplier industries and other related industries that are internationally competitive.

4. *Firm Strategy, Structure, and Rivalry.* The conditions in the nation governing how companies are created, organized, and managed, as well as the nature of domestic rivalry.

These determinants create the national environment in which companies are born and learn how to compete. (See Figure 6.1.) Each point on the diamond—and the diamond as a system—affects essential ingredients for achieving international competitive success: the availability of resources and skills necessary for competitive advantage in an industry; the information that shapes the opportunities that companies perceive and the directions in which they deploy their resources and skills; the

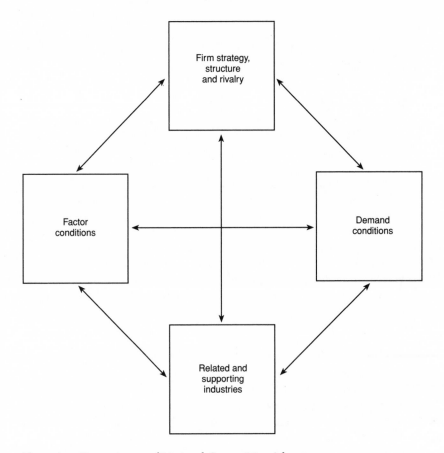

Figure 6.1   Determinants of National Competitive Advantage

goals of the owners, managers, and individuals in companies; and most important, the pressures on companies to invest and innovate. (See the insert "How the Diamond Works: The Italian Ceramic Tile Industry.")

When a national environment permits and supports the most rapid accumulation of specialized assets and skills—sometimes simply because of greater effort and commitment—companies gain a competitive advantage. When a national environment affords better ongoing information and insight into product and process needs, companies gain a competitive advantage. Finally, when the national environment pressures companies to innovate and invest, companies both gain a competitive advantage and upgrade those advantages over time.

How the Diamond Works: The Italian Ceramic Tile Industry

Michael J. Enright and Paolo Tenti

In 1987, Italian companies were world leaders in the production and export of ceramic tiles, a $10 billion industry. Italian producers, concentrated in and around the small town of Sassuolo in the Emilia-Romagna region, accounted for about 30 percent of world production and almost 60 percent of world exports. The Italian trade surplus that year in ceramic tiles was about $1.4 billion.

The development of the Italian ceramic tile industry's competitive advantage illustrates how the diamond of national advantage works. Sassuolo's sustainable competitive advantage in ceramic tiles grew not from any static or historical advantage but from dynamism and change. Sophisticated and demanding local buyers, strong and unique distribution channels, and intense rivalry among local companies created constant pressure for innovation. Knowledge grew quickly from continuous experimentation and cumulative production experience. Private ownership of the companies and loyalty to the community spawned intense commitment to invest in the industry.

Tile producers benefited as well from a highly developed set of local machinery suppliers and other supporting industries, producing materials, services, and infrastructure. The presence of world-class, Italian-related industries also reinforced Italian strength in tiles. Finally, the geographic concentration of the entire cluster supercharged the whole process. Today foreign companies compete against an entire subculture. The organic nature of this system represents the most sustainable advantage of Sassuolo's ceramic tile companies.

The Origins of the Italian Industry

Tile production in Sassuolo grew out of the earthenware and crockery industry, whose history traces back to the thirteenth century. Immediately after World War II, there were only a handful of ceramic tile manufacturers in and around Sassuolo, all serving the local market exclusively.

Demand for ceramic tiles within Italy began to grow dramatically in the immediate postwar years, as the reconstruction of Italy triggered a boom in building materials of all kinds. Italian demand for ceramic tiles was particularly great due to the climate, local tastes, and building techniques.

Because Sassuolo was in a relatively prosperous part of Italy, there were many who could combine the modest amount of capital and necessary organizational skills to start a tile company. In 1955, there were 14 Sassuolo area tile companies; by 1962, there were 102.

The new tile companies benefited from a local pool of mechanically trained workers. The region around Sassuolo was home to Ferrari, Maserati, Lamborghini, and other technically sophisticated companies. As the tile industry began to grow and prosper, many engineers and skilled workers gravitated to the successful companies.

The Emerging Italian Tile Cluster

Initially, Italian tile producers were dependent on foreign sources of raw materials and production technology. In the 1950s, the principal raw materials used to make tiles were kaolin (white) clays. Since there were red but no white-clay deposits near Sassuolo, Italian producers had to import the clays from the United Kingdom. Tile making equipment was also imported in the 1950s and 1960s: kilns from Germany, America, and France; presses for forming tiles from Germany. Sassuolo tile makers had to import even simple glazing machines.

Over time, the Italian tile producers learned how to modify imported equipment to fit local circumstances: red versus white clays, natural gas versus heavy oil. As process technicians from tile companies left

to start their own equipment companies, a local machinery industry arose in Sassuolo. By 1970, Italian companies had emerged as world-class producers of kilns and presses; the earlier situation had exactly reversed: were exporting their red-clay equipment for foreigners to use with white clays.

The relationship between Italian tile and equipment manufacturers was a mutually supporting one, made even more so by close proximity. In the mid-1980s, there were some 200 Italian equipment manufacturers; more than 60 percent were located in the Sassuolo area. The equipment manufacturers competed fiercely for local business, and tile manufacturers benefited from better prices and more advanced equipment than their foreign rivals.

As the emerging tile cluster grew and concentrated in the Sassuolo region, a pool of skilled workers and technicians developed, including engineers, production specialists, maintenance workers, service technicians, and design personnel. The industry's geographic concentration encouraged other supporting companies to form, offering molds, packaging materials, glazes, and transportation services. An array of small, specialized consulting companies emerged to give advice to tile producers on plant design, logistics, and commercial, advertising, and fiscal matters.

With its membership concentrated in the Sassuolo area, Assopiastrelle, the ceramic tile industry association, began offering services in areas of common interest: bulk purchasing, foreign-market research, and consulting on fiscal and legal matters. The growing tile cluster stimulated the formation of a new, specialized factor-creating institution: in 1976, a consortium of the University of Bologna, regional agencies, and the ceramic industry association founded the Centro Ceramico di Bologna, which conducted process research and product analysis.

Sophisticated Home Demand

By the mid-1960s, per-capita tile consumption in Italy was considerably higher than in the rest of the world. The Italian market was also the world's most sophisticated. Italian customers, who were generally the first to adopt new designs and features, and Italian producers, who constantly innovated to improve manufacturing methods and create new designs, progressed in a mutually reinforcing process.

The uniquely sophisticated character of domestic demand also extended to retail outlets. In the 1960s, specialized tile showrooms began opening in Italy. By 1985, there were roughly 7,600 specialized showrooms handling approximately 80 percent of domestic sales, far more than in other nations. In 1976, the Italian company Piemme introduced tiles by famous designers to gain distribution outlets and to build brand

name awareness among consumers. This innovation drew on another related industry, design services, in which Italy was world leader, with over $10 billion in exports.

Sassuolo Rivalry

The sheer number of tile companies in the Sassuolo area created intense rivalry. News of product and process innovations spread rapidly, and companies seeking technological, design, and distribution leadership had to improve constantly.

Proximity added a personal note to the intense rivalry. All of the producers were privately held, most were family run. The owners all lived in the same area, knew each other, and were the leading citizens of the same towns.

Pressures to Upgrade

In the early 1970s, faced with intense domestic rivalry, pressure from retail customers, and the shock of the 1973 energy crisis, Italian tile companies struggled to reduce gas and labor costs. These efforts led to a technological breakthrough, the rapid single-firing process, in which the hardening process, material transformation, and glaze-fixing all occurred in one pass through the kiln. A process that took 225 employees using the double-firing method needed only ninety employees using single-firing roller kilns. Cycle time dropped from sixteen to twenty hours to only fifty to fifty-five minutes.

The new, smaller, and lighter equipment was also easier to export. By the early 1980s, exports from Italian equipment manufacturers exceeded domestic sales; in 1988, exports represented almost 80 percent of total sales.

Working together, tile manufacturers and equipment manufacturers made the next important breakthrough during the mid and late 1970s: the development of materials-handling equipment that transformed tile manufacture from a batch process to a continuous process. The innovation reduced high labor costs—which had been a substantial selective factor disadvantage facing Italian tile manufacturers.

The common perception is that Italian labor costs were lower during this period than those in the United States and Germany. In those two countries, however, different jobs had widely different wages. In Italy, wages for different skill categories were compressed, and work rules constrained manufacturers from using overtime or multiple shifts. The restriction proved costly: once cool, kilns are expensive to reheat and are best run continuously. Because of this factor disadvantage, the Italian companies were the first to develop continuous, automated production.

Internationalization

By 1970, Italian domestic demand had matured. The stagnant Italian market led companies to step up their efforts to pursue foreign markets. The presence of related and supporting Italian industries helped in the export drive. Individual tile manufacturers began advertising in Italian and foreign home-design and architectural magazines, publications with wide global circulation among architects, designers, and consumers. This heightened awareness reinforced the quality image of Italian tiles. Tile makers were also able to capitalize on Italy's leading world export positions in related industries like marble, building stone, sinks, washbasins, furniture, lamps, and home appliances.

Assopiastrelle, the industry association, established trade-promotion offices in the United States in 1980, in Germany in 1984, and in France in 1987. It organized elaborate trade shows in cities ranging from Bologna to Miami and ran sophisticated advertising. Between 1980 and 1987, the association spent roughly $8 million to promote Italian tiles in the United States.

Michael J. Enright and
Paolo Tenti

Michael J. Enright, a doctoral student in business economics at the Harvard Business School, performed numerous research and supervisory tasks for The Competitive Advantage of Nations. *Paolo Tenti was responsible for the Italian part of research undertaken for the book. He is a consultant in strategy and finance for Monitor Company and Analysis F.A.—Milan.*

FACTOR CONDITIONS

According to standard economic theory, factors of production—labor, land, natural resources, capital, infrastructure—will determine the flow of trade. A nation will export those goods that make most use of the factors with which it is relatively well endowed. This doctrine, whose origins date back to Adam Smith and David Ricardo and that is embedded in classical economics, is at best incomplete and at worst incorrect.

In the sophisticated industries that form the backbone of any advanced economy, a nation does not inherit but instead creates the most important factors of production—such as skilled human resources or a scientific base. Moreover, the stock of factors that a nation enjoys at a particular time is less important than the rate and efficiency with which it creates, upgrades, and deploys them in particular industries.

The most important factors of production are those that involve sustained and heavy investment and are specialized. Basic factors, such as a pool of labor or a local raw-material source, do not constitute an advantage in knowledge-intensive industries. Companies can access them easily through a global strategy or circumvent them through technology. Contrary to conventional wisdom, simply having a general work force that is high school or even college educated represents no competitive advantage in modern international competition. To support competitive advantage, a factor must be highly specialized to an industry's particular needs—a scientific institute specialized in optics, a pool of venture capital to fund software companies. These factors are more scarce, more difficult for foreign competitors to imitate—and they require sustained investment to create.

Nations succeed in industries where they are particularly good at factor creation. Competitive advantage results from the presence of world-class institutions that first create specialized factors and then continually work to upgrade them. Denmark has two hospitals that concentrate in studying and treating diabetes—and a world-leading export position in insulin. Holland has premier research institutes in the cultivation, packaging, and shipping of flowers, where it is the world's export leader.

What is not so obvious, however, is that selective disadvantages in the more basic factors can prod a company to innovate and upgrade—a disadvantage in a static model of competition can become an advantage in a dynamic one. When there is an ample supply of cheap raw materials or abundant labor, companies can simply rest on these advantages and often deploy them inefficiently. But when companies face a selective disadvantage, like high land costs, labor shortages, or the lack of local raw materials, they must innovate and upgrade to compete.

Implicit in the oft-repeated Japanese statement, "We are an island nation with no natural resources,' is the understanding that these deficiencies have only served to spur Japan's competitive innovation. Just-in-time production, for example, economized on prohibitively expensive space. Italian steel producers in the Brescia area faced a similar set of disadvantages: high capital costs, high energy costs, and no local raw materials. Located in Northern Lombardy, these privately owned companies faced staggering logistics costs due to their distance from southern ports and the inefficiencies of the state-owned Italian transportation system. The result: they pioneered technologically advanced minimills that require only modest capital investment, use less energy, employ scrap metal as the feedstock, are efficient at small scale, and permit producers to locate close to sources of scrap and end-use customers. In other words, they converted factor disadvantages into competitive advantage.

Disadvantages can become advantages only under certain conditions. First, they must send companies proper signals about circumstances that will spread to other nations, thereby equipping them to innovate in advance of foreign rivals. Switzerland, the nation that experienced the first labor shortages after World War II, is a case in point. Swiss companies responded to the disadvantage by upgrading labor productivity and seeking higher value, more sustainable market segments. Companies in most other parts of the world, where there were still ample workers, focused their attention on other issues, which resulted in slower upgrading.

The second condition for transforming disadvantages into advantages is favorable circumstances elsewhere in the diamond—a consideration that applies to almost all determinants. To innovate, companies must have access to people with appropriate skills and have home-demand conditions that send the right signals. They must also have active domestic rivals who create pressure to innovate. Another precondition is company goals that lead to sustained commitment to the industry. Without such a commitment and the presence of active rivalry, a company may take an easy way around a disadvantage rather than using it as a spur to innovation.

For example, U.S. consumer-electronics companies, faced with high relative labor costs, chose to leave the product and production process largely unchanged and move labor-intensive activities to Taiwan and other Asian countries. Instead of upgrading their sources of advantage, they settled for labor-cost parity. On the other hand, Japanese rivals, confronted with intense domestic competition and a mature home market, chose to eliminate labor through automation. This led to lower assembly costs, to products with fewer components and to improved quality and reliability. Soon Japanese companies were building assembly plants in the United States—the place U.S. companies had fled.

DEMAND CONDITIONS

It might seem that the globalization of competition would diminish the importance of home demand. In practice, however, this is simply not the case. In fact, the composition and character of the home market usually has a disproportionate effect on how companies perceive, interpret, and respond to buyer needs. Nations gain competitive advantage in industries where the home demand gives their companies a clearer or earlier picture of emerging buyer needs, and where demanding buyers pressure companies to innovate faster and achieve more sophisticated competitive advantages than their foreign rivals. The size of home demand proves far less significant than the character of home demand.

Home-demand conditions help build competitive advantage when a particular industry segment is larger or more visible in the domestic market than in foreign markets. The larger market segments in a nation receive the most attention from the nation's companies; companies accord smaller or less desirable segments a lower priority. A good example is hydraulic excavators, which represent the most widely used type of construction equipment in the Japanese domestic market—but which comprise a far smaller proportion of the market in other advanced nations. This segment is one of the few where there are vigorous Japanese international competitors and where Caterpillar does not hold a substantial share of the world market.

More important than the mix of segments per se is the nature of domestic buyers. A nation's companies gain competitive advantage if domestic buyers are the world's most sophisticated and demanding buyers for the product or service. Sophisticated, demanding buyers provide a window into advanced customer needs; they pressure companies to meet high standards; they prod them to improve, to innovate, and to upgrade into more advanced segments. As with factor conditions, demand conditions provide advantages by forcing companies to respond to tough challenges.

Especially stringent needs arise because of local values and circumstances. For example, Japanese consumers, who live in small, tightly packed homes, must contend with hot, humid summers and high-cost electrical energy—a daunting combination of circumstances. In response, Japanese companies have pioneered compact, quiet air-conditioning units powered by energy-saving rotary compressors. In industry after industry, the tightly constrained requirements of the Japanese market have forced companies to innovate, yielding products that are *kei-haku-tan-sho*—light, thin, short, small—and that are internationally accepted.

Local buyers can help a nation's companies gain advantage if their needs anticipate or even shape those of other nations—if their needs provide ongoing "early-warning indicators" of global market trends. Sometimes anticipatory needs emerge because a nation's political values foreshadow needs that will grow elsewhere. Sweden's long-standing concern for handicapped people has spawned an increasingly competitive industry focused on special needs. Denmark's environmentalism has led to success for companies in water-pollution control equipment and windmills.

More generally, a nation's companies can anticipate global trends if the nation's values are spreading—that is, if the country is exporting its values and tastes as well as its products. The international success of U.S. companies in fast food and credit cards, for example, reflects not only the American desire for convenience but also the spread of these tastes to the rest of the world. Nations export their values and tastes through media, through training foreigners, through political influence, and through the foreign activities of their citizens and companies.

RELATED AND SUPPORTING INDUSTRIES

The third broad determinant of national advantage is the presence in the nation of related and supporting industries that are internationally competitive. Internationally competitive home-based suppliers create advantages in downstream industries in several ways. First, they deliver the most cost-effective inputs in an efficient, early, rapid, and sometimes preferential way. Italian gold and silver jewelry companies lead the world in that industry in part because other Italian companies supply two-thirds of the world's jewelry-making and precious-metal recycling machinery.

Far more significant than mere access to components and machinery, however, is the advantage that home-based related and supporting industries provide in innovation and upgrading—an advantage based on close working relationships. Suppliers and end-users located near each other can take advantage of short lines of communication, quick and constant flow of information, and an ongoing exchange of ideas and innovations. Companies have the opportunity to influence their suppliers' technical efforts and can serve as test sites for R&D work, accelerating the pace of innovation.

Figure 6.2, "The Italian Footwear Cluster," offers a graphic example of how a group of close-by, supporting industries creates competitive advantage in a range of interconnected industries that are all internationally competitive. Shoe producers, for instance, interact regularly with leather manufacturers on new styles and manufacturing techniques and learn about new textures and colors of leather when they are still on the drawing boards. Leather manufacturers gain early insights into fashion trends, helping them to plan new products. The interaction is mutually advantageous and self-reinforcing, but it does not happen automatically: it is helped by proximity, but occurs only because companies and suppliers work at it.

The nation's companies benefit most when the suppliers are, themselves, global competitors. It is ultimately self-defeating for a company or country to create "captive" suppliers who are totally dependent on

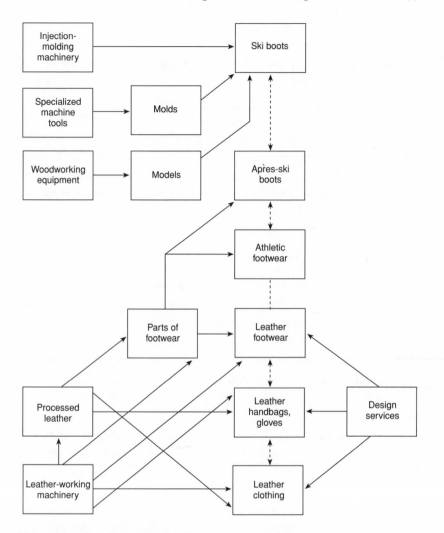

Figure 6.2   The Italian Footwear Cluster

the domestic industry and prevented from serving foreign competitors. By the same token, a nation need not be competitive in all supplier industries for its companies to gain competitive advantage. Companies can readily source from abroad materials, components, or technologies without a major effect on innovation or performance of the industry's products. The same is true of other generalized technologies—like electronics or software—where the industry represents a narrow application area.

Home-based competitiveness in related industries provides similar benefits: information flow and technical interchange speed the rate of innovation and upgrading. A home-based related industry also in-creases the likelihood that companies will embrace new skills, and it also provides a source of entrants who will bring a novel approach to competing. The Swiss success in pharmaceuticals emerged out of previous international success in the dye industry, for example; Japanese dominance in electronic musical keyboards grows out of success in acoustic instruments combined with a strong position in consumer electronics.

FIRM STRATEGY, STRUCTURE, AND RIVALRY

National circumstances and context create strong tendencies in how companies are created, organized, and managed, as well as what the nature of domestic rivalry will be. In Italy, for example, successful international competitors are often small or medium-sized companies that are privately owned and operated like extended families; in Germany, in contrast, companies tend to be strictly hierarchical in organization and management practices, and top managers usually have technical backgrounds.

No one managerial system is universally appropriate—notwithstanding the current fascination with Japanese management. Competitiveness in a specific industry results from convergence of the management practices and organizational modes favored in the country and the sources of competitive advantage in the industry. In industries where Italian companies are world leaders—such as lighting, furniture, footwear, woolen fabrics, and packaging machines—a company strategy that emphasizes focus, customized products, niche marketing, rapid change, and breathtaking flexibility fits both the dynamics of the industry and the character of the Italian management system. The German management system, in contrast, works well in technical or engineering-oriented industries—optics, chemicals, complicated machinery—where complex products demand precision manufacturing, a careful development process, after-sale service, and thus a highly disciplined management structure. German success is much rarer in consumer goods and services where image marketing and rapid new-feature and model turn-over are important to competition.

Countries also differ markedly in the goals that companies and individuals seek to achieve. Company goals reflect the characteristics of national capital markets and the compensation practices for managers. For example, in Germany and Switzerland, where banks comprise a substantial part of the nation's shareholders, most shares are held for long-term appreciation and are rarely traded. Companies do well in mature industries, where ongoing investment in R&D and new facilities is essential but returns may be only moderate. The United States is at the opposite extreme, with a large pool of risk capital but widespread trading of public companies and a strong emphasis by investors on quarterly and annual share-price appreciation. Management compensation is heavily based on annual bonuses tied to individual results. America does well in relatively new industries, like software and bio-technology, or ones where equity funding of new companies feeds active domestic rivalry, like specialty electronics and services. Strong pressures leading to underinvestment, however, plague more mature industries.

Individual motivation to work and expand skills is also important to competitive advantage. Outstanding talent is a scarce resource in any nation. A nation's success largely depends on the types of education its talented people choose, where they choose to work, and their commitment and effort. The goals a nation's institutions and values set for individuals and companies, and the prestige it attaches to certain industries, guide the flow of capital and human resources—which, in turn, directly affects the competitive performance of certain industries. Nations tend to be competitive in activities that people admire or depend on—the activities from which the nation's heroes emerge. In Switzerland, it is banking and pharmaceuticals. In Israel, the highest callings have been agriculture and defense-related fields. Sometimes it is hard to distinguish between cause and effect. Attaining international success can make an industry prestigious, reinforcing its advantage.

The presence of strong local rivals is a final, and powerful, stimulus to the creation and persistence of competitive advantage. This is true of small countries, like Switzerland, where the rivalry among its pharmaceutical companies, Hoffmann-La Roche, Ciba-Geigy, and Sandoz, contributes to a leading worldwide position. It is true in the United States in the computer and software industries. Nowhere is the role of fierce rivalry more apparent than in Japan, where there are 112 companies competing in machine tools, thirty-four in semiconductors, twenty-five in audio equipment, fifteen in cameras—in fact, there are usually double figures in the industries in which Japan boasts global dominance. (See Table 6.1.) Among all the points on the diamond, domestic rivalry is

Table 6.1   Estimated Number of Japanese Rivals in Selected Industries

Air conditioners	13
Audio Equipment	25
Automobiles	9
Cameras	15
Car Audio	12
Carbon Fibers	7
Construction Equipment*	15
Copiers	14
Facsimile Machines	10
Large-scale Computers	6
Lift Trucks	8
Machine Tools	112
Microwave Equipment	5
Motorcycles	4
Musical Instruments	4
Personal Computers	16
Semiconductors	34
Sewing Machines	20
Shipbuilding†	33
Steel‡	5
Synthetic Fibers	8
Television sets	15
Truck and Bus Tires	5
Trucks	11
Typewriters	14
Videocassette Recorders	10

Sources: Field interviews; *Nippon Kogyo Shinbun, Nippon Kogyo Nenkan,* 1987; Yano Research, *Market Share Jitan,* 1987; researchers' estimates.
*The number of companies varied by product area. The smallest number, ten, produced bulldozers. Fifteen companies produced shovel trucks, truck cranes, and asphalt-paving equipment. There were twenty companies in hydraulic excavators, a product area where Japan was particularly strong.
†Six companies had annual production exports in excess of 10,000 tons.
‡Integrated companies.

arguably the most important because of the powerfully stimulating effect it has on all the others.

Conventional wisdom argues that domestic competition is wasteful: it leads to duplication of effort and prevents companies from achieving economies of scale. The "right solution" is to embrace one or two national champions, companies with the scale and strength to tackle foreign competitors, and to guarantee them the necessary resources, with the government's blessing. In fact, however, most national champions are uncompetitive, although heavily subsidized and protected by their government. In many of the prominent industries in which there is only one national rival, such as aerospace and telecommunications, government has played a large role in distorting competition.

Static efficiency is much less important than dynamic improvement, which domestic rivalry uniquely spurs. Domestic rivalry, like any rivalry, creates pressure on companies to innovate and im-prove. Local rivals push each other to lower costs, improve quality and service, and create new products and processes. But unlike rivalries with foreign competitors, which tend to be analytical and distant, local rivalries often go beyond pure economic or business competition and become intensely personal Domestic rivals engage in active feuds; they compete not only for market share but also for people, for technical excellence, and perhaps most important, for "bragging rights." One domestic rival's success proves to others that advancement is possible and often attracts new rivals to the industry. Companies often attribute the success of foreign rivals to "unfair" advantages. With domestic rivals, there are no excuses.

Geographic concentration magnifies the power of domestic rivalry. This pattern is strikingly common around the world: Italian jewelry companies are located around two towns, Arezzo and Valenza Po; cutlery companies in Solingen, West Germany and Seki, Japan; pharmaceutical companies in Basel, Switzerland; motorcycles and musical instruments in Hamamatsu, Japan. The more localized the rivalry, the more intense. And the more intense, the better.

Another benefit of domestic rivalry is the pressure it creates for constant upgrading of the sources of competitive advantage. The presence of domestic competitors automatically cancels the types of advantage that come from simply being in a particular nation—factor costs, access to or preference in the home market, or costs to foreign competitors who import into the market. Companies are forced to move beyond them, and as a result, gain more sustainable advantages. Moreover, competing domestic tons. rivals will keep each other honest in obtaining government support. Companies are less likely to get hooked on the narcotic of government contracts or creeping industry protectionism. Instead, the industry will seek—and benefit from—more constructive forms of government support, such as assistance in opening foreign markets, as well as investments in focused educational institutions or other specialized factors.

Ironically, it is also vigorous domestic competition that ultimately pressures domestic companies to look at global markets and toughens them to succeed in them. Particularly when there are economies of scale, local competitors force each other to look out-ward to foreign markets to capture greater efficiency and higher profitability. And having been tested by fierce domestic competition, the stronger companies are well equipped to win abroad. If Digital Equipment can hold its own against IBM, Data General, Prime, and Hewlett-Packard, going up against Siemens or Machines Bull does not seem so daunting a prospect.

The Diamond as a System

Each of these four attributes defines a point on the diamond of national advantage; the effect of one point often depends on the state of others. Sophisticated buyers will not translate into advanced products, for example, unless the quality of human resources permits companies to meet buyer needs. Selective disadvantages in factors of production will not motivate innovation unless rivalry is vigorous and company goals support sustained investment. At the broadest level, weaknesses in any one determinant will constrain an industry's potential for advancement and upgrading.

But the points of the diamond are also self-reinforcing: they constitute a system. Two elements, domestic rivalry and geographic concentration, have especially great power to transform the diamond into a system— domestic rivalry because it promotes improvement in all the other determinants and geographic concentration because it elevates and magnifies the interaction of the four separate influences.

The role of domestic rivalry illustrates how the diamond operates as a self-reinforcing system. Vigorous domestic rivalry stimulates the development of unique pools of specialized factors, particularly if the rivals are all located in one city or region: the University of California at Davis has become the world's leading center of wine-making research, working closely with the California wine industry. Active local rivals also upgrade domestic demand in an industry. In furniture and shoes, for example, Italian consumers have learned to expect more and better products because of the rapid pace of new product development that is driven by intense domestic rivalry among hundreds of Italian companies. Domestic rivalry also promotes the formation of related and supporting industries. Japan's world-leading group of semiconductor producers, for instance, has spawned world-leading Japanese semiconductor-equipment manufacturers.

The effects can work in all directions: sometimes world-class suppliers become new entrants in the industry they have been supplying. Or highly sophisticated buyers may themselves enter a supplier industry, particularly when they have relevant skills and view the new industry as strategic. In the case of the Japanese robotics industry, for example, Matsushita and Kawasaki originally designed robots for internal use before beginning to sell robots to others. Today they are strong competitors in the robotics industry. In Sweden, Sandvik moved from specialty steel into rock drills, and SKF moved from specialty steel into ball bearings.

Another effect of the diamond's systemic nature is that nations are rarely home to just one competitive industry; rather, the diamond creates an environment that promotes clusters of competitive industries. Competitive industries are not scattered helter-skelter throughout the economy but are usually linked together through vertical (buyer-seller) or horizontal (common customers, technology, channels) relationships. Nor are clusters usually scattered physically; they tend to be concentrated geographically. One competitive industry helps to create another in a mutually reinforcing process. Japan's strength in consumer electronics, for example, drove its success in semiconductors toward the memory chips and integrated circuits these products use. Japanese strength in laptop computers, which contrasts to limited success in other segments, reflects the base of strength in other compact, portable products and leading expertise in liquid-crystal display gained in the calculator and watch industries.

Once a cluster forms, the whole group of industries becomes mutually supporting. Benefits flow forward, backward, and horizontally. Aggressive rivalry in one industry spreads to others in the cluster, through spin-offs, through the exercise of bargaining power, and through diversification by established companies. Entry from other industries within the cluster spurs upgrading by stimulating diversity in R&D approaches and facilitating the introduction of new strategies and skills. Through the conduits of suppliers or customers who have contact with multiple competitors, information flows freely and innovations diffuse rapidly. Interconnections within the cluster, often unanticipated, lead to perceptions of new ways of competing and new opportunities. The cluster becomes a vehicle for maintaining diversity and overcoming the inward focus, inertia, inflexibility, and accommodation among rivals that slows or blocks competitive upgrading and new entry.

The Role of Government

In the continuing debate over the competitiveness of nations, no topic engenders more argument or creates less understanding than the role of the government. Many see government as an essential helper or supporter of industry, employing a host of policies to contribute directly to the competitive performance of strategic or target industries. Others accept the "free market" view that the operation of the economy should be left to the workings of the invisible hand.

Both views are incorrect. Either, followed to its logical outcome, would lead to the permanent erosion of a country's competitive capabilities. On one hand, advocates of government help for industry frequently propose policies that would actually hurt companies in the long run and only create the demand for more helping. On the other hand, advocates of a diminished government presence ignore the legitimate role that government plays in shaping the context and institutional structure surrounding companies and in creating an environment that stimulates companies to gain competitive advantage.

Government's proper role is as a catalyst and challenger; it is to encourage—or even push—companies to raise their aspirations and move to higher levels of competitive performance, even though this process may be inherently unpleasant and difficult. Government cannot create competitive industries; only companies can do that. Government plays a role that is inherently partial, that succeeds only when working in tandem with favorable underlying conditions in the diamond. Still, government's role of transmitting and amplifying the forces of the diamond is a powerful one. Government policies that succeed are those that create an environment in which companies can gain competitive advantage rather than those that involve government directly in the process, except in nations early in the development process. It is an indirect, rather than a direct, role.

Japan's government, at its best, understands this role better than anyone—including the point that nations pass through stages of competitive development and that government's appropriate role shifts as the economy progresses. By stimulating early demand for advanced products, confronting industries with the need to pioneer frontier technology through symbolic cooperative projects, establishing prizes that reward quality, and pursuing other policies that magnify the forces of the diamond, the Japanese government accelerates the pace of innovation. But like government officials anywhere, at their worst Japanese bureaucrats can make the same mistakes: attempting to manage industry structure, protecting the market too long, and yielding to political pressure to insulate inefficient retailers, farmers, distributors, and industrial companies from competition.

It is not hard to understand why so many governments make the same mistakes so often in pursuit of national competitiveness: competitive time for companies and political time for governments are fundamentally at odds. It often takes more than a decade for an industry to create competitive advantage; the process entails the long upgrading of human skills, investing in products and processes, building clusters, and penetrating foreign markets. In the case of the Japanese auto industry, for instance, companies made their first faltering steps toward exporting in the 1950s— yet did not achieve strong international positions until the 1970s.

But in politics, a decade is an eternity. Consequently, most governments favor policies that offer easily perceived short-term benefits, such as subsidies, protection, and arranged mergers—the very policies that retard innovation. Most of the policies that would make a real difference either are too slow and require too much patience for politicians or, even worse, carry with them the sting of short-term pain. Deregulating a protected industry, for example, will lead to bankruptcies sooner and to stronger, more competitive companies only later.

Policies that convey static, short-term cost advantages but that unconsciously undermine innovation and dynamism represent the most common and most profound error in government industrial policy. In a desire to help, it is all too easy for governments to adopt policies such as joint projects to avoid "wasteful" R&D that undermine dynamism and competition. Yet even a 10 percent cost saving through economies of scale is easily nullified through rapid product and process improvement and the pursuit of volume in global markets—something that such policies undermine.

There are some simple, basic principles that governments should embrace to play the proper supportive role for national competitiveness: encourage change, promote domestic rivalry, stimulate innovation. Some of the specific policy approaches to guide nations seeking to gain competitive advantage include the following.

FOCUS ON SPECIALIZED FACTOR CREATION

Government has critical responsibilities for fundamentals like the primary and secondary education systems, basic national infrastructure, and research in areas of broad national concern such as health care. Yet these kinds of generalized efforts at factor creation rarely produce competitive advantage. Rather, the factors that translate into competitive advantage are advanced, specialized, and tied to specific industries or industry groups. Mechanisms such as specialized apprenticeship programs, research efforts in universities connected with an industry, trade association activities, and, most important, the private investments of companies ultimately create the factors that will yield competitive advantage.

AVOID INTERVENING IN FACTOR AND CURRENCY MARKETS

By intervening in factor and currency markets, governments hope to create lower factor costs or a favorable exchange rate that will help companies compete more effectively in international markets. Evidence from around the world indicates that these policies—such as the Reagan administration's dollar devaluation—are often counterproductive. They work against the upgrading of industry and the search for more sustainable competitive advantage.

The contrasting case of Japan is particularly instructive, although both Germany and Switzerland have had similar experiences. Over the past twenty years, the Japanese have been rocked by the sudden Nixon currency devaluation shock, two oil shocks, and, most recently, the yen shock—all of which forced Japanese companies to upgrade their competitive advantages. The point is not that government should pursue policies that intentionally drive up factor costs or the exchange rate. Rather, when market forces create rising factor costs or a higher exchange rate, government should resist the temptation to push them back down.

ENFORCE STRICT PRODUCT, SAFETY, AND ENVIRONMENTAL STANDARDS

Strict government regulations can promote competitive advantage by stimulating and upgrading domestic demand. Stringent standards for product performance, product safety, and environmental impact pressure companies to improve quality, upgrade technology, and provide features that respond to consumer and social demands. Easing standards, however tempting, is counterproductive.

When tough regulations anticipate standards that will spread internationally, they give a nation's companies a head start in developing products and services that will be valuable elsewhere. Sweden's strict standards for environmental protection have promoted competitive advantage in many industries. Atlas Copco, for example, produces quiet compressors that can be used in dense urban areas with minimal disruption to residents. Strict standards, however, must be combined with a rapid and streamlined regulatory process that does not absorb resources and cause delays.

SHARPLY LIMIT DIRECT COOPERATION AMONG INDUSTRY RIVALS

The most pervasive global policy fad in the competitiveness arena today is the call for more cooperative research and industry consortia. Operating on the belief that independent research by rivals is wasteful and duplicative, that collaborative efforts achieve economies of scale, and that individual companies are likely to underinvest in R&D because they cannot reap all the benefits, governments have embraced the idea of more direct cooperation. In the United States, antitrust laws have been modified to allow more cooperative R&D; in Europe, megaprojects such as ESPRIT, an information-technology project, bring together companies from several countries. Lurking behind much of this thinking is the fascination of Western governments with—and fundamental misunderstanding of—the countless cooperative research projects sponsored by the Ministry of International Trade and Industry (MITI), projects that appear to have contributed to Japan's competitive rise.

But a closer look at Japanese cooperative projects suggests a different story. Japanese companies participate in MITI projects to maintain good relations with MITI, to preserve their corporate images, and to hedge the risk that competitors will gain from the project—largely defensive reasons. Companies rarely contribute their best scientists and engineers to cooperative projects and usually spend much more on their own private research in the same field. Typically, the government makes only a modest financial contribution to the project.

The real value of Japanese cooperative research is to signal the importance of emerging technical areas and to stimulate proprietary company research. Cooperative projects prompt companies to explore new fields and boost internal R&D spending because companies know that their domestic rivals are investigating them.

Under certain limited conditions, cooperative research can prove beneficial. Projects should be in areas of basic product and process research, not in subjects closely connected to a company's proprietary sources of advantage. They should constitute only a modest portion of a company's overall research program in any given field. Cooperative research should be only indirect, channeled through independent organizations to which most industry participants have access. Organizational structures, like university labs and centers of excellence, reduce management problems and minimize the risk to rivalry. Finally, the most useful cooperative projects often involve fields that touch a number of industries and that require substantial R&D investments.

PROMOTE GOALS THAT LEAD TO SUSTAINED INVESTMENT

Government has a vital role in shaping the goals of investors, managers, and employees through policies in various areas. The manner in which capital markets are regulated, for example, shapes the incentives of investors and, in turn, the behavior of companies. Government should aim to encourage sustained investment in human skills, in innovation, and in physical assets. Perhaps the single most powerful tool for raising the rate of sustained investment in industry is a tax incentive for long-term(five years or more) capital gains restricted to new investment in corporate equity. Long-term capital gains incentives should also be applied to pension funds and other currently untaxed investors, who now have few reasons not to engage in rapid trading.

DEREGULATE COMPETITION

Regulation of competition through such policies as maintaining a state monopoly, controlling entry into an industry, or fixing prices has two strong negative consequences: it stifles rivalry and innovation as companies become preoccupied with dealing with regulators and protecting what they already have; and it makes the industry a less dynamic and less desirable buyer or supplier. Deregulation and privatization on their own, however, will not succeed without vigorous domestic rivalry—and that requires, as a corollary, a strong and consistent antitrust policy.

ENFORCE STRONG DOMESTIC ANTITRUST POLICIES

A strong antitrust policy—especially for horizontal mergers, alliances, and collusive behavior—is fundamental to innovation. While it is fashionable today to call for mergers and alliances in the name of globalization and the creation of national champions, these often undermine the creation of competitive advantage. Real national competitiveness requires governments to disallow mergers, acquisitions, and alliances that involve industry leaders. Furthermore, the same standards for mergers and alliances should apply to both domestic and foreign companies. Finally, government policy should favor internal entry, both domestic and international, over acquisition. Companies should, however, be allowed to acquire small companies in related industries when the move promotes the transfer of skills that could ultimately create competitive advantage.

REJECT MANAGED TRADE

Managed trade represents a growing and dangerous tendency for dealing with the fallout of national competitiveness. Orderly marketing agreements, voluntary restraint agreements, or other devices that set quantitative targets to divide up markets are dangerous, ineffective, and often enormously costly to consumers. Rather than promoting innovation in a nation's industries, managed trade guarantees a market for inefficient companies.

Government trade policy should pursue open market access in every foreign nation. To be effective, trade policy should not be a passive instrument; it cannot respond only to complaints or work only for those industries that can muster enough political clout; it should not require a long history of injury or serve only distressed industries. Trade policy should seek to open markets wherever a nation has competitive advantage and should actively address emerging industries and incipient problems.

Where government finds a trade barrier in another nation, it should concentrate its remedies on dismantling barriers, not on regulating imports or exports. In the case of Japan, for example, pressure to accelerate the already rapid growth of manufactured imports is a more effective approach than a shift to managed trade. Compensatory tariffs that punish companies for unfair trade practices are better than market quotas. Other increasingly important tools to open markets are restrictions that prevent companies in offending nations from investing in acquisitions or production facilities in the host country—thereby blocking the unfair country's companies from using their advantage to establish a new beachhead that is immune from sanctions.

Any of these remedies, however, can backfire. It is virtually impossible to craft remedies to unfair trade practices that avoid both reducing incentives for domestic companies to innovate and export and harming domestic buyers. The aim of remedies should be adjustments that allow the remedy to disappear.

The Company Agenda

Ultimately, only companies themselves can achieve and sustain competitive advantage. To do so, they must act on the fundamentals described above. In particular, they must recognize the central role of innovation—and the uncomfortable truth that innovation grows out of pressure and challenge. It takes leadership to create a dynamic, challenging environment. And it takes leadership to recognize the all-too-easy escape routes that appear to offer a path to competitive advantage, but are actually short-cuts to failure. For example, it is tempting to rely on cooperative research and development projects to lower the cost and risk of research. But they can divert company attention and resources from proprietary research efforts and will all but eliminate the prospects for real innovation.

Competitive advantage arises from leadership that harnesses and amplifies the forces in the diamond to promote innovation and upgrading. Here are just a few of the kinds of company policies that will support that effort:

CREATE PRESSURES FOR INNOVATION

A company should seek out pressure and challenge, not avoid them. Part of strategy is to take advantage of the home nation to create the impetus for innovation. To do that, companies can sell to the most sophisticated and demanding buyers and channels; seek out those buyers with the most difficult needs; establish norms that exceed the toughest regulatory hurdles or product standards; source from the most advanced suppliers; treat employees as permanent in order to stimulate upgrading of skills and productivity.

SEEK OUT THE MOST CAPABLE COMPETITORS AS MOTIVATORS

To motivate organizational change, capable competitors and respected rivals can be a common enemy. The best managers always run a little scared; they respect and study competitors. To stay dynamic, companies must make meeting challenge a part of the organization's norms. For example, lobbying against strict product standards signals the organization that company leadership has diminished aspirations. Companies that value stability, obedient customers, dependent suppliers, and sleepy competi tors are inviting inertia and, ultimately, failure.

ESTABLISH EARLY-WARNING SYSTEMS

Early-warning signals translate into early-mover advantages. Companies can take actions that help them see the signals of change and act on them, thereby getting a jump on the competition. For example, they can find and serve those buyers with the most anticipatory needs; investigate all emerging new buyers or channels; find places whose regulations foreshadow emerging regulations elsewhere; bring some outsiders into the management team; maintain ongoing relationships with research centers and sources of talented people.

IMPROVE THE NATIONAL DIAMOND

Companies have a vital stake in making their home environment a better platform for international success. Part of a company's responsibility is to play an active role in forming clusters and to work with its home-nation buyers, suppliers, and channels to help them upgrade and extend their own competitive advantages. To upgrade home demand, for example, Japanese musical instrument manufacturers, led by Yamaha, Kawai, and Suzuki, have established music schools. Similarly, companies can stimulate and support local suppliers of important specialized inputs—including encouraging them to compete globally. The health and strength of the national cluster will only enhance the company's own rate of innovation and upgrading.

In nearly every successful competitive industry, leading companies also take explicit steps to create specialized factors like human resources, scientific knowledge, or infrastructure. In industries like wool cloth, ceramic tiles, and lighting equipment, Italian industry associations invest in market information, process technology, and common infrastructure. Companies can also speed innovation by putting their headquarters and other key operations where there are concentrations of sophisticated buyers, important suppliers, or specialized factor-creating mechanisms, such as universities or laboratories.

WELCOME DOMESTIC RIVALRY

To compete globally, a company needs capable domestic rivals and vigorous domestic rivalry. Especially in the United States and Europe today, managers are wont to complain about excessive competition and to argue for mergers and acquisitions that will produce hoped-for economies of scale and critical mass. The complaint is only natural—but the argument is plain wrong. Vigorous domestic rivalry creates sustainable competitive advantage. Moreover, it is better to grow internationally than to dominate the domestic market. If a company wants an acquisition, a foreign one that can speed globalization and supplement home-based advantages or offset home-based disadvantages is usually far better than merging with leading domestic competitors.

GLOBALIZE TO TAP SELECTIVE ADVANTAGES IN OTHER NATIONS

In search of "global" strategies, many companies today abandon their home diamond. To be sure, adopting a global perspective is important to creating competitive advantage. But relying on foreign activities that supplant domestic capabilities is always a second-best solution. Innovating to offset local factor disadvantages is better than outsourcing; developing domestic suppliers and buyers is better than relying solely on foreign ones. Unless the critical underpinnings of competitiveness are present at home, companies will not sustain competitive advantage in the long run. The aim should be to upgrade home-base capabilities so that foreign activities are selective and supplemental only to over-all competitive advantage.

The correct approach to globalization is to tap selectively into sources of advantage in other nations' diamonds. For example, identifying sophisticated buyers in other countries helps companies understand different needs and creates pressures that will stimulate a faster rate of innovation. No matter how favorable the home diamond, moreover, important research is going on in other nations. To take advantage of foreign research, companies must station high-quality people in overseas bases and mount a credible level of scientific effort. To get anything back from foreign research ventures, companies must also allow access to their own ideas—recognizing that competitive advantage comes from continuous improvement, not from protecting today's secrets.

USE ALLIANCES ONLY SELECTIVELY

Alliances with foreign companies have become another managerial fad and cure-all: they represent a tempting solution to the problem of a company wanting the advantages of foreign enterprises or hedging against risk, without giving up independence. In reality, however, while alliances can achieve selective benefits, they always exact significant costs: they involve coordinating two separate operations, reconciling goals with an independent entity, creating a competitor, and giving up profits. These costs ultimately make most alliances short-term transitional devices, rather than stable, long-term relationships.

Most important, alliances as a broad-based strategy will only ensure a company's mediocrity, not its international leadership. No company can rely on another outside, independent company for skills and assets that are central to its competitive advantage. Alliances are best used as a selective tool, employed on a temporary basis or involving noncore activities.

LOCATE THE HOME BASE TO SUPPORT COMPETITIVE ADVANTAGE

Among the most important decisions for multinational companies is the nation in which to locate the home base for each distinct business. A company can have different home bases for distinct businesses or segments. Ultimately, competitive advantage is created at home: it is where strategy is set, the core product and process technology is created, and a critical mass of production takes place. The circumstances in the home nation must support innovation; otherwise the company has no choice but to move its home base to a country that stimulates innovation and that provides the best environment for global competitiveness. There are no half measures: the management team must move as well.

The Role of Leadership

Too many companies and top managers misperceive the nature of competition and the task before them by focusing on improving financial performance, soliciting government assistance, seeking stability, and reducing risk through alliances and mergers.

Today's competitive realities demand leadership. Leaders believe in change; they energize their organizations to innovate continuously; they recognize the importance of their home country as integral to their competitive success and work to upgrade it. Most important, leaders recognize the need for pressure and challenge. Because they are willing to encourage appropriate—and painful—government policies and regulations, they often earn the title "statesmen," although few see themselves that way. They are prepared to sacrifice the easy life for difficulty and, ultimately, sustained competitive advantage. That must be the goal, for both nations and companies: not just surviving, but achieving international competitiveness.

And not just once, but continuously.

CHAPTER 7

Clusters and Competition

New Agendas for
Companies, Governments,
and Institutions

Michael E. Porter

THINKING ABOUT COMPETITION and strategy at the company level has been dominated by what goes on inside companies. Thinking about the competitiveness of nations and states has focused on the economy as a whole, with national economic policy seen as the dominant influence. In both competition and competitiveness the role of location is all but absent. If anything, the tendency has been to see location as diminishing in importance.[1] Globalization allows companies to source capital, goods, and technology from anywhere and to locate operations wherever it is most cost effective. Governments are widely seen as losing their influence over competition to global forces.

This perspective, although widespread, does not accord with competitive reality. In *The Competitive Advantage of Nations* (1990), I put forward a theory of national, state, and local competitiveness within the context of a global economy. This theory gives clusters a prominent role. Clusters are geographic concentrations of interconnected companies, specialized suppliers, service providers, firms in related industries, and associated institutions (for example, universities, standards agencies, and trade associations) in particular fields that compete but also

This article has benefited from extensive research by Veronica H. Ingham and from research assistance by John Kelleher and Raymond Fisman. I am also grateful for comments by Joseph Babiec, Gregory Bond, Michael Fairbanks, Ifor Ffowcs-Williams, Anne Habiby, Bennett Harrison, David L. Kang, Lucia Marshall, Ian Smith, Claas van der Linde, and Marjorie Williams.

cooperate. Critical masses of unusual competitive success in particular business areas, clusters are a striking feature of virtually every national, regional, state, and even metropolitan economy, especially those of more economically advanced nations.

While the phenomenon of clusters in one form or another has been recognized and explored in a range of literatures, clusters cannot be understood independently of a broader theory of competition and the influence of location in the global economy. (See the insert "Historical and Intellectual Antecedents of Cluster Theory.") The prevalence of clusters in economies, rather than isolated firms and industries, reveals important insights into the nature of competition and the role of location in competitive advantage. Even though old reasons for clustering have diminished in importance with globalization, new roles of clusters in competition have taken on growing importance in an increasingly complex, knowledge-based, and dynamic economy.

The cluster concept represents a new way of thinking about national, state, and city economies, and points to new roles for companies, governments, and other institutions striving to enhance competitiveness. The presence of clusters suggests that much of competitive advantage lies outside a given company or even outside its industry, residing instead in the *locations* of its business units. The odds of building a world-class mutual fund company are much higher in Boston than in most any other location; a similar statement applies to textile-related companies in North and South Carolina, high performance auto companies in southern Germany, or fashion shoe companies in Italy.

The importance of clusters creates new management agendas that are rarely recognized. Companies have a tangible stake in the business environments where they are located in ways that go far beyond taxes, electricity costs, and wage rates. The health of the cluster is important to the health of the company. A company may actually benefit from the presence of local competitors. Trade associations can be competitive assets, as well as lobbying and social organizations.

Clusters also create new roles for government. The proper macroeconomic policies for fostering competitiveness are increasingly well understood but they are necessary and not sufficient. Government's more decisive influences are often at the microeconomic level. Removing obstacles to the growth and upgrading of existing and emerging clusters should be a priority. Clusters are a driving force in increasing exports and magnets for attracting foreign investment. They constitute a forum in which new types of dialogue can, and must, take place among firms, government agencies, and institutions (such as schools, universities, and public utilities).

Knowledge about cluster theory has advanced and continues to spread since publication of *The Competitive Advantage of Nations,* which triggered an ever growing number of formal cluster initiatives at the city, state, country, and even regional level (as in Central America, for example). In this essay, I will assess the current state of knowledge about clusters, their role in competition, and their implications. I will describe the theory of clusters, the process by which they grow and decline, the appropriate roles of the private sector, government, and other institutions in cluster upgrading, and some of the implications clusters hold for company strategy. Finally, I will draw on my participation in many cluster studies and initiatives and on other literature to explore the best ways to organize such initiatives to catalyze positive economic improvement. (An extensive bibliography on clusters and cluster initiatives appears at the end of this chapter.)

What Is a Cluster?

A cluster is a geographically proximate group of interconnected companies and associated institutions in a particular field, linked by commonalities and complementarities. The geographic scope of a cluster can range from a single city or state to a country or even a network of neighboring countries.[2] Clusters take varying forms depending on their depth and sophistication, but most include end-product or service companies; suppliers of specialized inputs, components, machinery, and services; financial institutions; and firms in related industries. Clusters also often include firms in downstream industries (that is, channels or customers); producers of complementary products; specialized infrastructure providers; government and other institutions providing specialized training, education, information, research, and technical support (such as universities, think tanks, vocational training providers); and standards-setting agencies. Government agencies that significantly influence a cluster can be considered part of it. Finally, many clusters include trade associations and other collective private sector bodies that support cluster members. (See the insert "Historical and Intellectual Antecedents of Cluster Theory.")

Identifying the constituent parts of a cluster involves starting with a large firm or concentration of like firms and then looking upstream and downstream in the vertical chain of firms and institutions. The next step is to look horizontally to identify industries that pass through common channels or that produce complementary products and services. Additional horizontal chains of industries are identified based on the use of similar specialized inputs or technologies or with other supply-side linkages. The next step after identification of a cluster's industries and firms involves isolating the institutions that provide it with specialized skills, technology, information, capital, or infrastructure and any collective bodies covering cluster participants. The final step is to seek out government or other regulatory bodies that significantly influence participants in the cluster.

Figures 7-1 and 7-2 present schematic diagrams of the Italian leather footwear and fashion cluster and the California wine cluster. While

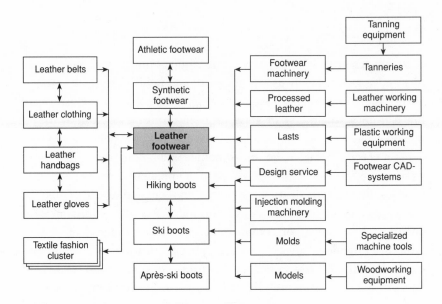

Figure 7-1   The Italian Footwear and Fashion Cluster
Source: Research by Claas van der Linde, 1993.

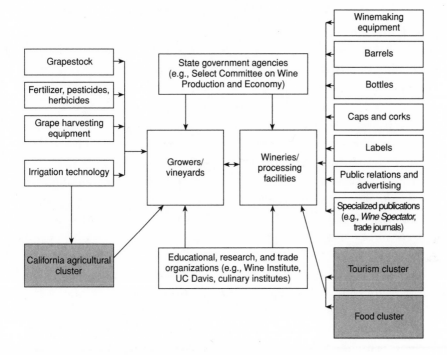

Figure 7-2   The California Wine Cluster
Sources: Based on research by Harvard MBA students R. Alexander, R. Arney,
N. Black, E. Frost, and A. Shivananda.

neither diagram can include all the entities comprising the respective clusters, each illustrates important cluster attributes. Figure 7-1, for example, demonstrates the several chains of related industries involved in the Italian leather footwear and fashion cluster, including those relating to different types of leather goods (complementary products, common, common inputs, similar technologies), different types of footwear (overlapping channels, similar inputs, and technologies), and different types of fashion goods (complementary products). These industries also employ common marketing media and compete with similar images in similar customer segments. The extraordinary strength of the Italian cluster can be attributed, at least in part, to the multiple cross-firm linkages and synergies that Italian firms enjoy.

The California wine cluster includes an extensive complement of supporting industries to both winemaking and grape growing. On the growing side, there are strong connections to the larger California agricultural cluster. On the winemaking side, the cluster enjoys strong links to both the California restaurant and food preparation industries (complementary products) and the tourism cluster in Napa and other wine-producing regions of the state. Figure 7-2 also illustrates the host of local institutions involved with wine, for example, the world-renowned viticulture and enology program at the University of California at Davis and special committees of the California senate and assembly.

Drawing cluster boundaries is often a matter of degree, and involves a creative process informed by understanding the most important linkages and complementarities across industries and institutions to competition. The strength of these "spillovers" and their importance to productivity and innovation determine the ultimate boundaries. The institutional furnishings cluster located in the Grand Rapids, Michigan, area illustrates the kinds of choices made when drawing cluster boundaries (see Figure 7-3). Office furniture and partitions clearly belong in the cluster, as does seating for stadia, classrooms, and transportation vehicles. These products have important commonalities in product attributes, features, components, and technology. Nearby metal parts and equipment manufacturers, plastics manufacturers, and printing companies are cluster suppliers. These supplier industries may also be part of other clusters, because they serve other customer industries such as automobile manufacturers. Particularly in metal parts, the prior existence of automotive suppliers serving the nearby Detroit automotive cluster contributed importantly to development of the furnishing cluster. Cluster boundaries should encompass all firms, industries, and institutions with strong linkages, whether vertical, horizontal, or institutional; those with weak or non-existent linkages can safely be left out.[3]

Clusters encompassing broad groupings, such as manufacturing, consumer goods, or high tech, have been too broadly conceived. Such aggregates exhibit, at best, weak connections among the industries included. Discussions about cluster constraints and bottlenecks in such groupings fall into generalities. Conversely, labeling a single industry as a cluster overlooks crucial cross-industry and institutional interconnections that strongly affect competitiveness.[4]

Clusters occur in many types of industries, in both larger and smaller fields, and even in some local businesses, such as restaurants, car dealers,

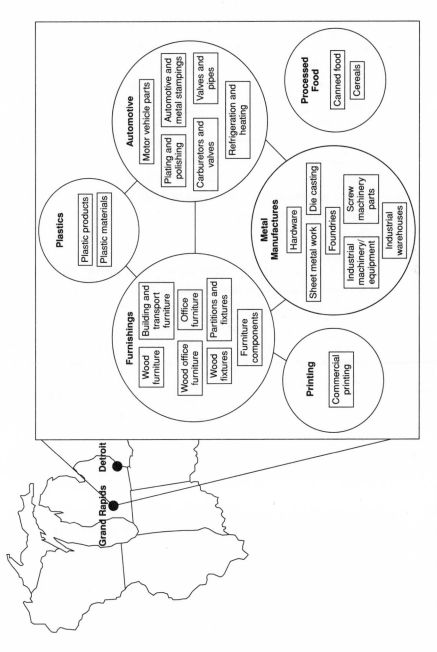

Figure 7-3 Greater Grand Rapids Clusters

and antique shops. They are present in large and small economies, in rural and urban areas, and at several geographic levels (for example, nations, states, metropolitan regions, and cities). Clusters occur in both advanced and developing economies, although clusters in advanced economies tend to be far better developed.

Cluster boundaries rarely conform to standard industrial classification systems, which fail to capture many important actors in competition as well as linkages across industries. Clusters normally consist of a combination of end-product, machinery, materials, and service industries, usually classified in separate categories. They often involve (or potentially involve) both traditional and high-tech industries. Clusters, then, represent a distinct way of organizing economic data and viewing the economy.

Because parts of a cluster often fall within different traditional industrial or service categories, significant clusters may be obscured or even go unrecognized. In Massachusetts, for example, more than four hundred companies, representing at least 39,000 high-paying jobs, were involved in some way in medical devices. The cluster long remained all but invisible, however, buried within several larger and overlapping industry categories, such as electronic equipment and plastic products. Executives in the cluster had never come together before despite the fact that firms shared many common constraints, problems, and opportunities. The discovery of this cluster, the subsequent organization of an association, MassMedic, and the initiation of a productive dialogue with government will be explored below.

Clusters vary in size, breadth, and state of development. Some clusters consist primarily of small- and medium-sized firms (for example, the Italian footwear and the North Carolina home furniture clusters).[5] Other clusters involve both large and small firms (for example, Hollywood or the German chemical clusters). Some clusters center on research universities, while others have no important university connection.[6] These differences in the nature of clusters reflect differences in the structures of their constituent industries. More developed clusters have deeper and more specialized supplier bases, a wider array of related industries, and more extensive supporting institutions.

The boundaries of clusters continually evolve as new firms and industries emerge, established industries shrink or decline, and local institutions develop and change. Technological and market developments spawn new industries, create new linkages, or alter served markets. Regulatory changes also contribute to shifting boundaries, as they have, for example, in telecommunications and transport.

Clusters can be examined at various levels of aggregation, thus exposing different issues. In California, for example, there is a large agribusiness cluster. Mapping and analyzing this broad cluster reveals important competitive insights. The wine cluster already discussed is embedded within the broad cluster. Analysis at this level reveals some more specific and distinct issues (for example, the linkage with the tourism clusters).

The appropriate definition of a cluster can differ in different locations, depending on the segments in which the member companies compete and the strategies they employ. The lower Manhattan multimedia cluster, for example, consists primarily of content providers and firms in related industries, such as publishing, broadcast media, and graphics and visual arts. The San Francisco Bay area multimedia cluster, in contrast, contains many hardware and software industries that provide enabling technology.

Why view economies through the lens of clusters rather than of more traditional groupings such as companies, industries, or sectors, such as manufacturing or services? Foremost because clusters align better with the nature of competition and the sources of competitive advantage. Clusters, broader than industries, capture important linkages, complementarities, and spillovers of technology, skills, information, marketing, and customer needs that cut across firms and industries. As will be discussed below, such connections are fundamental to competition, to productivity, and, especially, to the direction and pace of new business formation and innovation. Most cluster participants do not compete directly, but serve different industry segments. Yet they do share many common needs and opportunities and encounter many common constraints and obstacles to productivity. Viewing a group of companies and institutions as a cluster highlights opportunities for coordination and mutual improvement in areas of common concern without threatening or distorting competition or limiting the intensity of rivalry. The cluster provides a constructive and efficient forum for dialogue among related companies and their suppliers, government, and other salient institutions. Public and private investments to improve conditions for clusters benefit many firms.

Viewing the world in terms of industries or narrow sectors such as automotive products, in contrast, often degenerates into lobbying over subsidies and tax breaks by the participating companies. Resulting public investments create fewer spillover benefits for other industries and may, therefore, distort markets. Because a large proportion of participants directly compete, there is a very real threat that the intensity of rivalry will be diminished. Companies are also often hesitant about participating for fear of aiding direct competitors. An industry or narrow sectoral perspective tends to result in distorting competition, then, while a cluster perspective focuses on enhancing competition. I will return to these issues when I explore the implications of clusters for companies and governments.

Historical and Intellectual Antecedents of Cluster Theory

Clusters have long been part of the economic landscape, with geographic concentrations of trades and companies in particular industries dating back for centuries. However, the role of clusters was arguably more limited. The depth and breadth of clusters, however, have increased as competition has evolved and as modern economies have grown in complexity. Globalization, together with rising knowledge intensity, have greatly altered the role of clusters in competition.

Intellectual antecedents of cluster theory date back at least to Alfred Marshall, who included a fascinating chapter on the externalities of specialized industrial locations in his *Principles of Economics* (originally published in 1890). During the first fifty years of this century, economic geography was a recognized field with an extensive literature. With the mid-century advent of neoclassical economics, however, location moved out of the economics mainstream. More recently, increasing returns have started to play a central role in new theories of growth and international trade, and interest in the field of economic geography has been growing.[a]

In the management literature, as well, attention to geography or location has been minimal. If treated at all, consideration of geography has often been reduced to assessments of cultural and other differences when doing business in various countries. Corporate location has been treated as a narrow subspecialty of operations management. The recent preoccupation with globalization has, if anything, created a tendency to regard location as of diminished and diminishing importance.

A variety of bodies of literature have in some respects recognized and shed light on the phenomenon of clusters, including those on growth poles and backward and forward linkages,[b] agglomeration economies,[c] economic geography,[d] urban and regional economics,[e] national innovation systems,[f] regional science,[g] industrial districts,[h] and social networks.[i]

The literature on urban economics and on regional science focuses on generalized urban agglomeration economies, reflected in the infrastructure, communications technology, input access, diverse industrial base, and markets available in concentrated urban areas. These types of economies, which are independent of the types of firms and clusters present, appear to be most important in developing countries. Overall, however, generalized urban agglomeration economies seem to be diminishing in importance as the opening of trade and the fall in communication and transportation costs allow easier access to inputs and markets and as more locations and countries develop comparable infrastructures.[j]

Other studies focus on geographic concentrations of companies operating in particular fields, which can be seen as special cases of clusters. Italian-style industrial districts of small- and medium-sized firms dominating a local economy prevail in some types of industries. In other fields, a mixture of large domestic firms, large foreign-owned firms, and an array of smaller companies is the rule.

Some clusters center on research universities, while others draw little on the resources of formal technological institutions. Clusters occur both in high tech and traditional industries, in manufacturing as well as in service industries. Indeed, clusters often mix high tech, low tech, manufacturing, and services. Some regions contain a single dominant cluster, while others contain several. Clusters appear in both developing and advanced economies, though the lack of depth of clusters in developing nations is a characteristic constraint to development.

Earlier studies have, nonetheless, contributed to our understanding of the influence of clusters on competition. The literature on agglomeration economies stresses input cost minimization, input specialization made possible because of the extent of the local market, and the advantages of locating near markets. The economic development literature focuses on induced demand and supply, certainly an element of cluster formation. The normative implication of the concept of backward and forward linkages, however, emphasizes the need to build industries with linkages to many others. Cluster theory, in contrast, advocates building on emerging concentrations of companies and encouraging the development of those fields with the strongest linkages to or spillovers within each cluster.

Overall, most past theories address particular aspects of clusters or clusters of a particular type. Many traditional agglomeration arguments for the existence of clusters have been undercut by the globalization of supply sources and markets. Yet the modern, knowledge-based economy creates a far more textured role for clusters.

The broader role of clusters in competition is only now becoming widely recognized. To understand this role requires embedding clusters in a broader and dynamic theory of competition that encompasses both cost and differentiation and both static efficiency and continuous improvement and innovation, and that recognizes a world of global factor and product markets. Some of the most important agglomeration economies represent dynamic rather than static efficiencies and revolve around innovation and the rate of learning. Clusters occupy a more complex and integral role in the modern economy than has been previously recognized.

Clusters, then, constitute an important multi-organizational form, a central influence on competition, and a prominent characteristic of market economies. The state of an economy's clusters reveals important insights into its productive potential and the constraints on its future development. The role of clusters in competition raises important implications for companies, government, and other institutions.

---

a. See Krugman (1991A, 1991B).

b. Hirschman (1958).

c. There is an extensive literature on agglomeration including Weber (1929); Lösch (1954); Harris (1954); Isard (1956); Lloyd and Dicken (1977); Goldstein and Gronberg (1984); Rivera-Batiz (1988); McCann (1995B); Ciccone and Hall (1996); and Fujita and Thisse (1996).

d. See Storper and Salais (1997A, 1997B); Storper (1997); Amin and Thrift (1992); and papers by Storper, Gertler, Mair, Swyngedouw, and Cox in Cox (1993).

e. Scott (1991); Glaeser, Kallal, Sheinkman, and Shleifer (1992); Glaeser (1994); Henderson (1994); Glaeser, Scheinkman and Shleifer (1995); Henderson, Kuncoro, and Turner (1995); and Henderson (1996) are some interesting examples.

f. See Bengt-Åke (1992); Dosi, Gianetti, and Toninelli (1992); Nelson (1993); and Cimoli and Dosi (1995).

g. See, for example, Giarratani (1994) and Markusen (1995A).

h. This literature includes the work of Piore and Sabel (1984); Becattini (1987); Pyke, Becattini, and Sengenberger (1990);Pyke and Sengenberger (1992); and Harrison (1992).

i. See, for example, Burt (1997); Granovetter (1985); Henton, Melville, and Walesh (1997); Nohria (1992); Perrow (1992); Putnam, Leonardi, and Nanetti (1993); Fukuyama (1995); and Harrison and Weiss (1998).

j. Harrison, Kelley, and Grant (1996) construct an imaginative test of the relative importance of industry and urbanization economies in the diffusion of innovation in machining and find that urbanization effects are more significant. They acknowledge, however, that the test is far from definitive. This is because, among other reasons, they picked a widely applicable (versus specialized) innovation in a not very geographically concentrated field. Metalworking, indeed, is not normally a cluster itself but part of other clusters.

Location and Competition

In recent decades, thinking about the influence of location on competition has taken a relatively simple view of how companies compete. Competition has been seen as largely static and as resting on cost minimization in relatively closed economies. Here comparative advantage in factors of production (labor and capital) is decisive, or, in the most recent analyses, economies of scale.

Yet this picture fails to represent real competition. Competition is dynamic and rests on innovation and the search for strategic differences. Three conditions contribute to rendering factor inputs per se less valuable: the expanded input supply as more countries open to the global economy; the greater efficiency of national and international factor markets; and the diminishing factor intensity of competition. Instead, close linkages with buyers, suppliers, and other institutions contribute importantly not only to efficiency but to the rate of improvement and innovation. While extensive vertical integration (for example, in-house production of parts, services, or training) may have once been the norm, a more dynamic environment can render vertical integration inefficient, ineffective, and inflexible.

In this broader and more dynamic view of competition, location affects competitive advantage through its influence on *productivity* and especially on *productivity growth*. Productivity is the value created per day of work and unit of capital or physical resources employed. Generic factor inputs themselves are usually abundant and readily accessed. Prosperity depends on the productivity with which factors are used and upgraded in a particular location.

The productivity and prosperity of a location rest not on the industries in which its firms compete, but on *how* they compete. Firms can be more productive in any industry—shoes, agriculture, or semiconductors—if they employ sophisticated methods, use advanced technology, and offer unique products and services. All industries can employ high technology, all industries can be knowledge intensive. The term *high tech*, normally used to refer to fields such as information technology and biotechnology, thus has questionable relevance. A more descriptive term might be *enabling technology*, signifying fields providing tools that enhance technology in many industries.

Conversely, the mere presence of high tech in an industry does not by itself guarantee prosperity if the firms are unproductive. Traditional distinctions between industries, such as high or low tech, manufacturing or services, resource-based or knowledge-based have in themselves little relevance. The proper goal is to improve the productivity of *all* industries, enhancing prosperity both directly and indirectly, as the improved productivity of one industry increases the productivity of others.

The prosperity of a location depends, then, on the productivity of what firms located there choose to do. This sets the wages that can be sustained and the profits that can be earned. Both domestic and foreign firms contribute to the prosperity of a location, based on the productivity of their activities there. The presence of sophisticated foreign firms often enhances the productivity of domestic firms and vice versa.

The sophistication and productivity with which companies compete in a location is strongly influenced by the *quality of the business environment*. Firms cannot employ advanced logistical techniques, for example, unless a high-quality transportation infrastructure is available. Firms cannot compete using high-service strategies unless they can access well-educated people. Firms cannot operate efficiently under onerous amounts of regulatory red tape, requiring endless dialogue with government, or under a court system that fails to resolve disputes quickly and fairly. All of these situations consume resources and management time without contributing to customer value. The effects of some aspects of the business environment, such as the road system, corporate tax rates, and the legal system, cut across all industries. These economywide (or horizontal) areas can represent the binding constraints to competitiveness in developing economies. For both more advanced economies and, increasingly, everywhere, however, the more decisive aspects of the business environment are often *cluster specific* (for example, the presence of particular types of suppliers or university departments). Cluster thinking thus assumes an important role in both company strategy and economic policy.

Capturing the nature of the business environment in a location is challenging given the myriad of locational influences on productivity and productivity growth. In *The Competitive Advantage of Nations*, I modeled the effect of location on competition using four interrelated influences, graphically depicted in a diamond, a metaphor that has become a shorthand reference to the theory (see Figure 7-4).[7] A few elements of this framework deserve highlighting here because they are important to understanding the role of clusters in competition.

As Figure 7-4 shows, factor inputs include tangible assets (such as physical infrastructure), information, the legal system, and university research institutes that firms draw upon in competition. To increase productivity, factor inputs must improve in efficiency, quality, and, ultimately specialization to particular cluster areas. Specialized factors, especially those integral to innovation and upgrading (for example, a specialized university research institute), not only foster high levels of productivity but tend to be less tradable or available from elsewhere.

The context for firm strategy and rivalry refers to the rules, incentives, and norms governing the type and intensity of local rivalry. Economies with low productivity demonstrate little local rivalry: Most competition, if it is present at all, comes from imports; local rivalry, if it occurs at all, involves imitation. Price is the sole competitive variable, and firms

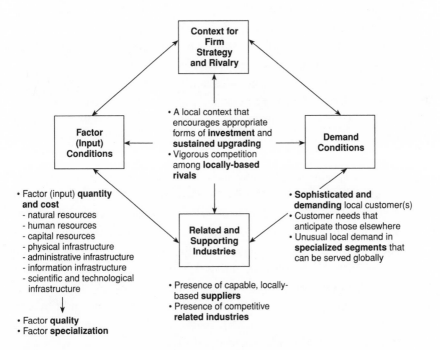

Figure 7-4 Sources of Locational Competitive Advantage

hold down wages to lower cost. Such competition involves minimal investment.

The move to an advanced economy requires developing vigorous local rivalry. Rivalry must shift from low wages to low total cost, which requires upgrading the efficiency of manufacturing and service delivery. Ultimately, rivalry must also evolve beyond cost to include differentiation. Competition must shift from imitation to innovation and from low investment to high investment, not only in physical assets but in intangibles such as skills and technology. Clusters, as will be evident, play an integral role in these transitions.

The context for strategy and rivalry can be divided into two primary dimensions. One is the climate for investment in its various forms. A rising investment intensity of competition is necessary for support of more sophisticated forms of competition and higher levels of productivity. Macroeconomic and political stability sets the context for investment, but microeconomic policies are also important: the structure of the tax system, the corporate governance system, labor market policies affecting workforce development incentives, and intellectual property rules and their enforcement, among others.

The other dimension of the context for competition is local policies affecting rivalry itself. Openness to trade and foreign investment, government ownership, licensing rules, antitrust policy, and the influence of corruption, among other things, have a vital role in setting the intensity of local rivalry. The character of rivalry is also strongly influenced by many other aspects of the business environment (such as the available factors and local demand conditions).

Demand conditions at home have much to do with whether firms can and will move from imitative, low-quality products and services to competing on differentiation. Firms in low productivity economies learn about demand primarily from foreign markets. Advancement requires the development of increasingly demanding local markets. The presence or emergence of sophisticated and demanding home customers presses firms to improve and provides insights into existing and future needs difficult to gain through foreign markets alone. Local demand can also reveal market segments in which firms can differentiate. In a global economy, the *quality* of local demand matters far more than its size.

Clusters of linked industries play a central role in setting demand conditions.

Clusters and Competitive Advantage

Clusters constitute one facet of the diamond (related and supporting industries), but they are best seen as a manifestation of the interactions among all four facets. Clusters affect competition in three broad ways: first, by increasing the productivity of constituent firms or industries; second, by increasing their capacity for innovation and thus for productivity growth; and third, by stimulating new business formation that supports innovation and expands the cluster. Many cluster advantages rest on external economies or spillovers across firms and industries of various sorts. (Many cluster advantages also apply to sub-units *within* firms, such as R&D and production.) A cluster may thus be defined as a system of interconnected firms and institutions whose value as a whole is greater than the sum of its parts.

As noted above, scholars have sought to explain concentrations of firms in terms of economies of agglomeration.[8] These have normally been seen as arising either at the industry level or in a diversified urban economy. Many treatments of agglomeration economies stress cost minimization due to proximity to inputs or proximity to markets. These explanations, though, have been undercut by the globalization of markets, technology, and supply sources, increased mobility, and lower transportation and communication costs. Today, economies of agglomeration have shifted in nature, becoming increasingly important at the cluster level and not just within narrowly-defined industries.

The competitive advantages of clusters will not be equally great in all fields, although clusters appear to occur quite broadly in economies. Generally, the stronger the advantages of clusters and the more tradable the products and services involved, the fewer the number of viable cluster locations. The importance of clusters rises with the sophistication of competition, meaning clusters tend to increase in number as economies develop.

Each of the three broad influences of clusters on competition depends to some extent on personal relationships, face-to-face communication, and interaction among networks of individuals and institutions. While the existence of a cluster makes such relationships more likely to develop and more effective once in place, the process is far from automatic. Formal and informal organizing mechanisms and cultural norms often play a role in the development and functioning of clusters, as will become more evident below.

CLUSTERS AND PRODUCTIVITY

Access to Specialized Inputs and Employees. Locating within a cluster can provide superior or lower-cost access to specialized inputs such as components, machinery, business services, and personnel, as compared to the alternatives—vertical integration, formal alliances with outside entities, or "importing" inputs from distant locations. The cluster, then, represents a spatial organizational form that can be an inherently more efficient or effective means of assembling inputs—if competitive local suppliers are available. Sourcing outside the cluster may be necessary where competent local suppliers are unavailable, but that is not the ideal arrangement.

Sourcing inputs from cluster participants ("local" outsourcing) can result in lower transactions costs than those incurred when using distant sources ("distant" outsourcing). Local outsourcing minimizes the need for inventory and eliminates importing costs and delays. It curbs opportunistic behavior by suppliers to overprice or renege on commitments because of the transparency and ongoing nature of local relationships and the adverse effect poor performance will have on their reputations with other cluster participants. Sourcing within the cluster eases communication, reduces the cost of tailoring, and facilitates the joint provision of ancillary or support services, such as installation, debugging, user training, troubleshooting, and timely repair. Other things being equal, then, local outsourcing often dominates distant outsourcing, especially for advanced and specialized inputs involving embedded technology, information, or service content. (Note that "local" refers to a firm with substantial investment within the cluster, including technical resources, even though the parent company is headquartered elsewhere.)

Formal alliances with distant suppliers can mitigate some of the disadvantages of distant outsourcing. However, forming formal alliances with either distant or nearby firms introduces complex bargaining and governance problems and can inhibit a firm's flexibility. The close, informal relationships possible between firms in a local cluster can offer a superior solution.

Access to inputs within a cluster can also be more efficient or effective than vertical integration. Outside specialists are often more cost effective and responsive than in-house units, not only in component production but also in areas such as training. Vertical integration consumes management attention that may be better spent elsewhere. In contrast, obtaining inputs from nearby vendors with whom a firm has close and special relationships offers cost and quality advantages. Proximity of vendors allows efficient quasi-vertical integration while preserving strong incentives.

Expanding the range of inputs available from specialized suppliers at a single location has long been observed to be one of the benefits of agglomeration.[9] This remains true, although the globalization of markets undercuts the traditional rationale. The division of labor is no longer limited by the extent of the market, because the market is international. Suppliers rarely need to rely on the local market for most of their volume.

In the modern economy, the greater depth and specialization of suppliers within clusters arises from the easier recognition of market opportunities and from risk reduction due to the presence of multiple local customers. Moreover, developed clusters consist not only of one industry but of a number of related industries. These industries frequently draw on common or very similar inputs, thus expanding opportunities for suppliers. For this reason, and because of the importance of externalities and spillovers within clusters, the breadth and depth of a cluster rather than the size of individual firms or industries within the cluster is often more significant for competitive advantage.

Clusters also offer advantages in obtaining inputs best sourced from a distance. The presence of a cluster can lower the costs of importing distant inputs because suppliers will price more aggressively and firms can use more efficient means of delivery. (Lower supplier prices will reflect not only the attractiveness of penetrating a large, concentrated potential market but also the efficiencies in serving it.) Suppliers may also be willing to make greater investments to make their products or services more available. Because of the depth of Boston's financial services cluster, for example, senior executives on road shows invariably visit Boston, substantially lowering the cost to Boston institutions of direct contact with the managements of the companies in which they invest.

Clusters offer similar, although not identical, sourcing advantages in the area of specialized and experienced employees. A cluster represents a pool of such employees. This lowers search and transactions costs for recruiting and makes possible more efficient matching of jobs to people. In addition, because a cluster signals opportunity and reduces the risk to employees of relocation, clusters may reduce the cost of sourcing specialized employees from other locations.[10]

Working against a cluster's advantages in assembling inputs and labor is the possibility that such concentration will render these resources scarce and bid up their cost. (Another potential cost of clustering, costs of congestion, apply more to large, diversified urban concentrations rather than to clusters per se.) Yet the ability to outsource many inputs limits any cost penalty relative to other locations. More importantly, the presence of a cluster not only increases the demand for specialized inputs but also increases their supply. Where a cluster exists, the availability of specialized personnel, services, and components and the number of entities creating them usually far exceeds the levels at other locations, a distinct benefit, despite the greater competition.

The absence of capable, locally based suppliers also works against cluster input advantages. If competitive suppliers or other institutions are entrenched elsewhere, distant outsourcing or formal alliances may be necessary. Given the inherent benefits of clusters, however, forces encouraging local suppliers to upgrade will be strong, and cluster constituent firms will have an incentive to encourage the entry of new suppliers or local investments by distant suppliers.

Access to Information. Extensive market, technical, and other specialized information accumulates within a cluster in firms and local institutions. This can be accessed better or at lower cost from within the cluster, thus allowing firms to enhance productivity and get closer to the productivity frontier. This effect also applies to the flow of information between units of the same company.[11] Proximity, supply and technological linkages, and the existence of repeated, personal relationships and community ties fostering trust facilitate the information flow within clusters. (These conditions all make sticky or impacted information more transferable.) An important special case of the informational benefits of clusters is the availability of information about current buyer needs. Sophisticated buyers are often part of clusters, and other cluster participants often gain and share information about buyer needs.[12]

Complementarities. A cluster enhances productivity not only via the acquisition and assembly of inputs but by facilitating complementarities between the activities of cluster participants. The most obvious form of complementarities are among products. In tourism, for example, the quality of the visitor's experience depends not only on the appeal of the primary attraction (for example, beaches or historical sites) but also on the comfort and service of area hotels, restaurants, souvenir outlets, airport and other transportation facilities, and so on. As this example illustrates, the parts of the cluster are often truly mutually dependent. Bad performance by one part of the cluster can undermine the success of the others.

Such complementarities across products to create buyer value are pervasive, not only in service delivery but in product design, logistics, and after-sales service. Coordination and internal pressures for improvement among parts of a cluster, made possible by co-location, can substantially improve its overall quality or efficiency. Co-location makes it easier to achieve technological linkages and accomplish ongoing coordination. As with access to inputs, achieving these and other complementarities internally within a cluster offers advantages over having to resort to formal alliances.

Marketing provides another form of complementarity within clusters. The presence of a group of related firms and industries in a location offers efficiencies in joint marketing (for example, firm referrals, trade fairs, trade magazines, and marketing delegations). It can also enhance the reputation of a location in a particular field, making it more likely that buyers will consider a vendor or manufacturer based there. Italy, for example, has established a strong reputation for fashion and design that benefits firms in footwear, leather goods, apparel, and accessories. This reputation constitutes a type of public good for all Italian-based companies in fashion-related industries.

The presence of a cluster also can enhance buying efficiency. Visiting buyers can see numerous firms in a single trip. The presence in a location of multiple sources for a product or service can also reduce perceived buying risk by offering buyers the potential to multisource or switch vendors if the need arises. Hong Kong thrives as a source of fashion apparel in part for this reason.[13]

Other complementarities arising within clusters involve the better alignment of activities among cluster participants. In the wood products cluster, for example, the efficiency of sawmills depends on a reliable supply of good-quality timber and the ability to maximize the utilization of timber in either furniture (highest quality), pallets and boxes (lower quality), or wood chips (lowest quality). Portuguese sawmills suffered from poor timber quality because landowners would not invest in timber management.[14] Hence most timber was processed for use in pallets and boxes, a lower value use that limited the price paid to landowners. Substantial improvement in productivity was possible, but only if several parts of the cluster changed simultaneously. Logging operations, for example, had to modify cutting and sorting procedures while sawmills had to develop the capacity to process in more sophisticated ways. Coordination to develop standard wood classifications and measures was an important enabling step. Such linkages can be recognized and captured more easily within clusters than among dispersed participants.

Access to Institutions and Public Goods. Clusters make many inputs that would otherwise be costly into public or quasi-public goods. The ability to recruit employees trained in local programs, for example, eliminates or lowers the cost of internal training. Firms can often access benefits, such as specialized infrastructure or advice from experts in local institutions at very low cost. Indeed, the information built up in a cluster can in itself be seen as a quasi-public good.

The public goods held in clusters may better be termed quasi-public goods, because accessing them involves some cost, although well below full cost. The analysis of public goods in economics has been limited to the pure cases of a fairly narrow range of largely governmental functions. Clusters create a far broader array of circumstances in which something approaching a public-good asset arises and include many instances in which *private* institutions and investments help create them.

Some of the public or quasi-public goods available in clusters are similar to conventional public goods in that they are closely linked to government and to public institutions. Public investment in specialized infrastructure, educational programs, information, trade fairs, and other forms that benefit a cluster is encouraged by the number and visibility of cluster participants and by the number of firms likely to experience spillover benefits from such investment. Other quasi-public goods available to cluster participants arise as natural by-products of competition. These include information and technology pools, the reputation accrued by the cluster location, and some of the marketing and sourcing advantages described above.

In addition, public or quasi-public goods at cluster locations often result from *private* investments in training programs, infrastructure, quality centers, and so on. While public goods are associated with public institutions, they may also arise in private or partially private institutions created at cluster locations (for example, testing laboratories or trade journals). Such private investments are common because cluster participants perceive the potential for collective benefits. Often such investments take place via trade associations or other collective mechanisms.

Incentives and Performance Measurement. Clusters help to solve or mitigate some agency problems that arise in more isolated locations and in more vertically integrated firms. Clusters improve the incentives within companies for achieving high productivity for several reasons. Foremost is competitive pressure. Rivalry with locally based competitors has particularly strong incentive effects because of the ease of constant comparison and because local rivals have similar general circumstances (for example, labor costs and local market access), so that competition must take place on other things. In addition, peer pressure amplifies competitive pressure within a cluster, even among indirectly competing or non-competing firms. Pride and the desire to look good in the local community motivate firms in their attempts to outdo each other.

Clusters also facilitate measurement of the performance of in-house activities because, often, other local firms perform similar functions. Managers gain wider opportunities to compare internal costs with arms-length transactions, and lower employee monitoring costs by comparing employee performance with others locally. The accumulation of cluster knowledge in financial institutions, for example, should make loan decisions and other financing choices better informed and improve customer monitoring. As mentioned above, clusters also offer the advantage of limiting opportunistic behavior as when one participant takes advantage of another or provides shoddy products or services.[15] Because of repeated interactions, the easy spread of information, the spread of reputation, and the desire to maintain a standing in the local community, cluster participants usually strive for constructive interactions that will positively affect their long-term interests.

* * *

As has been noted, many of these productivity advantages of clusters involve location-specific public goods or benefits that depend on physical proximity, face-to-face contact, close and ongoing relationships, and "insider" access to information. The benefits of cluster membership can thus be difficult if not impossible to access unless firms participate actively, with a significant local presence. Clusters can and do include foreign firms, but only when such firms make a permanent investment in achieving a significant local presence.

Many of the advantages of clustering also apply to sub-units *within a single company.* Co-locating R&D, component fabrication, assembly, marketing, customer support, and other activities can facilitate internal efficiencies in sourcing and information flow, as well as complementarities and other benefits. Companies sometimes disperse units in order to lower costs of labor, utilities, or taxes, thus unwittingly sacrificing the powerful system cost benefits of clusters and their advantages in fostering dynamism and innovation.

CLUSTERS AND INNOVATION

The benefits of clusters in innovation and productivity growth, compared to an isolated location, can be more important than those in current productivity, though there are some risks as well. Some of the same cluster characteristics that enhance current productivity are even more important to innovation.

Firms within a cluster are often able to more clearly and rapidly perceive new buyer needs. Just as with current buyer needs, firms in a cluster benefit from the concentration of firms with buyer knowledge and relationships, the juxtaposition of firms in related industries, the concentration of specialized information-generating entities, and buyer sophistication. Cluster firms can often discern buyer trends faster than can isolated competitors. Silicon Valley and Austin-based computer companies, for example, plug into customer needs and trends quickly and effectively, with an ease impossible to match elsewhere.

Cluster participation also offers advantages in perceiving new technological, operating, or delivery possibilities. Participants learn early and consistently about evolving technology, component and machinery availability, service and marketing concepts, and so on, facilitated by ongoing relationships with other cluster entities, the ease of site visits, and frequent face-to-face contacts. Cluster membership makes possible direct observation of other firms. The isolated firm, in contrast, faces higher costs and steeper impediments to acquiring information and a corresponding increase in the need to devote resources to generating such knowledge internally.[16]

The potential advantages of clusters in perceiving both the need and the opportunity for innovation are significant, but equally important can be the flexibility and capacity they provide to act rapidly on these insights. A firm within a cluster often can more rapidly source the new components, services, machinery, and other elements needed to implement innovations, whether a new product line, a new process, or a new logistical model. Local suppliers and partners can and do get closely involved in the innovation process, thus ensuring that the inputs they supply better meet the firm's requirements. New, specialized personnel can often be recruited locally to fill gaps required to pursue new approaches. The complementarities involved in innovating are more easily achieved among nearby participants.

Firms within a cluster can experiment at lower cost and can delay large commitments until they are more assured that a new product, process, or service will pan out. In contrast, a firm relying on distant outsourcing faces greater challenges in contracting, securing delivery, obtaining associated technical and service support, and coordinating across complementary entities, and a firm relying on vertical integration faces inertia, difficult tradeoffs if the innovation erodes the value of in-house assets, and constraints if current products or processes must be maintained while new ones are developed.

Reinforcing these other advantages for innovation is the sheer pressure —competitive pressure, peer pressure, and constant comparison— occurring in geographically concentrated clusters. The similarity of basic circumstances (for example, labor and utility costs) combined with the presence of multiple rivals forces firms to distinguish themselves creatively. The pressure to innovate is elevated. Individual firms in the cluster have difficulty staying ahead for long, but many firms progress faster than do those based at other locations.

Under certain circumstances, however, cluster participation can retard innovation. When a cluster shares a uniform approach to competing, a sort of groupthink often reinforces old behaviors, suppresses new ideas, and creates rigidities that prevent adoption of improvements.[17] Clusters also may not support truly radical innovation, which tends to invalidate the existing pools of talent, information, suppliers, and infrastructure. In these circumstances, a cluster participant may be no worse off, in principle, than an isolated firm (because both can outsource), but the firm in an established cluster may suffer from greater barriers to perceiving the need to change and from inertia against severing past relationships that no longer contribute to competitive advantage. I will explore these issues further in the context of the processes by which clusters emerge and decline.

*   *   *

The geographic concentration of clusters occurs because proximity serves to amplify many of the productivity and innovation benefits of clustering already described.[18] Transactions costs are reduced, the creation and flow of information improves, local institutions respond more readily to a cluster's specialized needs, and peer pressure and competitive pressure are more keenly felt.

Clusters clearly represent a combination of competition and cooperation. Vigorous competition occurs in winning customers and retaining them. The presence of multiple rivals and strong incentives often accentuates the intensity of competition among clusters. Yet cooperation must occur in a variety of areas I identified above. Much of it is vertical, involves related industries and is with local institutions. Competition and cooperation can coexist because they occur on different dimensions and between different players; cooperation in some dimensions aids successful competition in others.

A number of the mechanisms through which clusters affect productivity and innovation echo findings in other literatures. Management literature shows growing awareness of the importance of close linkages with suppliers and buyers and of the value of outsourcing or partnering. The literature on innovation highlights the role of customers, suppliers, and universities in the innovation process, while the literature on the diffusion of innovation stresses such notions as demonstration effects, contagion, experimentation, and ease of observability—all clearly influenced by the presence of clusters.[19] Many studies in economics highlight the importance of transactions costs, and others explore the organizational incentive problems that stand in the way of efficiency.

Little of this thinking, however, has been connected to location. It is as if linkages, transactions, and information flow took place outside time and space. Yet proximity clearly affects linkages and transactions costs. Incentive misalignments difficult to resolve with feasible contracts may right themselves under the strong influence of repeated interaction and other aspects of location and clusters. The resort to formal partnerships and alliances, undertaken despite complex incentive and governance problems, overlooks the relative ease of achieving many of the same benefits more simply and informally within clusters. Bringing these various theoretical approaches together with an understanding of location and clusters can extend their usefulness and deepen our understanding of the effect of clusters on competition.

More broadly, the geographically proximate cluster of independent and informally linked firms and institutions represents a robust organizational form in the continuum between markets and hierarchies—but one still little explored in theory. Location can powerfully shape the tradeoffs between markets and hierarchies. Clusters offer obvious advantages in transactions cost over other forms and seem to ameliorate many incentive problems. Repeated interactions and informal contracts within a cluster structure result from living and working in a circumscribed geographic area and foster trust, open communication, and lower the costs of severing and recombining market relationships.

CLUSTERS AND NEW BUSINESS FORMATION

Many if not most new businesses (that is, headquarters, not branch offices or ancillary facilities) form within existing clusters rather than at isolated locations. This occurs for a variety of reasons. First, clusters provide inducement to entry through better information about opportunities. The existence of a cluster in itself signals an opportunity. Individuals working somewhere in or near the cluster more easily perceive gaps in products, services, or suppliers to fill. Having had this insight, these individuals more readily leave established firms to start new ones aimed at filling the perceived gaps.

Opportunities perceived at cluster locations are pursued there because *barriers to entry are lower than elsewhere*. Needed assets, skills, inputs, and staff, often readily available at the cluster location, can be assembled more easily for a new enterprise. Local financial institutions and investors, already possessing familiarity with the cluster, may require a lower risk premium on capital. In addition, the cluster often presents a significant local market. The entrepreneur seeking to benefit from established relationships often prefers to stay in the same community. All of these factors—lower entry barriers, multiple potential local customers, established relationships, and the presence of other local firms that have "made it"— reduce the perceived risks of entry. The barriers to exit at a cluster can also be lower due to reduced need for specialized investment, deeper markets for specialized assets, and other factors.[20]

While local entrepreneurs are likely entrants to a cluster, entrepreneurs based outside a cluster frequently relocate, sooner or later, to a cluster location. The same lower entry barriers attract them, as does the potential to create more economic value from their ideas and skills at the cluster location or the ability to operate more productively.

Established companies based in non-cluster locations (foreign and domestic) often establish subsidiaries at clusters, seeking the productivity benefits and innovation advantages discussed above. The presence of an established cluster not only lowers the barriers to entry for outside firms, but it also reduces, as noted above, the perceived risk. (This is particularly the case where other "foreign" firms have already moved into the cluster.) Many firms have relocated entire business units to a cluster location or have designated their cluster-based subsidiary as their regional or world headquarters for that particular line of business.

The advantages of a cluster in new business formation can play a major role in speeding up the process of cluster innovation. Large companies often face constraints or impediments of various sorts to innovating. Spin-off companies often pick up the slack, sometimes with the blessing of the original company. (A large company, for example, may support a smaller firm serving a niche it cannot address economically.) Larger companies in a cluster develop close relationships with innovative smaller ones, helping in their establishment, and acquiring them if they become successful.

Because of new business formation, clusters often grow in depth and breadth over time, further enhancing cluster advantages. The intense competition within a cluster, together with lower entry and exit barriers, sometimes leads to high rates of both entry and exit at these locations. The net result is that many of the surviving firms in the cluster can gain position vis-à-vis rivals at other locations. Location and the state of clusters not only affect barriers to entry and exit but most other aspects of industry structure. Analysts are just beginning to explore the connections between location and industrial organization. (See the Introduction, pages 1–17.)

The Socioeconomy of Clusters

The mere presence of firms, suppliers, and institutions in a location creates the *potential* for economic value, but it does not necessarily ensure the realization of this potential. Social glue binds clusters together, contributing to the value creation process. Many of the competitive advantages of clusters depend on the free flow of information, the discovery of value-adding exchanges or transactions, the willingness to align agendas and to work across organizations, and strong motivation for improvement. Relationships, networks, and a sense of common interest undergird these circumstances. The social structure of clusters thus takes on central importance.

A growing economic and organizational literature examines the importance of network relationships found in effective companies and communities.[21] Economic activities are seen as "embedded" in ongoing social relationships. Much research undertakes to map these networks, to understand the number of nodes feasible, and to verify the importance of repeated interaction and of time in making networks effective. Examinations of the structure of networks has revealed that the social relationships among individuals, or their "social capital," greatly facilitates access to important resources and information.

Cluster theory focuses on how juxtaposition of economically linked firms and institutions in a specific geographic location affects competitiveness. While some cluster advantages are largely independent of social relationships (for example, available pools of capital or employees), most if not all have at least a relationship component. A firm's identification with and sense of community, derived from membership in a cluster, and its "civic engagement" beyond its own narrow confines as a single entity translate directly, according to cluster theory, into economic value. Cluster theory further extends notions of social capital by exploring the mechanisms through which a structure of network relationships within a geographic location produce benefits for particular firms. The benefits of trust and organizational permeability, fostered through repeated interactions and a sense of mutual dependence within a region or city, clearly grease the interactions within clusters that enhance productivity, spur innovation, and result in the creation of new businesses.

Cluster theory bridges network theory and competition. A cluster is a form of a network that occurs within a geographic location, in which the proximity of firms and institutions ensures certain forms of commonality and increases the frequency and impact of interactions. Well-functioning clusters move beyond hierarchical networks to become lattices of numerous overlapping and fluid connections among individuals, firms, and institutions. These connections are repeated, constantly shift, and often expand to related industries. Both "strong ties" and "weak ties" occur together. Modest changes in the pattern of relationships within a cluster may have significant consequences for productivity and the direction of innovation.

Network theory can greatly inform understanding of the way clusters work and of how clusters can become more productive. As will be discussed further, successful cluster upgrading depends on paying explicit attention to relationship building, an important characteristic of cluster development initiatives. Trade associations play important roles in facilitating the formation of networks.

For its part, cluster theory also provides a way to connect theories of networks, social capital, and civic engagements more tightly to business competition and economic prosperity—and to extend them. Cluster theory identifies who needs to be in the network for what relationships and why. Clusters offer a new way of exploring the mechanisms by which networks, social capital, and civic engagement affect competition and market outcomes. Cluster theory helps isolate the most beneficial forms of networks. Relationships and trust resulting in cartels, for example, undermine economic value, while those facilitating open information exchange between customers and suppliers enhance it. The workings of clusters also suggest the efficiency and flexibility possible in network structures built on proximity and informal local links compared to those defined by formal or hierarchical relationships between companies or between institutions and companies. Cluster theory may also reveal how network relationships form and how social capital is acquired, helping to unscramble questions of cause and effect; for example, do strong relationships and trust arise because a cluster exists or are clusters more likely to develop from existing networks? Cluster theory, then, helps illuminate the causes of network structure, the substance of network activity, and the link between network characteristics and outcomes.

Clusters and Economic Geography

Specialization characterizes the economic geography of cities, states, and nations, especially of prosperous ones, and appears to increase as an economy becomes more advanced.[22] A relatively small number of clusters usually account for a major share of the economy within a geographic area as well as an overwhelming share of the outward-oriented economic activity (for example, exports to other locations and investment in other locations by locally based firms).[23] Outward-oriented clusters are juxtaposed with two other types of business: localized industries and clusters that do not compete with other locations (for example, restaurants, entertainment, logistical services, real estate, and construction); and local subsidiaries of competitive firms based elsewhere that primarily serve the local market (for example, sales offices, customer support centers, branch offices, and assembly plants).

The outward-oriented clusters based in a geographic area constitute the area's primary *long-run* source of economic growth and prosperity. Such clusters can grow far beyond the size of the local market, absorbing workers from less productive firms and industries. The demand for local industries, in contrast, is inherently limited and derives primarily, either directly or indirectly, from the success of outward-oriented clusters.

The partial cluster map in Figure 7-5 illustrates the geographic distribution of clusters in the United States, a highly advanced economy. The map shows just a few of the many geographically concentrated clusters present in the United States, ranging from familiar ones, such as entertainment in Hollywood, finance in New York City, and household furniture in High Point, North Carolina, to less familiar clusters, such as golf equipment in Carlsbad, California, and optics in Arizona. Figure 7-6 shows regional clusters in a less advanced economy, Portugal. Figure 7-7 maps the dominant clusters in a single U.S. state, Massachusetts, and Figure 7-8 shows the clusters in a single U.S. metropolitan region, greater Pittsburgh. Not evident from these maps are the striking differences in cluster specialization even between nearby economic areas: The Massachusetts economy, for example, looks quite different from that of neighboring Connecticut.

In identifying clusters, outward-oriented industries must be distinguished from those that primarily serve the local market. Every economy will include local clusters, such as real estate and construction, as well as the local operations of exporting clusters based elsewhere. It is also important to recognize that the co-location of parts of a cluster does not ensure that linkages and interactions within the cluster function effectively. In Pittsburgh, for example, the potential for innovation within and across clusters has not been fully realized.

While cluster boundaries often fit within political boundaries, they may also cross state and even national borders, especially in smaller states and nations and in cities located near borders. A thriving photonics (or electro-optics) cluster in Massachusetts, centered around Sturbridge, for example, extends into Connecticut, where another 135 companies are based, about 50 of them in counties abutting the Massachusetts border. In another example, a European chemicals cluster encompasses

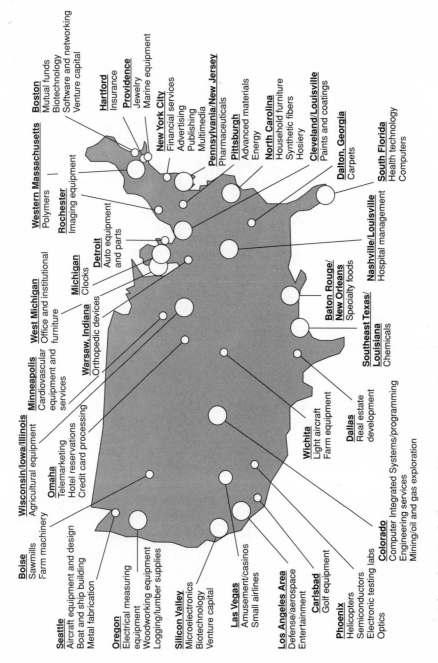

Boston
Mutual funds
Biotechnology
Software and networking
Venture capital

Hartford
Insurance

Providence
Jewelry
Marine equipment

New York City
Financial services
Advertising
Publishing
Multimedia

Western Massachusetts
Polymers

Pennsylvania/New Jersey
Pharmaceuticals

Pittsburgh
Advanced materials
Energy

North Carolina
Household furniture
Synthetic fibers
Hosiery

Cleveland/Louisville
Paints and coatings

Rochester
Imaging equipment

Dalton, Georgia
Carpets

South Florida
Health technology
Computers

Detroit
Auto equipment
and parts

Michigan
Clocks

Nashville/Louisville
Hospital management

West Michigan
Office and institutional
furniture

**Baton Rouge/
New Orleans**
Specialty foods

Minneapolis
Cardiovascular
equipment and
services

Warsaw, Indiana
Orthopedic devices

**Southeast Texas/
Louisiana**
Chemicals

Wisconsin/Iowa/Illinois
Agricultural equipment

Omaha
Telemarketing
Hotel reservations
Credit card processing

Dallas
Real estate
development

Wichita
Light aircraft
Farm equipment

Boise
Sawmills
Farm machinery

Seattle
Aircraft equipment and design
Boat and ship building
Metal fabrication

Oregon
Electrical measuring
equipment
Woodworking equipment
Logging/lumber supplies

Silicon Valley
Microelectronics
Biotechnology
Venture capital

Las Vegas
Amusement/casinos
Small airlines

Los Angeles Area
Defense/aerospace
Entertainment

Carlsbad
Golf equipment

Phoenix
Helicopters
Semiconductors
Electronic testing labs
Optics

Colorado
Computer Integrated Systems/programming
Engineering services
Mining/oil and gas exploration

Figure 7-5   Selected Regional Clusters of Competitive U.S. Industries

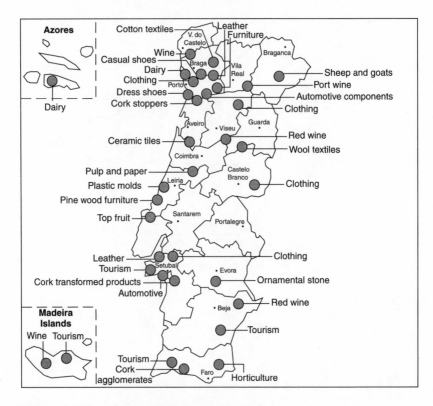

Figure 7-6 Selected Regional Clusters in Portugal
Source: Monitor Company, Cambridge, Massachusetts.

firms in both Germany and the German-speaking part of Switzerland. Clusters are more likely to span political borders where there is a common language, short physical distances (e.g., 200 miles or less between business locations), similar legal systems and other institutions, and minimal trade or investment barriers.

CLUSTERS AND DEVELOPING ECONOMIES

Clusters are normally most pronounced in advanced economies, where the depth and breadth of clusters is usually greater. In developing economies, a greater proportion of industries are locally based or are foreign

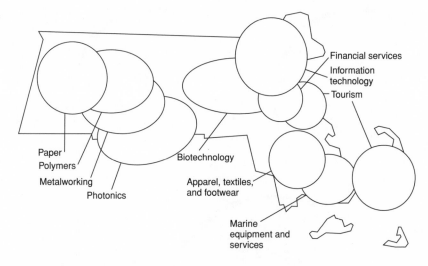

Financial services
Information
technology
Tourism

Paper
Polymers
Metalworking
Photonics

Biotechnology

Apparel, textiles,
and footwear

Marine
equipment and
services

Figure 7-7   Massachusetts Clusters

subsidiaries serving the local market. Exporting industries tend to ber-esource- or labor-intensive. Clusters in developing economies tend to be shallow and to rely primarily on foreign components, services, and technology. Firms in such locations must often vertically integrate, producing not only their own components but even back-up electricity as well; they must sometimes also build and operate not only physical infrastructure but their own schools and other services. The relatively competitive companies in developing economies tend to operate more like islands rather than as cluster participants.[24] Figure 7-9 contrasts the forest products cluster in Sweden, an advanced economy, with that of Portugal, a middle income economy, illustrating some of these differences.

As compared to those in advanced economies, clusters in developing economies not only involve fewer participants but often differ as well in their sociometrics. Many take the form of hierarchical, hub-and-spoke networks surrounding a few large companies, government entities, or distributors. Communication is limited, and linkages between existing firms and institutions are not well developed. In contrast, successful clusters in advanced economies involve a dense mesh of continually evolving relationships and linkages.

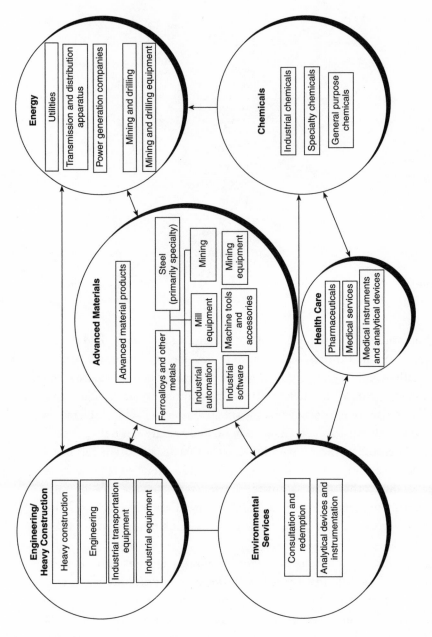

Figure 7-8 Greater Pittsburgh Clusters

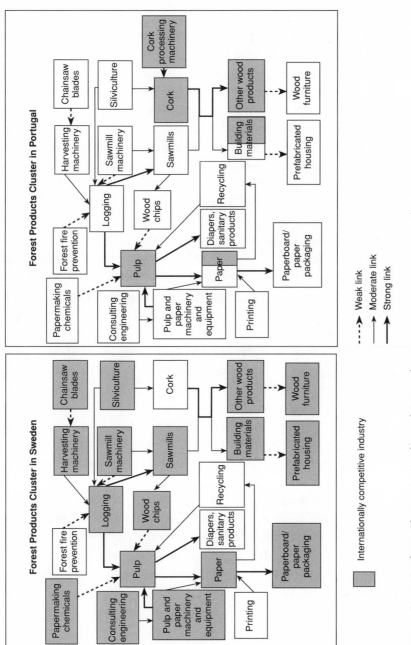

Forest Products Cluster in Sweden

Forest Products Cluster in Portugal

Internationally competitive industry

- - -> Weak link
——→ Moderate link
——▶ Strong link

Figure 7-9 Forest Products Clusters in Sweden and Portugal
Sources: Monitor Company (1994) and Porter, Sölvell, and Zander (1991).

The development of well-functioning clusters is one of the essential steps in moving to an advanced economy. In developing economies, cluster formation is impeded by low local education and skill levels, weaknesses in technology, lack of access to capital, and poorly developed institutions. Government policy may also work against cluster formation. Restrictions on industrial location and subsidies artificially spread out companies. University and technical school curricula, centrally dictated, fail to adapt to cluster needs. Finally, protected from competition, companies engage in monopolistic behavior that further retards cluster development.

The paucity of clusters in developing countries does not mean that such countries cannot compete, but it impedes upgrading and productivity improvement. While exports can grow for a time based on low-cost local labor or natural resources exploited with imported technology, such an approach is ultimately limiting. To improve profits, wages, and the standard of living, the challenge over time is to raise productivity and increase product value. To allow a location to become more productive, develop local capacity to improve products and processes, and, ultimately, to innovate, a cluster must build up over time. Otherwise, the natural tendency for local costs to rise over time cannot be counteracted, and other locations with lower factor costs or offering greater subsidies will take over production.

The successful deepening and broadening of clusters, then, is integral to successful economic development.[25] Cluster development seems to be a controlling factor in moving from a lower middle income (per capita income of $8,000 to 15,000) to an advanced economy. Even in advanced, high-wage economies, however, the need for cluster upgrading is never-ending. It remains essential to allow the continuing rise of productivity and incomes. The wealthier the economy, the more necessary becomes true innovation in products, services, and methods of production to support rising wages and to replace jobs freed up by improvements in efficiency.

INTERNAL TRADE AND INVESTMENT

While international trade and investment are widely recognized as powerful forces for productivity growth, the role of internal trade and investment has been largely ignored. The geographic dispersion of clusters and the specialization of geographic regions by cluster is normally greatest in advanced economies. In nations such as the United States, Italy, Switzerland, and Germany, internal specialization, trade, and investment contribute significantly to productivity and productivity growth. Internal competition motivates improvements by state and local governments and by local institutions, because these entities face far more competitive pressure than do federal government or institutional monopolies. Trading within a nation, made easier by proximity, national similarities, and, often, fewer trade barriers outside of a nation's control, provides a stepping-stone from which firms can build the skills needed to internationalize.

In developing economies, a large proportion of economic activity tends to concentrate around large capital cities, such as in Bangkok and Bogota. This concentration reflects the absence of infrastructure and institutions in outlying areas and the almost total lack of available suppliers. It may also reflect an intrusive role by the central government in controlling competition, a force that leads firms to locate near the seat of power and the agencies whose approval they require to do business. In many developing economies, industries crowd together, and little or no activity takes place in outlying areas, other than agriculture and resource production.

This pattern of economic geography inflicts high costs in terms of productivity as compared to geographic dispersion and specialization. Congestion, bottlenecks, and inflexibility lead to high administrative costs and major inefficiencies, not to mention a diminished quality of life. Companies cannot easily move out from the center, however, because neither infrastructure nor rudimentary clusters exist in the smaller cities and towns. The transition from a concentrated to a dispersed economy, with specialized industries and clusters, represents another essential challenge of economic development. (The building of a tourism cluster in developing economies can be a positive force in improving outlying infrastructure and dispersing economic activity.)

Even in advanced economies, however, economic activity may be concentrated in a few geographic areas. Japan offers a particularly striking case, with nearly 50 percent of total manufacturing shipments located around Tokyo and Osaka. This is due less to inadequacies in infrastructure in outlying areas and more to the powerful and intrusive central government, with its centralizing bias in policies and institutions. The Japanese case illustrates vividly the major inefficiencies and productivity costs resulting from such an economic geography even for advanced nations. Addressing its pattern of economic geography is a major policy issue facing Japan.

Traditional treatments of economic geography often stress the benefits of highly diversified metropolitan economies, citing advantages in terms of available inputs, infrastructure, communication, and access to a large local market. The forces of globalization have greatly diminished such generalized urbanization advantages, while cluster-specific advantages have increased. In advanced economies, even large metropolitan areas are often quite specialized in terms of exporting clusters. An economic geography characterized by a number of metropolitan areas, each specializing in an array of clusters, appears to be a far more productive industrial organization than one based on one or two huge, diversified cities. Most developing countries also suffer from the lack of multiple metropolitan areas that compete with one another.

THE LOCATION PARADOX

Economic geography in an era of global competition, then, involves a paradox. In an economy with rapid transportation and communication and accessible global markets, location remains fundamental to competition. It has been widely recognized that changes in technology and competition have diminished many of the traditional roles of location. Resources, capital, and other inputs can be efficiently sourced in global markets. Firms can access immobile inputs via corporate networks. They need no longer locate near large markets.

Naturally, perhaps, the first response to globalization has been to pursue these benefits by moving assembly plants and other factor cost-sensitive activities to low-cost locations. Anything that can be efficiently sourced from a distance, however, has been essentially *nullified* as a competitive advantage in advanced economies. Information and relationships that can be accessed and maintained via fax or e-mail are available to anyone. While global sourcing and communication mitigates disadvantages, it does not create advantages. Moreover, distant sourcing is normally a second-best solution compared to accessing a competitive local cluster, in terms of both total productivity and innovation.

Paradoxically, then, the enduring competitive advantages in a global economy are often heavily local, arising from concentrations of highly specialized skills and knowledge, institutions, rivals, related businesses, and sophisticated customers in a particular nation or region. Proximity in geographic, cultural, and institutional terms allows special access, special relationships, better information, powerful incentives, and other advantages in productivity and productivity growth that are difficult to tap from a distance. Standard inputs, information, and technologies are readily available via globalization, then, while more advanced dimensions of competition remain geographically bounded. Location matters, albeit in different ways at the turn of the twenty-first century than in earlier decades.[26]

Economic geography in many parts of the world, however, remains in a state of major transition. The relaxation of barriers to trade and investment, still comparatively recent in many countries, is incomplete. The fall of transportation and communication costs has been rapid, while investments in plant and equipment often last for many decades. As a result, many overly broad national and subnational economies persist, as do many clusters in countries and regions that lack a real competitive advantage.

The Birth, Evolution, and Decline of Clusters

A cluster's roots can often be traced to parts of the diamond that are present in a location due to historical circumstances.[27] One prominent motivation for the formation of early companies is the availability of pools of factors, such as specialized skills, university research expertise, an efficient physical location, or particularly good or appropriate infrastructure. Many Massachusetts clusters, for example, had their beginnings in research done at MIT or Harvard while a number of prominent Finnish clusters emerged from the presence of natural resources. The Dutch transportation cluster owes much to a central location within Europe, a network of waterways, the efficiency of the port of Rotterdam, and the skills accumulated by the Dutch through Holland's long maritime history.

Clusters may also arise from unusual, sophisticated, or stringent local demand. Israel's cluster in irrigation equipment and other advanced agricultural technologies reflects that nation's strong desire for a self-sufficient food supply, coupled with its scarcity of water and its hot, arid growing conditions. Finland's environmental cluster emerged from pollution problems created by local process industries (for example, metals, forestry, chemicals, energy), as did the environment cluster in greater Pittsburgh (see Figure 7-8).

Prior existence of supplier industries, related industries, or entire related clusters provides yet another seed for new clusters. The golf equipment cluster near San Diego, California, for example, has its roots in the southern California aerospace cluster. This cluster created a pool of available suppliers for castings and advanced materials and of engineers with the requisite experience in working with these technologies.

New clusters may also arise from one or two innovative companies that stimulate the growth of many others. Medtronic played this role in helping to create the Minneapolis medical devices cluster. Similarly, MCI and America OnLine have been spin-off hubs for the telecommunications cluster in the Washington, D.C., metropolitan area.

Chance events are often important to the birth of a cluster. The early formation of companies in a location often reflects acts of entrepreneurship not completely explainable by reference to favorable local circumstances. These companies, in other words, could have sprouted at any one of a number of comparable locations. The establishment of cluster pioneer Callaway Golf in Carlsbad rather than another southern California town had much to do with chance.

Chance, however, often has locational antecedents, making its role less than it at first appears. The location of pacemaker pioneer Medtronic in the Minneapolis area provides an interesting example. Medtronic, which now employs over twelve thousand people, provided the seed for the entire Minnesota medical devices cluster, now encompassing more than one hundred Minnesota companies—all with roots traceable to Medtronic employees or technologies.[28] In 1949, Earl Bakken, an electrical engineering graduate student working part time at a Minneapolis hospital, founded Medtronic, with Palmer Hermundslie, as a medical equipment repair company. By the early 1950s, Medtronic was building custom equipment for medical researchers. In the mid 1950s, the company developed a relationship with Dr. C. W. Lillehei, a pioneer in open heart surgery at the University of Minnesota Medical School. The university had a national reputation in both electrical engineering and surgery. Medtronic engineers worked with Dr. Lillehei to improve the bulky and dangerous devices then being used to stimulate heart activity. By 1957, the breakthrough Bakken battery-powered pacemaker was in use. The next breakthrough, in electrodes, was developed in 1958, the result of a collaboration with Dr. Samuel Hunter of St. Joseph Hospital in St. Paul. By 1960, Medtronic had evolved into a world-recognized pacemaker competitor. While the developments leading to the company's initial success arose partly by chance, the founding and success of the company were inextricably entwined with the area's local university and medical institutions.

Chance events can also be important in the chain of causality leading to company formation by creating advantageous factor or demand conditions. The telemarketing cluster in Omaha, Nebraska, for example, owes much to the decision by the U.S. Air Force to locate the Strategic Air Command (SAC) there. Charged with a key role in America's nuclear deterrence strategy, SAC was the site of the first installation of fiber-optic telecommunications cables in the United States. In addition, the local Bell operating company (now U.S. West) developed unusual capability through dealing with such a demanding customer. The extraordinary telecommunication infrastructure that consequently developed in Omaha, coupled with less unique attributes, such as its central time zone location and easy-to-understand local accent, provided the underpinnings of the area's telemarketing cluster.

Some recent treatments of industry evolution have emphasized chance, but chance must be considered in its locational context. What looks like chance may be as much the result of preexisting local circumstances, as the above examples, and others, suggest. Moreover, even when chance provides a central explanation for a development, it is almost never the sole explanation. The influences of location not only raise the odds that chance events will occur, they also raise the odds that chance events will lead to competitive firms and industries. Chance alone rarely explains why a cluster takes root or its subsequent growth and development.

The limited explanatory role of chance raises serious doubts about whether clusters can be seeded in locations where no important advantages already exist. The appropriate policy towards cluster development, then, should be to *build on existing or emerging fields* that have passed a market test, a subject to which I will return below.

CLUSTER DEVELOPMENT

While the birth of clusters has many causes, the development or lack of development of clusters is more predictable. Though there is no guarantee that a cluster will develop, once the process gets started it is like a chain reaction in which the lines of causality quickly become blurred. The process depends heavily on the efficacy of the diamond's arrows or feedback loops, on how well, for example, local educational, regulatory, and other institutions respond to the cluster's needs, or how rapidly capable suppliers respond to the cluster opportunity. Three particular areas deserve special attention: intensity of local competition, the location's overall environment for new business formation, and the efficacy of formal and informal mechanisms for bringing cluster participants together. Healthy rivalry is an essential driver of rapid improvement and entrepreneurship. The entrepreneurial climate is important because the creation of new firms and institutions is so integral to cluster development. Finally, organizational and relationship-building mechanisms are necessary because a cluster's advantages rely heavily on linkages and connections among individuals and groups.

In a healthy cluster, the initial critical mass of firms triggers a self-reinforcing process in which specialized suppliers emerge; information accumulates; local institutions develop specialized training, research, infrastructure and appropriate regulations; and cluster visibility and prestige grows. Perceiving a market opportunity and facing falling entry barriers, entrepreneurs create new companies. Spinoffs from existing companies develop, and new suppliers emerge. Recognition of the cluster's existence constitutes a milestone. As more institutions and firms recognize the cluster's importance, a growing number of specialized products and services become available and specialized expertise responsive to the cluster arises among local financial services providers, construction firms, and the like. Informal and formal organizations and modes of communication involving cluster participants develop.[29] As the cluster grows, it develops greater influence not only over what other firms do but also over public and private institutions and government policies. Policies that have deterred cluster upgrading are often modified.

From numerous case studies, it appears that clusters require a decade or more to develop depth and to gain real competitive advantage—one reason why government attempts to create clusters normally fail. Clusters at different locations often develop unique subspecializations, notably in product segment coverage, the array of suppliers and complementary industries, and the prevailing modes of competing.

Cluster development often becomes particularly vibrant at the intersection of clusters. Here, insights, skills, and technologies from different fields merge, sparking new businesses. The presence of multiple intersecting clusters further lowers barriers to entry, because potential entrants and spinoffs come from several directions. Diversity of learning stimulates innovation. Germany, for example, has both a home appliance cluster and a household furniture cluster. At the intersection of these clusters is built-in kitchens and built-in appliances, products in which Germany has a higher share of world exports than in either appliances or furniture overall. Figure 7-10 illustrates some cluster intersections in Massachusetts that have proven to be fertile breeding grounds for new companies.

In a national or global economy, cluster development can be greatly accelerated by attracting cluster participants from other states or nations. A growing cluster begins to attract in-bound foreign direct investment (FDI) in the form of manufacturing or service operations and supplier facilities. Companies relocate from less productive locations or invest in subsidiaries to access cluster expertise in particular segments. This occurred in golf equipment, for example, when east coast manufacturers established R&D centers and operations in Carlsbad, California. Suppliers move to the emerging location to gain better access and closer relationships with a growing customer base.

Developing clusters also attract—and cluster participants seek out—people and ideas that reinforce the cluster. Growing clusters attract

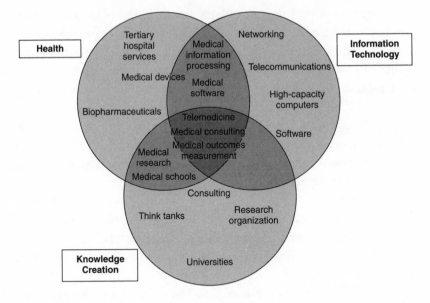

Figure 7-10 Cluster Intersections in Massachusetts

skilled people through offering greater opportunities. Entrepreneurs or individuals with ideas migrate to the cluster from other locations, as well, because a growing cluster signals opportunity. A cluster's success stories help attract the best talent.

As noted, cluster participants often play a role in this process, seeking out people, technologies, and even suppliers from elsewhere. The later history of Medtronic provides a good example. In 1960, two Buffalo, New York, physicians and an electrical engineer published a paper on a self-contained, transistorized, implantable pacemaker. Medtronic, working on the same problem, immediately recognized the significance of the work, and within months had contracted for exclusive rights to the new pacemaker. Lacking a local cluster, the Buffalo inventors quickly realized that the economic value of their idea would be much greater if an established company in a growing cluster commercialized it.

As a cluster evolves, cluster participants tend to develop increasingly global strategies. They market products in more and more countries, and sometimes source the more generic or basic inputs from other locations. Over time, less productive activities are internationalized to lower cost and improve access to foreign markets. As long as such internationalization results not from internal rigidities but from active pursuit of opportunities, this process makes the cluster more competitive. A cluster in which many participants compete globally is healthier because this not only opens up more growth opportunities but enriches knowledge and stimulates new ideas. Any effort to keep cluster participants local to protect advantages is misguided and ultimately counterproductive.

Nascent clusters can never develop if the market forces and feedback loops of the kind described here prove weak or nonfunctioning. Local institutions may have other agendas. Inbound foreign investments may be blocked by government policy. Dominant firms or cartels may keep out new competition. Dominant suppliers may be entrenched elsewhere. Artificial barriers to new business formation may stunt competition and retard innovation and specialization. Government policy can also impede clustering and cluster upgrading in a myriad of ways.

In a world economy in which many national and local markets are still protected to some extent or are only slowly opening, there are still numerous clusters lacking any competitive advantage. As more and more of the world economy opens to competition, however, these clusters will shrink and wither away.

CLUSTER DECLINE

Clusters can maintain vibrancy as competitive locations for centuries, and most successful clusters prosper at least for decades. Just as the development of a cluster is not assured, however, neither is its continued ability to compete.

The causes of cluster atrophy and decline can also be found in the elements of the diamond. They can be grouped into two broad categories: endogenous, or deriving from the location itself, and exogenous, or due to developments or discontinuities in the external environment.

Internal sources of decline stem from internal rigidities that diminish productivity and innovation. The onset of restrictive union rules or regulatory inflexibility can slow down productivity improvement. Overconsolidation, mutual understandings, cartels, or other barriers to competition can undermine local rivalry. Institutions such as schools and universities can suffer from their own rigidities and fail to upgrade and change. Groupthink among cluster participants, another form of rigidity, was discussed above.

Such rigidities in clusters tend to arise in locations in which government is prone to suspend or intervene in competition. When internal rigidities arise, the rate of improvement and innovation in a cluster falters. Increases in the cost of doing business begin to outrun the ability to upgrade. Such internal rigidities currently work against a variety of clusters in Switzerland and Germany.

As long as rivalry remains sufficiently vigorous, companies can partially compensate for local problems through globalization. Outsourcing can compensate for supplier problems, and foreign production can offset local wages that rise ahead of productivity. German firms in the 1990s, for example, have been rapidly outsourcing and outlocating to mitigate the effect of local cost problems. Unless internal rigidities ease, however, a cluster will eventually lose its productivity and dynamism. Competitive advantage will migrate to other locations.

External threats to cluster success arise in several areas. Technological discontinuities are perhaps the most significant, because they can neutralize many cluster advantages simultaneously. Market information, employee skills, scientific and technical expertise, and supplier bases may be rendered inappropriate. Unless the requisite new technologies and skills are available from other local institutions or can be rapidly developed, competitive advantage will shift to another location. The shift of golf equipment manufacturing from New England to California provides a good example. The New England cluster was based on steel shafts, steel irons, and wooden-headed woods. When the notion of making golf clubs with advanced materials was pioneered, east coast producers had difficulty competing. Some east coast firms joined the California cluster; others died or declined.

A shift in buyer needs, creating a divergence between local needs and needs elsewhere, constitutes another external threat to cluster productivity and innovation. American firms in a variety of clusters, for example, suffered when energy efficiency grew in importance in most parts of the world while the United States maintained low energy prices, retarding innovation. As this example illustrates, however, the threat posed by external developments often relates to local choices and policies.

As with internal threats to cluster competitiveness, aggressive firms in a location can, for a time, use globalization to compensate for external discontinuities. Technology can be licensed or sourced from other locations, product development can be moved elsewhere, and components and equipment can be outsourced. Over time, however, a location that fails to build up a critical mass in a major new technology or in meeting a major new need will wane as a home base for innovative companies.

The competitive decline of a cluster should not be confused with reductions in employment or total revenue that may result from upgrading. Rising local wages and profits reflect economic success. This means that less skilled and less productive activities *should* move to other locations. The ultimate test of the health or decline of a cluster is its rate of innovation. A cluster that is investing and innovating at home is of far less concern than one that improves productivity only through shrinking and outsourcing.

The Role of Government

Government inevitably plays a variety of roles in an economy. Identifying the broad types of these roles helps put government's proper policies toward clusters in context.

Goverment's most basic role in an economy is to achieve macroeconomic and political stability. It does this by establishing stable government institutions, a consistent basic economic framework, and sound macroeconomic policies, including prudent government finances and low inflation. Government's second role is to improve general microeconomic capacity of the economy by improving the efficiency and quality of the general purpose inputs to business identified in the diamond (an educated workforce, appropriate physical infrastructure, and accurate and timely economic information) and the institutions that provide them. Such inputs are required across the entire economy and are a foundation upon which everything else is built. Government's third role is to establish the overall microeconomic rules and incentives governing competition that will encourage productivity growth. Such rules and incentives, present throughout the diamond, include a competition policy enhancing rivalry, a tax system and intellectual property laws encouraging investment, a fair and efficient legal system, laws providing consumer recourse, corporate governance rules holding managers accountable for performance, and an efficient regulatory process promoting innovation rather than freezing the status quo.

While these roles of government are necessary for economic progress, however, they may not be sufficient. Especially as government begins to make headway in its more basic roles, a fourth role—that of facilitating cluster development and upgrading—takes on prominence. Government should aim to reinforce the development and upgrading of *all* clusters, not choose among them. While the general business environment is central to competitiveness, cluster circumstances are increasingly important in allowing an economy to move beyond factor-cost competition. Government policies inevitably affect the opportunities for upgrading clusters. At the same time, many of the productivity and innovation advantages of clusters rest on spillovers and externalities that involve government entities. In addition to modifying its own policies and practices, government can also motivate, facilitate, and provide incentives for collective action by the private sector. (Government's role in cluster development and upgrading is not the same as so-called industrial policy. See the insert "Clusters versus Industrial Policy.")

Government's final role in an economy is in developing and implementing a positive, distinctive, long-term economic action program or change process which mobilizes government, business, institutions, and citizens to upgrade both the general business environment and the array of local clusters. Economic progress is thwarted as much by inaction as by a lack of knowing what steps are necessary. Strong forces oppose economic upgrading, ranging from obsolete views about competitiveness to entrenched interests that prosper from the status quo. Only a long-term process, with accompanying institutions, can counteract these forces. The process must involve all key constituencies and rise above the politics of any particular administration or government. The process must encompass the general conditions affecting all industries as well as the upgrading of clusters. Ideally, such a process will occur not only at the national level but at the state and city level as well.

GOVERNMENT POLICY AT THE CLUSTER LEVEL

All clusters offer opportunities to improve productivity and support rising wages, even those that do not compete with other locations. Every cluster not only contributes directly to national productivity but can affect the productivity of *other* clusters as well. This means that traditional clusters, such as agriculture, should not be abandoned but upgraded. Efforts to upgrade clusters may have to be sequenced for practical reasons, but the goal should be to encompass all of them eventually. Not all clusters will succeed, of course, and upgrading in some clusters will reduce employment as firms move to more productive activities. These outcomes should be determined by market forces, however, not by government decisions.

Government should reinforce and build on established and emerging clusters, rather than attempt to create entirely new ones. New industries and new clusters emerge best from established ones. Businesses involving advanced technology do not succeed in a vacuum, but where there is already a base of less sophisticated activities in the field. Most clusters form independently of government action—and sometimes in spite of it. Clusters form where a foundation of locational advantages exists to build on. To justify cluster development efforts, some seeds of a cluster should have already passed a market test.

Cluster development efforts must embrace the pursuit of competitive advantage and specialization, rather than attempt to imitate exactly what is present in other locations. This requires building on local differences and sources of uniqueness where possible, turning them into strengths. Finding areas of specialization normally proves more effective than head-on competition with well-established rival locations. Specialization also offers the potential to meet new needs and expand the market.

Cluster development can be seeded and reinforced by inbound FDI. The most effective efforts at attracting FDI concentrate on attracting multiple companies in the same field, supported by parallel investments in specialized training, infrastructure, and other aspects of the business environment.

Cluster upgrading involves recognizing the presence of a cluster, and then removing obstacles, relaxing constraints, and eliminating inefficiencies that impede cluster productivity and innovation. Constraints include those of human resources, infrastructure, and regulation. Some can be addressed to varying degrees by private initiatives, but others result from government policies and institutions and must be addressed by government. Government regulations, for example, may create unnecessary inefficiencies; important infrastructure may be lacking; education and training policies may overlook cluster needs. Ideally, all government policies that inflict costs on firms without conferring any compensating, long-term competitive value should be minimized or eliminated. Upgrading clusters, then, requires going beyond improvements in the general business environment to evaluating and, if necessary, changing policies and institutions that affect particular concentrations of related firms and industries.

Governments are often drawn into developing policies, such as subsidiaries or technology grants, that attempt to enhance the competitiveness of individual firms. Much policy attention has also addressed the industry level, also narrower than clusters. Conversely, other policy thinking is concerned with broad sectors, such as machinery, manufacturing, or services. None of these approaches is well aligned with modern competition. Setting policies to benefit individual firms distorts markets and

---

Clusters versus Industrial Policy

A cluster-based approach to economic development is sometimes confused with industrial policy. In reality, cluster theory and industrial policy differ fundamentally in both their intellectual foundations and their implications for government policy.

Industrial policy rests on a view of international (or more generally, locational) competition in which some industries offer greater wealth-creating prospects than others. Desirable industries—that is, those that are growing or industries that employ high tech—should be "targeted" for support. Industrial policy sees competitive advantage as heavily determined by increasing returns to scale.

Given the importance of scale, governments should nurture priority emerging, "infant" industries until they reach a critical mass, through subsidies, eliminating "destructive" or "wasteful" internal competition, selective protection from imports, and restricting foreign investment. Subsidies and suspension of internal competition should concentrate on scale-sensitive areas, such as R&D and facilities investment. Through such intervention, government attempts to tilt competitive outcomes (and international market share) in a nation's favor. Sometimes the notion of industrial policy seems to reflect a zero-sum view of international competition, where there is a fixed pool of demand to be served and the goal is to gain a larger share for a particular nation.[a]

Cluster theory could hardly be more different. The concept of clusters rests on a broader, more dynamic view of competition among firms and locations based on the growth of productivity. Interconnections and spillovers within a cluster often influence productivity growth more than does the scale of individual firms.

All clusters can be desirable, and all offer the potential to contribute to prosperity. What matters is not what a nation (location) competes in, but how. Instead of targeting, therefore, all existing and emerging clusters deserve attention. All clusters can improve their productivity. Rather than recommending the exclusion of foreign firms, cluster theory calls for welcoming them. Foreign firms enhance cluster externalities and productivity, and their activities in a nation contribute directly to local employment and investment. Rather than advocate blocking imports, cluster theory stresses the need for timely and steady opening of the local market to imports that boost local efficiency, provide needed inputs, upgrade local demand conditions, and stimulate rivalry.

While industrial policy aims to distort competition in favor of a particular location, cluster theory focuses on removing constraints to productivity and productivity growth. Cluster theory emphasizes not market share but dynamic improvement. This results in a positive sum underlying view of competition, in which productivity improvements and trade expand the market and many locations prosper if they can become more productive and innovative.

---

a. The intellectual foundations of industrial policy go back for centuries and can be traced to works on mercantilism and arguments for protecting of infant industries, among others. Industrial policy received major impetus in work that viewed it as an important explanation for Japan's economic success. The intellectual rigor of industrial policy was also greatly enhanced by "strategic trade theory." See, for example, Krugman (1986) and Tyson (1992).

uses government resources inefficiently. Focusing policy at the industry level presumes that some industries are better than others and runs grave risks of distorting or limiting competition. Often, firms are wary of participating along with their competitors. Sectors, in contrast, are too broad to be competitively significant, and distinctions such as manufacturing versus services or high tech versus low tech no longer hold meaning.

A cluster focus highlights the externalities, linkages, spillovers, and supporting institutions so important to competition. By grouping together firms, suppliers, related industries, service providers, and institutions, government initiatives and investments address problems common to many firms and industries without threatening competition. A government role in cluster upgrading, then, will encourage competition rather than distort it. A cluster focus will also encourage the buildup of public or quasi-public goods that significantly impact many linked businesses. Government investments focused on improving the business environment in clusters, then, other things being equal, may well earn a higher return than those aimed at individual firms or industries or at the broad economy.

Emphasizing clusters might seem to encourage unhealthy economic specialization, but upgrading all clusters rather than choosing among them avoids this. Moreover, clusters function as powerful sources of new business formation, and new clusters often emerge out of existing ones. Also, the presence of clusters can facilitate the adjustment of local firms to changing economic conditions, reducing risk to the local economy rather than increasing it.[30]

More broadly, clusters represent a new and complementary way of dividing and understanding an economy, organizing economic development thinking and practice, and setting public policy. Clusters, together with the diamond model, reveal the process by which wealth is actually created in an economy and make competitiveness more concrete and operational. (Nonbusiness constituencies, especially, benefit from the demystification of competition.) Policy analyses and recommendations can address systematically the needs of business. In the Netherlands, for example, cluster development represents an important priority of government policy. Clusters provide a vehicle for bringing companies, government, and local institutions together in a constructive dialogue about upgrading and offer a new mechanism for business-government collaboration. Dialogue with more broadly defined business groupings inevitably gravitates toward discussion of the general business environment, and issues such as taxes, currency value, and overall complaints about the inefficiencies of government. Businesses get to vent their grievances against the government, but quickly lose patience. Government gains little useful information from such critiques and representatives quickly tire of listening to repetitive lobbying over the same old issues. A business-government dialogue convened around narrowly defined industries inhibits productive interchange as participants grow wary of revealing their needs and problems in front of competitors. Such discussions often gravitate toward subsidies, import protections, and limits to competition. Dialogues that engage cluster participants, in contrast, avoid these difficulties by bringing together all the affected players and focusing on common constraints and linkages among related firms. The presence of suppliers, channels, and often customers checks any incipient effort to suppress competition.

GOVERNMENT INFLUENCES ON CLUSTER UPGRADING

Figure 7-11 illustrates some specific government roles in cluster upgrading. Government influences on a cluster appear throughout the diamond. At one end of the spectrum, governments might convene forums of

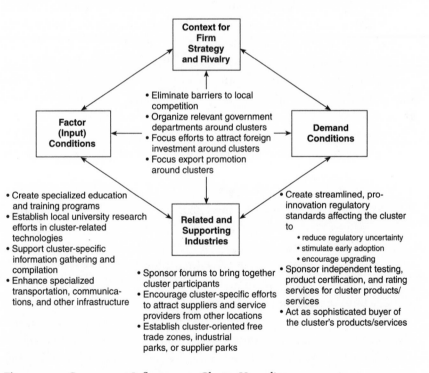

Figure 7-11   Government Influences on Cluster Upgrading

firms, institutions, and appropriate government agencies. At the other end, government has more direct roles such as collecting and compiling cluster-specific information; setting educational policies encouraging public universities and schools to respond to local cluster needs; clarifying and simplifying regulations significantly affecting the cluster; and improving the sophistication of local demand for cluster products and services. At times, cluster upgrading can be as simple as colocating public with private investments. In New Zealand forestry, for example, the cluster centers on the North Island, while the main university institution supporting the cluster, at the University of Canterbury, is on the South Island. (See the insert "Microclusters in Catalonia" for another specific case example.)

Clusters offer a new way for governments to collect and organize information. The Standard Industrial Classification System, for example, aligns poorly with clusters and with the actual nature of competition; dated groupings, such as machinery, products, and services, fail to capture the most important linkages among industries. Some regions, such as Massachusetts, have begun to retabulate economic data focusing on clusters, although much remains to be done.[31]

As clusters mature and develop and as the sources of their competitive advantage shift, the appropriate government priorities change. Early priorities involve improving infrastructure and eliminating diamond disadvantages. Later roles revolve more around removing constraints and impediments to innovation.

An important tool for encouraging cluster growth in developing countries is attracting foreign investment. Attracting one or two multinationals in a field can attract others, which in turn triggers local developments. In Costa Rica, for example, an Intel plant announced in November 1996 and a Microsoft investment announced in September 1997 have led to serious expressions of interest in the nation from other information technology producers. Foreign investment alone, however, is insufficient to build clusters. Also necessary are systematic efforts to improve local conditions throughout the diamond. Costa Rica's plan to create the conditions for growing an information technology cluster includes initiatives in areas such as improving training, enhancing the data communications infrastructure, and encouraging use of computers in schools.

Even when attempting to seed clusters with FDI, however, success requires the presence of prior locational advantages. Costa Rica spends 6 percent of GDP on education, one of the highest expenditures in the region. It also has an established network of research centers and enjoys the highest index of computers per capita in Latin America. These conditions, together with a long history of political stability, were what attracted Intel and Microsoft in the first place.

In developing economies, foreign investment promotion, free trade zones, and industrial parks also act as prominent policy levers favoring cluster growth. Free trade zones and industrial parks can better foster economic upgrading if they have a cluster rather than a general focus, supported by tailored regulations and supporting infrastructure. Free trade zones and industrial parks may have to begin as enclaves in an otherwise inefficient business environment, with virtually all inputs imported, all outputs exported, and little or no contact with the rest of the economy. Over time, however, such zones should build links with the rest of the economy. Programs and regulations must encourage the use and development of local suppliers, for example, and the forging of links with local educational and training institutions. In addition, government must move aggressively to improve infrastructure and reduce inefficiencies *throughout* the economy. The use of enclaves cannot be allowed to reduce the sense of urgency about needed improvements in the general business environment, still the only way to achieve sustained improvements in prosperity.

CLUSTERS AND OVERALL ECONOMIC POLICY

The cluster concept provides a way of organizing thinking about many policy areas that goes beyond the common needs of the entire economy, as shown in Figure 7-12. Cluster-based thinking can help guide policies in science and technology, education and training, and promotion of exports and foreign investment, among others. A location's best chance of attracting foreign investment and promoting exports, for example, lies in its existing or emerging clusters.

A cluster orientation highlights the fact that more parts of government have an influence on competitiveness, often not recognized within gov-

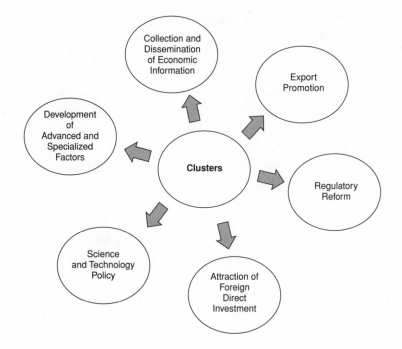

Figure 7-12   Clusters and Economic Policy

ernment itself. Cluster theory clarifies the impacts on competitive position of government policies and makes needed actions more operational.
Effective solutions often require collaboration among different parts of
government. (See the insert "Microclusters in Catalonia" for an example.)

In some locations, government agencies that relate to business have
begun to organize themselves internally to align with local clusters. In
Arizona, for example, the Department of Commerce now develops staff
as experts on particular clusters, in contrast to a past focus on individual
foreign countries (for example, Canada or Japan). A cluster orientation
in government also provides a mechanism through which officials can
become better informed about the practical costs and benefits of policies
and better motivated to make policies and government organizations
more cost effective. Ongoing cluster assessments represent a powerful
tool for identifying and validating economy-wide policy deficiencies
and for finding practical solutions. A problem that surfaces in several
different clusters clearly should be a priority.

Finally, cluster thinking also highlights the important roles of government at a number of geographic levels. The traditional focus of economic policy has been at the national level, where many aspects of the general business environment are best addressed. Recently, globalization has focused attention on worldwide multilateral institutions. State, metropolitan region, and local governments, however, also significantly influence the general business environment in a location. At the cluster level, these influences often dominate, and consideration of clusters should represent an important component of state and local economic policy.

Each level of government exerts an important influence on the overall business environment and on clusters. National policies should set minimum standards while pushing public investment choices down to smaller geographic levels, and they should avoid centralization and rigidities that obstruct policies tailored for implementation at the state and local level.[32] Economic development programs should increasingly involve parallel efforts at multiple geographic levels. In New Zealand, for example, cluster development began at the national level but has spread to the state and local level. Almost three-quarters of all local economic development agencies in New Zealand have adopted the identification and upgrading of clusters as an integral part of their activities.[33]

Finally, while far less common, influences on productivity—and clusters themselves—sometimes cross national borders. Coordination among transportation systems, energy networks, and other areas among neighboring countries can benefit productivity in ways that go well beyond customs unions and free trade zones. Groups of neighboring countries, then, also have a joint role to play in formulating economic policy. Figure 7-13 illustrates the broadening geographic units of policy analysis important in modern competition.

The Corporate Role in Cluster Development

The existence of clusters suggests that much of a company's potential to achieve competitive advantage, both in operational effectiveness and in establishing a unique strategy, lies outside the company and even outside the industry. The presence of a well-developed cluster provides

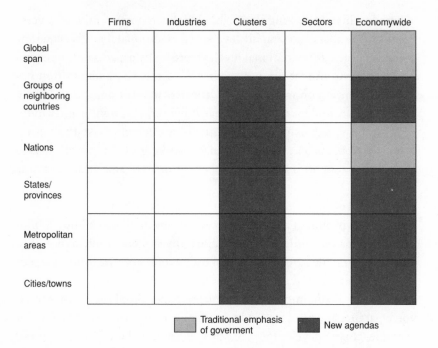

Figure 7-13   Government Influences on Competitiveness

powerful benefits to productivity and to the capacity for innovation that are difficult for firms based elsewhere to match. Often, for a given field, only a few locations in the world can achieve such an environment.

Even though clusters offer tangible competitive benefits, the first reaction of managers is often to be wary of them. There are concerns that the expansion of a cluster will invite unwanted competition and drive up the costs of employees and inputs. Managers have nightmare visions of losing valued employees to rivals or spinoffs. As their understanding of the cluster concept grows, however, managers realize that many cluster participants do not directly compete. Although a company may face competition for employees and other inputs, the presence of the cluster expands their supply. The net access to specialized skills, services, technology, and information in a cluster often increases. Any increases in competition comes with cluster benefits in productivity, flexibility, and innovation.

Cluster theory suggests new tasks and roles for companies. Cluster analysis must become part of competitive assessments, along with company and industry analysis. Private sector roles in cluster upgrading can be found in all parts of the diamond, as shown in Figure 7-14. Improving factor conditions provides the most obvious example, with efforts possible in enhancing the supply of appropriately trained personnel, the quality and appropriateness of local university research activities, the creation of specialized physical infrastructure, and the supply of cluster-specific information. Ongoing relationships with government bodies and local institutions, such as utilities, schools, and research groups, are necessary to attain these benefits. There is also a role for private investment by cluster participants to establish common specialized infrastructure, such as port or handling facilities, satellite communication links, and testing laboratories. Often such investments can be made and administered through third parties, for example, universities or trade associations.

In the area of related and supporting industries, firms have a role in attracting suppliers, services, and complementary-product producers to the cluster, as well as in forming supplier businesses to fill gaps. Joint

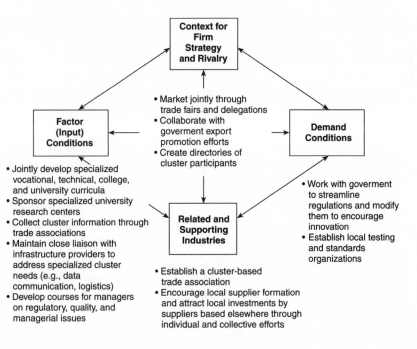

Figure 7-14   Private Sector Influences on Cluster Upgrading

ventures are sometimes used to establish local capability in essential supporting industries.

The need for cluster participants to inform and prod government to address the constraints or weaknesses under its control cuts across all parts of the diamond. Individual departments or units of government that impact the cluster must be engaged and educated on the effect of regulations and policies and on the quality of government services. An open, constructive dialogue must replace self-serving lobbying or paternalism in these relationships.

THE ROLE OF TRADE ASSOCIATIONS AND COLLECTIVE BODIES

Individual companies can independently influence cluster development, and cluster pioneers or leading firms often play this role because they gain major benefits. Given the important externalities and public goods involved in clusters, however, informal networks and formal trade associations, consortia, and other collective bodies often become necessary and appropriate. Trade associations representing all or most cluster participants can command greater attention and achieve greater influence than can individual members, and an association or collective body (for example, a joint research center or testing laboratory) creates a vehicle for cost sharing.

Many trade associations do little more than lobby government, compile some statistics, and host social functions. The opportunity for associations to enhance cluster competitiveness, however, is much greater. Associations or collective bodies institutionalize cluster linkages. In addition to providing a neutral forum for identifying common needs, constraints, and opportunities, associations can serve as focal points for efforts to address them. Associations often take the lead in organizing national and international fairs and delegations; they create training programs in conjunction with local institutions, manage purchasing consortia, establish university-based research programs and testing facilities, collect cluster-related information, offer forums on common managerial problems, investigate solutions to environmental issues, and pursue many other common interests. These activities are in addition to performance of the traditional task of interfacing with local, state, and national government, guiding regulatory reform, and representing the cluster with other business groups.

Associations fulfill especially important functions for clusters consisting of many small- and medium-sized firms (for example, tourism, apparel, or agriculture). Such clusters have a particularly great need for a collective body to take on scale-sensitive functions. In the Netherlands, for example, grower cooperatives built the specialized auction and handling facilities that constitute one of the Dutch flower cluster's greatest competitive advantages. The Dutch Flower Council and the Association of Dutch Flower Growers Research Groups, in which most growers participate, have taken on other functions as well, such as marketing and applied research.

At times, cluster-based trade associations may not exist. Or, existing associations may be too narrow, including industry participants but not suppliers, companies in related industries, or local institutions. Existing trade organizations may be national rather than local in scope. National associations have been the norm, as most associations have seen their primary role as lobbying government, with the national government viewed as most important. National associations, however, are rarely effective in addressing many of the training, infrastructure, and other issues most important to cluster productivity. Another typical pattern among a location's business organizations is chambers of commerce, roundtables, or councils cutting across the entire economy or large parts of it. Once again, these inevitably focus primarily on government lobbying and general business issues. Cluster-based associations are also needed. In other cases, several associations may be present that would be more useful if combined or at least coordinated. Given individuals' and companies' limited time and money for participation in associations, the more integrated the efforts of various groups, the better.

Surprisingly often, cluster participants never meet, and there is little public or government recognition of the cluster's significance to the local economy. Both situations existed in the Massachusetts medical-devices cluster. Where absent, the formation of associations should be part of a location's economic development agenda. In Massachusetts, this effort was undertaken by the Governor's Council on Economic Growth and Technology. This private-sector advisory body, composed of leaders from firms, universities, and other entities, convened a series of task forces to examine Massachusetts clusters that led to the formation of new and permanent associations where they did not yet exist, as in telecommunications and medical devices.

CORPORATE LOCATION

Globalization and the ease of transportation and communication have led to a surge of outsourcing, with companies relocating many facilities to locations with low wages, low taxes, and low utility costs. Outsourcing some activities to tap lower cost inputs can indeed reduce locational disadvantages. Cluster theory, however, suggests a more complex view of corporate locational choices: Corporate location involves far more than simply building offices or factories.

First, cluster theory suggests that locational choices should weigh overall productivity potential, not just input costs or taxes. In locating activities, the aim is low total cost. Locations with low wages and low taxes, however, often lack efficient infrastructure, available suppliers, timely maintenance, and other conditions that clusters offer. Logistical costs and costs of introducing new models may be substantial. Many companies have discovered that such productivity disadvantages can be more than offsetting. Yet the effects of low wages, low taxes, and low utility costs are easy to measure up front, while productivity costs remain hidden and unanticipated.

Locating in an existing or developing cluster, then, often involves lower total systems cost and greatly improved capacity for innovation. A shift back toward clusters is beginning among companies who once believed in the cost savings of highly dispersed activities. This trend is evident in choices of international locations (with activities being moved back to places such as the United States) and locations within nations (with clusters gaining in appeal over remote Sun Belt or other sites).

Second, firms must capture the cost advantages of spreading activities across locations while *also* harnessing advantages of clusters. (See Chapter 9 for a full treatment of global strategy, or, more broadly, of competition across locations.) The determinants of location differ markedly for various activities. For activities such as assembly plants, manufacture of stable, labor-intensive components, and software translation, locational choices often should be driven by factor cost and market access. For what I term "home base" activities, however, the basis for choice should be very different. Home base activities are those involved in the creation and renewal of the firm's product, processes, and services. This includes activities, such as fabrication of frequently redesigned components, that involve substantial, ongoing changes.

The location of home base activities should be heavily driven by total systems cost and by innovation potential. Clusters usually provide conditions favorable for innovation. Home base activities should sometimes move to locations outside the company's nation of principal ownership or the nation containing its corporate headquarters—if a more vibrant cluster exists elsewhere. This rule applies especially to product lines, but also to entire business units. The siting of regional headquarters should also involve consideration of clusters, not just of tax considerations or the convenience of executives.

Cluster thinking also underscores the desirability of moving groups of linked activities to the same place rather than spreading them across numerous states and nations. Grouping in this way lowers total system costs, eases sharing of internal information, facilitates and spreads innovation, creates critical mass for supporting company infrastructure and facilities, and extends deeper roots into local clusters that increase the ability to capture externalities and spillovers.

Finally, activities located in places isolated from other firms in the same field require firms to begin building a cluster. The process calls for wooing suppliers, encouraging local institutions to make supporting investments, and finding ways to build the local stock of specialized inputs. Corporate location, then, is not something to be delegated to operations departments but is part of overall strategy.

Organizing Cluster Development Initiatives

Numerous cluster-related initiatives—to organize participants, assess advantages and disadvantages, and catalyze public and private action— have arisen at the national, state, and city levels, as illustrated by the examples in Table 7-1. Some relatively recent efforts have begun to develop initiatives around clusters that cross the borders of neighboring

Table 7-1   Examples of Cluster Initiatives*

Multi-Country Regions	Nations	Regions/States/ Provinces	Cities/ Metropolitan Areas
Central America	Andorra	Arizona	Bogota
Middle East	Bermuda	Atlantic region	Charlotte
	Bolivia	(Canada)	Christchurch
	Bulgaria	Basque Region	Long Island
	Canada	(Spain)	Minneapolis
	Colombia	California	Rotterdam
	Costa Rica	Catalonia	Silicon Valley
	Denmark	Connecticut	Sonoma, CA
	Egypt	Chihuahua	Tampa
	El Salvador	Massachusetts	Wellington
	Finland	Minnesota	Worcester, MA
	Hong Kong	North Carolina	
	India	Ohio	
	Israel	Oregon	
	Jordan	Scotland	
	Malaysia	Quebec	
	Morocco		
	Northern Ireland		
	Norway		
	Netherlands		
	New Zealand		
	Panama		
	Portugal		
	Peru		
	Republic of Ireland		
	South Africa		
	Sweden		
	Tatarstan		
	Venezuela		

*Citations of the published output of many of these initiatives appear in the references at the end of this chapter.

countries in Central America and in the Middle East, a practice that would benefit other regions, as well.

Cluster initiatives provide a new way of organizing economic development efforts that go beyond traditional efforts to reduce the cost of doing business and enhance the overall business environment. Efforts focusing on clusters draw firms to become much more interested and engaged than in broad, economy-wide efforts that must necessarily gravitate to general issues, such as tax policy and export promotion. Business-government-university dialogue tends to take place on a more concrete level, making action possible. Cluster initiatives can not only bring focus to discussions of government policy, but can reveal and help address issues within the private sector, as well.[34]

One cluster initiative is profiled in the insert "Microclusters in Catalonia." Similar profiles of other efforts in Arizona, Chihuahua, the Netherlands, and New Zealand are available.[35]

These and other successful cluster initiatives have a number of common characteristics:

- *A shared understanding of competitiveness and the role of clusters in competitive advantage.* Productivity and innovation, not low wages, low taxes, or a devalued currency, are the definition of competitiveness. Participants understand the influences that bear on productivity and how clusters enhance it. Roles for both business and government are well understood, and not confused with market distortion or with picking winners. Early and ongoing communication and discussion educates cluster participants about competitiveness and helps to shift mindsets. In addition to government and businesses, other constituencies share the understanding of competitiveness. Labor unions and non-governmental organizations that may fear lost jobs, lower pay, and watered-down regulations concerning safety, working conditions, and environmental impact are brought to recognize that competitiveness depends on productivity, which supports rising wages, and on an improved quality of life.

- *A focus on removing obstacles and easing constraints to cluster upgrading.* Explicit, upfront discussion of goals at the beginning of a cluster initiative and regular reinforcement of those goals helps overcome the urge to seek subsidies or limit competition. The presence of suppliers and customers in the cluster process provides a natural check to these tendencies. Some participants may cling to the status quo and may join the cluster initiative only to influence its efforts in that direction. Successful cluster initiatives remain alert against these tendencies.

- *A structure that embraces all clusters in a nation or state.* Setting priorities among clusters is not only bad economics, it disenfranchises large parts of the private sector. Successful cluster initiatives include traditional clusters, such as agriculture and tourism, and even declining clusters. They include emerging clusters as well as established ones. To avoid misguided attempts at creating clusters that have no assets on which to build, emerging clusters should have a demonstrable local foundation and a base of firms that have met a market test. Practical considerations may require the sequencing of cluster projects, but early clusters where work is undertaken should involve a representative spectrum of the types of clusters present (for example, a traditional cluster, an emerging cluster and a declining cluster) and should strive to demonstrate the value of the cluster approach. Careful choices early on help disseminate the concepts and processes to clusters that will be included in later initiatives.

- *Appropriate cluster boundaries.* By definition, clusters include industries and institutions with important linkages or spillovers, rather than broad sectors (for example, manufacturing or high tech) or individual industries (for example, plastic machinery or Italian restaurants). Cluster boundaries should reflect economic reality, not necessarily political boundaries. In the Atlantic provinces of Canada, for example, several clusters cross provincial borders, and the cluster initiative there was structured accordingly.

- *Wide involvement of cluster participants and associated institutions.* Cluster initiatives should include firms of all sizes, as well as representatives of all important constituencies. Excluding individuals, even (or especially) difficult ones, invites opposition. While any effort will have its share of the skeptical, parochial, self-serving, and opportunistic, the most successful cluster initiatives make an effort to reach out and educate them. Individuals who then choose not to participate have less ground for criticizing or opposing recommendations. Ultimately, cluster initiatives must carry on with those who are willing to work to improve conditions for all.

• *Private-sector leadership.* Active government participation in a private-led effort, rather than an initiative controlled by government, will have a better chance of success. Companies can usually better identify the obstacles and constraints in their path, as well as the opportunities, than can government. Letting the private sector lead also reduces the initiative's political content, while taking advantage of the private sector's often superior implementation ability. Cluster initiatives should be as nonpartisan as possible and remain independent of any party or administration's political agenda. Legislators and the executive branch, the opposition parties, and those in power must all be involved. Ideally, the cluster initiative will take place through an entity *independent* of government. Otherwise, promising efforts may be dropped when a new government takes office.[36]

• *Close attention to personal relationships.* In itself, the presence of an established or emerging cluster does not guarantee functioning cluster linkages. Many of the benefits of clusters flow from the personal relationships which facilitate linkages, foster open communication, and build trust. Information is essential to productivity, and relationships that improve its flow will endure and even strengthen after a cluster project ends. Instigating communications is the essence of successful cluster initiatives. Neutral facilitators often help with this where trust is lacking and relationships are undeveloped. From the outset, major efforts will be required to ensure efficient and regular communication, both internal and external. Successes should be widely publicized.

• *A bias towards action.* Cluster initiatives must be motivated by the desire to achieve results; they should not be driven by academic institutions, think tanks, or government agencies that see research as an end in itself. Diagnosis and a broad vision for the future must be combined with concrete, active steps. Strong, senior champions are needed in both government and the private sector. Entrepreneurial leadership and the involvement of opinion leaders characterize virtually all successful initiatives.

• *Institutionalization.* Cluster upgrading is a long-term process that must have a life beyond a one-shot effort. It requires institutionalization of concepts, relationships, and linkages among constituencies. In the private sector, new or revitalized trade associations often take leading roles in the continuing upgrading of clusters. In government, cluster upgrading can be institutionalized by appropriately organizing government agencies, organization through the gathering and dissemination of economic statistics, and by controlling the structure and membership of business advisory groups.

Summary

A cluster is a system of interconnected firms and institutions the whole of which is greater than the sum of the parts. Clusters play an important role in competition, and these raise important implications for companies, governments, universities, and other institutions in an economy.

Clusters represent a new and complementary way of understanding an economy, organizing economic development, and setting public policy. Understanding the state of clusters in a location provides important insights into the productive potential of its economy and the constraints on its future development. Paradoxically, then, the most enduring competitive advantages in a global economy will often be local.

Microclusters in Catalonia

History

Catalonia, one of Spain's seventeen autonomous regions, accounts for 13 percent of the national population but almost 20 percent of its GDP and about 40 percent of its industrial exports. In December 1989, Antoni Subirà was appointed Catalonia's Minister of Industry, Trade and Commerce. Soon after, he obtained a manuscript copy of *The Competitive Advantage of Nations* and circu-

lated several chapters within the ministry. With Spain facing entry into the European Common Market in 1992, Subirà sought to develop a new approach to industrial policy in Catalonia. He chose clusters as a central element.

Since then, approximately twenty Catalan clusters have been studied in detail. As of 1997, clusters continued to be used in Catalonia as the main methodology for assessing the region's industrial competitiveness and for identifying areas in which the government could improve the environment for companies.

Actors

Initially, Subirà asked Professors Eduard Ballarin and Josep Faus from IESE, a top business school based in Barcelona, to apply the cluster methodology to the study of Catalonia's industry. Their preliminary work set the stage for a larger report, prepared together with Monitor Company, a consulting firm.[a] The report offered an overall diagnosis of Catalonia's strengths and weaknesses and was well received. It defined groups of clusters (for example, mass-market consumption goods) and provided some general guidelines about what was needed to enhance their competitive advantage.

Subirà decided to take this work one step further and to study discrete clusters in more detail. Already-existing capabilities within the Ministry of Industry, Trade and Commerce were reorganized, and a local consulting firm—CLUSTER Competitiveness—was asked to lead a series of cluster initiatives. Each study involved companies, suppliers, trade associations, business schools, universities, and many government departments.

Cluster Definition

Catalan clusters included wooden toys, agricultural machinery, jewelry, leather, knitting, processed meats, publishing, consumer electronics, and furniture.[b] Specific clusters were defined relatively narrowly. In furniture, for example, three separate clusters were isolated in different parts of Catalonia, each competing in different segments and facing different challenges. Estimates indicate that Catalonia has more than one hundred such narrowly defined clusters, or microclusters.

Each microcluster study included firms, suppliers, universities, and a wide range of other interested participants. Cluster boundaries and participation emerged as a result of the study process. Self-selection was the rule: All firms interested in participating were considered part of the cluster.

All clusters were viewed as equally desirable. For practical reasons, however, cluster studies were sequenced. Some clusters were initially much better organized than others. One goal of the process was to establish effective trade organizations to serve each cluster.

Process of Change

The cluster studies in Catalonia took place in three stages. In the first, the cluster's problems and opportunities were identified and the basic concepts of cluster upgrading, such as the goal of enhancing rather than suppressing competition, were laid out. At times, the study revealed a view of the cluster's problems that differed from that presented by conventional wisdom. Members of the Catalan leather-tanning cluster, for example, had attributed their decline in competitiveness to the laxity of environmental regulations in LDCs.[c] Research revealed, however, that the environmental regulations of their most significant rivals, the Italians, were, in fact, more stringent than those in Catalonia. As a result, Catalan leather tanners who had previously been asking for a relaxation of government environmental legislation decided to set up a joint cleaning and tanning plant and an R&D center. The cluster process convinced them that caring for the environment would actually improve their competitiveness.

The second stage of the study process involved the attempt to achieve a consensus vision of the cluster's future that would unite all participants and facilitate change. In the third stage, cluster participants created strategies and action steps for fulfilling the vision. Specific individuals were identified to lead the action initiatives.

Results

The cluster process equipped the Catalan government with the knowledge it needed to influence Spanish national policy more effectively. More importantly, however, it resulted in a new and more productive dialogue between government and business within Catalonia. Previously, broad, sector-wide organizations had sought general measures, such as subsidies and tax cuts. The cluster process allowed businesses to assess competitive position in specific, operational terms. Companies requested more specific and pro-competitive government support, such as help in establishing research laboratories or promoting foreign trade. Participants agreed that the competitive advantage of the region's industries had clearly benefited from taking a cluster perspective.

The cluster approach helped numerous firms (many of them small and medium sized) to think more strategically about their problems. Examples of resulting initiatives included the transfer of a leather research center from the Universidad de Barcelona to a location near the leather cluster in Igualada; a series of seminars that helped textile producers make the transition from a production to a retailing focus; and a project for developing a common sub-assembly facility to serve the local Honda, Yamaha, and Derbi motorcycle factories. Some clusters initially lacked effective associations (for example, the furniture cluster in Montsia); others were part of organizations that represented a too broad constituency (for example, lathe operators); still others had ineffective associations (for example, the leather tanners' cluster in Igualada). Following the cluster effort, new and more cluster-specific associations were created and old associations were revived.

Catalan government policies shifted toward cluster upgrading: improving the market access of clusters; facilitating foreign direct investment; introducing product certification programs; and instituting policies for upgrading technology. Based on cluster studies, for example, the government provided assistance for a cork research and applications center in Parafrugell (currently developing an international standard for cork quality). In follow-up discussions, however, some firms expressed the view that the best service provided by the government was the stimulation of dialogue among cluster participants.

In one of the major benefits of the cluster process, government officials were transformed into an informed audience for firms. The dialogue among various agencies and departments within the Catalan government also increased and coordination improved.

Catalonia's experience offers many lessons about applying cluster

methodology. First, one of the major benefits of convening a cluster is to explore common opportunities, not just discuss common problems. Second, leaders stressed the value to the cluster process of keeping a low profile; limiting publicity during the early stages helped avoid creating premature, unrealistic expectations and helped minimize formation of political and other opposition. Third, the particular leaders that emerged in a given cluster had much to do with its success in improving. Finally, the cluster initiative benefited greatly from the close and aggressive support and follow-up by Minister Subirà, who, with his business training and orientation, insulated the process from politics.

---

a. See Monitor Company (1992).

b. See Conejos, et al. (1997).

c. See Rodriguez, Prats, Enright, and Ballarin (1995).

NOTES

1. For a recent example, see Cairncross (1997).

2. See Enright (1993B) for examples illustrating clusters' varying geographic scope.

3. Enright (1993C) offers an interesting discussion of how to draw cluster boundaries.

4. While industry analysis properly involves suppliers, channels, and customers, cluster analysis widens the scope considerably to include chains or related industries at all levels, as well as a wide range of institutions.

5. The case of Italy, where such clusters are quite common, helped spawn a literature on industrial districts. Industrial districts are a special case of clusters.

6. The literature about such cases uses a number of alternate terms, such as *technopoles* and *science cities*. See A. Advani (1997) for one example.

7. See Porter (1990), Chapters 3 and 4.

8. See Harrison, Kelley, and Gant (1996) for a good summary. Static agglomeration economies consist of a local concentration of customers (or downstream firms) suffi-

cient to permit suppliers to achieve economies of scale in production or distribution, great enough for local firms to amass sufficient demand to warrant the provision (usually by or via local governments) of specialized infrastructure, and large enough to realize a specialized local division of labor. So-called dynamic agglomeration economies consist of advantages in terms of technological learning and improvement.

9. Stigler (1951). For a more recent re-statement, see Krugman (1991B).

10. An extensive literature has explored these advantages, including Pascal and McCall (1980), Angel (1990), Rauch (1993), and Glaeser and Maré (1994).

11. Adams and Jaffe (1996), for example, found that the influence of parent firm R&D on plant-level productivity diminishes with geographic distance.

12. Saxenian (1994) describes the workings of the remarkable information flow within Silicon Valley.

13. For a model capturing some of these elements, see Stahl (1982).

14. See Monitor Company (1994).

15. Enright (1990).

16. Strong empirical support exists for the spillover effects among firms and between universities and firms in R&D and innovation. Jaffe, Trajtenberg, and Henderson (1993) show geographic localization of knowledge spillovers. Audretsch and Feldman (1996) find a strong association between the importance of new knowledge and spatial clustering. Harrison, Kelley, and Gant (1996) also highlight the geographic dimension of innovation.

17. For an example drawn from the Swiss watch industry, see Glasmeier (1991).

18. Enright (1990), building on Porter (1990), provides the foundational treatment of the role of geographic concentration. See also Enright (1993A).

19. See, for example, von Hippel (1988), Case (1992), and Rogers (1995).

20. See Porter and Caves (1977).

21. See, for example, Burt (1997); Granovetter (1985); Henton, Melville, and Walesh (1997); Nohria (1992); Perrow (1992); Putnam, Leonard, and Naneth (1993); Fukuyama (1995); and Harrison and Weiss (1998).

22. Some empirical research is beginning to explore the effect of clustering on the rate of growth of cities. Glaeser et al. (1992) and Henderson, Kuncoro, and Turner (1995) find support for a positive association.

23. I use the term *exports* to apply to industries that compete outside a geographic area, even if destined for another state and not a foreign country. Note that most exports actually move to other locations, while other exporting industries (mainly services) attract outside customers to the home location.

24. See Ingham (1995).

25. More efforts are under way to bring cluster thinking into the mainstream of economic development. Cluster development has become a core approach in the World Bank's Private Sector Development Department, for example. See also Fairbanks and Lindsay (1997B) and Rosenfeld (1997).

26. Interesting recent work by economic geographers explores the synthesis between globalization and location. See Cox (1997) and Storper (1997).

27. My book *The Competitive Advantage of Nations* (1990) contains the basic treatment of the life cycle of clusters. Many other cluster studies provide some

historical perspective, as well. A particularly detailed historical analysis of the development of an array of Swedish clusters is contained in Porter, Sölvell, and Zander (1993). See also van der Linde (1992) and Hernesniemi, Lammi, and Ylä-Anttila (1996).

28. See Metropolitan Council (1995B).

29. For some interesting examples, see Rosenfeld (1997).

30. See Rosenfeld (1996B).

31. My research team has created a classification that regroups all SIC and SITC industries into clusters; this system is designed to serve as a consistent starting point for statistical research, recognizing that local modifications will usually be needed. The classification is available from the author.

32. See Markusen (1995B) and Porter (1995A).

33. See Ffowcs-Williams (1996) and Mitchell (1997).

34. See Waits (1996) for a discussion of the cluster approach taken in Arizona. See Jacobs and de Man (1996) for a discussion of some of the practical considerations that arise when formulating cluster-based economic policies and strategies.

35. Contact the author for more information.

36. See Andorra, Govern d', *Andorra Pla Estratégic* (1993).

Bibliography

General References

Abrams, M. "Emerging Clusters in Regional Economies." Paper presented at the Technopolis '97 conference, Ottawa, Canada, September 1997.

Adams, J., and A. Jaffe. "Bounding the Effects of R&D: An Investigation Using Matched Establishment-Firm Data." *Rand Journal of Economics* 27, no. 4 (1996):700–721.

Advani, A. "Industrial Clusters: A Support System for Small and Medium Sized Enterprises." Private Sector Development Department, occasional paper no. 32, The World Bank, April 1997.

Amin, A., and N. Thrift. "Neo-Marshallian Nodes in Global Networks." *International Journal of Urban and Regional Research* 16, no. 4 (1992):571–587.

Andorra, Govern d'. *Andorra Pla Estratègic.* Govern d'Andorra, 1993.

Angel, D. "New Firm Formation in the Semiconductor Industry: Elements of a Flexible Manufacturing System." *Regional Studies* 24, no. 3 (1990):211–221.

Arthur, P. "Industry Location Patterns and the Importance of History." Technical paper no. 84, Center for Economic Policy Research, Stanford University, Stanford, Calif., 1986.

Audretsch, D., and M. Feldman. "Innovative Clusters and the Industry Life Cycle." Discussion paper no. 1161, Centre for Economic Policy Research, London, 1995.

———. "R&D Spillovers and the Geography of Innovation and Production." *American Economic Review* 86, no. 3 (1996):630–640.

Babiec, J., with M. Fairbanks. *Pink Sand: Strategies for Tourism Clusters in the Age of Competitive Advantage.* Cambridge, Mass.: Monitor Company, in press.

Bartik, T. "Business Location Decisions in the United States: Estimates of the Effects of Unionization, Taxes, and Other Characteristics of States." *Journal of Business and Economic Statistics* 3, no. 1 (1985):14–22.

Becattini, G. "The Marshallian Industrial District as a Socio-Economic Notion." In *Industrial Districts and Inter-Firm Cooperation in Italy,* edited by F.

Pyke, G. Becattini and W. Sengenberger. Geneva: International Institute for Labour Studies, 1990.

Becattini, G., ed. *Mercato e Forze Locali: Il Distretto Industriale.* Bologna: Il Mulino, 1987.

———. *Modelli locali di Sviluppo.* Bologna: Il Mulino, 1989.

Becker, G., and K. Murphy. "The Division of Labor, Coordination Costs and Knowledge." *Quarterly Journal of Economics* 107, no. 4 (1992):1137–1160.

Beckmann, M., and J. F. Thisse. "The Location of Production Activities." In *Handbook of Regional and Urban Economics,* Vol. 1, edited by P. Nijkamp, Chapter 2. Amsterdam: Elsevier Science, 1987.

Benabou, R. "Workings of a City: Location, Education and Production." *Quarterly Journal of Economics* 108, no. 3 (1993):619–652.

Bengt-Åke, L., ed. *National Systems of Innovation: Towards a Theory of Innovation and Interactive Learning.* London: Pinte, 1992.

Bergman, E., E. Feser, and S. Sweeney. "Targeting North Carolina Manufacturing: Understanding the State's Economy Through Industrial Cluster Analysis." University of North Carolina Institute for Economic Development, Chapel Hill, North Carolina, 1996.

Breault, R. "The Evolution of Clusters or Structured Economic Development Regions and Their Future." Breault Research Organization, Inc., Tucson, Arizona, 1997.

Breault, R., ed. *Global Networking of Regional Optics Clusters.* Denver, Colo.: The International Society for Optical Engineering, 1996.

Burt, R. "The Contingent Value of Social Capital." *Administrative Science Quarterly* 42, no. 2 (1997):339–365.

Cairncross, F. *The Death of Distance: How the Communications Revolution Will Change Our Lives.* Boston, Mass.: Harvard Business School Press, 1997.

Carlton, D. "The Location and Employment Decisions of New Firms: An Econometric Analysis with Discrete and Continuous Exogenous Variables." *Review of Economics and Statistics* 65, no. 3 (1983):440–449.

Case, A. "Neighborhood Influence and Technological Change." *Regional Science and Urban Economics* 22, no. 4 (1992):491–508.

Ciccone, A., and R. Hall. "Productivity and the Density of Economic Activity." *American Economic Review* 86, no. 1 (1996):54–70.

Cimoli, M., and G. Dosi. "Technological Paradigms, Patterns of Learning and Development: An Introductory Roadmap." *Journal of Evolutionary Economics* 5, no. 3 (1995):243–268.

Conejos, J., E. Duch, J. Fontrodona, J. M. Hernández, A. Luzárraga, and E. Terré. *Cambio Estratégico y Clusters en Cataluña.* Barcelona: Gestión 2000, 1997.

Cox, K. R. "Globalization and the Politics of Distribution: A Critical Assessment." In *Spaces of Globalization: Reasserting the Power of the Local,* edited by K. R. Cox. New York: Guilford, 1997.

Cox, K. R., ed. *Spaces of Globalization: Reasserting the Power of the Local.* New York: Guilford, 1997.

Davis, D., and D. Weinstein. "Does Economic Geography Matter for International Specialization?" Working paper 5706, National Bureau of Economic Research, Cambridge, Mass., 1996.

———. "Economic Geography and Regional Production Structure: An Empirical Investigation." Working paper 6093, National Bureau of Economic Research, Cambridge, Mass., 1997.

Dodge, W. R. "Regional Excellence: Governing Together to Compete Globally and Flourish Locally." Washington, D.C.: National League of Cities, 1996.

Doeringer, B., and D. G. Terkla. "Business Strategy and Cross-Industry Clusters." *Economic Development Quarterly* 9, no. 3 (1995):225–237.

Dosi, G., R. Giannetti, and P. Toninelli. *Technology and Enterprise in Historical Perspective.* Oxford: Oxford University Press, 1992.

DRI/McGraw-Hill. *America's Clusters.* Conference Building Industry Clusters, DRI/McGraw-Hill, Lexington, Mass., 1995.

DRI/McGraw-Hill and FOCS. *Le Maroc Compétitif: A Cluster Development Initiative in Morocco.* Washington, D.C.: DRI/McGraw-Hill and FOCS, 1996.

Ellison, G., and E. Glaeser. "Geographic Concentration in U.S. Manufacturing Industries: A Dartboard Approach." *Journal of Political Economy* 105, no. 5 (1997):889–927.

Englmann, F., and U. Walz. "Industrial Centers and Regional Growth in the Presence of Local Inputs." *Journal of Regional Science* 35 (1995):3–27.

Enright, M. "The Determinants of Geographic Concentration in Industry." Working paper 93-052, Division of Research, Harvard Business School, Boston, Mass., 1993 (A).

———. "The Geographic Scope of Competitive Advantage." In *Stuck in the Region? Changing Scales of Regional Identity,* edited by E. Dirven, J. Groenewegen and S. van Hoof, 87–102. Utrecht: Netherlands Geographical Studies 155, 1993(B).

———. "Geographical Concentration and Industrial Organization." Ph.D. diss., Harvard University, 1990.

————. "Organization and Coordination in Geographically Concentrated Industries." In *Coordination and Information: Historical Perspectives on the Organization of Enterprise,* edited by D. Raff and N. Lamoreux, 103–142. Chicago: University of Chicago Press, 1995.

————. "Regional Clusters and Economic Development: A Research Agenda." Paper presented at the Conference on Regional Clusters and Business Networks, Fredericton, New Brunswick, November 1993 (C).

————. "Why Local Clusters Are the Way to Win the Game." *World Link* 5, no. 4 (1992):24–25.

Enright, M., and R. Weder. *Studies in Swiss Competitive Advantage.* Bern: European Academic Publishers, 1995.

Eriksson, A. "Emerging Clusters in Regional Economies." Paper presented at the Technopolis '97 Conference, Ottawa, Canada, September 1997.

Fairbanks, M., and S. Lindsay. "Choosing Prosperity: An Agenda for Emerging Markets." *Economic Reform Today.* Washington, D.C.: Center for International Private Enterprise, 1997 (A).

————. *Plowing the Sea: Nurturing the Hidden Sources of Growth in the Developing World.* Boston: Harvard Business School Press, 1997 (B).

Feldman, M. "An Examination of the Geography of Innovation." *Industrial and Corporate Change* 2, no. 3 (1993):451–470.

————. *The Geography of Innovation.* Dordrecht: Kluwer Academic Publishers, 1994.

Ffowcs-Williams, I. "Hard and Soft Networks: Helping Firms Cooperate for Export Growth." *New Zealand Strategic Management* 2, no. 2 (1996):30–36.

————. "Stimulating Local Clusters." Paper prepared for the Workshop for Practitioners in Cluster Formation, Chihuahua, Mexico, November 1997.

Fitzgerald, R., ed. *The Competitive Advantage of Far Eastern Business.* Studies in Far Eastern Business No. 1. Essex, Great Britain: Frank Cass, 1994.

Fujita, M., and J. F. Thisse. "Economics of Agglomeration." *Journal of the Japanese and International Economies* 10, no. 4 (1996):339–378.

Fukuyama, F. *Trust: The Social Virtues and the Creation of Prosperity.* New York: Free Press, 1995.

Gabszewicz, J., and J. F. Thisse. "Spatial Competition and the Location of Firms." In *Location Theory,* edited by J. Gabszewicz, J. F. Thisse, M. Fujita, and U. Schweizer, 1–71. Chur (Switzerland): Harwood Academic, 1986.

Gagné, P., M. Lefevre, and G. Tremblay. *The Québec Industrial Atlas.* Montreal: Publi-Relais, 1993.

Gertler, M. "Between the Global and the Local: The Spatial Limits to Productive Capital." In *Spaces of Globalization: Reasserting the Power of the Local,* edited by K. R. Cox. New York: Guilford, 1997.

Giarratani, F. "Nurture the Symbiosis Between Economics and Regional Science (It's Worth the Trouble)." *International Regional Science Review* 17, no. 3 (1994):343–346.

Giersch, H. "Economic Union Between Nations and the Location of Industries." *Review of Economic Studies* 17 (1949):87–97.

Glaeser, E. "Cities, Information, and Economic Growth." *Cityscape: A Journal of Policy Development and Research* 1, no. 1 (1994):9–47.

Glaeser, E., H. Kallal, J. Scheinkman, and A. Shleifer. "Growth in Cities." *Journal of Political Economy* 100, no. 6 (1992):1126–1152.

Glaeser, E., and D. Maré. "Cities and Skills." Working paper 4728, National Bureau of Economic Research, 1994.

Glaeser, E., J. Scheinkman, and A. Shleifer. "Economic Growth in a Cross-Section of Cities." Working paper 5013, National Bureau of Economic Research, 1995.

Glasmeier, A. "Factors Governing the Development of High Tech Industry Agglomerations: A Tale of Three Cities." *Regional Studies* 22, no. 4 (1988):287–301.

———. "High-Tech Industries and the Regional Division of Labor." *Industrial Relations* 25, no. 2 (1986):197–211.

———. "The Role of Merchant Wholesalers in Industrial Agglomeration Formation." *Annals of the Association of American Geographers* 80, no. 3 (1990):394–417.

———. Technological Discontinuities and Flexible Production Networks: The Case of Switzerland and the World Watch Industry." *Research Policy* 20, no. 5 (1991):469–485.

Glasmeier, A., and R. Leichenko. "From Free Market Rhetoric to Free Market Reality: The Future of the U.S. South in an Era of Globalization." *International Journal of Urban and Regional Research* 20, no. 4 (1996):601–615.

Glasmeier, A., J. Thompson, and A. Kays. "The Geography of Trade Policy: Trade Regimes and Location Decisions in the Textile and Apparel Complex." *Transactions of British Geographers* 18 (Spring 1993):19–35.

Goldstein, G., and T. Gronberg. "Economies of Scale and Economies of Agglomeration." *Journal of Urban Economics* 16, no. 1 (1984):91–104.

Gotchev, A., ed. *The Competitiveness of Bulgarian Export Industries.* Sofia: Albatross, 1997.

Granovetter, M. "Economic Action and Social Structure: The Problem of Embeddedness." *American Journal of Sociology* 91 (1985):481–510.

Hagstrom, P. "Unshackling Corporate Geography." *Human Geography.* Geografiska Anneler, Series B, vol. 72, B(1990):3–12.

Hall, P., and A. Markusen. *Silicon Landscapes.* Boston: Allen and Unwin, 1985.

Hanson, G. "Agglomeration, Dispersion, and the Pioneer Firm." *Journal of Urban Economics* 39, no. 3 (1996):255–281.

Harris, C. "The Market as a Factor on the Localization of Industry in the United States." *Annals of the Association of American Geographers* 64 (1954):315–348.

Harrison, B. "Industrial Districts: Old Wine in New Bottles?" *Regional Studies* 26 (1992):469–483.

Harrison, B., M. Kelley, and J. Gant. "Innovative Firm Behavior and Local Milieu: Exploring the Intersection of Agglomeration, Firm Effects, Industrial Organization, and Technological Change." *Economic Geography* 72, no. 3 (1996):233–258.

Harrison, B., and M. Weiss. *Workforce Development Networks.* Thousand Oaks, Calif.: Sage, 1998.

Henderson, V. "Ways to Think About Urban Concentration: Neoclassical Urban Systems versus the New Economic Geography." *International Regional Science Review* 19, no. 1-2 (1996):31–36.

———. "Where Does an Industry Locate?" *Journal of Urban Economics* 35, no. 1 (1994):83–104.

Henderson, V., A. Kuncoro, and M. Turner. "Industrial Development in Cities." *Journal of Political Economy* 103, no. 5 (1995):1067–1090.

Henton, D., J. Melville, and K. Walesh. *Grassroots Leaders for a New Economy.* San Francisco: Jossey-Bass, 1997.

Hernesniemi, H., M. Lammi, and P. Ylä-Anttila. *Advantage Finland: The Future of Finnish Industries.* Helsinki: ETLA, Taloustieto Oy, 1996.

Hill, E., and Z. Austrian. "Creating Competitive Industries in Northeast Ohio by Strengthening Industrial Clustering Behavior within the Region." Proposal to The Greater Cleveland Growth Association and Cleveland Tomorrow, 1996.

Hirschman, A. *The Strategy of Economic Development.* New Haven: Yale University Press, 1958.

Hyvärinen, J., and J. Borsos. *Emerging Estonian Industrial Transformation: Towards a Dual Industrial Strategy for Estonia.* Helsinki: ETLA, Taloustieto Oy, 1994.

Ingham, V. "The Competitiveness of Argentina: From Sheltered Markets to Global Rivalry." Ph.D. diss., Tufts University, 1995.

Isard, W. *Location and Space-Economy*. Cambridge, Mass.: MIT Press, 1956.

Jacobs, D., P. Boekholt, and W. Zegveld. *De Economische Kracht van Nederland: een toepassing van Porters benadering van de concurrentiekracht van landen*. SMO-Boek, TNO-Beleidsstudies. S-Gravenhage: Stichting Maatschappij en Onderneming, 1990.

Jacobs, D., and M. W. de Jong. "Industrial Clusters and the Competitiveness of the Netherlands: Empirical and Conceptual Issues." *De Economist* 140, no. 2 (1992):233–252.

Jacobs, D., and A. P. de Man. "Clusters, Industrial Policy and Firm Strategy: A Menu Approach." *Technology Analysis and Strategic Management* 8, no. 4 (1996):425–437.

Jaffe, A., M. Trajtenberg, and R. Henderson. "Geographic Localization of Knowledge Spillovers as Evidenced by Patent Citations." *Quarterly Journal of Economics* CVIII, no. 3 (1993):577–598.

Krugman, P. *Development, Geography, and Economic Theory*. Cambridge, Mass.: MIT Press, 1995.

———. "Increasing Returns and Economic Geography." *Journal of Political Economy* 99, no. 3 (1991A):483–499.

———. *Strategic Trade Policy and the New International Economics*. Cambridge, Mass.: MIT Press, 1986.

———. *Trade and Geography*. Cambridge, Mass.: MIT Press, 1991(B).

Leymaire, S., and J. Tripier. *Maroc: Le Prochain Dragon*. Paris: Karthala, 1993.

Lloyd, P., and P. Dicken. *Location in Space*. London: Harper & Row, 1977.

Lösch, A. *The Economics of Location*. New Haven: Yale University Press, 1954.

McCann, Philip. "Logistics Costs and the Location of the Firm: A One-Dimensional Comparative Static Approach." *Location Science* 4, no. 1/2 (1996):101–116.

———. "On Regional Science: Some Thoughts From a Recent Observer." *International Regional Science Review* 18, no. 2 (1995A):249–252.

———. "Rethinking the Economics of Location and Agglomeration." *Urban Studies* 32, no. 3 (1995B):563–577.

Mair, A. "Strategic Localization: The Myth of the Postnational Enterprise." In *Spaces of Globalization: Reasserting the Power of the Local*, edited by K. R. Cox. New York: Guilford, 1997.

Markusen, A. "Growing Pains: Thoughts on Theory, Method, and Politics for a Regional Science of the Future." *International Regional Science Review* 17, no. 3 (1995A):319–326.

———. "The Interaction Between Regional and Industrial Policies: Evidence from Four Countries." In *Proceedings of The World Bank Annual Conference on Development Economics 1994*, Supplement to The World Bank Economic Review and The World Bank Research Observer, edited by Michael Bruno and Boris Pleskovic. Washington, D.C.: The International Bank for Reconstruction and Development/The World Bank, 1995(B).

———. *Profit Cycles, Oligopoly, and Regional Development.* Cambridge, Mass.: MIT Press, 1985.

Marshall, Alfred. *Industry and Trade.* 3d ed. London: Macmillan, 1920.

———. *Principles of Economics.* 8th ed. London: Macmillan, 1920.

Metropolitan Council. *Twin Cities Industry Cluster Study.* Minneapolis/St. Paul, Minn.: Metropolitan Council, 1995.

Ministry of Economic Affairs. *Economie met open grenzen.* The Hague: Sdu, 1990.

———. *Kennis in beweging.* The Hague: Sdu, 1995.

Mitchell, C. "Identifying and Stimulating Clusters: A Local Initiative with National Import." *Firm Connections* 5, no. 5 (1997):11–12.

Monitor Company. *The Competitiveness of Portugal: Building Self-Confidence.* Cambridge, Mass.: Monitor Company, 1994(A).

———. *Creación de la ventaja para Colombia.* Bogotá, Colombia: Colombia Camara de Comercio de Bogotá, 1994(B).

———. *La estrategia competitiva para Bogotá.* Bogotá, Colombia: Colombia Camara de Comercio de Bogotá, 1995(A).

———. *Estudi Sobre els Avantatges Competitius de Catalunya.* Cambridge, Mass.: Monitor Company, 1992.

———. *El valle del cauca de cara al mundo.* Cali, Colombia: Camara de comercio de Cali, 1995(B).

Nadvi, K., and H. Schmitz. "Industrial Clusters in Less Developed Countries: Review of Research Experiences and Research Agenda." Discussion paper 339, Institute of Development Studies, University of Sussex, U. K., 1994.

Nelson, R., ed. *National Innovation Systems, A Comparative Analysis.* New York: Oxford University Press, 1993.

Nohria, N. "Information and Search in the Creation of New Business Ventures: The Case of the 128 Venture Group." In *Networks and Organizations:*

Structure, Form and Action, edited by N. Nohria and R. Eccles. Boston: Harvard Business School Press, 1992.

Oakey, R. "High Technology Industry and Agglomeration Economies." In *Silicon Landscapes,* edited by P. Hall and A. Markusen, 94–117. Boston: Allen & Unwin, 1985.

Pari Sabety, J., and J. Griffin. "Pro-Competitive Alliances: New Vehicles for Regional, State and Community Based Economic Development." *Economic Development Review* 14, no. 2 (1996):2–6.

Pascal, A., and J. McCall. "Agglomeration Economies, Search Costs, and Industrial Location." *Journal of Urban Economics* 8, no. 3 (1980):383–388.

Perrow, C. "Small-Firm Networks." In *Networks and Organizations: Structure, Form and Action,* edited by N. Nohria and R. Eccles. Boston: Harvard Business School Press, 1992.

Piore, M., and C. Sabel. *The Second Industrial Divide.* New York: Basic Books, 1984.

Porter, M. "Comment on 'Interaction Between Regional and Industrial Policies: Evidence from Four Countries,' by Markusen." In *Proceedings of The World Bank Annual Conference on Development Economics 1994,* Supplement to The World Bank Economic Review and The World Bank Research Observer, edited by Michael Bruno and Boris Pleskovic, 303–307. Washington, D.C.: The International Bank for Reconstruction and Development/The World Bank, 1995(A).

———. "Competitive Advantage, Agglomeration Economies, and Regional Policy." *International Regional Science Review* 19, nos. 1 & 2 (1996):85–94.

———. "The Competitive Advantage of the Inner City." *Harvard Business Review* 73, no. 3 (1995B):55–71.

———. *The Competitive Advantage of Nations.* New York: Free Press, 1990.

———. "The Role of Location on Competition." *Journal of the Economics of Business* 1, no. 1 (1994):35–39.

Porter, M., and J. Armstrong. "Canada at the Crossroads." *Business Quarterly* 56, no. 4 (1992):6–10.

Porter, M., S. Borner, R. Weder, and M. Enright. *Internationale Wettbewerbsvorteile: Ein Strategisches Konzept fur die Schweiz.* Frankfurt/New York: Campus Verlag, 1991.

Porter, M., and R. Caves. "From Entry Barriers to Mobility Barriers: Conjectural Decisions and Contrived Deterrence to New Competition." *Quarterly Journal of Economics* (1977):241–262.

Porter, M., G. Crocombe, and M. Enright. *Upgrading New Zealand's Competitive Advantage.* Auckland: Oxford University Press, 1991.

Porter, M., Ö. Sölvell, and I. Zander. *Advantage Sweden,* 2d ed. Stockholm, Sweden: Norstedts Juridik, 1993.

Porter, M., H. Takeuchi, and M. Sakakibara. *Two Japans: Competitive Advantage and Disadvantage of the Japanese Economy,* in press.

Pade, H. *Voekst og dynamik I dansk erhvervsliv.* København: Danmarks Internationale Koncurrenceevne, Schultz, 1991.

Preer, R. *The Emergence of Technopolis: Knowledge-Intensive Technologies and Regional Development.* New York: Praeger, 1992.

Puga, D. "The Rise and Fall of Regional Inequalities." Discussion paper 314, Centre for Economic Performance, London School of Economics, U.K., 1996.

Puga, D., and A. Venables. "The Spread of Industry: Spatial Agglomeration in Economic Development." *The Journal of the Japanese and International Economies* 10, no. 4 (1996):440–464.

Putnam, R. D., R. Leonardi, and R. Y. Nanetti. *Making Democracy Work: Civic Traditions in Modern Italy.* Princeton, N.J.: Princeton University Press, 1993.

Pyke, F., G. Becattini, and W. Sengenberger, eds. *Industrial Districts and Interfirm Cooperation in Italy.* Geneva: International Institute for Labour Studies, 1990.

Pyke, F., and W. Sengenberger, eds. *Industrial Districts and Local Economic Regeneration.* Geneva: International Institute for Labour Studies, 1992.

Quah, D. "Regional Convergence Clusters Across Europe." Discussion paper 1286, Centre for Economic Policy Research, London, 1996.

Rauch, J. "Productivity Gains from Geographic Concentration of Human Capital: Evidence from the Cities." *Journal of Urban Economics* 34, no. 3 (1993):380–400.

Rivera-Batiz, F. "Increasing Returns, Monopolistic Competition, and Agglomeration Economies in Consumption and Production." *Journal of Regional Science and Urban Economics* 18 (1988):125–153.

Rodriguez, M. D., M. Prats, M. Enright, and E. Ballarin. "The Catalan Leather Industry." Case 9-795-105. Boston: Harvard Business School, 1995.

Rogers, E. M. *Diffusion of Innovations.* 4th ed. New York: Free Press, 1995.

Rosenfeld, S. "Bringing Business Clusters into the Mainstream of Economic Development." *European Planning Studies* 5, no. 1 (1997):3–23.

———. *Industrial-Strength Strategies, Regional Business Clusters, and Public Policy.* Washington, D.C.: The Aspen Institute Rural Economic Policy Program, 1995.

———. "Overachievers, Business Clusters that Work: Prospects for Regional Development." Paper presented at The Graylyn Center, Winston-Salem, North Carolina, May 1996(A).

———. "United States: Business Clusters." In *Networks of Enterprises and Local Development,* 179–202. Paris: OECD, 1996(B).

Saxenian, A. "The Cheshire Cat's Grin: Innovation, Regional Development and the Cambridge Case." Working paper 497, Institute of Urban and Regional Development, University of California, Berkeley, 1989.

———. *Regional Advantage: Culture and Competition in Silicon Valley and Route 128.* Cambridge, Mass.: Harvard University Press, 1994.

Schmitz, H. "Small Shoemakers and Fordist Giants: Tale of a Supercluster." *World Development* 23, no. 1 (1995):9–28.

Scotchmer, S., and J. F. Thisse. "Space and Competition: A Puzzle." *Annals of Regional Science* 26 (1992):269–286.

Scott, A. "The Aerospace-Electronics Industrial Complex of Southern California: The Formative Years, 1940–1960." *Research Policy* 20, no. 5 (1991):439–456.

———. "Industrial Organization and Location: Division of Labor, the Firm, and Spatial Process." *Economic Geography* 63 (1987):214–231.

Sears, G. "Technopole Survey: Interviews with Community Leaders." Paper presented at the Technopolis '97 Conference, Ottawa, Canada, September 1997.

Stahl, K. "Differentiated Products, Consumer Search, and Locational Oligopoly." *Journal of Industrial Economics* 31, no. 1/2 (1982):97–114.

Steinbock, D. *The Competitive Advantage of Finland: From Cartels to Competition?* Helsinki: ETLA, Taloustieto Oy, 1998.

Sternberg, E. "The Sectoral Cluster in Economic Development Policy: Lessons from Rochester and Buffalo," *Economic Development Quarterly* 5, no. 4 (1991):342–356.

Stigler, G. "The Division of Labor Is Limited by the Extent of the Market." *Journal of Political Economy* 59, no. 3 (1951):185–193.

Storper, M. "Territories, Flows, and Hierarchies in the Global Economy." In *Spaces of Globalization: Reasserting the Power of the Local,* edited by K. R. Cox. New York: Guilford Press, 1997.

Storper, M., and R. Salais. *The Regional World: Territorial Development in the Global Economy.* New York: Guilford Press, 1997(A).

———. *Worlds of Production: The Action Frameworks of the Economy.* Cambridge, Mass.: Harvard University Press, 1997(B).

Swyngedouw, E. "Neither Global Nor Local: 'Glocaliation' and the Politics of Scale." In *Spaces of Globalization: Reasserting the Power of the Local,* edited by K. R. Cox, 137–166. New York: Guilford Press, 1997.

Tyson, L. *Who's Bashing Whom? Trade Conflict in High-Technology Industries.* Washington, D. C.: Institute for International Economics, 1992.

Ullring, S. "Challenges in International Shipping." Paper presented at the Massachusetts Institute of Technology, Cambridge, Mass., January 1995.

van den Bosch, F. A. J., and A. P. de Man. "Government's Impact on the Business Environment and Strategic Management." *Journal of General Management* 19, no. 3 (1994):50–59.

———, eds. *Perspectives on Strategy: Contributions of Michael E. Porter.* Dordrecht: Kluwer Academic Publishers, 1997.

van der Linde, C. *The Competitive Advantage of Germany.* Ph.D. diss., University of St. Gallen, 1991.

———. *Deutsche Wettbewerbsvorteile.* Düsseldorf: Econ, 1992.

von Hippel, E. *The Sources of Innovation.* New York: Oxford University Press, 1988.

Voyer, R. "Can High-Tech Clusters be Created?" Paper presented at the Technopolis '97 Conference, Ottawa, Canada, September 1997.

———. "Emerging High-Technology Industrial Clusters in Brazil, India, Malaysia, and South Africa." Paper presented at the Technopolis '97 Conference, Ottawa, Canada, September 1997.

Waits, M. J. "State of Cluster-Based Economic Development in Arizona." In *Global Networking of Regional Optics Clusters,* edited by R. Breault, 1–10. Denver, Colo.: The International Society for Optical Engineering, 1996.

Waits, M. J., and G. Howard. "Industry Clusters: A Multipurpose Tool for Economic Development." *Economic Development Commentary* 20, no. 3 (1996):5–11.

Weber, A. *Theory of the Location of Industries,* trans. Carl J. Friedrich. Chicago: University of Chicago Press, 1929.

Zieminski, J., and J. Warda. "What Makes Technopoles Tick: A Corporate Perspective." Paper presented at the Technopolis '97 Conference, Ottawa, Canada, September 1997.

Cluster-Based Reports and Case Studies

Appalachia

"Exports, Competitiveness, and Synergy in Appalachian Industry Clusters: A Report to the Appalachian Regional Commission." Regional Technology Strategies, Inc., Chapel Hill, N.C., February 1997.

Arizona

Arizona Optics Industry Association. "Arizona Optics Industry Resource Directory and Industry Analysis." Arizona Optics Industry Association, Tucson, Ariz., May 1996.

"New Foundations for Arizona's Future: Defining Economic Development for the 1990s." Governor's Strategic Partnership for Economic Development, 1990.

"Greater Tucson Strategic Economic Plan." Greater Tucson Economic Council, Tucson, Ariz., July 1996.

"Greater Tucson Legislative Agenda." Greater Tucson Strategic Partnership for Economic Development, Tucson, Ariz., January 1997.

Brazil

Chadha, S., M. Harrison, R. Parsley, and V. Serra. "The Brazilian Financial Cluster." Student report prepared for Seminar on Competition and Competitiveness, Harvard Business School, Boston, Mass., May 1997.

California

Alexander, R., R. Arney, N. Black, E. Frost, and A. Shivananda. "The California Wine Cluster." Student report prepared for Seminar on Competition and Competitiveness, Harvard Business School, Boston, Mass., May 1997.

Center for Economic Competitiveness. "An Economy at Risk." Menlo Park, Calif.: Center for Economic Competitiveness, SRI International, 1992.

Evans, D., N. Hugh, T. Kazinos, and P. Teague. "The Hollywood Filmed Entertainment Cluster." Student report prepared for Seminar on Competition and Competitiveness, Harvard Business School, Boston, Mass., May 1997.

Joint Venture, Silicon Valley Network. "Blueprint for a Twenty-first Century Community." San Jose, Calif.: Joint Venture, Silicon Valley Network, Phase II Report, June 1993.

———. "The Joint Venture Way: Lessons for Regional Rejuvenation." San Jose, Calif.: Joint Venture, Silicon Valley Network, 1995.

———. "Joint Venture's Index of Silicon Valley: Measuring Progress Toward a Twenty-first Century Community." San Jose, Calif.: Joint Venture, Silicon Valley Network, 1995, 1996, 1997. [An annual publication.]

Canada

Porter, M., and Monitor Company. "Canada at the Crossroads: The Reality of a New Competitive Environment." Ottawa: Business Council on National Issues and the Government of Canada, 1991.

Central America

Andrade, M., A. Espejel, D. Lazarus, V. Silhy, and M. Velasco. "Textiles and Apparel in Central America." Student report prepared for Seminar on Competition and Competitiveness, Harvard Business School, Boston, Mass., May 1997.

Connecticut

Department of Economic and Community Development. "Connecticut: The International State." Department of Economic and Community Development International Strategic Plan, Hartford, Conn., 1991.

Chandra, R., R. Becherer, D. Young, and A. De Maria. "Review of the CONNECT Program Progress and the Connecticut Photonics Cluster." In *Global Networking of Regional Optics Clusters*, edited by R. Breault, 63–69. Bellingham, Wash.: The International Society for Optical Engineering, 1996.

Ireland

Industrial Policy Review Group. "A Time for Change: Industrial Policy for the 1990s." Dublin: The Stationery Office, 1992.

O'Malley, E., K. A. Kennedy, and R. O'Donnell. *Report to the Industrial Policy Review Group on the Impact of the Industrial Development Agencies.* Dublin: The Stationery Office, 1992.

Massachusetts

Porter, M., and Monitor Company. "The Competitive Advantage of Massachusetts." Boston, Mass.: Office of the Secretary of State, 1991.

Porter, M., R. Wayland, and C. J. Grogan, in collaboration with Challenge to Leadership. "Toward a Shared Economic Vision for Massachusetts." December 1992.

Minnesota

Metropolitan Council. "The Financial Services Cluster of the Twin Cities: A Follow-Up to the Twin Cities Industry Cluster Study." Minneapolis/St. Paul: Metropolitan Council, October 1995(A).

——. "Twin Cities Industry Cluster Study." Minneapolis/St. Paul: Metropolitan Council, 1995(B).

"Southeastern Minnesota Industrial Cluster Study." The Initiative Fund of Southeastern and South Central Minnesota, Owatonna, Minn., September 1996.

Morocco

DRI/McGraw-Hill and FOCS. *Le Maroc Compétitif: A Cluster Development Initiative in Morocco.* Washington, D.C.: DRI/McGraw Hill and FOCS, September 1996.

——. *Le Maroc Compétitif: Plan d'Action Stratégique.* Washington, D.C.: DRI/McGraw Hill and FOCS, November 1996.

Netherlands

Ministry of Economic Affairs. *Economie met Open Grenzen.* The Hague: Sdu, 1990.

——. *Kennis is Beweging.* The Hague: Sdu, 1995.

New York City

Aslett, M., J. Kondo, S. Pannu, K. Park, and A. Rodriguez. "New York Fashion: Recommendations from a Global Cluster Analysis." Student report prepared for Seminar on Competition and Competitiveness, Harvard Business School, Boston, Mass., May 1997.

Beauchamp, C., D. Bodor, M. Capur, E. Kuo, and T. Shoeb. "Multimedia in Manhattan." Student report prepared for Seminar on Competition and Competitiveness, Harvard Business School, Boston, Mass., May 1997.

New Zealand

Graduate School of Business and Government Management. *Partnership and Enterprise: Putting Porter into Practice.* Auckland: GMBGM Special Report Series No. 3, 1991.

Northern Ireland

Northern Ireland Growth Challenge. *North Ireland Growth Challenge: Interim Summary of Progress.* Northern Ireland Growth Challenge, Belfast, Northern Ireland, May 1995.

Pennsylvania

Pittsburgh High Technology Council and Southwestern Pennsylvania Industrial Resource Center. "Thinking Differently About the Region: Southwestern Pennsylvania's Manufacturing and Technology Assets." Pittsburgh: Pittsburgh High Technology Council and Southwestern Pennsylvania Industrial Resource Center, 1994.

Portugal

Forum para a Competitividade. *A Competitividade da Economia Portuguesa.* Lisboa: Forum para a Competitividade, 1995.

Ministério da Industria e Energia. *O Projecto Porter: A aplicaçao a Portugal 1993/1994.* Lisboa: Ministério da Industrio e Energia, 1995.

Monitor Company, under the direction of M. Porter. "Construir as Vantagens Competitivas de Portugal." Lisboa: Forum para a Competitividade, 1994.

CHAPTER 8

How Global Companies Win Out

Thomas Hout

Michael E. Porter

Eileen Rudden

HOLD THAT OBITUARY ON American manufacturers. Some not only refuse to die but even dominate their businesses worldwide. At the same time Ford struggles to keep up with Toyota, Caterpillar thrives in competition with another Japanese powerhouse, Komatsu. Though Zenith has been hurt in consumer electronics, Hewlett-Packard and Tektronix together profitably control 50 percent of the world's industrial test and measurement instrument market. American forklift truck producers may retreat under Japanese pressure, but two U.S. chemical companies—Du Pont and Dow—dramatically outperform their competitors.

How do these American producers hold and even increase profitability against international competitors? By forging integrated, global strategies to exploit their potential; and by having a long-term outlook, investing aggressively, and managing factories carefully.

The main reason is that today's international competition in many industries is very different from what it has been. To succeed, an international company may need to change from a multidomestic competitor, which allows individual subsidiaries to compete independently in differ-

We acknowledge that this article is based in part on a paper coauthored by Eric Vogt.

September–October 1992

ent domestic markets, to a global organization, which pits its entire worldwide system of product and market position against the competition. (For a more complete discussion of this distinction, see the insert "What Is a Global Industry?")

What Is a Global Industry?

The nature of international competition among multinationals has shifted in a number of industries. *Multinational* generally denotes a company with significant operations and market interests outside its home country. The universe of these companies is large and varied, encompassing different kinds of organizations operating in different types of industries. From a strategic point of view, however, there are two types of industries in which multinationals compete: *multidomestic* and *global.* They differ in their economics and requirements for success.

In *multidomestic* industries a company pursues separate strategies in each of its foreign markets while viewing the competitive challenge independently from market to market. Each overseas subsidiary is strategically independent, with essentially autonomous operations. The multinational headquarters will coordinate financial controls and marketing (including brand name) policies worldwide and may centralize some R&D and component production. But strategy and operations are decentralized. Each subsidiary is a profit center and expected to contribute earnings and growth commensurate with market opportunity.

In a multidomestic industry, a company's management tries to operate effectively across a series of worldwide positions, with diverse product requirements, growth rates, competitive environments, and political risks. The company prefers that local managers do whatever is necessary to succeed in R&D, production, marketing, and distribution but holds them responsible for results. In short, the company competes with other multinationals and local competitors on a market-by-market basis. A large number of successful U.S. companies are in multidomestic industries, including Procter & Gamble in household products, Honeywell in controls, Alcoa in aluminum, and General Foods in branded foods.

A *global* industry, in contrast, pits one multinational's entire worldwide system of product and market positions against another's. Various country subsidiaries are highly interdependent in terms of operations and strategy. A country subsidiary may specialize in manufacturing only part of its product line, exchanging products with others in the system. Country profit targets vary, depending on individual impact on the cost position or effectiveness of the entire worldwide system—or on the subsidiary's position relative to a key global competitor. A company may set prices in one country to have an intended effect in another.

A large number of U.S. multinationals are in global industries. Among them, along with their principal competitors, are: Caterpillar and Komatsu in large construction equipment; Timex, Seiko, and Citizen in watches; General Electric, Siemens, and Mitsubishi in heavy electrical equipment.

In a global business, management competes worldwide against a small number of other multinationals in the world market. Strategy is centralized, and various aspects of operations are decentralized or centralized as economics and effectiveness dictate. The company seeks to respond to particular local market needs, while avoiding a compromise of efficiency of the overall global system.

The multidomestic and global labels apply to distinct industries and industry segments, not necessarily to whole industry groups. For example, within the electrical equipment industry, heavy apparatus such as steam turbine generators and large electric motors is typically global while low-voltage building controls and electrical fittings are multidomestic in nature.

The global company—whatever its nationality— tries to control leverage points, from cross-national production scale economies to the foreign competitors' sources of cash flow. By taking unconventional action, such as lowering prices of an important product or in key markets, the company makes the competitor's response more expensive and difficult. Its main objective is to improve its own effectiveness while eroding that of its competitors.

Not all companies can or should forge a global strategy. While the rewards of competing globally are great, so are the risks. Major policy and operating changes are required. Competing globally demands a number of unconventional approaches to managing a multinational business to sometimes allow:

Major investment projects with zero or even negative ROI.

Financial performance targets that vary widely among foreign subsidiaries.

Product lines deliberately overdesigned or underpriced in some markets.

A view of country-by-country market positions as interdependent and not as independent elements of a worldwide portfolio to be increased or decreased depending on profitability.

Construction of production facilities in both high and low labor-cost countries.

Not all international businesses lend themselves to global competition. Many are multidomestic in nature and are likely to remain so, competing on a domestic-market-by-domestic-market basis. Typically these businesses have products that differ greatly among country markets and have high transportation costs, or their industries lack sufficient. scale economies to yield the global competitors a significant competitive edge.

Before entering the global arena, you must first decide whether your company's industry has the right characteristics to favor a global competitor. A careful examination of the economies of the business will highlight its ripeness for global competition.[1] Simply put, the potential for global competition is greatest when significant benefits are gained from worldwide volume—in terms of either reduced unit costs or superior reputation or service—and are greater than the additional costs of serving that volume.

Identifying potential economies of scale requires considerable insight. Advantages to increased volume may come not only from larger production plants or runs but also from more efficient logistics networks or higher volume distribution networks. Worldwide volume is also particularly advantageous in supporting high levels of investment in research and development; many industries requiring high levels of R&D, such as pharmaceuticals or jet air craft, are global. The level of transport or importing costs will also influence the business's tendency to become global. Transport is a relatively small portion of highly traded optical goods, for example, while it is a barrier in trading steel reinforcing bars.

Many businesses will not be able to take the global step precisely because their industries lack these characteristics. Economies of scale may be too modest or R&D spending too closely tied to particular markets. Products may differ significantly across country boundaries, or the industry may emphasize distribution, installation, and other local activities. Lead times may be short, as in fashion-oriented businesses and in many service businesses, including printing. Also, transportation costs and government barriers to trade may be high, and distribution maybe fragmented and hard to penetrate. Many consumer nondurable businesses or low-technology assembly companies fall into this category, as do many heavy raw-material processing industries and wholesaling and service businesses.

Our investigation into the strategies of successful global companies leads us to believe that a large group of international companies have global potential, even though they may not know it. Almost every industry that is now global—automobiles and TV sets, for example—was not at one time. A company must see the potential for changing competitive interaction in its favor to trigger a shift from multidomestic to global competition. And because there is no guarantee that the business can become global, the company must be willing to risk the heavy investment that global competition requires.

A company that recognizes its business as potentially global but not yet so must ask itself whether it can innovate effectively and must understand its impact on the competition to find the best answers to these three questions:

What kind of strategic innovation might trigger global competition?

Is it in the best position among all competitors to establish and defend the advantages of global strategy?

What kind of resources—over how long a period—will be required to establish the leading position?

The Successful Global Competitor

If your industry profile fits the picture we've drawn, you can better judge your ability to make these kinds of unconventional decisions by looking at the way three global companies have succeeded. These organizations (American, European, and Japanese) exemplify the global competitor. They all perceive competition as global and formulate strategy on an integrated, worldwide basis. Each has developed a strategic innovation to change the rules of the competitive game in its particular industry. The innovation acts as a lever to support the development of an integrated global system but demands a market position strong enough to implement it.

Finally, the three companies have executed their strategies more aggressively and effectively than their competitors. They have built barriers to competitive responses based on careful assessment of competitors' behavior. All three have the financial resources and commitment needed to compete unconventionally and the organizational structure to manage an integrated system.

We will take a careful look at each of these three and how they developed the strategic innovation that led, on the one hand, to the globalization of their industries and, on the other, to their own phenomenal success. The first company's innovation was in manufacturing; the second, in technology; and the third, in marketing.

THE CATERPILLAR CASE: WARRING WITH KOMATSU

Caterpillar Tractor Company turned large-scale construction equipment into a global business and achieved world leadership in that business even when faced with an able Japanese competitor. This accomplishment was difficult for a variety of reasons. For one thing, specifications of construction equipment varied widely across countries. Also, machines are expensive to transport, and field distribution—including user financing, spare parts inventories, and repair facilities—is demanding and best managed locally.

Navy Seabees who left their Caterpillar equipment in other countries following World War II planted the seeds of globalization. The company established independent dealerships to service these fleets, and this base of units provided a highly profitable flow of revenue from spare parts, which paid for inventorying new units. The Caterpillar dealers quickly became self-sustaining and to this day are larger, better financed, and do a more profitable parts business than their competitors. This global distribution system is one of Cat's two major barriers against competition.

The company used its worldwide production scale to create its other barrier. Two-thirds of the total product cost of construction equipment is in heavy components—engines, axles, transmissions, and hydraulics—whose manufacturing costs are capital intensive and highly sensitive to economies of scale. Caterpillar turned its network of sales in different countries into a cost advantage by designing product lines that use identical components and by investing heavily in a few large-scale, state-of-the-art component manufacturing facilities to fill worldwide demand.

The company then augmented the centralized production with assembly plants in each of its major markets—Europe, Japan, Brazil, Australia, and so on. At these plants Cat added local product features, avoiding the high transportation cost of end products. Most important, Cat became a direct participant in local economies. The company achieved lower costs without sacrificing local product flexibility and became a friend rather than a threat to local governments. No single "world model" was forced on the customer, yet no competitor could match Caterpillar's production and distribution cost.

Not that they haven't tried. The most recent—and greatest—challenge to Caterpillar has come from Komatsu (see Table 8.1 for a financial comparison). Japan's leading construction equipment producer forged its own global strategy based on exporting high-quality products from centralized facilities with labor and steel cost advantages. Over the last decade Komatsu has gained some 15 percent of the world construction-

---

Table 8.1   Financial Comparison of Caterpillar and Komatsu

	Caterpillar	Komatsu
1980 estimated sales of construction equipment	$7.2 billion	$2.0 billion
1974–1979 averages:		
Return on capital employed	13.6%	4.0%
Debt/equity	0.4 times	2.1 times
Return on equity	19.1%	12.2%
Percent of earnings retained	69%	65%
Spare parts as percent of total revenue (estimated)	30% to 35%	15% to 20%
Cash flow available from operations	$681 million	$140 million

Source: Financial statements.

equipment market, with a significant share of sales in nearly every product line in competition with Cat.

Caterpillar has maintained its position against Komatsu and gained world share. The two companies increasingly dominate the market vis-á-vis their competitors, who compete on a domestic or regional basis. What makes Caterpillar's strategy so potent? The company has fostered the development of four characteristics essential to defending a leading world position against a determined competitor.

1. **A global strategy of its own.** Caterpillar's integrated global strategy yields a competitive advantage in cost and effectiveness. Komatsu simply plays catch-up ball rather than pulling ahead. Facing a competitor that has consciously devised a global strategy, Komatsu is in a much weaker position than were Japanese TV and automobile manufacturers when they took off.

2. **Willingness to invest in manufacturing**. Caterpillar's top management appears committed to the kind of flexible automated manufacturing systems that allow full exploitation of the economies of scale from its worldwide sales volume.

3. **Willingness to commit financial resources**. Caterpillar is the only Western company that matches Komatsu in capital spending per employee; in fact, its overall capital spending is more than three times that of the Japanese company. Caterpillar does not divert resources into other businesses or dissipate the financial advantage against Komatsu by paying out excessive dividends. Because Komatsu's profitability is lower than Caterpillar's, it must exhaust debt capacity in trying to match Cat's high investment rates.

4. **Blocking position in the Japanese market**. In 1963, Caterpillar formed a joint venture in Japan with Komatsu's long-standing but weaker competitor, Mitsubishi. Operationally, the venture serves the Japanese market. Strategically, it acts as a check on the market share and cash flow of Komatsu. Japan accounts for less than 20 percent of the world market but yields over 80 percent of Komatsu's worldwide cash flow. The joint venture is number two in market position, serving to limit Komatsu's profits. Japanese tax records indicate that the Cat-Mitsubishi joint ven-

ture has earned only modest profits, but it is of great strategic value to Caterpillar.[2]

L.M. ERICSSON: CAN SMALL BE BEAUTIFUL?

L.M. Ericsson of Sweden has become a successful global competitor by developing and exploiting a technological niche. Most major international telephone-equipment producers operated first in large, protected home markets that allowed the most efficient economies of scale. The additional profits helped underwrite R&D and provided good competitive leverage. Sweden's home market is relatively small, yet Ericsson translated the advent of electronic switching technology into a powerful global lever that befuddled competitors in its international market niche. In the electromechanical era of the 1960s, the telephone switching equipment business was hardly global. Switching systems combine hardware and software. In the electromechanical stage, 70 percent of total installed costs lay in hardware and 70 percent of hardware cost was direct labor, manufacturing overhead, and installation of the equipment.

Each country's telephone system was unique, economies of scale were low, and the wage rate was more important than the impact of volume on costs. In the late 1960s, major international companies (including Ericsson) responded by moving electro-switching production to LDCs not only to take advantage of cheaper labor but also to respond to the desire of government telephone companies to source

Eventually, each parent company centrally sourced only the core software and critical components and competed on a domestic-market-by domestic-market basis. For its part, Ericsson concentrated investment in developing countries without colonial ties to Europe and in smaller European markets that lacked national suppliers and that used the same switching systems as the Swedish market.

The telecommunications industry became global when, in the 1970s, electronic switching technology emerged, radically shifting cost structures and threatening the market position Ericsson had carved for itself. Software is now 60 percent of total cost; 55 percent of hardware cost is in sophisticated electronic components whose production is highly scale sensitive. The initial R&D investment required to develop a system has jumped to more than $100 million, which major international compa-

298 The Competitiveness of Locations

Table 8.2   Ericsson's Technology Lever: Reduction of Software Cost through Modular Design

	Representative Systems	New Modules Required	Existing Modules Used
Year 1	Södertalje, Sweden	57	0
Year 2	Orleans, France	22	57
Year 3	Åbo, Finland	0	77

Source: Boston Consulting Group, *A Framework for Swedish Industrial Policy* (Uberforlag, Stockholm, 1978).

nies could have amortized more easily than Ericsson. In addition, the move to electronics promised to destroy the long-standing relationships Ericsson enjoyed with smaller government telephone companies. And it appeared that individual electronic switching systems would require a large fixed-cost software investment for each country, making the new technology too expensive for the smaller telephone systems, on which Ericsson thrived.

Ericsson knew that the electronic technology would eventually be adapted to small systems. In the meantime, it faced the possibility of losing its position in smaller markets because of its inability to meet the ante for the new global competition.

The company responded with a preemptive strategic innovation—a modular technology that introduced electronics to small telephone systems. The company developed a series of modular software packages that could be used in different combinations to meet the needs of diverse telephone systems at an acceptable cost. Moreover, each successive system required fewer new modules. As Table 8.2 shows, the first system—Södertalje in Sweden—required all new modules, but by the third year, the Åbo system in Finland required none at all. Thus the company rapidly amortized development costs and enjoyed economies of scale that steepened as the number of software systems sold increased. As a result, Ericsson was able to compete globally in small systems.

Ericsson's growth is accelerating as small telephone systems convert to electronics. The company now enjoys an advantage in software cost and variety that continually reinforces itself. Through this technology

Ericsson has raised a significant entry barrier against other companies in the small-system market.

HONDA'S MARKETING GENIUS

Before Honda became a global company, two distinct motorcycle industries existed in the world. In Asia and other developing countries, large numbers of people rode small, simple motorcycles to work. In Europe and America, smaller numbers of people. drove big, elaborate machines for play. Since the Asian motorcycle was popular as an inexpensive means of transportation, companies competed on the basis of price. In the West, manufacturers used styling and brand image to differentiate their products. No Western market exceeded 100,000 units; wide product lines and small volumes meant slight opportunities for economies of scale. Major motorcycle producers such as Harley-Davidson of the United States, BMW of West Germany, and Triumph and BSA of the United Kingdom traded internationally but in only modest volumes.

Honda made its industry global by convincing middle-class Americans that riding motorcycles could be fun. Because of the company's marketing innovations, Honda's annual growth rate was greater than 20 percent from the late 1950s to the late 1960s. The company then turned its attention to Europe, with a similar outcome. Honda invested for seven full years before sustaining profitability in Europe, financing this global effort with cash flows earned from a leading market position at home and in the United States.

Three crucial steps were decisive in Honda's achievement. First, Honda turned market preference around to the characteristics of its own products and away from those of American and European competitors. Honda targeted new consumers and used advertising, promotions, and trade shows to convince them that its motorbikes were inexpensive, reliable, and easy to use. A large investment in the distribution network —2,000 dealerships, retail missionaries, generous warranty and service support, and quick spare-parts availability—backed up the marketing message.

Second, Honda sustained growth by enticing customers with the upper levels of its product line. Nearly half of new bike owners purchased larger, more expensive models within 12 months. Brand loyalty proved very high. Honda exploited these trends by expanding from its line of a few small motorcycles to one covering the full range of size and features by 1975. The result: self-sustaining growth in dollar volume and a model mix that allowed higher margins. The higher volume reduced marketing and distribution costs and improved the position of Honda and other Japanese producers who invaded the 750cc "super bike" portion of the market traditionally reserved for American and European companies. Here Honda beat the competition with a bike that was better engineered, lower priced, and whose development cost was shared over the company's wide product line.

The third step Honda took was to exploit economies of scale through both centralized manufacturing and logistics. The increasing volume of engines and bike assemblies sold (50,000 units per month and up) enabled the company to use less costly manufacturing techniques unavailable to motorcycle producers with lower volumes (see Table 8.3). Over a decade, Honda's factory productivity rose at an average annual rate of

Table 8.3   The Effect of Volume on Manufacturing Approaches in Motorcycle Production

Cost Element	Low Volume	High Volume
Machine tools	Manual, general purpose	Numerical control, special purpose
Changeover time	Manual, slow (hours)	Automatic positioning, fast (minutes)
Work-in-process inventory	High (days of production)	Low (hours of production)
Materials handling	Forklift trucks	Automated
Assembly	Bay assembly	Motorized assembly line
Machine tool design	Designed outside the company, available throughout industry	Designed in-house, proprietary
Rework	More	Less

Source: *Strategy Alternatives for the British Motorcycle Industry*, a report prepared for the British Secretary of State for Industry by the Boston Consulting Group, July 30, 1975.

13.1 percent—several times higher than European and American producers. Combined with lower transportation cost, Honda's increased output gave it a landed cost per unit far lower than the competition's. In turn, the lower production cost helped fund Honda's heavy marketing and distribution investment. Finally, economies of scale in marketing and distribution, combined with low production cost, led to the high profits that financed Honda's move into automobiles.

WHAT CAN WE LEARN?

Each of these successful global players changed the dynamics of its industry and pulled away from its major competitors. By achieving economies of scale through commonality of design, Caterpillar exploited both its worldwide sales volume and its existing market for parts revenues. Competitors could not match its costs or profits and therefore could not make the investment necessary to catch up. Ericsson created a cost advantage by developing a unique modular technology perfectly adapted to its segment of the market. Its global strategy turned electronics from a threat to Ericsson into a barrier to its competitors. Honda used marketing to homogenize worldwide demand and unlock the potential for economies of scale in production, marketing, and distribution. The competition's only refuge was the highly brand-conscious, small-volume specialty market.

In each case, the industry had the potential for a worldwide system of products and markets that a company with a global strategy could exploit. Construction equipment offered large economies of scale in component manufacture, allowing Caterpillar to neutralize high transportation costs and government barriers through local assembly. Ericsson unlocked scale economies in software development for electronic switches. The modular technology accommodated local product differences and governments' desire to use local suppliers. Once Honda's marketing techniques raised demand in major markets for products with similar characteristics, the industry's economies of scale in production combined with low transportation costs and low tariff barriers to turn it into a global game.

In none of the cases did success result from a "world product." The companies accommodated local differences without sacrificing production costs. The global player's position in one major market strengthened its position in others. Caterpillar's design similarities and central compo-nent facilities allowed each market to contribute to its already favorable cost structure. Ericsson's shared modules led to falling costs each time a system was sold in a new country. Honda drew on scale economies from the centralized production of units sold in each market and used its U.S. marketing and distribution experience to succeed in Europe.

In addition to superior effectiveness and cost advantages, a winning global strategy always requires abilities in two other dimensions. The first is timing. The successful global competitor uses a production cost or distribution advantage as a leverage point to make it more difficult or expensive for the competitor to respond. The second is financial. The global innovator commits itself to major investment before anyone else, whether in technology, facilities, or distribution. If successful, it then reaps the benefits from increased cash flows from either higher volume (Honda and Ericsson) or lower costs (all three companies). The longer the competitor takes to respond, the larger the innovator's cash flows. The global company can then deploy funds either to increase investment or lower prices, creating barriers to new market entrants.

A global player should decide against which of its major competitors it must succeed first in order to generate broad-based success in the future. Caterpillar located in the Far East not only to source products locally but also to track Komatsu. (Cat increasingly sources product and manufacturing technology from Japan.) Ericsson's radical departure in technology was aimed squarely at ITT and Siemens, whose large original market shares would ordinarily have given them an advantage in the smaller European and African markets. Honda created new markets in the United States and Europe because its most powerful competitors, Yamaha and Kawasaki, were Japanese. By exploiting the global opportu-nity first, Honda got a head start, and it remained strong even when competitors' own international ambitions came to light.

Playing the Global Chess Game

Global competition forces top management to change the way it thinks about and operates its businesses. Policies that made sense when the company was multidomestic may now be counterproductive. The most powerful moves are those that improve the company's worldwide cost position or ability to differentiate itself and weaken key worldwide competitors. Let us consider two potential moves.

The first is preempting the leading positions in major newly industrializing countries (NICs). Rapid growth in, for example, Mexico, Brazil, and Indonesia has made them an important part of the worldwide market for many capital goods. If its industry has the potential to become global, the company that takes a leading position in these markets will have made a decisive move to bar its competitors. Trade barriers are often prohibitively high in these places, and a company that tries to penetrate the market through a *self-contained* local subsidiary is likely to fall into a trap.

The astute global competitor will exploit the situation, however, by building a specialized component manufacturing facility in an NIC which will become an integral part of a global sourcing network. The company exports output of the specialized facility to offset importing complementary components. Final assembly for the domestic and smaller, neighboring markets can be done locally. (Having dual sources for key items can minimize the risk of disruption to the global sourcing network.)

A good illustration of this strategy is Siemens's circuit breaker operation in Brazil. When the company outgrew its West German capacity for some key components, it seized the opportunity presented by Brazilian authorities seeking capital investments in the heavy electrical equipment industry. Siemens now builds a large portion of its common components there, swaps them for other components made in Europe, and is the lowest-cost and leading supplier of finished product in Brazil.

Another move that can be decisive in a global industry is to establish a solid position with your largest customers to block competitors. Many businesses have a few customers that dominate the global market. The global competitor recognizes their importance and prevents current or prospective competitors from generating any sales.

A good example is a British company, BSR, the world's largest producer of automatic record changers. In the 1970s, when Japanese exports of audio equipment were growing rapidly, BSR recognized that it could lose its market base in the United States and Europe if the Japanese began marketing record changers. BSR redesigned its product to Japanese specifications and offered distributors aggressive price discounts and inventory support. The Japanese could not justify expanding their own capacity. BSR not only stalled the entry of the Japanese into the record-changer market but it also moved ahead of its existing competitor, Garrard.

A global company can apply similar principles to block the competition's access to key distributors or retailers. Many American companies have failed to seize this opportunity in their unwillingness to serve large, private-label customers (e.g., Sears, Roebuck) or by neglecting the less expensive end of their product line and effectively allowing competitors access to their distributors. Japanese manufacturers in particular could then establish a toehold in industries like TV sets and farm equipment.

The decision on prices for pivotal customers must not be made solely on considerations of ROI. Equally important in global competition is the impact of these prices on prospective entrants and the cost of failing to protect and expand the business base. One way to control the worldwide chess game in your favor is to differentiate prices among countries.

Manage Interdependently

The successful global competitor manages its business in various countries as a single system, not a portfolio of independent positions. In the view of portfolio planning theory, a market's attractiveness and the strength of a company's position within it determine the extent of corporate resources devoted to it. A company should defend strong positions and try to turn weak ones around or abandon them. It will pursue high-profit and/or high-growth markets more aggressively than lower-profit or lower-growth ones, and it will decide on a stand-alone basis whether to compete in a market.

Accepting this portfolio view of international competition can be disastrous in a global industry. The global competitor focuses instead on its ability to leverage positions in one country market against those in other markets. In the global system, the ability to leverage is as important as market attractiveness; the company need not turn around weak positions for them to be useful.

The most obvious leverage a company obtains from a country market is the volume it contributes to the company's overall cost or effectiveness. Du Pont and Texas Instruments have patiently won a large sales volume in the sophisticated Japanese market, for example, which supports their efforts elsewhere. Winning a share of a market that consistently supports product innovation ahead of other markets—like the United States in long-haul jet aircraft—is another leverage point. The competitor with a high share of such a market can always justify new product investment. Or a market can contribute leverage if it supports an efficient scale manufacturing facility for a region—like Brazil for Siemens. Finally, a market can contribute leverage if a position in it can be used to affect a competitor's cash flow.

Organization: The Achilles Heel

Organizational structure and reporting relationships present subtle problems for a global strategy. Effective strategic control argues for a central product-line organization; effective local responsiveness, for a geographic organization with local autonomy. A global strategy demands that the product-line organization have the *ultimate* authority, because without it the company cannot gain systemwide benefits. Nevertheless, the company still must balance product and area needs. In short, there is no simple solution. But there are some guidelines to help.

No one organization structure applies to all of a company's international businesses. It may be unnecessarily cumbersome, for example, to impose a matrix structure on all business. Organizational reporting lines should probably differ by country market depending on that market's role. An important market that offers high leverage, as in the foregoing examples, must work closely with the global business-unit managers at headquarters. Coordination is crucial to success. But the manager of a market outside the global system will require only sets of objectives under a regional reporting system.

Another guideline is that organizational reporting the lines and structures should change as the nature of the international business changes. When a business becomes global, the emphasis should shift toward centralization. As countries increase in importance, they must be brought within the global manager's reach. Over time, if the business becomes less global, the company's organization may emphasize local autonomy.

The common tendency to apply one organizational structure to all operations is bound to be a disadvantage to some of them. In some U.S. companies, this approach inhibited development of the global strategy their industries required.

Match Financial Policies to Competitive Realities

If top management is not careful, adherence to conventional financial management and practices may constrain a good competitive response in global businesses. While capital budgeters use such standard financial tools as DCF return analysis or risk profiles to judge investments and creditors and stock analysts prefer stable debt and dividend policies, a global company must chart a different course.

ALLOCATING CAPITAL

In a global strategy, investments are usually a long-term, interdependent series of capital commitments, which are not easily associated with returns or risks. The company has to be aware of the size and timing of the total expenditures because they will greatly influence competitors' new investment response. Most troublesome, however, is that revenues from investments in several countries may have to buildup to a certain point before the company earns *any* return on investment.

A global strategy goes against the traditional tests for capital allocation: project-oriented DCF risk-return analysis and the country manager's record of credibility. Global competition requires a less mechanical approach to project evaluation. The successful global competitor develops at least two levels of financial control. One level is a profit and cost center for self-contained projects; the other is a strategy center for tracking interdependent efforts and competitors' performance and reactions. Global competitors operate with a short time frame when monitoring the execution of global strategy investments and a long time frame when evaluating such investments and their expected returns.

DEBT AND DIVIDENDS

Debt and dividend policies should vary with requirements of the integrated investment program of the whole company. In the initial stages, a company with a strong competitive position should retain earnings to build and defend its global position. When the industry has become global and growth slows or the returns exceed the reinvestment needed to retain position, the company should distribute earnings to the rest of the corporation and use debt capacity elsewhere, perhaps in funding another nascent global strategy.

Honda's use of debt over the last twenty-five years illustrates this logic (see Table 8.4). In the mid-1950s, when Honda held a distant second place in a rapidly growing Japanese motorcycle industry, the company had to leverage its equity 3.5 times to finance growth. By 1960, the Japanese market had matured and Honda emerged dominant. The debt-equity ratio receded to 0.5 times but rose again with the company's international expansion in motorcycles. In the late 1960s, Honda made

---

Table 8.4   Honda Motor Company's Financial Policy from 1954 to 1980

Period	Interest-bearing debt-to-equity ratio	Strategic phase
1954–55	3.5 times	Rapid growth in domestic motorcycle market; Honda is low-margin, number two producer
1959–60	0.5	Domestic motorcycle market matured; Honda is dominant high-margin producer
1964–65	0.7	Honda makes major penetration of U.S. motorcycle market
1969–70	1.6	Honda begins major move in doemstic auto market
1974–75	1.3	Investment pause due to worldwide recession; motorcycle is major cash generator
1978–80	1.0	Auto exports are highly profitable, as are motorcycles

Source: Annual reports.

a major move to the automobile market, requiring heavy debt. At that time, motorcycle cash flows funded the move.

Which Strategic Road to Take?

There is no safe formula for success in international business. Industry structures continuously evolve. The Caterpillar, Ericsson, and Honda approaches will probably not work forever. Competitors will try to push industrial trends away from the strengths of the industry leaders, and technological or political changes may force the leading companies to operate in a multidomestic fashion once again.

Strategy is a powerful force in determining competitive outcomes, whether in international or domestic business. And although adopting a global strategy is risky, many companies can dramatically improve their positions by fundamentally changing the way they plan, control, and operate their businesses. But a global strategy requires that managers think in new ways. Otherwise the company will not be able to recognize the nature of competition, justify the required investments, or sustain the change in everyday behavior needed.

If the company can successfully execute a global strategy, it may find itself joining the ranks of the truly successful international companies. Whether they be Japanese, American, European, or otherwise, the strategic thread that ties together companies like IBM, Matsushita, K. Hattori (Seiko), Du Pont, and Michelin clearly shows that the rules of the international competitive game have changed.

NOTES

1. For a more detailed look at globalization see Michael E. Porter, *Competitive Strategy.*

2. For more on this subject, see Craig M. Watson, "Counter-Competition Abroad to Protect Home Markets," *Harvard Business Review* 60, no. 5 (1982): 40.

CHAPTER 9

Competing Across Locations

Enhancing Competitive
Advantage through a
Global Strategy

Michael E. Porter

ONE OF THE MOST POWERFUL forces affecting companies since World War II has been the globalization of competition. We have seen transport and communication costs fall, the flow of information and technology across borders increase, national infrastructures grow more similar, and trade and investment barriers ease. The result has been marked growth in international trade and investment. In an ever-widening range of industries a global, as opposed to a domestic, strategy is a necessity.

Unsurprisingly, as the globalization of competition has become more apparent, research and corporate practice in international strategy has taken on greater prominence. Thinking about international strategy has focused by and large on the power of the multinational company to create competitive advantage through globalness. A global strategy, involving operations spread among many countries, has been seen as a powerful means of reaping economies of scale, assimilating and responding to international market needs, and efficiently assembling resources such

This article draws on an earlier article, "Global Competition and the Localization of Competitive Advantage," written with Rebecca E. Wayland, published in *Proceedings of the Integral Strategy Collegium*, Graduate School of Business, Indiana University (Greenwich, Connecticut: JAI Press, 1995). The article benefited from research by Hernan Cristerna and joint work with Michael Enright, of the University of Hong Kong, and Örjan Sölvell and Ivo Zander, both of Stockholm School of Economics. I am also grateful for the helpful comments offered by David Collis and Hans Thorelli.

as capital, labor, raw materials, and technology from around the world. Authors as diverse as Ohmae, Reich, and Bartlett and Ghoshal see the global firm as transcending national boundaries. The national identity of a corporation must be replaced, in this view, by a strategic paradigm that knows no borders.

When considering the globalization of competition, however, one must confront an apparent paradox: Although companies do indeed compete globally and inputs such as raw materials, capital, and scientific knowledge now move freely around the world, strong evidence shows that location continues to play a crucial role in competitive advantage. First, striking differences persist in the economic performance of nations and of states and cities within nations. Second, in a wide variety of industries, the world's leading competitors are all based in one or two countries; this tendency is especially marked if *industry* is defined narrowly in terms meaningful for setting strategy and if industries are excluded in which government policy heavily distorts competition. This geographic concentration of competitive advantage appears not only in established industries such as automobiles and machine tools but also in new industries such as software, biotechnology, and advanced materials. Third, global companies have indeed dispersed activities to many countries, but they continue to concentrate in one location a critical mass of their most important activities for competing in each of their major product lines or businesses. Interestingly, however, these "home bases," as I call them, are not all located in the home country or even in the same country.

This article aims to reconcile these seemingly divergent perspectives into a framework for understanding the nature of international competition and the shift from domestic to global strategy in particular businesses. In creating competitive advantage, global strategy must integrate the roles of both location and a global network of activities. To bring the framework to life, I employ extended examples drawn from three premier global competitors: the Novo-Nordisk Group, based in Denmark; Hewlett-Packard, based in the United States; and Honda, based in Japan. (See the insert "Case Studies of Three Global Competitors.") This article concludes by examining how its framework can be employed to develop a concrete global strategy for a particular business.

While the discussion here frames the issues in terms of global competition, the principles can be applied much more generally. The same

Case Studies of Three Global Competitors

To bring life to this discussion of global strategy, I have drawn on the international activities of three prototypical global corporations. For each of these successful international leaders, headquartered variously in Europe, Japan, and the United States, profiles of their international operations probe the international configuration and coordination of their activities.

• *Novo-Nordisk Group (Novo)*. Headquartered in Denmark, Novo is the world's leading exporter of insulin and industrial enzymes.[a] Novo generates more than 90 percent of its revenues outside its home country and has strong positions in Europe, the United States, and Japan. Data for 1991 show that 27 percent of its employees were based outside Denmark and 19 percent of its total assets were located outside Europe. Novo had seven R&D locations and nine production sites outside Denmark. The company distributes its products in one hundred countries and had its own marketing subsidiaries in forty-three countries. Novo sourced animal pancreases, a key raw material for insulin, in more than twenty countries. It also sourced its capital from around the world, funding 83 percent of its short-term debt and 54 percent of its long-term debt in currencies other than the Danish kroner. The company was listed on the London and the New York stock exchanges.

• *Honda*. Headquartered in Japan, Honda is one of the world's leading producers of automobiles and is the world leader in motorcycles.[b] Honda generated 61 percent of its revenues outside Japan in 1991 and held particularly strong market positions in Asia and North America. It based 22 percent of its employees and 39 percent of its total assets outside Japan, maintained production and assembly facilities in thirty-nine countries, and distributed its automobiles and motorcycles in 150 countries. Inputs and capital were sourced worldwide; the company was listed on the Tokyo and the New York stock exchanges.

• *Hewlett-Packard (HP)*. Headquartered in the United States, HP is the world's largest and most diversified manufacturer of electronic measurement and testing equipment as well as a leader in other products such as printers, medical instruments, and computers.[b] HP generated 54 percent of its revenues outside the United States in 1991. It based 38 percent of its 93,000 employees and 50 percent of its total assets outside the United States and operated 600 sales and support offices and distributorships in 110 countries. It was listed on the London, Paris, Tokyo, Frankfurt, Stuttgart, Switzerland, and Pacific stock exchanges.

Globalization has led each of these firms to spread activities extensively around the world. Hewlett-Packard's location philosophy is instructive. HP locates low-skilled manufacturing activities with high direct-labor content in low-cost areas, at an estimated savings of 40 to 75 percent compared to U.S. locations. Some component assembly and manufacturing for personal computers (PCs), for example, is conducted in Singapore, and electronic component manufacturing is conducted in Malaysia. Hewlett-Packard also locates some medium-skilled activities in lower-cost countries; for example, some product and process engi-neering activities (such as manufacturing cost reduction programs) are conducted at the PC manufacturing facilities in Singapore, process engi-neering for some new electronic component products has been transferred to the manufacturing plant in Malaysia, and some software coding and maintenance has been subcontracted to countries such as India, China, Eastern Europe, and the former Soviet Union, where college-educated programmers work for 40 to 60 percent lower wages than those in the United States.

a. Information on Novo draws on Enright (1989) and field research.
b. The profiles of Honda and of Hewlett-Packard are based on Porter and Wayland (1995). Most figures are taken from 1991 annual reports and other corporate filings.

framework applies in examining *competition across locations* at any level—cities, states, regions, or even groups of neighboring countries. The same thought process can be used by a local competitor seeking to compete nationally or by a national competitor seeking to compete regionally.

A General Framework for Global Strategy

Most issues in competitive strategy are the same for domestic and global companies; in both cases, success is a function of the attractiveness of the industries in which the firm competes and of the firm's relative position in those industries.[1] The firm's performance within the industry depends on its competitive advantages (or disadvantages) vis-à-vis its rivals. Competitive advantage is manifested either in lower costs than those of rivals or in the ability to differentiate and command a premium price that exceeds the extra cost of differentiating. Some competitive advantages arise because of differences in operational effectiveness, but the most sustainable advantages come from occupying a unique competitive position. Both domestic and global companies must understand the structure of their industry, identify their sources of competitive advantage, and analyze competitors.

"Global" strategy, then, refers to the special issues that arise when firms compete across nations. The need for a global strategy depends on the nature of international competition in a particular industry. There is not one single pattern of international competition, but many. Not all industries require a global strategy. The nature of international competition in industries can be arrayed along a spectrum. At one end are *multidomestic* industries, present in many countries (even every country) but industries in which competition takes place on a country-by-country basis with little or no linkage. Examples include most types of retailing, metal fabrication, construction, and many services. Indeed, numerous industries are regional within nations or even local. At the other end of the spectrum are truly *global industries*, in which competition in different countries is linked because a firm's position in a given country significantly affects its position elsewhere. Prominent examples are commercial aircraft, consumer electronics, and many types of industrial machinery.

In multidomestic industries, there is no need for a global strategy. Here, the international strategy should be a series of distinct domestic strategies. Country operating units should be given wide latitude and autonomy. In global industries, however, firms must create integrated strategies involving all countries simultaneously. Just because a firm is multinational, therefore, does not mean that it has or should have a global strategy. The essential question in global strategy is this: When and how is the international whole more than the sum of the domestic parts?

To understand the underpinnings of competitive advantage and what a global strategy might contribute requires that what a firm does is disaggregated into its *value chain* (see Figure 9.1).[2] A firm competing in a particular business performs an array of discrete but interrelated economic activities; for example, it assembles products, its salespeople make sales visits, it processes orders, it recruits and trains, staff and it purchases inputs. All activities normally involve some procedures or routines, human resources, physical assets, enabling technologies, and the creation and use of information. A firm's "strengths," "competen-

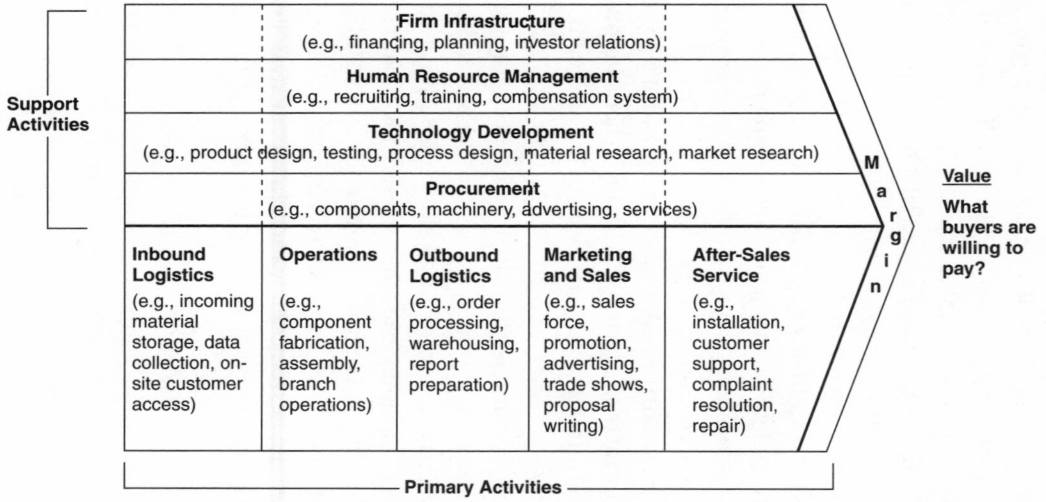

Figure 9.1 The Value Chain

cies," "capabilities," and "resources,"—common phrases in discussions of strategy—can best be understood in terms of the particular activities to which they apply.

The value chain groups a firm's activities into several categories, distinguishing between those directly involved in producing, marketing, delivering, and supporting a product or service; those that create, source, and improve inputs and technology; and those performing overarching functions such as raising capital or overall decisionmaking. Within each of these categories appears an array of discrete activities or economic/ organizational processes, at the level of field repair, inbound materials receiving and storage, billing, and reviewing and rewarding employees. The particular activities performed depend at least partly on the business.

Activities form the basic foundation of competitive advantage in either cost or differentiation. As noted above, competitive advantage results when a firm has the ability to perform the required activities at a collectively lower cost than rivals or to perform some activities in unique ways that create non-price buyer value and support a premium price. Creating buyer value depends, in turn, on how a firm influences the activities of its channels and end-users.

Competitive advantage in activities can arise from both operational effectiveness and strategy. Operational effectiveness refers to performing given or similar activities at the state of best practice. This includes the use of the most cost-effective purchased inputs, managerial practices, and the like. Part of the need for a global strategy is to enhance operational effectiveness through such things as global sourcing and transfer of knowledge.

A firm's strategy defines its particular configuration of activities and how they fit together. Different strategic positions involve tailoring activities to produce particular product/service varieties, to address the special needs of particular customer groups, or to access most efficiently certain types of customers. Broadly targeted competitors seek to gain advantages by sharing activities across an array of industry segments. Narrowly targeted competitors (which I term *focusers*) seek advantage by tailoring activities to the needs of one (or a few) particular segment(s). Global strategy also bears on strategic positioning by affecting the tradeoffs underlying a position or the ability to tailor activities to it.

The value chain provides the basic tool to highlight the strategy issues unique to a global strategy. Both domestic firms and global firms have value chains. The domestic (or multidomestic) company performs all the activities in the home (or in each) country. What distinguishes a global strategy, however, is the latitude to spread parts of the value chain among countries. The basic choices can be grouped into two areas:

1. *Configuration:* Configuration focuses on *where* each of the activities in a firm's value chain are located; assembly can be in one country, for example, and product R&D in another. Moreover, a given activity can occur in one location or be dispersed to many.
2. *Coordination:* Coordination focuses on the nature and extent to which dispersed activities are *coordinated* in a network or remain *autonomous,* that is, tailored to local circumstances.

Any firm that competes internationally must sell in many countries. Some activities, such as many of those involved in sales and distribution, necessarily are tied to the customer's location. A firm seeking to sell in a country must either establish its own marketing and sales and physical distribution activities there or rely on others (for example, distributors or joint venture partners). Other activities in the value chain, however, can be uncoupled from the customer, giving the international firm discretion over the number and location of such activities. In multidomestic strategy, the company performs the entire value chain in each country, and each country subsidiary has near or complete autonomy to tailor the activities to the country. In a global strategy, the company selectively locates activities in different countries and coordinates among them to harness and extend the competitive advantage of the network.

CONFIGURATION

The international configuration of a firm's activities creates competitive advantage through the choice of *where* to locate each activity and the *number of sites.* One motivation for locating an activity is *comparative advantage* in performing the activity, such as a location with the most cost-effective pool of raw materials or people. Some multinational software firms locate software debugging and program maintenance activities in India, for example, to access low-cost but good-quality programmers. Because the location with comparative advantage varies by activity, the global firm has the potential to gain the benefits of arbitraging comparative advantages across locations.

A second and less understood motivation for the choice of location is *competitive* or *productivity advantage*. Here, as will be discussed further, activities or groups of activities are located in the countries with the most attractive environments for innovation and productivity growth.

Choice of location includes deciding not only where to locate but how many sites to maintain. The firm might *concentrate* an activity in one location to serve the world or *disperse* the activity to several or many locations. By concentrating an activity, firms may gain economies of scale or may progress rapidly down the learning curve. Concentrating a group of linked activities in one location may also allow a firm to better coordinate among them. Dispersing activities to a number of locations, in contrast, may be justified by the need to minimize transportation and storage costs, hedge against the risks of a single activity site, tailor activities sensitive to local market differences, facilitate learning about country and market conditions that can be transmitted to headquarters, or respond to local government pressure or incentives to locate in a country in order to sell or produce there.

The global firm should disperse only those activities necessary to obtain these benefits, and no more. Both efficiency and the ease of innovation are enhanced, other things being equal, if as many activities as possible are co-located. This minimizes coordination and transshipment costs. Sometimes, a firm must disperse one activity to a country in order to gain the ability (or permission from local government) to concentrate other activities elsewhere. Establishing local assembly plants in a variety of countries, for example, may allow a company to import scale-sensitive components into each of the countries and thus to concentrate more scale-sensitive component production elsewhere. The particular activities to be dispersed should be those incurring the least sacrifice in terms of economies of scale or learning and requiring the least close coordination with other activities.

COORDINATION

A global strategy can also contribute to competitive advantage by coordinating activities across locations. Coordinating methods, technology, and output decisions across dispersed activities contributes a number of potential competitive advantages. These include the ability to respond to shifting comparative advantages (for example, raw materials prices or exchange rates); to share learning among countries; to reinforce the corporate brand reputation for mobile buyers who encounter the firm in different places (for example, McDonald's or Coca-Cola); to differentiate with or more efficiently serve multinational buyers who simultaneously deal with several of the firm's country units; to bargain more effectively with governments by using the carrot and stick of expanding or contracting local operations; or to respond more cost effectively to competitive threats by choosing the location at which to do battle. Some of these benefits relate to operational effectiveness, while others reinforce a company's unique position. Successful coordination is important to gaining the benefits of dispersing activities. These potential advantages of coordination are weighed against the benefits of allowing each dispersed unit to act autonomously and tailor its activities to local circumstances. An international strategy involving high levels of autonomy for dispersed units is favored where local needs and conditions vary, all customers are local, or few economies of scale are present. In practice, the balance between coordination and autonomy varies by activity.

A number of forms of coordination across locations are possible, including setting common standards, exchanging information, and allocating responsibility among sites. Coordination that involves allocating responsibilities across countries, such as assigning worldwide responsibility for producing particular models to different locations, can unleash economies of scale. Coordination involving information exchange reaps the benefits of worldwide learning. Coordination, then, can allow a firm to realize the advantages of dispersing its activities; conversely, the failure to coordinate activities can lessen those advantages. A central issue in coordination is how and where information, technology, and other knowledge gained from disparate locations becomes integrated into and reflected in products, processes, and other activities. The home base performs these essential functions.

Coordination across geographically dispersed locations involves daunting organization challenges, among them those of language and cultural differences and of aligning individual managers' and subsidiaries' incentives with those of the global enterprise as a whole. Some forms of coordination, such as allocating responsibilities for component production to different locations, require less ongoing interchange than others.

PATTERNS OF GLOBAL STRATEGY

Some competitive advantages of a global strategy arise from location; others arise from the overall global network and the way it is managed. Every global strategy normally begins with some kind of advantage in location, reflected in the company's competitive position. This advantage allows the firm to penetrate international markets and to overcome the inherent disadvantages of competing in another country. Without some asymmetry among firms based in different countries, competition will remain multidomestic.

The initial location-based advantages are extended and supplemented through a global network. The advantages of other locations can also be tapped by dispersing activities. Global competition has not one but many patterns, depending on the particular activities concentrated or dispersed, the location of various activities, and how activities are coordinated. In multidomestic industries, industry structure favors a highly dispersed configuration in which each country contains virtually the entire value chain. In such industries, strong benefits follow from allowing country units nearly full strategic autonomy. Competition in an industry globalizes when the competitive advantages of a global network are substantial enough to overcome the local focus and local knowledge of domestic or country-centered competitors.

Global strategy thus takes many forms. The particular global strategy utilized by McDonald's in the fast food industry differs a good deal from that of Intel in the microprocessor industry or Boeing in commercial aircraft. Figure 9-2, which sketches Citibank's global strategy in retail banking, illustrates this. As in many service businesses, Citibank disperses many activities, including branch operations, marketing, and even many forms of processing. Active coordination occurs on image,

Concentrated	Dispersed
• Common brand name • Product development • Software development • Global information infrastructure • Credit-card clearing system • Human resource training program development	• Branch and ATM networks • Tele-banking centers • Advertising and promotion • Regional processing centers
Coordinated	**Decentralized**
• Consistent corporate image • Consistent branch office design • Consistent service delivery	• Adaptation to local language and business customs • Regulatory compliance

Figure 9.2   Citicorp: Global Configuration and Coordination in Retail Banking

branch design, and service standards, however, and local autonomy is narrowly drawn.

Firms can play a major role in shaping the benefits and costs of a global versus a domestic strategy. Firms can redefine competition through strategic innovations that increase the advantages of a global strategy or that reduce its disadvantages. Becton Dickinson, for example, created worldwide demand for disposable syringes in favor of reusable glass syringes. Partly by being the first mover, Becton Dickinson emerged as the world leader. Other firms have triggered globalization by pioneering new approaches to competing that increased economies of scale or by inventing product designs or production processes that reduced the cost of tailoring products to differing country needs. Many global industry leaders have emerged because they were early to perceive and act on these levers. Theodore Levitt's 1983 work on the globalization of markets is typically seen as arguing the merits of world products.[3] Yet often unrecognized is the essay's more important emphasis on the ability of the firm to *create* world products by pioneering new approaches to segmentation and marketing rather than by passively responding to preexisting needs.

Location and Global Competition

The globalization of competition allows firms to gain competitive advantages independent of location by coordinating activities across a wide range of countries. Globalization has not eliminated the importance of location in competition, however. In hundreds of industries that have been studied, including services and newly emerging fields such as software, advanced materials, and biotechnology, the world leaders are typically headquartered in just a few countries and sometimes in only one country.[4] The three case studies of companies presented in the insert "Case Studies of Three Global Competitors" all fit this rule. Honda is not the only Japanese success story in the automotive and motorcycle industries: Nine of the world's automobile companies and the four dominant global motorcycle companies are all based in Japan. Similarly, Hewlett-Packard is not the only successful U.S. firm in its industries: U.S. firms are preeminent in workstations, PCs, medical instruments, and test and instrumentation equipment. Two Denmark-based companies, merged into Novo-Nordisk only in 1989, dominated insulin exports. Novo is also a world leader in industrial enzymes, a field in which other Danish firms compete as well.

The geographic concentration of leading firms *within* nations demonstrates the importance of location to competition even more clearly. The United States presents a particularly interesting example. Despite free trade among the states, a common language and laws, and great similarities across states along many dimensions, successful competitors in particular businesses are far from evenly distributed. Publishing concentrates heavily in New York City; movies and television production, in Hollywood; office furniture, in western Michigan; pharmaceuticals, in Philadelphia and New Jersey; hosiery and home furnishings, in North Carolina; artificial hips and joints, in Indiana: Countless other examples could be added.[5] A similar pattern of geographic concentration can be found, in varying degrees, in every advanced nation.[6]

A close look at the configuration and coordination of activities in global companies also reveals the strong influence of location, including Novo, Hewlett-Packard, and Honda. Accounts emphasizing the widespread geographic dispersion of activities by multinationals can be misleading. Company diversification often means extensive foreign activities, but these may span many entirely different product areas. In a given business, activities are far less dispersed.

A more important distinction in assessing geographic dispersion is that between the *types* of activities located in different countries. International firms tend to concentrate their most sophisticated activities in a single country—often, though less so over time, in their home country. Novo markets its insulin products around the world and sources some inputs globally, but it conducts the most strategically important activities in the value chain—all production and core product and process R&D—in Denmark. Honda has extensive worldwide manufacturing and distribution, but Japan remains the home base for strategy, design, and the production of Honda's most sophisticated components, including all core engine research. Hewlett-Packard's operations encompass more than sixteen thousand product lines sold around the world, yet it concentrates worldwide responsibility (HP refers to this as "worldwide re") for each product line, including core manufacturing, R&D, and decision making, in one particular location.

Additional evidence comes from Asea Brown Boveri (ABB), often cited as the prototype of a company with no national identity.[7] ABB has multiple operations located throughout the world, but it bases global responsibility for establishing business strategy, selecting product development priorities, and allocating production among countries in each product line in a particular geographic location. Leadership for power transformers is based in Germany, for example; electric drives in Finland; and process automation in the United States. Moreover, multinationals seem to be relocating headquarters of particular businesses from one nation to another with increasing frequency.

COMPARATIVE ADVANTAGE VS. COMPETITIVE ADVANTAGE

The apparent paradox between the globalization of competition and a strong national or even local role in competitive advantage can be resolved by recognizing that the paradigm that governs the competition among locations has shifted from *comparative advantage* to the broader notion of *competitive advantage*.

Comparative advantage due to lower factor costs (for example, labor, raw materials, capital, or infrastructure) or size still exists, but it no longer confers competitive advantage in most industries nor supports high wages. Globalization now allows firms to match comparative advantages by sourcing inputs such as raw materials, capital, and even generic scientific knowledge from anywhere and to disperse selective activities overseas to take advantage of low-cost labor or capital. The global firm must do these things to attain operational effectiveness. Failure to disperse activities to access comparative advantages will lead to a competitive *dis*advantage, but doing so yields the firm no advantage.

Similarly, the size of the home market is far less important than the ability to penetrate the much larger world market. Moreover, advancing technology has given firms the capacity to reduce, nullify, or circumvent many weaknesses in comparative advantage. Japanese firms, for example, have prospered in many industries, despite the high local costs of energy and land, by pioneering energy-saving and space-saving innovations such as lean production. New technology also diminishes economies of scale,[8] while vertical integration now gives way to greater outsourcing to specialized suppliers.

The competitive advantage of locations arises not from the availability of low cost inputs or size per se, but from superior productivity in using inputs: Basic inputs create competitive disadvantages, not advantages. The enduring advantages of a location come from providing an environment in which firms can operate productively and continuously innovate and upgrade their ways of competing to more sophisticated levels, thereby allowing rising productivity. Innovation refers not only to technology in the narrow sense but also to ways of marketing, product positioning, and providing service. The most dynamic and innovative companies in such locations can outpace their rivals elsewhere, even entrenched competitors enjoying low-cost factors or economies of scale in older methods of operating. In productivity competition, firms spread activities globally to source inputs and access markets but competitive advantage arises from a process of innovation and productivity growth heavily localized at the firm's "home base" for a particular product line: the location of its strategy development, core product and process R&D, and a critical mass of the firm's sophisticated production (or service provision).[9] At the home base reside the essential skills and technology; it is the integration site for inputs and information sourced from global activities; and the most productive jobs are located there.

The location of a firm's owners or of its corporate headquarters becomes far less significant than the location of the home-based activities for each strategically distinct business.

THE COMPETITIVE ADVANTAGE OF LOCATIONS

The competitive advantages of a location lie in the quality of the environment it provides for achieving high and rising levels of productivity in a particular field. While we tend to think of the sources of competitive advantage as primarily arising within a company, a company's potential for advantage and many of the necessary inputs resides in its proximate environment. Only this can explain why so many successful companies in particular fields emerge in the same country and even in the same region within a country.

My research has highlighted four aspects of a national (and state or local) environment that define the context for growth and innovation and productivity: factor (input) conditions; the context for strategy and rivalry; demand conditions; and related and supporting industries. These four areas, which I collectively term the *diamond*, help explain why companies based in particular locations can achieve consistent innovation and upgrading in particular fields (see Figure 9-3). Diamond theory is treated in greater detail in Chapters 6 and 7. Here I sketch an outline designed to lay the foundation for discussing global strategy.[10]

Factor (Input) Conditions. Factors of production are the basic inputs to competition; they include land, labor, capital, physical infrastructure, commercial or administrative infrastructure, natural resources, and scientific knowledge. The notion of comparative advantage normally refers to the cost and availability of inputs. General purpose inputs, such as sound roads and ports or a cadre of college-educated employees, are necessary to avoid a competitive disadvantage, but they are no longer sufficient for gaining a locational advantage.

The advantages of a location for productivity competition arise instead from high quality inputs and especially from *specialized* inputs, such as pools of skills, applied technology, physical infrastructure, regulatory regimes, legal processes, information, and sources of capital tailored to

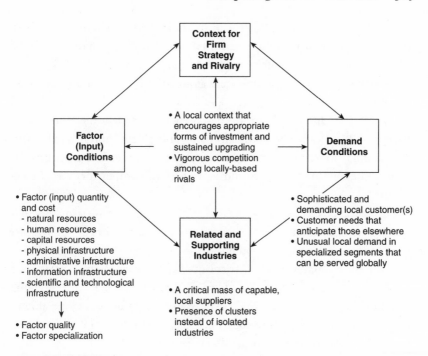

Figure 9.3 Sources of Locational Competitive Advantage

the needs of particular industries. In the United States, for example, preeminence in software rests on a unique concentration of highly trained programmers and other computer science professionals, unparalleled research programs in computer-related disciplines, an efficient body of rules governing software licensing and use, and well-developed and expert sources of risk capital for software firms (many American venture capital firms specialize in software). Hewlett-Packard benefits from some of these advantages in its computer-related businesses. Nations and regions do not inherit the most important factors of production for sophisticated competition; they must create them. This, in turn, depends on the local presence and quality of specialized institutions in education, training, research, data collection, and other areas. Such institutions become a potent source of locational advantage.

More paradoxical as a locational advantage is the role of selective *disadvantages* in basic inputs, such as high costs of land or local raw material shortages. These can lead to competitive advantages because they trigger innovation and/or stimulate the development of specialized institutions. In Holland, for example, a poor climate and land shortages have led to innovations in such areas as greenhouse cultivation methods, breeding technology, and handling techniques for cut flowers, a product for which the Dutch hold more than 60 percent of world exports. Conversely, in locations with abundant labor, cheap debt capital, and bountiful natural resources, firms tend to use these resources less productively, raising their vulnerability to more productive competitors based elsewhere.

The presence of pools of specialized inputs, and the institutions that create and renew them, become an external advantage or collective asset of a location. This public good builds up over time through cumulative investment by many firms, institutions, and government entities. The presence of the external advantage obviates the need for individual companies to bear the internal costs. While a company may be able to gain access to some of the locational assets through global sourcing, many are hard to access from a distance.

Context for Strategy and Rivalry. Locations have advantages in productivity competition if the context of rules, social norms, and incentives there foster sustained investment in forms appropriate to a particular industry. Forms of investment include not only fixed assets but R&D, training, and market development.

The tax system, intellectual property rules, and the stability of the macroeconomic and political environment clearly influences the investment climate in a location. Corporate ownership and governance rules also have an important influence. The American system of venture capital and public offerings constitutes a major advantage in array of industries, for example, while institutional ownership and frequent trading make it more difficult for American companies to compete in lower growth, longer life-cycle fields. Cultural factors can sometimes raise or lower the prestige of various occupations and fields and thereby the investment devoted to them.

The intensity of local rivalry forms another major dimension of the competitive context in a location. Combined with a favorable investment climate, local rivalry is perhaps the most potent advantage of a location. Firms can rarely succeed abroad, for example, unless they have competed with some capable rivals at home. Honda, for example, faces competition from eight other Japanese auto companies, all of which compete internationally. Rivalry among a group of locally-based competitors heightens pressure to innovate and upgrade. Relative performance comparisons among local rivals stimulates rapid improvement. Local rivals, faced with comparable input costs and access to the home market, are forced to seek other ways to compete. In locations with a poor investment climate, rivalry can degenerate to price cutting. Where local conditions support investment, however, rivalry fosters upgrading. Since no firm can comfortably dominate the home market, rivals are forced to compete internationally.[11] Novo, for example, was pushed to export early because it had a strong Danish rival; most other insulin producers were effectively national monopolies. Intense local rivalry creates a situation where individual companies have difficulty staying ahead for long, but the entire local industry progresses more rapidly than competitors based elsewhere.[12]

Demand Conditions. A third type of locational advantage arises from the character of the local market. Advantage arises from having sophisticated and demanding local customers, or customers with unusually intense needs for specialized varieties also in demand elsewhere. Sophisticated, demanding buyers pressure companies to meet high standards, provide a window into evolving customer needs, and prod companies to innovate and move to more advanced segments. Home customers are particularly valuable if their needs anticipate or shape those of other nations, thereby providing "early-warning indicators" of global market trends. Local demand also creates advantages when it highlights industry segments ignored elsewhere. In productivity competition, the character of home demand is far more important than its size.

Home demand conditions reflect local needs, sophistication levels, purchasing power, and even cultural affinities for particular products. Government policies can directly and indirectly influence demand conditions in a variety of ways, such as product, safety, and environmental regulations mandating certain attributes of products or processes. Strict environmental or energy-efficiency standards can stimulate innovation and productivity improvement, for example, if standards are flexible enough to accommodate new methods.[13]

The advantages of home demand are rooted in information and incentives difficult to obtain from a distance. Local customers offer high visibility, ease in communication, and the opportunity for joint working relationships. All three of the global leaders discussed in the insert above benefit from sophisticated demand at home. Novo, for example, sells to perhaps the most sophisticated group of medical specialists in the treatment of diabetes in the world and operates in the context of a national health care system providing generous reimbursement for new treatments.

Related and Supporting Industries. The final type of locational advantages in productivity competition arises from the local presence of capable specialized suppliers and related industries. Proximity to local suppliers of the specialized components, machinery, and services and related firms is not necessary to gain access to inputs, which can be sourced globally. Instead, the advantage arises from efficiency, knowledge, and the ease of innovation.

The presence of capable local suppliers reduces the often considerable transaction cost and delay of importing and dealing with distant vendors and facilitiates repair and problem solving. Companies also have more discretion in choosing appropriate levels of vertical integration. The presence of capable local firms in related fields further contributes to efficiency by making it easier to gain complementarities in R&D, distribution, and marketing.

The efficiency gains from local suppliers and related industries are often less significant, however, than the benefits in terms of innovation and dynamism. Nearby suppliers and firms in related businesses foster the rapid flow of information, scientific collaboration, and joint development efforts. Speed and flexibility in introducing new products increase because companies can readily farm out parts of the process. More broadly, companies can more readily influence their suppliers' technical efforts and serve as test sites for new developments, accelerating the pace of innovation. Honda benefited from a strong local supplier network in both automobiles and motorcycles, as did HP in all its principal businesses. Novo enjoyed particular advantages from the presence in Denmark of related fields, such as brewing and dairy products, which employed related technology, skills, and machinery.

As with demand advantages, the benefits of home-based suppliers and related industries for innovation are difficult to replicate from a distance. Highly applied technology and specialized skills are difficult to codify, accumulate, and transfer. Global sourcing works best for raw materials, standard components, and general purpose equipment and machinery with little need for associated information and technical exchange. Here, foreign sourcing involves lower transaction costs and little impact on the innovation process, although it may reduce flexibility.

The importance of local suppliers and firms in related fields, coupled with local demand conditions, underlies the fundamental role of *clusters* of interconnected industries. An extensive discussion of clusters is the subject of Chapter 7. Clusters include specialized suppliers, service providers, downstream (for example, channel or customer) industries, information providers, infrastructure providers, and firms in related fields. Associated institutions such as trade associations, standards-setting agencies, and university departments constitute part of the cluster as well. The cluster represents a collective asset, creating an environment in which firms can easily and efficiently assemble knowledge, skills, and inputs. This raises productivity and speeds the rate of innovation.

THE DIAMOND AS A LOCAL SYSTEM

Together, the four types of location-based advantages in the diamond constitute a dynamic system more important than its parts. The effect on productivity of one part of the diamond depends on the state of the other parts. Vigorous local rivalry stimulates productivity growth— provided that the local context supports investment (context for strategy and rivalry) and that local buyers seek quality products (demand conditions). Otherwise, rivalry can degenerate into destructive price cutting. Similarly, improving the supply of skilled engineers (factor conditions) will not boost productivity unless firms invest in R&D and process improvements and an adequate supplier base supports innovation-based strategies. Serious weakness in any part of the diamond will constrain an industry's potential for productivity growth.

Given appropriate institutional and other linkages, the four types of location advantages are strongly reinforcing. Vigorous domestic rivalry contributes, for example, to the development of unique pools of specialized skills and technology. The presence of a number of rivals encourages local institutions, such as universities, colleges, and training providers, to adapt and support the industry's distinctive needs. Active local rivalry also promotes the formation and upgrading of local supplier industries, which find a ready local market.

The processes of cluster formation and upgrading are not inevitable. The health of the feedback loops depend on the strength of local relationships, the openness of information flow, and the mutual responsiveness of the various firms and institutions. The intensity of local rivalry and the climate for investment play particularly important roles because they have much to do with whether firms act. Some locations are far better organized to facilitate improvement and upgrading than others. Because of the cumulative and self-reinforcing nature of the diamond and the time required to build specialized institutions, knowledge, and a critical mass of firms, normally only a small number of locations will favor competition in a particular business. Foreign firms and specialized suppliers will be drawn to invest in these locations. Often, these newcomers are relocating from weaker diamonds. In pharmaceuticals, for example, the Philadelphia/New Jersey diamond attracts substantial investment by German, Swiss, British, and Japanese pharmaceutical firms because of its superior demand conditions and excellent access to specialized factors. Finally, individuals with good ideas and specialized skills will be drawn to these locations as well because they offer the greatest excitement and rewards. The cycle is interrupted only when major technological changes invalidate past skills, suppliers, and other local advantages or when pressures to upgrade dissipate because local rivalry is eliminated or buyer sophistication lags.

Competition is becoming increasingly national and global, then, but the crucial sources of competitive advantage often remain local. They reside in critical masses of highly specialized and interconnected skills, applied technologies, firms, suppliers, and institutions in particular locations.[14] While the advantages of locations for input cost competition can be easily tapped through global networks, the advantages of a location for productivity competition require proximity. Anything that can be sourced from a distance or via a global network becomes accessible to rivals and ceases to be a robust source or competitive advantage. The important location advantages increasingly lie in local things— knowledge relationships, motivation—that distant rivals cannot match.

Competing Across Locations: From Local to Global Strategy

We are now in a position to bring together the competitive advantages of global networks and the competitive advantages of locations into an integrated conception of global strategy. Competing across locations involves a series of choices that will be illustrated using our three company examples: Novo, Hewlett-Packard, and Honda.

Build Globalization on the Foundation of a Unique Competitive Position. A global (or multilocation) strategy must begin with a unique competitive position that results in a clear competitive advantage. A company will not be able to overcome the barriers to penetrating unfamiliar markets unless it brings a meaningful advantage in either cost or differentiation to the table. Novo, for example, was a clear differentiator in the insulin industry. It pioneered high purity insulins, led in purity and in insulin delivery technology, and sought scientific excellence through its research institute, affiliated diabetes hospital, and hosting of international medical meetings. Novo's differentiation allowed it to make headway in selling its product to doctors and health authorities in each new country whose market it entered.

A corollary to this principle is that companies should globalize first in those businesses and product lines where they have the most unique advantages. These product areas present the greatest odds of international competitive success.

Penetrate International Markets with a Consistent Positioning. Internationalization opens up huge and growing international markets. A global strategy requires a patient, long-term campaign to enter every significant foreign market while maintaining and leveraging the company's unique strategic positioning. Novo-Nordisk, Honda, and HP all followed this approach. The portion of the foreign market available, given a company's particular strategy, will vary from country to country, depending on local purchasing power and the array of local needs (this can guide the order of entering country markets). Maintaining a consistent strategy from country to country, however, will reinforce a company's competitive advantage. Over time, the target market of a company's strategy will often grow, based on economic development in the country as well as efforts to educate the market about the benefits of a company's unique offering.

Efforts to internationalize based on opportunistic modifications of a company's competitive positioning from country to country rarely succeed. Neither does making a string of acquisitions of differently positioned companies, unless these companies are maintained as separate entities or, alternatively, repositioned to align them with the company's strategy and integrated. Without a consistent position, the company lacks a real competitive advantage, and its reputation does not cumulate. Moreover, efforts to integrate activities across countries will often be frustrated or ineffective.

Properly conceived, geographic expansion remains one of the best ways to grow without compromising a company's distinctive strategy. Expanding globally with a consistent position should reinforce a company's advantages. In contrast, broadening the strategy within existing markets runs the risk of compromising the company's uniqueness. One of the greatest barriers to the success of firms based in smaller countries is the perceived need to serve all segments and offer all varieties to capture the limited market opportunity. Instead, the imperative should be to stay focused and pursue the much larger international opportunity.

Establish a Clear Home Base for Each Distinct Business. A firm must have a clear home base for competing in each strategically distinct business. (The location of overall *corporate headquarters* is less significant, and can reflect historical factors or convenience.) The home base for a business is the location where strategy is set, core product and process technology is created and maintained, and a critical mass of sophisticated production and service activities reside. A coordinating center is not enough. Co-locating a critical mass of such activities at one location fosters rapid progress by allowing easier communication, better cross-functional coordination, and more rapid decision making. Firms are also better placed to capture the productivity and innovation benefits of the local cluster because these cut across many activities. The home base should have clear worldwide responsibility for the business unit and should serve as the coordinating and integrating point for inputs, production activities, information, and technology sourced elsewhere.

The home base should be located in the nation or region with the most favorable diamond for the particular business. This will provide the best environment for innovation and productivity growth. The most favorable home base may not necessarily be the country of ownership. Novo, Hewlett-Packard, and Honda each has a clear home base for each of its major businesses. Denmark serves as the home base of Novo's insulin business (and of both Novo's and Nordisk's insulin businesses prior to the merger). Even though 95 percent of sales is generated outside Denmark, all insulin purification facilities, which comprise the most critical activities in production process, are based in Denmark. Denmark's large pig-farming industry initially provided all of the crucial raw material, pig pancreases. Insulin purification requires not only a large investment but also highly specialized machinery, skilled technicians, and quality-control systems. Denmark is home to suppliers of critical machinery and other specialized production inputs, in part because of its strong position in the dairy and beer industries, which utilize related technologies and skills. All of Novo's core product and process R&D is also conducted in Denmark, which is the location of an array of world-class diabetes research institutes and two leading diabetes hospitals. The demand conditions for insulin in Denmark are also advanced. The country's generous health care system provided early funding for new diabetes testing and treatments. Danish doctors not only examine patients but also conduct and monitor programs that train diabetes patients in eating and cooking habits. Novo-Nordisk personnel interact directly with hospital doctors to gain quick feedback on the success of new products and on emerging issues facing diabetics.

Honda's home base for both motorcycles and automobiles is in Japan, where most of Honda's sophisticated activities are conducted. Japan accounts for 76 percent of Honda's production capacity in motorcycles and 68 percent of its automobile production. Foreign production plants are primarily assembly facilities, employing sophisticated parts from Japan. Honda's Japanese motorcycle plants have an average capacity of 396,000 units, for example, compared to 75,000 for those located elsewhere. R&D is even more concentrated: All core engine research and 95 percent of R&D employees and are located in Japan. R&D personnel based outside Japan must undergo two years' training at the Tochigi Research Center in Tokyo before beginning work in their native country.

Hewlett-Packard, which is far more diversified than Novo or Honda, also has a clear home base for each business. Worldwide responsibility for each product line—including core research, the most sophisticated production activities, and decision making—are concentrated in a particular location. The United States hosts 43 percent of HP's physical space dedicated to marketing but 77 percent of the space dedicated to manufacturing, R&D, and administration. At the home base, engineers with specialized expertise are designated worldwide experts; they transfer their knowledge either electronically or through periodic trips to subsidiaries. Regional subsidiaries take responsibility for some process-oriented R&D, product localization, and local marketing.

Leveraged Product-Line Home Bases at Different Locations. As a firm's product range broadens, the home bases for some product lines may best be located in different countries. A firm should specialize its international activity by assigning lead product line responsibility to the country with the most favorable home diamond in that particular segment. This approach is far superior to replicating production and R&D activities for a wide product line in several countries, an inefficient approach that dulls innovation. Instead, each major subsidiary should specialize in models for which it has the most favorable diamond, and serve those segments worldwide. Instead of dispersing activities individually, groups of activities comprising product-line home bases should be located in countries with locational advantage.

Hewlett-Packard provides an interesting example of these notions. HP locates many product line home bases outside the United States. It concentrates inkjet printer operations in Vancouver, British Columbia, for example, with localization for regional markets and assembly in

Barcelona (Spain). Worldwide responsibility for a new line of compact inkjet printers is based in Singapore. This product line combines printer technology transferred from Vancouver with Asian expertise in designing space-saving office products. Within the United States, HP similarly concentrates product line responsibility. It bases responsibility for personal computers and workstations in California (home to almost all of the world's leading personal computer and workstation firms) and medical instruments in Massachusetts (which has an extraordinary concentration of world-renowned research hospitals and numerous leading medical instrument companies).

Honda's home base for automobiles has been entirely in Japan; however, Honda has begun the process of creating a product-line home base for station wagons in the United States. Adapted from a sedan designed and engineered in Japan, the Accord station wagon was conceived, designed, and developed in the United States. The United States, considered the most advanced market for station wagons, has a well-established network of station wagon component suppliers. Honda's California R&D design facility created the models and life-size mock-ups of the wagon; the Ohio R&D facility fabricated the metal prototype; and major production tooling, including stamping dies, was made by American Honda Engineering. Honda has stated that the United States will become its world headquarters for station wagons and that U.S. designers and engineers will continue to develop and upgrade the product. American Honda also has worldwide responsibility for development of a two-door Civic coupe.[15] By the end of the 1990s, American Honda plans to export 70,000 automobiles from the United States to more than twenty countries.

Disperse Activities to Extend Home Base Advantages. While the home base is the location of core activities, other activities can and should be dispersed to extend the company's competitive position. Each activity in the value chain should be systematically examined for these opportunities, which will take one of the following three forms.

- **Sourcing comparative advantages.** Inputs not integral to the innovation process, such as low skilled assembly labor, raw materials, general purpose components or capital, can and must be sourced from the most cost-effective location. In this way, the global competitor harnesses the input cost advantages of various locations. The global competitor can thus exploit the comparative advantage of many locations, while nullifying the cost disadvantages of its home base.

- **Securing or improving foreign market access.** Locating selected activities near the market signals commitment to foreign customers and may allow a company to better address local needs and tailor offerings to local preferences. To this aim, many companies disperse some R&D activities to support product adaptation and compliance with local regulations. Modern flexible manufacturing systems and the increased power of information and communications technologies, however, work to lessen the need to dispersed activities to support local tailoring. Greater harmonization of technical standards and diminishing trade barriers have the same effect. Customization to serve local needs can often be most easily accomplished from a single facility.

  Some activities may need to be dispersed not to enhance competitiveness but in order to respond to actual or threatened government mandates. Much Japanese auto and consumer electronics assembly in the United States, for example, reflects such considerations. When a firm must respond to government pressures, it should disperse some less scale-sensitive activities or activities requiring less coordination and integration with others. The goal should be to deal with government mandates at the least possible sacrifice to efficiency and especially to the rate of innovation.

- **Selectively tapping competitive advantages at other locations.** The home base rarely offers all valuable expertise and promising technologies, no matter how favorable the location. To gain access to their benefits, global competitors can locate activities in other centers of innovation. When tapping the capabilities of other diamonds, however, the home base must be supplemented, not replicated or replaced. The firm's ultimate aim should be to improve capabilities in important skills or technologies at home in order to facilitate more rapid innovation. Relying too heavily on advantages sourced elsewhere threatens the capacity to innovate.

Overall, firms should disperse *only* those activities needed to achieve these three classes of benefits.

Novo illustrates all these motivations in different activities in the value chain. In procurement, Novo sources its traditional raw material, pig pancreases, from twenty countries. Worldwide sourcing not only allows access to larger supplies but hedges risk and allows Novo to capitalize on favorable price and currency fluctuations in particular farming countries. To access low cost capital, Novo funds 83 percent of its long-term debt in currencies other than the Danish kroner and taps foreign equity markets, including the United States. To facilitate market access and lower transportation costs, and, in several cases, to deal with government barriers, Novo has dispersed four insulin processing plants to France, South Africa, Japan, and the United States. These plants—the only Novo production facilities outside Denmark— are not full-scale production sites but units that dilute concentrated insulin crystals imported from Denmark and then package products for final sale. Dispersing these less scale-sensitive processing plants saves modestly on transport costs. More importantly, however, it has allowed Novo to continue to concentrate its more scale- and skill-dependent primary production in Denmark. In marketing and sales, Novo has established marketing joint ventures with local companies in a number of countries to improve access to local medical communities and government health care systems. Finally, in R&D, Novo has established a limited number of highly specialized research centers outside Denmark to tap particular skills or technologies not available at home. Zymotech, based in Seattle, Washington, was acquired to access expertise in genetic engineering (a U.S. strength). A Japanese research facility was established as well. After repeated delays in gaining regulatory approval in Denmark, Novo established a genetically engineered insulin production facility in Japan, where approval was more rapid. Novo has not ceded this core technology to its foreign operations, however. Novo's own genetic engineering capabilities have been expanded in Denmark. The company transfers the knowledge acquired in the United States and Japan back to its Danish home base and has established genetic insulin production there as well.

Honda has also dispersed activities for all three reasons. Automobiles are assembled in eleven countries and motorcycles in thirty countries, to reduce transportation and tariff costs and to source lower-cost labor. To ensure continued market access in the face of rising concern over Japanese automobile imports, Honda has invested more than $2 billion in facilities in the United States: two assembly plants; a manufacturing facility for engines, transmissions, and suspension parts; an engineering center; and an R&D facility. Honda's U.S. activities enjoy lower operating costs and focus on adaptation of products and processes to the U.S. market. Innovation remains centered in Japan. Finally, Honda taps styling expertise available in California and high performance design capabilities in Germany, via small, local design centers that transfer knowledge back to the Japanese home base, where it is incorporated into model development.

Coordinate and Integrate Dispersed Activities. Unlocking the competitive advantage from dispersed activities requires that activities be coordinated globally. Coordination ensures consistency and reinforcement across countries, to enhance differentiation. Coordination is also necessary to allow learning and technology gained from dispersed activities to be integrated at the home base.

The particular advantages of coordination in its various forms were described earlier. All three of our example companies exhibit these benefits, but Novo's case is particularly interesting. In raw material procurement, Novo's sourcing is dispersed to twenty countries, but coordinated centrally to take advantage of price and currency shifts. In marketing, all subsidiaries, agents, and distributors use consistent promotional materials, and Novo trains them in consistent selling approaches. Novo works hard to ensure a common image worldwide and reinforces it with periodic sponsorship of physicians' conferences on diabetes in Denmark.

Coordinating across disparate country locations, however, raises formidable organizational challenges. Language, culture, and distance work against communication and common ways of thinking. Country subsidiaries have a natural tendency to want autonomy, and to extensively tailor their activities to local circumstances. Successful global competitors overcome these challenges in a variety of ways. First, they establish clear positioning and a well understood concept for global strategy. Second, subsidiary managers recognize the overall global position as a difficult to match source of advantage in their particular country. Thus, they are careful to tailor local activities in ways that do not undermine the global strategy. Third, information and accounting systems are made consistent worldwide, right down to part numbers and client codes, facilitating operational coordination, the exchange of information comparisons across locations, and making appropriate tradeoffs. Fourth, the company makes active efforts to encourage personal relationships and the exchange of learning among subsidiary managers, both to foster mutual understanding and to give coordination a human face. Finally, any company that seeks a global strategy must put in place an incentive system that weights overall contribution to the company in addition to subsidiary performance.[16]

Preserve National Identity in Business Units. A firm's national identity in a particular business is not something to overcome, as some observers have suggested, but something to preserve. Competitive advantage in a business often arises from distinctive attributes of a firm's home environment; location places an imprint on the firm and shapes its method of competing. Foreign customers value national identity and culture, and the company characteristics they connote. Most Americans, for example, appreciate German cars because *German* has come to connote high standards of design, performance, and craftsmanship, not because German car companies have become "American" or "global."

When accessing foreign markets, a firm must adapt—in the sense that it tailors its product to local needs and shows sensitivity to local business practices. Yet the company should not lose its distinctive positioning and identity, which should, indeed, be nurtured and inculcated in foreign subsidiaries. At Honda, for example, managers hired to run international subsidiaries train for two years at the Japanese headquarters before assuming their responsibilities.

Alliances as Enabling Devices for Globalization, but Not as Strategy.
Once a company understands how to configure its global network in a business, alliances with firms based elsewhere can be a means of more effectively or more rapidly achieving the desired configuration. Alliances are a means to build a network of dispersed activities not an end, and can make activities outside the home base more effective. Market access,

for example, can often be enhanced by a local partner. The ability to source inputs or to tap advanced skills and technologies in a new location may require a partner's well-established presence. Alliances, however, can blur a company's positioning and get in the way of a consistent positioning in every market. They complicate coordination and can slow innovation.

The best alliances are highly selective: They focus on particular activities and on obtaining a particular competitive benefit. Novo, for example, formed joint ventures with a variety of firms to gain access to particular national markets. Broad alliances, covering many activities and markets, tend to stunt a company's own development. They inhibit or relieve the sense of urgency about building the brand or developing the firm's own products. The best alliances are often transitional devices, assisting a firm to build on its strengths and to learn. In the long run, the partners may go their separate ways or upgrade the alliance to a full merger. A firm cannot rely on a partner for assets crucial to its competitive advantage.[17]

Business Extension in Industries and Segments with Location Advantages. A location's competitive advantages provide a means for identifying the industries in which a firm can gain a unique competitive advantage vis-à-vis rivals based elsewhere, as well as those industry segments where the home-base environment provides the greatest benefits. New business development should concentrate in these areas.

The new paradigm of productivity competition raises cautions about extensive vertical integration. Vertical integration consumes resources and creates inflexibilities, and should be restricted to activities tightly connected to the overall strategy. Elsewhere, a company may be better served by developing strong relationships with local suppliers of specialized machinery and inputs.

Diversification should proceed along cluster lines. By diversifying, companies will better leverage not only their own internal assets but also the unique assets of locations to which they have special access, such as suppliers, research centers, and skill pools. HP's diversification from measurement and test equipment into information systems and medical instruments has followed these principles, in each case involving a field in which the United States has unique strengths. Novo's move from insulin to industrial enzymes also followed cluster lines, as did Honda's diversification from motorcycles to automobiles. Innovations often originate at the interstices between industries and clusters, when related technologies and skills are combined. To get its start in automobiles, for example, Honda drew on its small-engine technology expertise, nurtured in motorcycle manufacture. It combined this with assets in the Japanese automobile cluster, including a strong supplier base and demand conditions encouraging compact designs and energy efficiency.

Upgrade the Home Bases. An important part of a firm's competitive advantage in a business clearly resides in the local environment where that business is based, not merely within the firm itself. Without a fundamentally healthy home base, a business's capacity for productivity growth and rapid innovation will diminish. The firm will be unable to assemble the resources, skills, technologies, and information most essential to competitive advantage. While dispersing sophisticated production or outsourcing critical components and machinery can often offset home base weaknesses and improve performance in the short run, the firm's ability to innovate over the long run will be threatened.

The presence of external competitive advantages adds new and often unfamiliar dimensions to a company's strategic agenda. Firms should support specialized training programs and should promote university research in areas relevant to their particular business. Local suppliers should be nurtured and upgraded (depending heavily on distant suppliers nullifies a potential competitive advantage). Firms must guide and pressure local infrastructure providers to meet their needs and ensure that government regulations enhance productivity. Industry associations can play an important role in sponsoring training programs, research on standards and enabling technologies, and the collection of market information. Chapter 7 provides a more extensive discussion of these opportunities. Unfortunately, few companies see their local environment as a vital competitive resource. In the United States, for example, many companies take their suppliers for granted and see education and training as the responsibility of government.

The example of Novo illustrates how global leaders take an active role in upgrading their home environment. Before the merger of Nordisk and Novo, Nordisk established the Nordic Insulin Fund (in 1926) to support insulin research projects in Scandinavia and the Steno Memorial Hospital (in 1932) as a center for research and treatment of diabetes. Novo founded the Hvidore Diabetes Hospital soon after and later (in 1957) founded the Hagedoorn Research Institute to conduct basic research on diabetes. The Novo Research Institute was created (in 1964) to investigate the causes and origins of diabetes. Today, the Steno Diabetes Center and Hvidore Diabetes Hospital treat 6,000 diabetes patients and conduct 25,000 diabetes consultations each year. Novo also sponsors international conferences on diabetes in Denmark, bringing together local experts and specialists from around the world.[18]

The history of the Danish insulin industry illustrates the power of active local rivalry to motivate continual innovation. The companies recognized one of the risks of their merger as the possibility that, while achieving some efficiencies, it would undermine dynamism. The parent company hopes to address this and other risks by keeping the two operations separate. The broader principle, however, remains: The presence of local rivals creates advantages. Seeking to eliminate local competition, under most circumstances, is a misguided effort.

Relocate the Home Base if Necessary. If the vitality of a firm's home base for a particular business deteriorates because of lagging customer sophistication, a requirement for new types of suppliers, ineffective local institutions, or for other reasons, the first response should be to upgrade at home. If such efforts are exhausted without success, however, a firm may need to shift its home base to a more favorable location. This is perhaps the ultimate manifestation of global competition.

Shifts of home bases from country to country occur with increasing frequency in multinational companies. As global competition exposes companies to the world's best rivals and nullifies traditional comparative advantages in access to capital, raw materials, and labor, the penalty of an unfavorable home diamond increases. Yet, the decision to relocate a home base must be approached reluctantly, because it entails becoming accepted as a true insider in a new location and a new culture.

Firms rarely shift an entire company's home base. Instead, they relocate the home base of particular product lines or business segments. One common catalyst (and enabler) of such shifts is acquisition of a foreign firm already established in a more vibrant location. Such acquisitions provide the critical mass for new home bases, which, over time, gain increasing worldwide responsibility in particular segments or businesses. Nestlé, for example, has relocated the world headquarters for its confectionery business to England, associating it with the acquired Rowntree MacIntosh company. England, with its sweet-toothed consumers, sophisticated retailers, advanced advertising agencies, and highly competitive media companies, constitutes a more dynamic environment for competing in mass-market candy than Switzerland. Similarly, Nestlé has moved its headquarters for bottled water to France, the most competitive location in that industry.

Although each of our example companies, Novo, Hewlett-Packard, and Honda, continues to enjoy a strong home diamond in its principal businesses, not all firms are so fortunate. The Canadian manufacturer Northern Telecom, for example, has relocated the home base for its digital central-office switching equipment from Canada to the United States.[19] Northern Telecom manufactured and installed the first local digital switch, the DMS-10, in the United States in 1977. The subsequent AT&T divestiture and mandate for equal access reconfigured the U.S. diamond for telecommunications service and equipment and led Northern Telecom to expand its U.S. operations dramatically. By 1991, the company had relocated its world headquarters for central-office switching to the United States. It now conducts all R&D activities for this product line in the United States, with a work force of more than one thousand employees. Virtually all of the company's central-office switching manufacturing is also conducted in North Carolina.

The rationale behind Northern Telecom's move to the United States can be seen in the strength of the U.S. telecommunications equipment diamond. Compared to Canada, the United States presents a unique array of highly specialized factors, including sophisticated software engineering and world-class university research programs in computer science and telecommunications. American buyers and end-users are among the most sophisticated in the world, and the existence of twenty to twenty-five major independent U.S. switch buyers leads to intense competition that encourages Northern Telecom's customers to continuously upgrade their central-office switching capabilities. American firms in integrated circuit manufacturing and systems-level software design

provide strong capabilities in related industries. The openness of the
U.S. market to foreign rivals further intensifies the local rivalry within
the U.S. market. (In telecommunications equipment, governments have
tended to protect local markets and support monopoly suppliers.)

In another interesting example, Wesson (1993) describes Hyundai's
shift of its home base in personal computers from Korea to Silicon
Valley, when it discovered that it simply could not "keep up" from a
Korean location. With all competitors sourcing low-cost parts internationally, crucial competitive imperatives were the rapid introduction
of new models that met evolving customer needs and the ability to
successfully access evolving distribution channels. In these areas, the
United States was far ahead of other locations. Traditionally, foreign
direct investment (FDI) has been seen as exploiting home base advantages. Wesson employs statistical evidence to confirm the prevalence
of home-base *seeking* FDI, that is, FDI directed at accessing the sophisticated advantages of other locations, even to the extent of relocating the
firm's home base elsewhere.

Competing Globally from a Developing Country

Developing countries have become a growing part of the international
economy, and many firms based in developing countries are exporters.
The platform of a developing country, however, raises some particular
issues for the move to a global strategy.

The basic challenge is to shift from comparative advantage to competitive advantage. Most firms based in developing countries have internationalized through exports of resource- or labor-intensive commodities
or via OEM agreements with multinationals that rest on resource labor
costs. Such exports have been primarily directed to advanced economies.
Opportunities to expand into other developing markets, including neighboring countries, have been limited by similarities in factor conditions
and circumscribed by protectionist government policies.

Moving beyond the traditional modes of internationalization requires
that firms based in developing countries create distinctive strategies.
Without their own product or service varieties, production methods, or
reputations, they find it difficult to penetrate foreign markets. At the

same time, firms must extend their value chains to include international distribution, marketing, sourcing, and ultimately production. The best opportunities for true international strategies emanating from developing countries often lie within the region and with other like economies. While exports to advanced economies based on comparative advantage can continue, firms must take advantage of the opening of neighboring markets to build regional networks. The challenge becomes one of building distinctive product varieties and production methods while gaining knowledge and control of international marketing and distribution. Over time, the firm must build innovative capacity sufficient to enter more and more advanced markets based on competitive rather than comparative advantage.

Integrating Location and Global Competition

Since the 1950s, globalization has exerted an ever-increasing influence on competitive strategy. Aggregate statistics confirm the popular view that firms have become increasingly global in their sales and operations. The traditional role of comparative advantage has been superseded, and it is tempting to conclude that many corporations now transcend national boundaries.

Deeper investigation reveals, however, a striking localization of competitive advantage. This apparent paradox can be explained by recognizing the new paradigm of international competition which makes productivity and innovation paramount. Firms must harness the comparative advantages from many locations to avoid a disadvantage. Firms' advantages over others, however, often lie in their locations' competitive advantage for raising productivity. This paradigm must guide a new generation of thinking about global strategy, one that integrates localization and globalization in wholly new ways.

Localization was once seen as a necessary evil to be balanced against the compelling benefits of a global strategy. Instead, the home base location should be seen as the root of competitive advantage. Global strategies can extend this advantage through dispersing activities to source comparative advantages, access markets, or tap particular skills or technologies. To play this role, however, dispersed activities must be coordinated. This new synthesis, which recognizes the complex role of location in competitive advantage, will drive competition in the coming decades.

NOTES

1. See Porter (1980).

2. See Porter (1985).

3. See Theodore Levitt, "Globalization of Markets," *Harvard Business Review* 61, no. 3 (1983): 92–102.

4. See, for example, Porter (1990); Crocombe, Enright, and Porter (1991); and Sölvell, Zander, and Porter (1991).

5. See Figure 7-5 in Chapter 7.

6. See also Enright (1993 and 1994).

7. See Cristerna (1993).

8. See, for example, Jaikumar and Upton (1993).

9. This group of activities, which varies in composition from industry to industry, will be termed *home-based activities* or *core activities*.

10. See also Porter (1990).

11. Thomas (1993) confirms this result in pharmaceuticals, where firms facing local rivals (and strict product approval regulation, see below) are the most innovative.

12. Some observers have cited collaboration rather than competition as an important basis of competitiveness, referring most often to Japan and to the industrial districts of Italy. This view confuses *vertical* collaboration with buyers, suppliers, and local institutions, which diamond theory stresses, with *horizontal* collaboration among competitors. Horizontal collaboration is rare in successful Japanese and Italian industries (*keiretsu*, for example, do not contain direct competitors).

13. See, for example, Porter and van der Linde (1995).

14. See also Kogut (1991). Such location-based advantages are inconsistent with Reich's (1991) views of mobile resources, information, and technology. Reich's notion of symbolic analyst zones, which focuses only on skilled employees, attempts to bridge this inconsistency.

15. Honda's movement toward greater local content relates to its establishment of new product-line home bases.

16. For a useful discussion of other organizational issues in global companies, see Bartlett and Ghoshal (1989).

17. For further discussion, see Porter and Fuller (1986) and Porter and Ghemawat (1986).

18. Enright (1989).

19. Wesson (1993) discusses the Northern Telecom case.

Bibliography

Bartlett, C. A., and S. Ghoshal. *Managing Across Borders: The Transnational Solution.* Boston: Harvard Business School Press, 1989.

Cristerna, H. "The Role of Home-Based Advantages in Global Expansion: Five Case Studies." Unpublished MBA research report, Harvard Business School, Boston, Mass., 1993.

Crocombe, G. T., M. J. Enright, and M. E. Porter. *Upgrading New Zealand's Competitive Advantage.* Auckland, New Zealand: Oxford University Press, 1991.

Enright, M. J. "The Determinants of Geographic Concentration in Industry." Working paper 93-052, Harvard Business School, Boston, Mass., 1993.

———. "Novo Industri." Case 9-389-148. Boston: Harvard Business School, 1989.

———. "Organization and Coordination in Geographically Concentrated Industries." In *Coordination and Information: Historical Perspectives on the Organization of Enterprise,* edited by Naomi R. Lamoreaux and Daniel G. M. Raff (Chicago: University of Chicago Press/NBER, 1994).

Jaikumar, R., and D. M. Upton. "The Coordination of Global Manufacturing." In *Globalization, Technology, and Competition: The Fusion of Computers and Telecommunications in the 1990s,* edited by S. P. Bradley, J. A. Hausman, and R. L. Nolan. Boston: Harvard Business School Press, 1993.

Kogut, B. "Country Capabilities and the Permeability of Borders." *Strategic Management Journal* (Summer 1991), 33–47.

Porter, M. E. "Competition in Global Industries: A Conceptual Framework." In *Competition in Global Industries,* edited by M. E. Porter. Boston: Harvard Business School Press, 1986.

———. *Competitive Advantage: Creating and Sustaining Superior Performance.* New York: Free Press, 1985.

———. *The Competitive Advantage of Nations.* New York: Free Press, 1990.

———. *Competitive Strategy: Techniques for Analyzing Industries and Competitors.* New York: Free Press, 1980.

Porter, M. E., and M. B. Fuller. "Coalitions and Global Strategy." In *Competition in Global Industries*, edited by M. E. Porter. Boston: Harvard Business School Press, 1986.

Porter, M. E., and P. Ghemawat. "Patterns of International Coalition Activity." In *Competition in Global Industries*, edited by M. E. Porter. Boston: Harvard Business School Press, 1986.

Porter, M. E., and C. van der Linde. "Green and Competitive: Ending the Stalemate." *Harvard Business Review* 73, no. 5 (1995): 120–134.

Porter, M. E., and R. E. Wayland. "Global Competition and the Localization of Competitive Advantage." Published in the proceedings of the Integral Strategy Collegium, Graduate School of Business, Indiana University. Greenwich, CT: JAI Press, 1995.

Reich, R. B. "Who Is Us?" *Harvard Business Review* 68, no. 1 (1990): 53–64.

Sölvell, Ö., I. Zander, and M. E. Porter. *Advantage Sweden*. Stockholm, Sweden: Norstedts, 1991.

Thomas, L. G. "Spare the Road and Spoil the Industry: Vigorous Regulation and Vigorous Competition Promote International Competitive Advantage." Working paper, Emory University, Atlanta, Georgia, 1993.

Wesson, T. "The Determinants of Foreign Direct Investment in U.S. Manufacturing Industries." Ph.D. diss., Harvard Business School, 1993.

Part III   Competitive Solutions to Societal Problems

CHAPTER 10

Green and Competitive

Ending the Stalemate

Michael E. Porter

Claas van der Linde

THE NEED FOR REGULATION to protect the environment gets widespread but grudging acceptance: widespread because everyone wants a livable planet, grudging because of the lingering belief that environmental regulations erode competitiveness. The prevailing view is that there is an inherent and fixed trade-off: ecology versus the economy. On one side of the trade-off are the *social* benefits that arise from strict environmental standards. On the other are industry's *private* costs for prevention and cleanup—costs that lead to higher prices and reduced competitiveness. With the argument framed this way, progress on environmental quality has become a kind of arm-wrestling match. One side pushes for tougher standards; the other tries to roll them back. The balance of power shifts one way or the other depending on the prevailing political winds.

This static view of environmental regulation, in which everything except regulation is held constant, is incorrect. If technology, products, processes, and customer needs were all fixed, the conclusion that regulation must raise costs would be inevitable. But companies operate in the real world of dynamic competition, not in the static world of much

The authors are grateful to Benjamin C. Bonifant, Daniel C. Esty, Donald B. Marron, Jan Rivkin, Nicolaj Siggelkow, and R. David Simpson for their extremely helpful comments; to the Management Institute for Environment and Business for joint research; and to Reed Hundt for ongoing discussions that have greatly benefited the thinking behind this article.

September–October 1995

economic theory. They are constantly finding innovative solutions to pressures of all sorts—from competitors, customers, and regulators.

Properly designed environmental standards can trigger innovations that lower the total cost of a product or improve its value. Such innovations allow companies to use a range of inputs more productively—from raw materials to energy to labor—thus offsetting the costs of improving environmental impact and ending the stalemate. Ultimately, this enhanced *resource productivity* makes companies more competitive, not less.

Consider how the Dutch flower industry has responded to its environmental problems. Intense cultivation of flowers in small areas was contaminating the soil and groundwater with pesticides, herbicides, and fertilizers. Facing increasingly strict regulation on the release of chemicals, the Dutch understood that the only effective way to address the problem would be to develop a closed-loop system. In advanced Dutch greenhouses, flowers now grow in water and rock wool, not in soil. This lowers the risk of infestation, reducing the need for fertilizers and pesticides, which are delivered in water that circulates and is reused.

The tightly monitored closed-loop system also reduces variation in growing conditions, thus improving product quality. Handling costs have gone down because the flowers are cultivated on specially designed platforms. In addressing the environmental problem, then, the Dutch have innovated in ways that have raised the productivity with which they use many of the resources involved in growing flowers. The net result is not only dramatically lower environmental impact but also lower costs, better product quality, and enhanced global competitiveness. (See the insert "Innovating to Be Competitive: The Dutch Flower Industry.")

Innovating to Be Competitive: The Dutch Flower Industry

The Dutch flower industry is responsible for about 65 percent of world exports of cut flowers—an astonishing figure given that the most important production inputs in the flower business would seem to be land and climate. Anyone who has been to the Netherlands knows its disadvantages on both counts. The Dutch have to reclaim land from the sea, and the weather is notoriously problematic.

How can the Dutch be the world's leaders in the flower business when they lack comparative advantage in the traditional sense? The answer, among other reasons, is that they have innovated at every step in the value chain, creating technology and highly specialized inputs that enhance resource productivity and offset the country's natural disadvantages.

In selling and distribution, for example, the Netherlands has five auction houses custom designed for the flower business. Carts of flowers are automatically towed on computer-guided paths into the auction room. The buying process occurs in a few seconds. Buyers sit in an amphitheater, and the price on the auction clock moves down until the first buyer signals electronically. That buyer's code is attached to the cart, which is routed to the company's shipping and handling area. Within a few minutes, the flowers are on a truck to regional markets or in a specialized, precooled container on their way to nearby Schiphol airport. Good airports and highway systems may be plentiful elsewhere, too. But the Netherlands' innovative, spe-

cialized infrastructure is a competitive advantage. It leads to very high productivity. It is so successful that growers from other countries actually fly flowers there to be processed, sold, and reexported.

Paradoxically, having a *shortage* of general-purpose or more basic inputs can sometimes be turned into an advantage. If land were readily available and the climate more favorable, the Dutch would have competed the same way other countries did. Instead they were forced to innovate, developing a high-tech system of year-round greenhouse cultivation. The Dutch continually improve the unique, specialized technology that creates high resource productivity and underpins their competitiveness.

In contrast, an abundance of labor and natural resources or a lack of environmental pressure may lead a country's companies to spend the national resources unproductively. Competing based on cheap inputs, which could be used with less productivity, was sufficient in a more insular, less global economy. Today, when emerging nations with even cheaper labor and raw materials are part of the global economy, the old strategy is unsustainable.

This example illustrates why the debate about the relationship between competitiveness and the environment has been framed incorrectly. Policy makers, business leaders, and environmentalists have focused on the static cost impacts of environmental regulation and have ignored the more important offsetting productivity benefits from innovation. As a result, they have acted too often in ways that unnecessarily drive up costs and slow down progress on environmental issues. This static mind-set has thus created a self-fulfilling prophecy leading to ever more costly environmental regulation. Regulators tend to set regulations in ways that deter innovation. Companies, in turn, oppose and delay regulations instead of innovating to address them. The whole process has spawned an industry of litigators and consultants that drains resources away from real solutions.

Pollution = Inefficiency

Are cases like the Dutch flower industry the exception rather than the rule? Is it naïve to expect that reducing pollution will often enhance competitiveness? We think not, and the reason is that pollution often is a form of economic waste. When scrap, harmful substances, or energy forms are discharged into the environment as pollution, it is a sign that resources have been used incompletely, inefficiently, or ineffectively. Moreover, companies then have to perform additional activities that add cost but create no value for customers: for example, handling, storage, and disposal of discharges.

The concept of resource productivity opens up a new way of looking at both the full systems costs and the value associated with any product. Resource inefficiencies are most obvious within a company in the form of incomplete material utilization and poor process controls, which result in unnecessary waste, defects, and stored materials. But there also are many other hidden costs buried in the life cycle of the product. Packaging discarded by distributors or customers, for example, wastes resources and adds costs. Customers bear additional costs when they use products that pollute or waste energy. Resources are lost when products that contain usable materials are discarded and when customers pay—directly or indirectly—for product disposal.

Environmental improvement efforts have traditionally overlooked these systems costs. Instead, they have focused on pollution control through better identification, processing, and disposal of discharges or waste—costly approaches. In recent years, more advanced companies and regulators have embraced the concept of pollution prevention, sometimes called source reduction, which uses such methods as material substitution and closed-loop processes to limit pollution before it occurs.

But, although pollution prevention is an important step in the right direction, ultimately companies must learn to frame environmental improvement in terms of resource productivity.[1] Today managers and regulators focus on the actual costs of eliminating or treating pollution. They must shift their attention to include the opportunity costs of pollution—wasted resources, wasted effort, and diminished product value to the customer. At the level of resource productivity, environmental improvement and competitiveness come together.

This new view of pollution as resource inefficiency evokes the quality revolution of the 1980s and its most powerful lessons. Today we have little trouble grasping the idea that innovation can improve quality while actually lowering cost. But as recently as fifteen years ago, managers believed there was a fixed trade-off. Improving quality was expensive because it could be achieved only through inspection and rework of the "inevitable" defects that came off the line. What lay behind the old view was the assumption that both product design and production processes were fixed. As managers have rethought the quality issue, however, they have abandoned that old mind-set. Viewing defects as a sign of inefficient product and process design—not as an inevitable by-product of manufacturing—was a breakthrough. Companies now strive to build quality into the entire process. The new mind-set unleashed the power of innovation to relax or eliminate what companies had previously accepted as fixed trade-offs.

Like defects, pollution often reveals flaws in the product design or production process. Efforts to eliminate pollution can therefore follow the same basic principles widely used in quality programs: Use inputs more efficiently, eliminate the need for hazardous, hard-to-handle materials, and eliminate unneeded activities. In a recent study of major process changes at ten manufacturers of printed circuit boards, for example, pollution-control personnel initiated thirteen of thirty-three major changes. Of the thirteen changes, twelve resulted in cost reduction, eight in quality improvements, and five in extension of production capabilities.[2] It is not surprising that total quality management (TQM) has become a source of ideas for pollution reduction that can create offsetting benefits. The Dow Chemical Company, for example, explicitly identified the link between quality improvement and environmental performance by using statistical-process control to reduce the variance in processes and to lower waste.

Innovation and Resource Productivity

To explore the central role of innovation and the connection between environmental improvement and resource productivity, we have been collaborating since 1991 with the Management Institute for Environment and Business (MEB) on a series of international case studies of industries and sectors significantly affected by environmental regulation: pulp and paper, paint and coatings, electronics manufacturing, refrigerators, dry cell batteries, and printing inks. (See Table 10.1.) The data clearly show that the costs of addressing environmental regulations can be minimized, if not eliminated, through innovation that delivers other competitive benefits. We first observed the phenomenon in the course of our research for a study of national competitiveness, *The Competitive Advantage of Nations* (The Free Press, 1990).

Consider the chemical sector, where many believe that the ecology-economy trade-off is particularly steep. A study of activities to prevent waste generation at twenty-nine chemical plants found innovation offsets that enhanced resource productivity. Of 181 of these waste prevention activities, only one resulted in a net cost increase. Of the seventy activities with documented changes in product yield, sixty-eight reported increases; the average for twenty initiatives documented with specific data was 7 percent. These innovation offsets were achieved with surprisingly low investments and very short payback times. One-quarter of the forty-eight initiatives with detailed capital cost information required no capital investment at all; of the thirty-eight initiatives with data on the payback period, nearly two-thirds recouped their initial investments in six months or less. The annual savings per dollar spent on source reduction averaged three dollars and forty-nine cents for the twenty-seven activities for which this information could be calculated. The study also found that the two main motivating factors for source reduction activities were waste disposal costs and environmental regulation.

Table 10.1   Environmental Regulation Has Competitive Implications

Sector/Industry	Environmental Issues	Innovative Solutions	Innovation Offsets
Pulp and paper	Dioxin released by bleaching with chlorine	Improved cooking and washing processes Elimination of chlorine by using oxygen, ozone, or peroxide for bleaching Closed-loop processes (still problematic)	Lower operating costs though greater use of by-product energy sources 25% initial price premium for chlorine-free paper
Paint and coatings	Volatile organic compounds (VOCs) in solvents	New paint formulations (low-solvent-content paints, water-borne paints) Improved application techniques Powder or radiation-cured coatings	Price premium for solvent-free paints Improved coatings quality in some segments Worker safety benefits Higher coatings-transfer efficiency Reduced coating costs through materials savings
Electronics manufacturing	Volatile organic compounds (VOCs) in cleaning agents	Semiaqueous, terpene-based cleaning agents Closed-loop systems No-clean soldering where possible	Increase in cleaning quality and thus in product quality 30% to 80% reduction in cleaning costs, often for one-year payback periods Elimination of an unnecessary production step
Refrigerators	Chlorofluorocarbons (CFCs) used as refrigerants Energy usage Disposal	Alternative refrigerants (propane-isobutane mix) Thicker insulation Better gaskets Improved compressors	10% better energy efficiency at same cost 5% to 10% initial price premium for "green" refrigerator
Dry cell batteries	Cadmium, mercury, lead, nickel, cobalt, lithium, and zinc releases in landfills or to the air (after incineration)	Rechargeable batteries of nickel-hydride (for some applications) Rechargeable lithium batteries (now being developed)	Nearly twice as efficient at same cost Higher energy efficiency Expected to be price competitive in the near future
Printing inks	VOCs in petroleum inks	Water-based inks and soy inks	Higher efficiency, brighter colors, and better printability (depending on application)

Sources: Benjamin C. Bonifant, Ian Ratcliffe, and Claas van der Linde.

Innovation in response to environmental regulation can fall into two broad categories. The first is new technologies and approaches that minimize the cost of dealing with pollution once it occurs. The key to these approaches often lies in taking the resources embodied in the pollution and converting them into something of value. Companies get smarter about how to process toxic materials and emissions into usable forms, recycle scrap, and improve secondary treatment. For example, at a Rhône-Poulenc plant in Chalampe, France, nylon by-products known as diacids used to be incinerated. Rhône-Poulenc invested 76 million francs and installed new equipment to recover and sell these diacids as additives for dyes and tanning and as coagulation agents. The new recovery process has generated annual revenues of about 20.1 million francs. New de-inking technologies developed by Massachusetts-based Thermo Electron Corporation, among others, are allowing more extensive use of recycled paper. Molten Metal Technology of Waltham, Massachusetts, has developed a cost-saving catalytic extraction method to process many types of hazardous waste.

The second and far more interesting and important type of innovation addresses the root causes of pollution by improving resource productivity in the first place. Innovation offsets can take many forms, including more efficient utilization of particular inputs, better product yields, and better products. (See the insert "Environmental Improvement Can Benefit Resource Productivity.") Consider the following examples.

Resource productivity improves when less costly materials are substituted or when existing ones are better utilized. Dow Chemical's California complex scrubs hydrochloric gas with caustic to produce a wide range of chemicals. The company used to store the wastewater in evaporation ponds. Regulation called for Dow to close the evaporation ponds by 1988. In 1987, under pressure to comply with the new law, the company redesigned its production process. It reduced the use of caustic soda, decreasing caustic waste by 6,000 tons per year and hydrochloric acid waste by eighty tons per year. Dow also found that it could capture a portion of the waste stream for reuse as a raw material in other parts of the plant. Although it cost only $250,000 to implement, the process gave Dow an annual savings of $2.4 million.[3]

3M also improved resource productivity. Forced to comply with new regulations to reduce solvent emissions by 90 percent, 3M found a way

Environmental Improvement Can Benefit Resource Productivity

Process Benefits

- materials savings resulting from more complete processing, substitution, reuse, or recycling of production inputs

- increases in process yields

- less downtime through more careful monitoring and maintenance

- better utilization of by-products

- conversion of waste into valuable forms

- lower energy consumption during the production process

- reduced material storage and handling costs

- savings from safer workplace conditions

- elimination or reduction of the cost of activities involved in discharges or waste handling, transportation, and disposal

- improvements in the product as a by-product of process changes (such as better process control)

Product Benefits

- higher quality, more consistent products

- lower product costs (for instance, from material substitution)

- lower packaging costs

- more efficient resource use by products

- safer products

- lower net costs of product disposal to customers

- higher product resale and scrap value

to avoid the use of solvents altogether by coating products with safer, water-based solutions. The company gained an early-mover advantage in product development over competitors, many of whom switched significantly later. The company also shortened its time to market because its water-based product did not have to go through the approval process for solvent-based coatings.[4]

3M found that innovations can improve process consistency, reduce downtime, and lower costs substantially. The company used to produce adhesives in batches that were then transferred to storage tanks. One bad batch could spoil the entire contents of a tank. Lost product, downtime, and expensive hazardous-waste disposal were the result. 3M developed a new technique to run rapid quality tests on new batches. It reduced hazardous wastes by 110 tons per year at almost no cost, yielding an annual savings of more than $200,000.[5]

Many chemical-production processes require an initial start-up period after production interruptions in order to stabilize output and bring it within specifications. During that time, only scrap material is produced. When regulations raised the cost of waste disposal, Du Pont was motivated to install higher-quality monitoring equipment, which in turn reduced production interruptions and the associated production start-ups. Du Pont lowered not only its waste generation but also cut the amount of time it wasn't producing anything.[6]

Process changes to reduce emissions and use resources more productively often result in higher yields. As a result of new environmental standards, Ciba-Geigy Corporation reexamined the waste-water streams at its dye plant in Tom's River, New Jersey. Engineers made two changes to the production process. First, they replaced sludge-creating iron with a less harmful chemical conversion agent. Second, they eliminated the release of a potentially toxic product into the wastewater stream. They not only reduced pollution but also increased process yields by 40 percent, realizing an annual cost savings of $740,000. Although that part of the plant was ultimately closed, the example illustrates the role of regulatory pressure in process innovation.

Process innovations to comply with environmental regulation can even improve product consistency and quality. In 1990, the Montreal Protocol and the U.S. Clean Air Act required electronics companies to eliminate ozone-depleting chlorofluorocarbons (CFCs). Many companies used them as cleaning agents to remove residues that occur in the manufacture of printed circuit boards. Scientists at Raytheon confronted the regulatory challenge. Initially, they thought that complete elimination of CFCs would be impossible. After research, however, they found an alternate cleaning agent that could be reused in a closed-loop system. The new method improved average product quality—which the old CFC-based cleaning agent had occasionally compromised—while also lowering operating costs. Responding to the same regulation, other researchers identified applications that did not require any cleaning at all and developed so-called no-clean soldering technologies, which lowered operating costs without compromising quality. Without environmental regulation, that innovation would not have happened.

Innovations to address environmental regulations can also lower product costs and boost resource productivity by reducing unnecessary packaging or simplifying designs. A 1991 law in Japan set standards to make products easier to recycle. Hitachi, along with other Japanese appliance producers, responded by redesigning products to reduce disassembly time. In the process, it cut back the number of parts in a washing machine by 16 percent and the number of parts in a vacuum cleaner by 30 percent. Fewer components made the products easier not only to disassemble but also to assemble in the first place. Regulation that requires such recyclable products can lower the user's disposal costs and lead to designs that allow a company to recover valuable materials more easily. Either the customer or the manufacturer who takes back used products reaps greater value.

Although such product innovations have been prompted by regulators instead of by customers, world demand is putting a higher value on resource-efficient products. Many companies are using innovations to command price premiums for "green" products and to open up new market segments. Because Germany adopted recycling standards earlier than most other countries, German companies have first-mover advantages in developing less packaging-intensive products, which are both lower in cost and sought after in the marketplace. In the United States, Cummins Engine Company's development of low-emissions diesel engines for such applications as trucks and buses—innovation that U.S. environmental regulations spurred—is allowing it to gain position in international markets where similar needs are growing.

These examples and many others like them do not prove that companies always can innovate to reduce environmental impact at low cost. However, they show that there are considerable opportunities to reduce pollution through innovations that redesign products, processes, and methods of operation. Such examples are common in spite of companies' resistance to environmental regulation and in spite of regulatory standards that often are hostile to innovative, resource-productive solutions. The fact that such examples are common carries an important message: Today a new frame of reference for thinking about environmental improvement is urgently needed.

Do We Really Need Regulation?

If innovation in response to environmental regulation can be profitable—if a company can actually offset the cost of compliance through
improving resource productivity—why is regulation necessary at all? If
such opportunities exist, wouldn't companies pursue them naturally
and wouldn't regulation be unnecessary? That is like saying there will
rarely be ten-dollar bills to be found on the ground because someone
already will have picked them up.

Certainly, some companies do pursue such innovations without, or
in advance of, regulation. In Germany and Scandinavia, where both
companies and consumers are very attuned to environmental concerns,
innovation is not uncommon. As companies and their customers adopt
the resource productivity mind-set and as knowledge about innovative
technologies grows, there may well be less need for regulation over time
in the United States.

But the belief that companies will pick up on profitable opportunities
without a regulatory push makes a false assumption about competitive
reality—namely, that all profitable opportunities for innovation have
already been discovered, that all managers have perfect information
about them, and that organizational incentives are aligned with innovating. In fact, in the real world, managers often have highly incomplete
information and limited time and attention. Barriers to change are numerous. The Environmental Protection Agency's Green Lights program,
which works with companies to promote energy-saving lighting, shows
that many ten-dollar bills are still waiting to be picked up. In one audit,
nearly 80 percent of the projects offered paybacks within two years or
less, and yet the companies considering them had not taken action.[7]
Only after companies joined the program and benefited from the EPA's
information and cajoling were such highly profitable projects implemented.

We are now in a transitional phase of industrial history in which
companies are still inexperienced in handling environmental issues creatively. Customers, too, are unaware that resource inefficiency means
that they must pay for the cost of pollution. For example, they tend to
see discarded packaging as free because there is no separate charge for
it and no current lower-cost alternative. Because there is no direct way

to recapture the value of the wasted resources that customers already have paid for, they imagine that discarding used products carries no cost penalty for them.

Regulation, although a different type than is currently practiced, is needed for six major reasons:

- To create pressure that motivates companies to innovate. Our broader research on competitiveness highlights the important role of outside pressure in overcoming organizational inertia and fostering creative thinking.

- To improve environmental quality in cases in which innovation and the resulting improvements in resource productivity do not completely offset the cost of compliance; or in which it takes time for learning effects to reduce the overall cost of innovative solutions.

- To alert and educate companies about likely resource inefficiencies and potential areas for technological improvement (although government cannot know better than companies how to address them).

- To raise the likelihood that product innovations and process innovations in general will be environmentally friendly.

- To create demand for environmental improvement until companies and customers are able to perceive and measure the resource inefficiencies of pollution better.

- To level the playing field during the transition period to innovation-based environmental solutions, ensuring that one company cannot gain position by avoiding environmental investments. Regulation provides a buffer for innovative companies until new technologies are proven and the effects of learning can reduce technological costs.

Those who believe that market forces alone will spur innovation may argue that total quality management programs were initiated without regulatory intervention. However, TQM came to the United States and Europe through a different kind of pressure. Decades earlier, TQM had been widely diffused in Japan—the result of a whole host of government efforts to make product quality a national goal, including the creation of the Deming Prize. Only after Japanese companies had devastated them in the marketplace did Americans and Europeans embrace TQM.

The Cost of the Static Mind-Set

Regulators and companies should focus, then, on relaxing the trade-off between environmental protection and competitiveness by encouraging innovation and resource productivity. Yet the current adversarial climate drives up the costs of meeting environmental standards and circumscribes the innovation benefits, making the trade-off far steeper than it needs to be.

To begin with, the power struggle involved in setting and enforcing environmental regulations consumes enormous amounts of resources. A 1992 study by the Rand Institute for Civil Justice, for example, found that 88 percent of the money that insurers paid out between 1986 and 1989 on Superfund claims went to pay for legal and administrative costs, whereas only 12 percent was used for actual site cleanups.[8] The Superfund law may well be the most inefficient environmental law in the United States, but it is not the only cause of inefficiency. We believe that a substantial fraction of environmental spending as well as of the revenues of environmental products and services companies relates to the regulatory struggle itself and not to improving the environment.

One problem with the adversarial process is that it locks companies into static thinking and systematically pushes industry estimates of the costs of regulation upward. A classic example occurred during the debate in the United States on the 1970 Clean Air Act. Lee Iacocca, then executive vice president of the Ford Motor Company, predicted that compliance with the new regulations would require huge price increases for automobiles, force U.S. production to a halt by 1975, and severely damage the U.S. economy. The 1970 Clean Air Act was subsequently enacted, and Iacocca's dire predictions turned out to be wrong. Similar stories are common.

Static thinking causes companies to fight environmental standards that actually could enhance their competitiveness. Most distillers of coal tar in the United States, for example, opposed 1991 regulations requiring substantial reductions in benzene emissions. At the time, the only solution was to cover the tar storage tanks with costly gas blankets. But the regulation spurred Aristech Chemical Corporation of Pittsburgh, Pennsylvania, to develop a way to remove benzene from tar in the first processing step, thereby eliminating the need for gas blankets. Instead of suffering a cost increase, Aristech saved itself $3.3 million.

Moreover, company mind-sets make the costs of addressing environmental regulations appear higher than they actually are. Many companies do not account for a learning curve, although the actual costs of compliance are likely to decline over time. A recent study in the pulp-and-paper sector, for example, found the actual costs of compliance to be four dollars to five dollars and fifty cents per ton, whereas original industry estimates had been as high as sixteen dollars and forty cents.[9] Similarly, the cost of compliance with a 1990 regulation controlling sulfur dioxide emissions is today only about half of what analysts initially predicted, and it is heading lower. With a focus on innovation and resource productivity, today's compliance costs represent an upper limit.

There is legitimate controversy over the benefits to society of specific environmental standards. Measuring the health and safety effects of cleaner air, for example, is the subject of ongoing scientific debate. Some believe that the risks of pollution have been overstated. But whatever the level of *social* benefits proves to be, the *private* costs to companies are still far higher than necessary.

Good Regulation versus Bad

In addition to being high-cost, the current system of environmental regulation in the United States often deters innovative solutions or renders them impossible. The problem with regulation is not its strictness. It is the way in which standards are written and the sheer inefficiency with which regulations are administered. Strict standards can and should promote resource productivity. The United States' regulatory process has squandered this potential, however, by concentrating on cleanup instead of prevention, mandating specific technologies, setting compliance deadlines that are unrealistically short, and subjecting companies to unnecessarily high levels of uncertainty.

The current system discourages risk taking and experimentation. Liability exposure and the government's inflexibility in enforcement, among other things, contribute to the problem. For example, a company that innovates and achieves 95 percent of target emissions reduction while also registering substantial offsetting cost reductions is still 5 percent out of compliance and subject to liability. On the other hand, regulators would reward it for adopting safe but expensive secondary treatment. (See the insert "Innovation-Friendly Regulation.")

Just as bad regulation can damage competitiveness, good regulation can enhance it. Consider the differences between the U.S. pulp-and-paper sector and the Scandinavian. Strict early U.S. regulations in the

---

Innovation-Friendly Regulation

Regulation, properly conceived, need not drive up costs. The following principles of regulatory design will promote innovation, resource productivity, and competitiveness:

Focus on outcomes, not technologies. Past regulations have often prescribed particular remediation technologies, such as catalysts or scrubbers for air pollution. The phrases "best available technology" (BAT) and "best available control technology" (BACT) are deeply rooted in U.S. practice and imply that one technology is best, discouraging innovation.

Enact strict rather than lax regulation. Companies can handle lax regulation incrementally, often with end-of-pipe or secondary treatment solutions. Regulation, therefore, needs to be stringent enough to promote real innovation.

Regulate as close to the end user as practical, while encouraging upstream solutions. This will normally allow more flexibility for innovation in the end product and in all the production and distribution stages. Avoiding pollution entirely or, second best, mitigating it early in the value chain is almost always less costly than late-stage remediation or cleanup.

Employ phase-in periods. Ample but well-defined phase-in periods tied to industry-capital-investment cycles will allow companies to develop innovative resource-saving technologies rather than force them to implement expensive solutions hastily, merely patching over problems. California imposed such short compliance deadlines on its wood-furniture industry that many manufacturers chose to leave the state rather than add costly control equipment.

Use market incentives. Market incentives such as pollution charges and deposit-refund schemes draw attention to resource inefficiencies. In addition, tradable permits provide continuing incentives for innovation and encourage creative use of technologies that exceed current standards.

Harmonize or converge regulations in associated fields. Liability exposure in the United States leads companies to stick to safe, BAT approaches, and inconsistent regulation on alternative technologies deters beneficial innovation. For example, one way to eliminate refrigerator cooling agents suspected of damaging the ozone layer involves replacing them with small amounts of propane and butane. But narrowly conceived safety regulations covering these gases seem to have impeded development of the new technology in the United States, while several leading European companies are already marketing the new products.

Develop regulations in sync with other countries or slightly ahead of them. It is important to minimize possible competitive disadvantages relative to foreign companies that are not yet subject to the same standard. Developing regulations slightly ahead of other countries will also maximize export potential in the pollution-control sector by raising incentives for innovation. When standards in the United States lead world developments, domestic companies get opportunities for valuable early-mover advantages. However, if standards are too far ahead of, or too different in character from, those that are likely to apply to foreign competitors, industry may innovate in the wrong directions.

Make the regulatory process more stable and predictable. The regulatory process is as important as the standards. If standards and phase-in periods are set and accepted early enough and if regulators commit to keeping standards in place for, say, five years, industry can lock in and tackle root-cause solutions instead of hedging against the next twist or turn in government philosophy.

Require industry participation in setting standards from the beginning. U.S. regulation differs sharply from European in its adversarial approach. Industry should help in designing phase-in periods, the content of regulations, and the most effective regulatory process. A predetermined set of information requests and interactions with industry representatives should be a mandatory part of the regulatory process. Both industry and regulators must work toward a climate of trust because industry needs to provide genuinely useful information and regulators need to take industry input seriously.

Develop strong technical capabilities among regulators. Regulators must understand an industry's economics and what drives its competitiveness. Better information exchange will help avoid costly gaming in which ill-informed companies use an array of lawyers and consultants to try to stall the poorly designed regulations of ill-informed regulators.

Minimize the time and resources consumed in the regulatory process itself. Time delays in granting permits are usually costly for companies. Self-regulation with periodic inspections would be more efficient than requiring formal

approvals. Potential and actual litigation creates uncertainty and consumes resources. Mandatory arbitration procedures or rigid arbitration steps before litigation would lower costs and encourage innovation.

For an extended discussion of the ways in which environmental regulation should change, see Michael E. Porter and Claas van der Linde, "Toward a New Conception of the Environment-Competitiveness Relationship," Journal of Economic Perspectives 9, no. 4 (fall 1995).

1970s were imposed without adequate phase-in periods, forcing companies to adopt best available technologies quickly. At that time, the requirements invariably meant installing proven but costly end-of-pipe treatment systems. In Scandinavia, on the other hand, regulation permitted more flexible approaches, enabling companies to focus on the production process itself, not just on secondary treatment of wastes. Scandinavian companies developed innovative pulping and bleaching technologies that not only met emission requirements but also lowered operating costs. Even though the United States was the first to regulate, U.S. companies were unable to realize any first-mover advantages because U.S. regulations ignored a critical principle of good environmental regulation: Create maximum opportunity for innovation by letting industries discover how to solve their own problems.

Unfortunately for the U.S. pulp-and-paper industry, a second principle of good regulation was also ignored: Foster continuous improvement; do not lock in on a particular technology or the status quo. The Swedish regulatory agency took a more effective approach. Whereas the United States mandated strict emissions goals and established very tight compliance deadlines, Sweden started out with looser standards but clearly communicated that tougher ones would follow. The results were predictable. U.S. companies installed secondary treatment systems and stopped there. Swedish producers, anticipating stricter standards, continually incorporated innovative environmental technologies into their normal cycles of capacity replacement and innovation.

The innovation-friendly approach produced the residual effect of raising the competitiveness of the local equipment industry. Spurred by Scandinavian demand for sophisticated process improvements, local pulp-and-paper-equipment suppliers, such as Sunds Defibrator and Kamyr, ultimately made major international gains in selling innovative pulping and bleaching equipment.

Eventually, the Scandinavian pulp-and-paper industry was able to reap innovation offsets that went beyond those directly stemming from regulatory pressures. By the early 1990s, producers realized that growing public awareness of the environmental problems associated with pulp-mill effluents was creating a niche market. For a time, Scandinavian companies with totally chlorine-free paper were able to command significant price premiums and serve a rapidly growing market segment of environmentally informed customers.

Implications for Companies

Certainly, misguided regulatory approaches have imposed a heavy burden on companies. But managers who have responded by digging in their heels to oppose all regulation have been shortsighted as well. It is no secret that Japanese and German automobile makers developed lighter and more fuel-efficient cars in response to new fuel consumption standards, while the less competitive U.S. car industry fought such standards and hoped they would go away. The U.S. car industry eventually realized that it would face extinction if it did not learn to compete through innovation. But clinging to the static mind-set too long cost billions of dollars and many thousands of jobs.

To avoid making the same mistakes, managers must start to recognize environmental improvement as an economic and competitive opportunity, not as an annoying cost or an inevitable threat. Instead of clinging to a perspective focused on regulatory compliance, companies need to ask questions such as What are we wasting? and How could we enhance customer value? The early movers—the companies that can see the opportunity first and embrace innovation-based solutions—will reap major competitive benefits, just as the German and Japanese car makers did. (See the insert "The New Environmentalists.")

At this stage, for most companies, environmental issues are still the province of outsiders and specialists. That is not surprising. Any new management issue tends to go through a predictable life cycle. When it first arises, companies hire outside experts to help them navigate. When practice becomes more developed, internal specialists take over. Only after a field becomes mature do companies integrate it into the ongoing role of line management.

Many companies have delegated the analysis of environmental problems and the development of solutions to outside lawyers and environmental consultants. Such experts in the adversarial regulatory process, who are not deeply familiar with the company's overall technology and operations, inevitably focus on compliance rather than innovation. They invariably favor end-of-pipe solutions. Many consultants, in fact, are associated with vendors who sell such technologies. Some companies are in the second phase, in which environmental issues are assigned to

---

The New Environmentalists

Environmentalists can foster innovation and resource productivity by speaking out for the right kind of regulatory standards and by educating the public to demand innovative environmental solutions. The German section of Greenpeace, for example, noted in 1992 that a mixture of propane and butane was safer for cooling refrigerators than the then-prevalent cooling agents—hydrofluorocarbons or hydrochlorofluorocarbons—that were proposed as replacements for chlorofluorocarbons. Greenpeace for the first time in its history began endorsing a commercial product. It ac-

tually ran an advertising campaign for a refrigerator designed by Foron, a small refrigerator maker on the verge of bankruptcy. The action was greatly leveraged by extensive media coverage and has been a major reason behind the ensuing demand for Foron-built propane-butane refrigerators and the switch that the established refrigerator producers in Germany later made to the same technology.

Environmental organizations can support industry by becoming sources of information about best practices that may not be well known outside of a few pioneering companies. When it realized that German magazine publishers and readers alike were unaware of the much improved quality of chlorine-free paper, Greenpeace Germany issued a magazine printed on chlorine-free paper. It closely resembled the leading German political weekly, *Der Spiegel,* and it encouraged readers to demand that publishers switch to chlorine-free paper. Shortly after, *Der Spiegel* and several other large magazines did indeed switch. Other environmental organizations could shift some resources away from litigation to focus instead on funding and disseminating research on innovations that address environmental problems.

Among U.S. environmental groups, the Environmental Defense Fund (EDF) has been an innovator in its willingness to promote market-based regulatory systems and to

work directly with industry. It supported the sulfur-dioxide trading system that allows companies either to reduce their own emissions or to buy emissions allowances from companies that have managed to exceed their reduction quotas at lower cost. The EDF-McDonald's Waste Reduction Task Force, formed in 1990, led to a substantial redesign of McDonald's packaging, including the elimination of the polystyrene-foam clamshell. EDF is now working with General Motors on plans to remove heavily polluting cars from the road and with Johnson & Johnson, McDonald's, NationsBank, The Prudential Insurance Company of America, Time Warner, and Duke University to promote the use of recycled paper.

Source: Benjamin C. Bonifant and Ian Ratcliffe, "Competitive Implications of Environmental Regulation in the Pulp and Paper Industry," working paper, Management Institute for Environment and Business, Washington, D.C., 1994.

internal specialists. But these specialists—for example, legal, governmental-affairs, or environmental departments—lack full profit responsibility and are separate from the line organization. Again, the result is almost always narrow, incremental solutions.

If the sorts of process and product redesigns needed for true innovation are even to be considered, much less implemented, environmental strategies must become an issue for general management. Environmental impact must be embedded in the overall process of improving productivity and competitiveness. The resource-productivity model, rather than the pollution-control model, must govern decision making.

How can managers accelerate their companies' progress toward a more competitive environmental approach? First, they can measure their direct and indirect environmental impacts. One of the major reasons that companies are not very innovative about environmental problems is ignorance. A large producer of organic chemicals, for example, hired a consultant to explore waste reduction opportunities in its 40 waste streams. A careful audit uncovered 497 different waste streams—the company had been wrong by a factor of more than ten.[10] Our research indicates that the act of measurement alone leads to enormous opportunities to improve productivity.

Companies that adopt the resource-productivity framework and go beyond currently regulated areas will reap the greatest benefits. Companies should inventory all unused, emitted, or discarded resources or packaging. Within the company, some poorly utilized resources will be held within plants, some discharged, and some put in dumpsters. Indirect resource inefficiencies will occur at the level of suppliers, channels, and customers. At the customer level, resource inefficiencies show up in the use of the product, in discarded packaging, and in resources left in the used-up product.

Second, managers can learn to recognize the opportunity cost of underutilized resources. Few companies have analyzed the true cost of toxicity, waste, and what they discard, much less the second-order impacts that waste and discharges have on other activities. Fewer still look beyond the out-of-pocket costs of dealing with pollution to the opportunity cost of the resources they waste or the productivity they forgo. There are scarcely any companies that think about customer value and the opportunity cost of wasted resources at the customer level.

Many companies do not even track environmental spending carefully, and conventional accounting systems are ill equipped to measure underutilized resources. Companies evaluate environmental projects as discrete, stand-alone investments. Straightforward waste- or discharge-reduction investments are screened using high hurdle rates that presume the investments are risky—leaving ten-dollar bills on the ground. Better information and evaluation methods will help managers reduce environmental impact while improving resource productivity.

Third, companies should create a bias in favor of innovation-based, productivity-enhancing solutions. They should trace their own and their customers' discharges, scrap, emissions, and disposal activities back into company activities to gain insight about beneficial product design, packaging, raw material, or process changes. We have been struck by the power of certain systems solutions: Groups of activities may be reconfigured, or substitutions in inputs or packaging may enhance utilization and potential for recovery. Approaches that focus on treatment of discrete discharges should be sent back to the organization for re-thinking.

Current reward systems are as anti-innovation as regulatory policies. At the plant level, companies reward output but ignore environmental costs and wasted resources. The punishment for an innovative, economically efficient solution that falls short of expectations is often far greater than the reward for a costly but "successful" one.

Finally, companies must become more proactive in defining new types of relationships with both regulators and environmentalists. Businesses need a new mind-set. How can companies argue shrilly that regulations harm competitiveness and then expect regulators and environmentalists to be flexible and trusting as those same companies request time to pursue innovative solutions?

The World Economy in Transition

It is time for the reality of modern competition to inform our thinking about the relationship between competitiveness and the environment. Traditionally, nations were competitive if their companies had access to the lowest cost inputs—capital, labor, energy, and raw materials. In industries relying on natural resources, for example, the competitive companies and countries were those with abundant local supplies. Because technology changed slowly, a comparative advantage in inputs was enough for success.

Today globalization is making the notion of comparative advantage obsolete. Companies can source low-cost inputs anywhere, and new, rapidly emerging technologies can offset disadvantages in the cost of inputs. Facing high labor costs at home, for example, a company can automate away the need for unskilled labor. Facing a shortage of a raw material, a company can find an alternative raw material or create a synthetic one. To overcome high space costs, Japanese companies pioneered just-in-time production and avoided storing inventory on the factory floor.

It is no longer enough simply to have resources. Using resources productively is what makes for competitiveness today. Companies can improve resource productivity by producing existing products more efficiently or by making products that are more valuable to customers—products customers are willing to pay more for. Increasingly, the nations and companies that are most competitive are not those with access to the lowest-cost inputs but those that employ the most advanced technology and methods in using their inputs. Because technology is constantly changing, the new paradigm of global competitiveness requires the ability to innovate rapidly.

This new paradigm has profound implications for the debate about environmental policy—about how to approach it, how to regulate, and how strict regulation should be. The new paradigm has brought environmental improvement and competitiveness together. It is important to use resources productively, whether those resources are natural and physical or human and capital. Environmental progress demands that companies innovate to raise resource productivity—and that is precisely what the new challenges of global competition demand. Resisting innovation that reduces pollution, as the U.S. car industry did in the 1970s, will lead not only to environmental damage but also to the loss of competitiveness in the global economy. Developing countries that stick with resource-wasting methods and forgo environmental standards because they are "too expensive" will remain uncompetitive, relegating themselves to poverty.

How an industry responds to environmental problems may, in fact, be a leading indicator of its overall competitiveness. Environmental regulation does not lead inevitably to innovation and competitiveness or to higher productivity for all companies. Only those companies that innovate successfully will win. A truly competitive industry is more likely to take up a new standard as a challenge and respond to it with innovation. An uncompetitive industry, on the other hand, may not be oriented toward innovation and thus may be tempted to fight all regulation.

It is not at all surprising that the debate pitting the environment against competitiveness has developed as it has. Indeed, economically destructive struggles over redistribution are the norm in many areas of public policy. But now is the time for a paradigm shift to carry us forward into the next century. International competition has changed dramatically over the last few decades. Senior managers who grew up at a time when environmental regulation was synonymous with litigation will see increasing evidence that environmental improvement is good business. Successful environmentalists, regulatory agencies, and companies will reject old trade-offs and build on the underlying economic logic that links the environment, resource productivity, innovation, and competitiveness.

NOTES

1. One of the pioneering efforts to see environmental improvement this way is Joel Makower's *The E-Factor: The Bottom-Line Approach to Environmentally Responsible Business* (New York: Times Books, 1993).

2. Andrew King, "Improved Manufacturing Resulting from Learning from Waste: Causes, Importance, and Enabling Conditions," working paper, Stern School of Business, New York University, New York, 1994.

3. Mark H. Dorfman, Warren R. Muir, and Catherine G. Miller, *Environmental Dividends: Cutting More Chemical Wastes* (New York: INFORM, 1992).

4. Don L. Boroughs and Betsy Carpenter, "Helping the Planet and the Economy," *U.S. News and World Report* 110, no. 11, March 25, 1991, p. 46.

5. John H. Sheridan, "Attacking Wastes and Saving Money. . .Some of the Time," *Industry Week*, February 17, 1992, p. 43.

6. Gerald Parkinson, "Reducing Wastes Can Be Cost-Effective," *Chemical Engineering* 97, no. 7, July 1990, p. 30.

7. Stephen J. DeCanio, "Why Do Profitable Energy-Saving Projects Languish?" working paper, Second International Research Conference of the Greening of Industry Network, Cambridge, Massachusetts, 1993.

8. Jan Paul Acton and Lloyd S. Dixon, "Superfund and Transaction Costs: The Experiences of Insurers and Very Large Industrial Firms," working paper, Rand Institute for Civil Justice, Santa Monica, California, 1992.

9. Norman Bonson, Neil McCubbin, and John B. Sprague, "Kraft Mill Effluents in Ontario," report prepared for the Technical Advisory Committee, Pulp and Paper Sector of MISA, Ontario Ministry of the Environment, Toronto, March 29, 1988, p. 166.

10. Parkinson, p. 30.

CHAPTER 11

The Competitive
Advantage of
the Inner City

Michael E. Porter

THE ECONOMIC DISTRESS of America's inner cities may be the most pressing issue facing the nation. The lack of businesses and jobs in disadvantaged urban areas fuels not only a crushing cycle of poverty but also crippling social problems, such as drug abuse and crime. And, as the inner cities continue to deteriorate, the debate on how to aid them grows increasingly divisive.

The sad reality is that the efforts of the past few decades to revitalize the inner cities have failed. The establishment of a sustainable economic base—and with it employment opportunities, wealth creation, role models, and improved local infrastructure—still eludes us despite the investment of substantial resources.

Past efforts have been guided by a social model built around meeting the needs of individuals. Aid to inner cities, then, has largely taken the form of relief programs such as income assistance, housing subsidies, and food stamps, all of which address highly visible—and real—social needs.

The research that this article is based on would not have been possible without the generous support of the Harvard Business School and the assistance of many individuals. Whitney Tilson, Michael Marubio, and Barbara Paige were integrally involved in preparing this article. I would also like to thank the many M.B.A. students from both the Harvard Business School and other schools who have been involved in the research effort that made this article possible.

May–June 1995

Programs aimed more directly at economic development have been fragmented and ineffective. These piecemeal approaches have usually taken the form of subsidies, preference programs, or expensive efforts to stimulate economic activity in tangential fields such as housing, real estate, and neighborhood development. Lacking an overall strategy, such programs have treated the inner city as an island isolated from the surrounding economy and subject to its own unique laws of competition. They have encouraged and supported small, subscale businesses designed to serve the local community but ill equipped to attract the community's own spending power, much less *export* outside it. In short, the social model has inadvertently undermined the creation of economically viable companies. Without such companies and the jobs they create, the social problems will only worsen.

The time has come to recognize that revitalizing the inner city will require a radically different approach. While social programs will continue to play a critical role in meeting human needs and improving education, they must support—and not undermine—a coherent economic strategy. The question we should be asking is how inner city-based businesses and nearby employment opportunities for inner city residents can proliferate and grow. A sustainable economic base *can* be created in the inner city, but only as it has been created elsewhere: through private, for-profit initiatives and investment based on economic self-interest and genuine competitive advantage—not through artificial inducements, charity, or government mandates.

We must stop trying to cure the inner city's problems by perpetually increasing social investment and hoping for economic activity to follow. Instead, an economic model must begin with the premise that inner city businesses should be profitable and positioned to compete on a regional, national, and even international scale. These businesses should be capable not only of serving the local community but also of exporting goods and services to the surrounding economy. The cornerstone of such a model is to identify and exploit the competitive advantages of inner cities that will translate into truly profitable businesses.

Our policies and programs have fallen into the trap of redistributing wealth. The real need—and the real opportunity—is to create wealth.

Toward a New Model: Location and Business Development

Economic activity in and around inner cities will take root if it enjoys a competitive advantage and occupies a niche that is hard to replicate elsewhere. If companies are to prosper, they must find a compelling competitive reason for locating in the inner city. A coherent strategy for development starts with that fundamental economic principle, as the contrasting experiences of the following companies illustrate.

Alpha Electronics (the company's name has been disguised), a twenty-eight-person company that designed and manufactured multimedia computer peripherals, was initially based in lower Manhattan. In 1987, the New York City Office of Economic Development set out to orchestrate an economic "renaissance" in the South Bronx by inducing companies to relocate there. Alpha, a small but growing company, was sincerely interested in contributing to the community and eager to take advantage of the city's willingness to subsidize its operations. The city, in turn, was happy that a high-tech company would begin to stabilize a distressed neighborhood and create jobs. In exchange for relocating, the city provided Alpha with numerous incentives that would lower costs and boost profits. It appeared to be an ideal strategy.

By 1994, however, the relocation effort had proved a failure for all concerned. Despite the rapid growth of its industry, Alpha was left with only eight of its original twenty-eight employees. Unable to attract high-quality employees to the South Bronx or to train local residents, the company was forced to outsource its manufacturing and some of its design work. Potential suppliers and customers refused to visit Alpha's offices. Without the city's attention to security, the company was plagued by theft.

What went wrong? Good intentions notwithstanding, the arrangement failed the test of business logic. Before undertaking the move, Alpha and the city would have been wise to ask themselves why none of the South Bronx's thriving businesses was in electronics. The South Bronx as a location offered no specific advantages to support Alpha's business, and it had several disadvantages that would prove fatal. Isolated from the lower Manhattan hub of computer-design and software companies, Alpha was cut off from vital connections with customers, suppliers, and electronic designers.

In contrast, Matrix Exhibits, a $2.2 million supplier of trade-show exhibits that has thirty employees, is thriving in Atlanta's inner city. When Tennessee-based Matrix decided to enter the Atlanta market in 1985, it could have chosen a variety of locations. All the other companies that create and rent trade-show exhibits are based in Atlanta's suburbs. But the Atlanta World Congress Center, the city's major exhibition space, is just a six-minute drive from the inner city, and Matrix chose the location because it provided a real competitive advantage. Today Matrix offers customers superior response time, delivering trade-show exhibits faster than its suburban competitors. Matrix benefits from low rental rates for warehouse space—about half the rate its competitors pay for similar space in the suburbs—and draws half its employees from the local community. The commitment of local police has helped the company avoid any serious security problems. Today Matrix is one of the top five exhibition houses in Georgia.

Alpha and Matrix demonstrate how location can be critical to the success or failure of a business. Every location—whether it be a nation, a region, or a city—has a set of unique local conditions that underpin the ability of companies based there to compete in a particular field. The competitive advantage of a location does not usually arise in isolated companies but in clusters of companies—in other words, in companies that are in the same industry or otherwise linked together through customer, supplier, or similar relationships. Clusters represent critical masses of skill, information, relationships, and infrastructure in a given field. Unusual or sophisticated local demand gives companies insight into customers' needs. Take Massachusetts's highly competitive cluster of information-technology industries: it includes companies specializing in semiconductors, workstations, supercomputers, software, networking equipment, databases, market research, and computer magazines.

Clusters arise in a particular location for specific historical or geographic reasons—reasons that may cease to matter over time as the cluster itself becomes powerful and competitively self-sustaining. In successful clusters such as Hollywood, Silicon Valley, Wall Street, and Detroit, several competitors often push one another to improve products and processes. The presence of a group of competing companies contributes to the formation of new suppliers, the growth of companies in related fields, the formation of specialized training programs, and the emergence of technological centers of excellence in colleges and universities. The clusters also provide newcomers with access to expertise, connections, and infrastructure that they in turn can learn and exploit to their own economic advantage.

If locations (and the events of history) give rise to clusters, it is clusters that drive economic development. They create new capabilities, new companies, and new industries. I initially described this theory of location in *The Competitive Advantage of Nations* (Free Press, 1990), applying it to the relatively large geographic areas of nations and states. But it is just as relevant to smaller areas such as the inner city. To bring the theory to bear on the inner city, we must first identify the inner city's competitive advantages and the ways inner city businesses can forge connections with the surrounding urban and regional economies.

The True Advantages of the Inner City

The first step toward developing an economic model is identifying the inner city's true competitive advantages. There is a common misperception that the inner city enjoys two main advantages: low-cost real estate and labor. These so-called advantages are more illusory than real. Real estate and labor costs are often higher in the inner city than in suburban and rural areas. And even if inner cities were able to offer lower-cost labor and real estate compared with other locations in the United States, basic input costs can no longer give companies from relatively prosperous nations a competitive edge in the global economy. Inner cities would inevitably lose jobs to countries like Mexico or China, where labor and real estate are far cheaper.

Only attributes that are unique to inner cities will support viable businesses. My ongoing research of urban areas across the United States identifies four main advantages of the inner city: strategic location, local market demand, integration with regional clusters, and human resources. Various companies and programs have identified and exploited each of those advantages from time to time. To date, however, no systematic effort has been mounted to harness them.

Inner cities are located in what *should* be economically valuable areas. They sit near congested high-rent areas, major business centers, and transportation and communications nodes. As a result, inner cities can offer a competitive edge to companies that benefit from proximity to downtown business districts, logistical infrastructure, entertainment or tourist centers, and concentrations of companies.

For example, Boston's food processing and distribution industry gains a competitive edge from its inner city location in Newmarket Square (see Figure 11.1). The industry consists of such businesses as seafood importers, meat processors, bakeries, and food distributors. Because they are near downtown Boston, these businesses can make rapid deliveries, and downtown buyers have a convenient location at which to purchase goods. Land, although more costly than in the suburbs, is cheaper in the inner city than it is downtown, and zoning regulations permit food processing operations. Newmarket Square has excellent access to trucking as well as sea and air transport, which provides it with a particular competitive advantage in the export of seafood. The combination of those factors has produced a dense concentration of processors, caterers, truckers, wholesalers, distributors, and other suppliers in the inner city.

Although the location of Boston's food processing cluster has historic roots that predate the modern inner city, examples of newly formed companies underscore how critical an advantage proximity can be. Consider the catering supplier Be Our Guest. Founded in 1984, the company rents linens, party equipment, and other hard goods associated with the catering business. Located in Boston's inner city neighborhood of Roxbury, the company enjoys immediate and easy access to downtown Boston. As a result, it is able to offer a higher level of service to customers than its competitors can. To reinforce its service strategy, Be Our Guest maintains sufficient inventory levels to meet peaks in demand. Today the company has thirty-six full-time employees and annual sales of $1.2 million.

In Boston and Los Angeles, it is striking how many of the businesses that have remained in the inner city in the face of numerous difficulties are ones for which location matters. For example, both cities have a concentration of logistics and storage businesses. Advances in transpor-

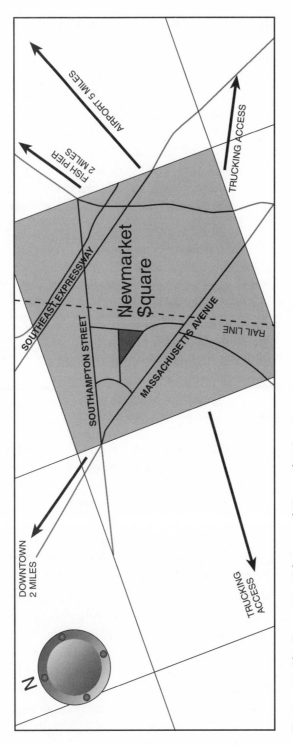

Figure 11.1 The Competitive Advantage of Newmarket Square

tation and communications may have reduced the importance of location for some kinds of businesses. However, the increasing importance of regional clusters and of such concepts as just-in-time delivery, superior customer service, and close partnerships between customers and suppliers are making location more critical than ever before.

There is significant potential, then, for expanding the inner-city business base by building on the advantage of strategic location. Among the initial prospects are location-sensitive industries now situated elsewhere, nearby companies and industries that face space constraints, and back-office or support functions amenable to relocation or outsourcing. Consider Boston's Longwood medical area, a huge concentration of world-class health care facilities. Longwood is located near the inner city neighborhoods of Roxbury and Jamaica Plain. Today such activities as laundry services, building maintenance, and just-in-time delivery of supplies are performed in-house or by suburban vendors. But, because of Longwood's proximity to the inner city, activities like these could be shifted to businesses based in Roxbury or Jamaica Plain—especially if basic infrastructure such as roads could be improved.

LOCAL MARKET DEMAND

The inner city market itself represents the most immediate opportunity for inner-city-based entrepreneurs and businesses. At a time when most other markets are saturated, inner city markets remain poorly served—especially in retailing, financial services, and personal services. In Los Angeles, for example, retail penetration per resident in the inner city compared with the rest of the city is 35 percent in supermarkets, 40 percent in department stores, and 50 percent in hobby, toy, and game stores.

The first notable quality of the inner city market is its size. Even though average inner city incomes are relatively low, high population density translates into an immense market with substantial purchasing power. Boston's inner city, for example, has an estimated total family income of $3.4 billion. Spending power per acre is comparable with the rest of the city despite a 21 percent lower average household income level than in the rest of Boston, and, more significantly, higher than in the surrounding suburbs. In addition, the market is young and growing rapidly, owing in part to immigration and relatively high birth rates.

A handful of forward-looking entrepreneurs have recognized the opportunities for profit and growth in this large, underdeveloped market and have opened retail outlets in the inner city. Chicago's historic retailer Goldblatt Brothers found new life after bankruptcy with a strategy built on inner city stores. In 1981, the company closed all its stores but six profitable ones located in the inner city. Focusing on cash-and-carry items and offering goods at closeout prices, Goldblatt Brothers has re-emerged as a competitive retailer. Today the company has fourteen stores, most of which are located in Chicago's inner city. Similarly, Stop & Shop and Purity Supreme are opening new stores in the inner city of Boston.

Another important quality of the inner city market is its character. Most products and services have been designed for white consumers and businesses. As a result, product configurations, retail concepts, entertainment, and personal and business services have not been adapted to the needs of inner city customers. Although microsegmentation has been slow to come to the inner city, it holds promise for creating thriving businesses.

Inner city consumers, in fact, represent a major growth market of the future, and companies based in the inner city have a unique ability to understand and address their needs. For example, Miami-based, Latino-owned CareFlorida has rapidly expanded its HMO business by tailoring its marketing to Latino customers. And Detroit's Universal Casket has grown to $3 million in sales by focusing on African-American-owned funeral homes. Many of the largest and most enduringly successful minority-owned (although not necessarily inner city-based) businesses have drawn their advantages from serving inner city residents' cultural and ethnic needs in fields such as food products (Parks Sausage and Brooks Sausages); beauty care (Soft Sheen, Proline, Dudley, Luster Products, and Johnson Products); and media (Essence, Earl Graves, Johnson Publishing, and Black Entertainment Television). Although inner city businesses need not be limited to serving local needs, this kind of focused strategy is one way to gain a clear competitive advantage over established businesses such as Procter & Gamble, Safeway, and Levi Strauss.

More important, businesses catering to local demand have the potential to expand beyond the inner city and become major players. Companies can target and sell not only to their own local communities but also to similar communities nationally and even internationally. Consider

Americas' Food Basket, a Cuban-owned supermarket based in Boston's inner city. In its second year of operation, the company has reached sales of $8 million annually and is profitable. It has developed a product mix that satisfies local demand better than mainstream supermarkets do. Its management's strong relationship with the community has reduced security problems and employee turnover. Unlike other nearby mom-and-pop stores, Americas' Food Basket has developed a partnership with a leading national wholesaler that provides goods and financing at competitive rates. As a result, its selection, prices, and service are far superior to those of smaller competitors. More important, Americas' Food Basket shows signs of becoming a major regional business by seeking ways to export its goods to the surrounding region. It is currently expanding into wholesaling with a start-up called Selmac Corporation. Selmac will supply mainly Latino products to Americas' Food Basket and to small *bodegas* throughout the inner city and the surrounding region. It also plans to bid on contracts to supply wholesale food services to schools, prisons, and other institutions throughout Massachusetts.

Tailored retailing concepts in a broad range of areas such as food, clothing, pharmaceuticals, toys, books, and restaurants could also set off a chain reaction of opportunities: Companies create demand for new types of products, which in turn creates new opportunities for manufacturers of specialized products. For example, tailored supermarkets are increasing the demand for established ethnic food producers and distributors such as Goya Foods, a supplier of Latino foods with annual sales of approximately $500 million. Such stores also represent a critical distribution channel for recent start-ups such as Glory Foods, which sells canned foods targeted at African-American consumers.

The most intriguing attribute of the inner city market is its potential to be a leading indicator of major nationwide trends. The tastes and sensibilities of inner city communities are cutting-edge in a number of respects and often become mainstream. Popular music is one example. Or consider Parks Sausage, based in Baltimore, Maryland, which developed its food products for African-American consumers but has found a receptive market nationally. Today it is competing head-to-head with Jimmy Dean Sausage, the industry leader.

Ultimately, what will attract the inner city consumer more than anything else is a new breed of company that is not small and high-cost but a professionally managed major business employing the latest in technology, marketing, and management techniques. This kind of company, much more than exhortation, will attract spending power and recycle capital within the inner city community.

INTEGRATION WITH REGIONAL CLUSTERS

The most exciting prospects for the future of inner city economic development lie in capitalizing on nearby regional clusters: those unique-to-a-region collections of related companies that are competitive nationally and even globally. For example, Boston's inner city is next door to world-class financial-services and health-care clusters. South Central Los Angeles is close to an enormous entertainment cluster and a large logistical-services and wholesaling complex.

The ability to access competitive clusters is a very different attribute—and one much more far-reaching in economic implication—than the more generic advantage of proximity to a large downtown area with concentrated activity. Competitive clusters create two potential advantages. The first is for business formation. Companies providing supplies, components, and support services could be created to take advantage of the inner city's proximity to multiple nearby customers in the cluster. For example, Detroit-based Mexican Industries has emerged as one of the most respected suppliers of head rests, arm rests, air bags, and other auto parts by forging close relationships with General Motors, Ford, Chrysler, and Volkswagen of America. Last year, the company had more than 1,000 employees, most of whom live in the inner city, and revenues of more than $100 million. Bing Steel, a fifty-four-person company with $57 million in sales, has made similar connections, supplying flat roll steel and coils to the auto industry.

The second advantage of these clusters is the potential they offer inner city companies to compete in downstream products and services. For example, an inner city company could draw on Boston's strength in financial services to provide services tailored to inner city needs—such as secured credit cards, factoring, and mutual funds—both within and outside the inner city in Boston and elsewhere in the country. Boston Bank of Commerce (BBOC) is a trusted local institution in the inner city with strong ties to the community. It has many small nonprofit customers, such as the Dimock Community Health Center in Roxbury, which has a $1 million endowment. There are many nonprofit organizations like Dimock whose funds are sitting idle in low-interest savings accounts because they lack the investment savvy and size to attract sophisticated money managers. In toto, however, such organizations represent a significant pool of capital. BBOC sees an opportunity here to take advantage of the trust it enjoys within the community and the proximity of world-class asset managers in the city's nearby financial services cluster. The company is developing a product to do asset management for nonprofits in its service area; it will pool funds from its clients and then subcontract their management to companies in the nearby cluster.

Few of these opportunities are currently being pursued. Most of today's inner city businesses either have not been export oriented, selling only within the local community rather than outside it, or have seen their opportunities principally in terms defined by government preference programs. Consequently, networks and relationships with surrounding companies are woefully underdeveloped. New private sector initiatives will be needed to make these connections and to increase inner city entrepreneurs' awareness of their value. Integration with regional clusters is potentially the inner city's most powerful and sustainable competitive advantage over the long term. It also provides tremendous leverage for development efforts: By focusing on upgrading existing and nascent clusters, rather than on supporting isolated companies or industries, public and private investments in training, infrastructure, and technology can benefit multiple companies simultaneously.

HUMAN RESOURCES

The inner city's fourth advantage takes on a number of deeply entrenched myths about the nature of its residents. The first myth is that inner city residents do not want to work and opt for welfare over gainful employment. Although there is a pressing need to deal with inner city residents who are unprepared for work, most inner city residents are industrious and eager to work. For moderate-wage jobs (six to ten dollars per hour) that require little formal education (for instance, warehouse workers, production-line workers, and truck drivers), employers report that they find hardworking, dedicated employees in the inner city. For example, a company in Boston's inner city neighborhood of Dorchester bakes and decorates cakes sold to supermarkets throughout the region. It attracts and retains area residents at seven to eight dollars per hour (plus contributions to pensions and health insurance) and has almost 100 local employees. The loyalty of its labor pool is one of the factors that has allowed the bakery to thrive.

Admittedly, many of the jobs currently available to inner city residents provide limited opportunities for advancement. But the fact is that they are jobs; and the inner city and its residents need many more of them close to home. Proposals that workers commute to jobs in distant suburbs—or move to be near those jobs—underestimate the barriers that travel time and relative skill level represent for inner city residents. Moreover, in deciding what types of businesses are appropriate to locate in the inner city, it is critical to be realistic about the pool of potential employees. Attracting high-tech companies might make for better press, but it is of little benefit to inner city residents. Recall the contrasting experiences of Alpha Electronics and Matrix Exhibits. In the case of Alpha, there was a complete mismatch between the company's need for highly skilled professionals and the available labor pool in the local community. In contrast, Matrix carefully considered the available workforce when it established its Atlanta office. Unlike the Tennessee headquarters, which custom-designs and creates exhibits for each client, the Atlanta office specializes in rentals made from prefabricated components—work requiring less-skilled labor, which can be drawn from the inner city. Given the workforce, low-skill jobs are realistic and economically viable: they represent the first rung on the economic ladder for many individuals who otherwise would be unemployed. Over time, successful job creation will trigger a self-reinforcing process that raises skill and wage levels.

The second myth is that the inner city's only entrepreneurs are drug dealers. In fact, there is a real capacity for legitimate entrepreneurship among inner city residents, most of which has been channeled into the provision of social services. For instance, Boston's inner city has numerous social service providers as well as social, fraternal, and religious organizations. Behind the creation and building of those organizations is a whole cadre of local entrepreneurs who have responded to intense local demand for social services and to funding opportunities provided by government, foundations, and private sector sponsors. The challenge is to redirect some of that talent and energy toward building for-profit businesses and creating wealth.

The third myth is that skilled minorities, many of whom grew up in or near inner cities, have abandoned their roots. Today's large and growing pool of talented minority managers represents a new generation of potential inner city entrepreneurs. Many have been trained at the nation's leading business schools and have gained experience in the nation's leading companies. Approximately 2,800 African Americans and 1,400 Hispanics graduate from M.B.A. programs every year compared with only a handful twenty years ago. Thousands of highly trained minorities are working at leading companies such as Morgan Stanley, Citibank, Ford, Hewlett-Packard, and McKinsey & Company. Many of these managers have developed the skills, network, capital base, and confidence to begin thinking about joining or starting entrepreneurial companies in the inner city. Two Harvard Business School graduates, for example, have launched Delray Farms with the aim of creating a national chain of small inner city supermarkets that focus on produce and other perishables. Backed by significant private-equity capital, Delray Farms is operating its first store in Chicago and is planning to open six new stores within a year.

The Real Disadvantages of the Inner City

The second step toward creating a coherent economic strategy is addressing the very real disadvantages of locating businesses in the inner city. The inescapable fact is that businesses operating in the inner city face greater obstacles than those based elsewhere. Many of those obstacles are needlessly inflicted by government. Unless the disadvantages are addressed directly, instead of indirectly through subsidies or mandates, the inner city's competitive advantages will continue to erode.

LAND

Although vacant property is abundant in inner cities, much of it is not economically usable. Assembling small parcels into meaningful sites can be prohibitively expensive and is further complicated by the fact that a number of city, state, and federal agencies each control land and fight over turf. For example, development of the Jeffrey Plaza shopping center in Chicago's South Side required government efforts over eight years to assemble twenty-one contiguous parcels. Similarly, attempts to rebuild South Central Los Angeles after the 1992 riots have been hampered because only nine of 200 vacant or underutilized properties are larger than one acre. (By comparison, Wal-Mart requires four to six acres for a single store.) Once assembled, an inner city site often requires expensive demolition, environmental cleanup, and extensive litigation. Private developers and banks tend to avoid sites with even a hint of environmental problems because of punitive liability laws.

BUILDING COSTS

The cost of building in the inner city is significantly higher than in the suburbs because of the costs and delays associated with logistics, negotiations with community groups, and strict urban regulations: restrictive zoning, architectural codes, permits, inspections, and government-required union contracts and minority set-asides. Ironically, despite the desperate need for new projects, construction in inner cities is far more regulated than it is in the suburbs—a legacy of big city politics and entrenched bureaucracies.

More damaging than regulatory costs is the uncertainty that the regulatory process creates for potential investors. Managers interviewed in Boston, Los Angeles, and Chicago expressed frustration with the three-year to five-year waiting periods necessary to obtain the numerous permit and site approvals required to build, expand, or improve facilities. Undeniably, the wait is expensive; but the uncertainty about whether an application will be approved or when a ruling will be made makes forming a financial strategy nearly impossible.

OTHER COSTS

Compared with the suburbs, inner cities have high costs for water, other utilities, workers' compensation, health care, insurance, permitting and other fees, real estate and other taxes, OSHA compliance, and neighborhood hiring requirements. For example, Russer Foods, a manufacturing company located in Boston's inner city, operates a comparable plant in upstate New York. The Boston plant's expenses are 55 percent higher for workers' compensation, 50 percent higher for family medical insurance, 166 percent higher for unemployment insurance, 340 percent higher for water, and 67 percent higher for electricity. High costs like these drive away companies and hold down wages. Some costs, such as those for workers' compensation, apply to the state or region as a whole. Others, such as real estate taxes, apply citywide. Still others, such as property insurance, are specific to the inner city. All are devastating to maintaining fragile inner city companies and to attracting new businesses.

It is an unfortunate reality that many cities—because they have a greater proportion of residents dependent on welfare, Medicaid, and other social programs—require higher government spending and, as a result, higher corporate taxes. The resulting tax burden feeds a vicious cycle—driving out more companies while requiring even higher taxes from those that remain. Cities have been reluctant to challenge entrenched bureaucracies and unions, as well as inefficient and outdated government departments, all of which unduly raise city costs.

Finally, excessive regulation not only drives up building and other costs but also hampers almost all facets of business life in the inner city, from putting up an awning over a shop window to operating a pushcart to making site improvements. Regulation also stunts inner city entrepreneurship, serving as a formidable barrier to small and start-up companies. Restrictive licensing and permitting, high licensing fees, and archaic safety and health regulations create barriers to entry into the very types of businesses that are logical and appropriate for creating jobs and wealth in the inner city.

SECURITY

Both the reality and the perception of crime represent profound impediments to urban economic development. First, crime against property raises costs. For example, the Shops at Church Square, an inner city strip shopping center in Cleveland, Ohio, spends two dollars per square foot more than a comparable suburban center for a full-time security guard, increased lighting, and continuous cleaning—raising overall costs by more than 20 percent. Second, crime against employees and customers creates an unwillingness to work in and patronize inner city establishments and restricts companies' hours of operation. Fear of crime ranks among the most important reasons why companies opening new facilities failed to consider inner city locations and why companies already located in the inner city left. Currently, police devote most of their resources to the security of residential areas, largely overlooking commercial and industrial sites.

INFRASTRUCTURE

Transportation infrastructure planning, which today focuses primarily on the mobility of residents for shopping and commuting, should consider equally the mobility of goods and the ease of commercial transactions. The most critical aspects of the new economic model—the importance of the location of the inner city, the connections between inner city businesses and regional clusters, and the development of export-oriented businesses—require the presence of strong logistical links between inner city business sites and the surrounding economy. Unfortunately, the business infrastructure of the inner city has fallen into disrepair. The capacity of roads, the frequency and location of highway on-ramps and off-ramps, the links to downtown, and the access to railways, airports, and regional logistical networks are inadequate.

EMPLOYEE SKILLS

Because their average education levels are low, many inner city residents lack the skills to work in any but the most unskilled occupations. To make matters worse, employment opportunities for less-educated workers have fallen markedly. In Boston between 1970 and 1990, for example, the percentage of jobs held by people without high school diplomas dropped from 29 percent to 7 percent, while those held by college graduates climbed from 18 percent to 44 percent. And the unemployment rate for African-American men aged sixteen to sixty-four with less than a high school education in major northeastern cities rose from 19 percent in 1970 to 57 percent in 1990.

MANAGEMENT SKILLS

The managers of most inner city companies lack formal business training. That problem, however, is not unique to the inner city; it is a characteristic of small businesses in general. Many individuals with extensive work histories but little or no formal managerial training start businesses. Inner city companies without well-trained managers experience a series of predictable problems that are similar to those that affect many small businesses: weaknesses in strategy development, market segmentation, customer-needs evaluation, introduction of information technology, process design, cost control, securing or restructuring financing, interaction with lenders and government regulatory agencies, crafting business plans, and employee training. Local community colleges often offer management courses, but their quality is uneven, and entrepreneurs are hard-pressed for time to attend them.

CAPITAL

Access to debt and equity capital represents a formidable barrier to entrepreneurship and company growth in inner city areas.

First, most inner city businesses still suffer from poor access to debt funding because of the limited attention that mainstream banks paid them historically. Even in the best of circumstances, small-business lending is only marginally profitable to banks because transaction costs are high relative to loan amounts. Many banks remain in small-business lending only to attract deposits and to help sell other more profitable products.

The federal government has made several efforts to address the inner city's problem of debt capital. As a result of legislation like the Community Reinvestment Act, passed in order to overcome bias in lending, banks have begun to pay much more attention to inner city areas. In Boston, for example, leading banks are competing fiercely to lend in the inner city—and some claim to be doing so profitably. Direct financing efforts by government, however, have proved ineffective. The proliferation of government loan pools and quasi-public lending organizations has produced fragmentation, market confusion, and duplication of overhead. Business loans that would provide scale to private sector lenders are siphoned off by these organizations, many of which are high-cost, bureaucratic, and risk-averse. In the end, the development of high-quality private sector expertise in inner city business financing has been undermined.

Second, equity capital has been all but absent. Inner city entrepreneurs often lack personal or family savings and networks of individuals to draw on for capital. Institutional sources of equity capital are scarce for minority-owned companies and have virtually ignored inner city business opportunities.

ATTITUDES

A final obstacle to companies in the inner city is antibusiness attitudes. Some workers perceive businesses as exploitative, a view that guarantees poor relations between labor and management. Equally debilitating are the antibusiness attitudes held by community leaders and social activists. These attitudes are the legacy of a regrettable history of poor treatment of workers, departures of companies, and damage to the environment. But holding on to these views today is counterproductive. Too often, community leaders mistakenly view businesses as a means of directly meeting social needs; as a result, they have unrealistic expectations for corporate involvement in the community. For example, some businesses interested in locating in Boston's inner city decided against it because of demands to build playgrounds, fund scholarships, and cede control of hiring and training to community-based organizations. Such demands on existing and potential businesses rarely help the community; instead, they drive businesses—and jobs—to other locations.

Demanding linkage payments and contributions and stirring up antibusiness sentiment are political tools that brought questionable results in the past when owners had less discretion about where they chose to locate their companies. In today's increasingly competitive business environment, such tactics will serve only to stunt economic growth.

Changing Roles and Responsibilities for Inner City Development

Overcoming the business disadvantages of the inner city as well as building on its inherent advantages will require the commitment and involvement of business, government, and the nonprofit sector. Each will have to abandon deeply held beliefs and past approaches. Each must be willing to accept a new model for the inner city based on an economic rather than a social perspective. The private sector, not government or social service organizations, must be the focus of the new model. (See Table 11.1.)

THE NEW ROLE OF THE PRIVATE SECTOR

The economic model challenges the private sector to assume the leading role. First, however, it must adopt new attitudes toward the inner city. Most private sector initiatives today are driven by preference programs or charity. Such activities would never stand on their own merits in the marketplace. It is inevitable, then, that they contribute to growing cynicism. The private sector will be most effective if it focuses on what it does best: creating and supporting economically viable businesses built on true competitive advantage. It should pursue four immediate opportunities as it assumes its new role.

Table 11.1   Inner City Economic Development

New Model	Old Model
Economic: create wealth	Social: redistribute wealth
Private sector	Government and social service organizations
Profitable businesses	Subsidized businesses
Integration with the regional economy	Isolation from the larger economy
Companies that are export oriented	Companies that serve the local community
Skilled and experienced minorities engaged in building businesses	Skilled and experienced minorities engaged in the social service sector
Mainstream, private sector institutions enlisted	Special institutions created
Inner city disadvantages addressed directly	Inner city disadvantages counterbalanced with subsidies
Government focused on improving the environment for business	Government involved directly in providing services or funding

Create and expand business activity in the inner city. The most important contribution companies can make to inner cities is simply to do business there. Inner cities hold untapped potential for profitable businesses. Companies and entrepreneurs must seek out and seize those opportunities that build on the true advantages of the inner city. In particular, retailers, franchisers, and financial services companies have immediate opportunities. Franchises represent an especially attractive model for inner city entrepreneurship because they provide not only a business concept but also training and support.

Businesses can learn from the mistakes that many outside companies have made in the inner city. One error is the failure of retail and service businesses to tailor their goods and services to the local market. The needs and preferences of the inner city market can vary greatly—something that companies like Goldblatt Brothers have recognized. The Chicago retailer understands that its inner city customers buy to meet immediate needs, and it has tailored its retail merchandise and purchasing planning to its customers' buying habits. For example, unlike most stores, which stock winter coats in the fall, Goldblatt Brothers stocks its coats in the winter.

Another common mistake is the failure to build relationships within the community and to hire locally. Hiring local residents builds loyalty from neighborhood customers, and local employees of retail and service businesses can help stores customize their products. Evidence suggests that companies that were perceived to be in touch with the community had far fewer security problems, whether or not the owners lived in the community. For example, Americas' Food Basket hires locally and is widely viewed as a good citizen of the community. As a result, management reports that it has not had to hire a security guard and that neighbors often call if they witness anything amiss.

Companies have discovered a number of other effective tactics for dealing with security. For instance, large concentrations of businesses spread security costs and reinforce perceptions of safety. MetroTech, a back-office operations complex serving nearby Wall Street, is located in a high-poverty and high-crime area near the federal buildings in downtown Brooklyn. The developers created an 18-acre campus that could support 4 million to 8 million square feet of office space. The complex is so large that tenants pay only 33 cents per square foot for twenty-four-hour private security. Because transportation infrastructure adds to perceptions of safety in traveling to and from business locations, MetroTech enlisted the city government to renovate the local subway stations and to locate a police branch near the site. Crime has been insignificant, and MetroTech is fully occupied by leading financial institutions.

In other cases, companies have organized themselves into associations to increase the effectiveness of security and to spread costs. The associations work closely with the police department and with members of the community to identify and address security problems. In some cities, special neighborhood-managed tax-assessment districts—such as New York City's many Business Improvement Districts—have been established to provide funds for supplemental security protection and other services.

Establish business relationships with inner city companies. By entering into joint ventures or customer-supplier relationships, outside companies will help inner city companies by encouraging them to export and by forcing them to be competitive. In the long run, both sides will benefit. For example, AB&W Engineering, a Dorchester-based metal fabricator, has built a close working relationship with General Motors. GM has given AB&W management assistance and a computerized ordering system and has referred a lot of new business to AB&W. In turn, AB&W has become a high-performing and reliable supplier. Such relationships, based not on charity but on mutual self-interest, are sustainable ones; every major company should develop them.

Redirect corporate philanthropy from social services to business-to-business efforts. Countless companies give many millions of dollars each year to worthy inner-city social-service agencies. But philanthropic efforts will be more effective if they also focus on building business-to-business relationships that, in the long run, will reduce the need for social services.

First, corporations could have a tremendous impact on training. The existing system for job training in the United States is ineffective. Training programs are fragmented, overhead intensive, and disconnected from the needs of industry. Many programs train people for nonexistent jobs in industries with no projected growth. Although reforming training will require the help of government, the private sector must determine how and where resources should be allocated to ensure that the specific employment needs of local and regional businesses are met. Ultimately, employers, not government, should certify all training programs based on relevant criteria and likely job availability.

Training programs led by the private sector could be built around industry clusters located in both the inner city (for example, restaurants, food service, and food processing in Boston) and the nearby regional economy (for example, financial services and health care in Boston). Industry associations and trade groups, supported by government incentives, could sponsor their own training programs in collaboration with local training institutions.

Programs that help inner city residents with the school-to-work transition could also take advantage of regional clusters. Project ProTech in Boston lets high school students compete for apprentice-like positions in the health care cluster. The program mixes classroom work and internship training during the school year and over the summer, beginning in the junior year of high school. Project ProTech is currently expanding to include other clusters, such as utilities and financial services.

Second, the private sector could make an equally substantial impact by providing management assistance to inner city companies. As with training, current programs financed or operated by the government are inadequate. Outside companies have much to offer companies in the inner city: talent, know-how, and contacts. One approach to upgrading management skills is to emphasize networking with companies in the regional economy that either are part of the same cluster (customers, suppliers, and related businesses) or have expertise in needed areas. An inner city company could team up with a partner in the region who provides management assistance; or a consortium of companies with a required expertise, such as information technology, could provide assistance to inner city businesses in need of upgrading their systems.

Professional associations could develop advisory programs for inner city managers. Business schools could develop and teach custom-designed short and practical executive programs or assist inner city companies through field studies programs. The Harvard Business School, for example, offers a for-credit course that matches teams of M.B.A. students with inner city companies. We are encouraging the development of such programs elsewhere.

Adopt the right model for equity capital investments. The investment community—especially venture capitalists—must be convinced of the viability of investing in the inner city. There is a small but growing number of minority-oriented equity providers (although none specifically focus on inner cities). A successful model for inner city investing will probably not look like the familiar venture-capital model created primarily for technology companies. Instead, it may resemble the equity funds operating in the emerging economies of Russia or Hungary— investing in such mundane but potentially profitable projects as supermarkets and laundries. Ultimately, inner-city-based businesses that follow the principles of competitive advantage will generate appropriate returns to investors—particularly if aided by appropriate incentives, such as tax exclusions for capital gains and dividends for qualifying inner city businesses.

THE NEW ROLE OF GOVERNMENT

To date, government has assumed primary responsibility for bringing about the economic revitalization of the inner city. Existing programs at the federal, state, and local levels designed to create jobs and attract businesses have been piecemeal and fragmented at best. Still worse, these programs have been based on subsidies and mandates rather than on marketplace realities. Unless we find new approaches, the inner city will continue to drain our rapidly shrinking public coffers.

Undeniably, inner cities suffer from a long history of discrimination. However, the way for government to move forward is not by looking behind. Government can assume a more effective role by supporting the private sector in new economic initiatives. It must shift its focus from direct involvement and intervention to creating a favorable environment for business. This is not to say that public funds will not be necessary. But subsidies must be spent in ways that do not distort business incentives, focusing instead on providing the infrastructure to support genuinely profitable businesses. Government at all levels should focus on four goals as it takes on its new role.

Direct resources to the areas of greatest economic need. The crisis in our inner cities demands that they be first in line for government assistance. This may seem an obvious assertion. But the fact is that many programs in areas such as infrastructure, crime prevention, environmental cleanup, land development, and purchasing preference spread funds across constituencies for political reasons. For example, most transportation infrastructure spending goes to creating still more attractive suburban areas. In addition, a majority of preference-program assistance does not go to companies located in low-income neighborhoods.

Investments that boost the economic potential of inner cities must receive priority. For example, Superfund cleanup dollars should go to sites in high-unemployment inner city areas before they go to low-unemployment suburban sites. Infrastructure improvements should go to making inner city areas more attractive business locations. And crime prevention resources should go to high-crime inner city areas. Spending federal, state, and local money in that way will have the added benefit of easing critical social problems, thus reducing social service spending.

Unfortunately, the qualifying criteria for current government assistance programs are not properly designed to channel resources where they are most needed. Preference programs support business based on the race, ethnicity, or gender of their owners rather than on economic need. In addition to directing resources away from the inner city, such race-based or gender-based distinctions reinforce inappropriate stereotypes and attitudes, breed resentment, and increase the risk that programs will be manipulated to serve unintended populations. Location in an economically distressed area and employment of a significant percentage of its residents should be the qualification for government assistance and preference programs. Shifting the focus to economic distress in this way will help enlist all segments of the private sector in the solutions to the inner city's problems.

Increase the economic value of the inner city as a business location. In order to stimulate economic development, government must recognize that it is a part of the problem. Today its priorities often run counter to business needs. Artificial and outdated government-induced costs must be stripped away in the effort to make the inner city a profitable location for business. Doing so will require rethinking policies and programs in a wide range of areas. There is early evidence that self-inflicted regulatory costs can be overcome. Consider the success of the Indianapolis Regulatory Study Commission in Indiana. In two short years, Indianapolis ended its taxi monopoly, streamlined its building permitting process, and eliminated a wide range of needless regulations.

Indeed, there are numerous possibilities for reform. Imagine, for example, policy aimed at eliminating the substantial land and building cost penalties that businesses face in the inner city. Ongoing rent subsidies run the risk of attracting companies for which an inner city location offers no other economic value. Instead, the goal should be to provide building-ready sites at market prices. A single government entity could be charged with assembling parcels of land and with subsidizing demolition, environmental cleanup, and other costs. The same entity could also streamline all aspects of building—including zoning, permitting, inspections, and other approvals.

That kind of policy would require further progress on the environmental front. A growing number of cities—including Detroit, Chicago, Indianapolis, Minneapolis, and Wichita, Kansas—have successfully developed so-called brownfield urban areas by making environmental cleanup standards more flexible depending on land use, indemnifying land owners against additional costs if contamination is found on a site after a cleanup, and using tax-increment financing to help fund cleanup and redevelopment costs.

Government entities could also develop a more strategic approach to developing transportation and communications infrastructures, which would facilitate the fluid movement of goods, employees, customers, and suppliers within and beyond the inner city. Two projects in Boston are prime examples: first, a new exit ramp connecting the inner city to the nearby Massachusetts Turnpike, which in turn connects to the surrounding region and beyond; and a direct access road to the harbor tunnel, which connects to Logan International Airport. Though inexpensive, both projects are stalled because the city does not have a clear vision of their economic importance.

Deliver economic development programs and services through mainstream, private sector institutions. There has been a tendency to rely on small community-based nonprofits, quasi-governmental organizations, and special-purpose entities, such as community development banks and specialized small-business investment corporations, to provide capital and business-related services. Social service institutions have a role, but it is not this. With few exceptions, nonprofit and government organizations cannot provide the quality of training, advice, and support to substantial companies that mainstream, private sector organizations can. Compared with private sector entities such as commercial banks and venture capital companies, special-purpose institutions and nonprofits are plagued by high overhead costs; they have difficulty attracting and retaining high-quality personnel, providing competitive compensation, or offering a breadth of experience in dealing with companies of scale.

Consider access to capital. Government must help create the conditions necessary for private, mainstream financial institutions to lend and invest profitably in inner city businesses. Efforts to eliminate discrimination are vital but are not sufficient. Financing in the inner city must be profitable, or private sector institutions will never have the enthusiasm to develop it aggressively. Some conventional lenders claim that the reason they have not found inner city loans profitable is not higher default rates, as is commonly assumed, but the high transaction costs of finding and actually making inner city loans. Government should address those costs head on through better information and relaxed paperwork requirements and regulations. In addition, it could provide direct incentives, giving banks a transaction fee rather than a loan guarantee for closing a qualifying inner-city-based business loan. Such an approach would encourage banks to make and maintain good loans, instead of forcing capital into bad loans to fill lending quotas based on race, ethnicity, or gender.

The most important way to bring debt and equity investment to the inner city is by engaging the private sector. Resources currently going to government or quasi-public financing would be better channeled through other private financial institutions or directed at recapitalizing minority-owned banks focusing on the inner city, provided that there were matching private sector investors. Minority-owned banks that have superior knowledge of the inner city market could gain a competitive advantage by developing business-lending expertise in inner city areas.

As in lending, the best approach to increase the supply of equity capital to the inner cities is to provide private sector incentives consistent with building economically sustainable businesses. One approach would be for both federal and state governments to eliminate the tax on capital gains and dividends from long-term equity investments in inner-city-based businesses or subsidiaries that employ a minimum percentage of inner city residents. Such tax incentives, which are based on the premise of profit, can play a vital role in speeding up private sector investment. Private sector sources of equity will be attracted to inner city investment only when the creation of genuinely profitable businesses is encouraged.

Align incentives built into government programs with true economic performance. Aligning incentives with business principles should be the goal of every government program. Most programs today would fail such a test. For example, preference programs in effect guarantee companies a market. Like other forms of protectionism, they dull motivation and retard cost and quality improvement. A 1988 General Accounting Office report found that within six months of graduating from the Small Business Association's purchasing preference program, 30 percent of the companies had gone out of business. An additional 58 percent of the remaining companies claimed that the withdrawal of the SBA's support had had a devastating impact on business. To align incentives with economic performance, preference programs should be rewritten to require an increasing amount of non-set-aside business over time.

Direct subsidies to businesses do not work. Instead, government funds should be used for site assembly, extra security, environmental cleanup, and other investments designed to improve the business environment. Companies then will be left to make decisions based on true profit.

THE NEW ROLE OF COMMUNITY-BASED ORGANIZATIONS

Recently, there has been renewed activity among community-based organizations (CBOs) to become directly involved in business development. CBOs can, and must, play an important supporting role in the process. But choosing the proper strategy is critical, and many CBOs will have to change fundamentally the way they operate. While it is difficult to make a general set of recommendations to such a diverse group of organizations, four principles should guide community-based organizations in developing their new role.

Identify and build on strengths. Like every other player, CBOs must identify their unique competitive advantages and participate in economic development based on a realistic assessment of their capabilities, resources, and limitations. Community-based organizations have played a much-needed role in developing low-income housing, social programs, and civic infrastructure. However, while there have been a few notable successes, the vast majority of businesses owned or managed by CBOs have been failures. Most CBOs lack the skills, attitudes, and incentives to advise, lend to, or operate substantial businesses. They were able to master low-income housing development, in which there were major public subsidies and a vacuum of institutional capabilities. But, when it comes to financing and assisting for-profit business development, CBOs simply can't compete with existing private sector institutions.

Moreover, CBOs naturally tend to focus on community entrepreneurship: small retail and service businesses that are often owned by neighborhood residents. The relatively limited resources of CBOs, as well as their focus on relatively small neighborhoods, is not well-suited to developing the more substantial companies that are necessary for economic vitality.

Finally, the competitive imperatives of for-profit business activity will raise inevitable conflicts for CBOs whose mission rests with the community. Turning down local residents in favor of better-qualified outside entrepreneurs, supporting necessary layoffs or the dismissal of poorly performing workers, assigning prime sites for business instead of social uses, and approving large salaries to successful entrepreneurs and managers are only a handful of the necessary choices. Given these organizations' roots in meeting the social needs of neighborhoods, it will be difficult for them to put profit ahead of their traditional mission.

Work to change workforce and community attitudes. Community-based organizations have a unique advantage in their intimate knowledge of and influence within inner city communities, and they can use that advantage to help promote business development. CBOs can help create a hospitable environment for business by working to change community and workforce attitudes and acting as a liaison with residents to quell unfounded opposition to new businesses. When BayBank wanted to open a new branch in Dorchester, for example, a local community development corporation was instrumental in smoothing relations with a few vocal critics who could have delayed the project or even driven the bank away.

Create work-readiness and job-referral systems. Community-based organizations can play an active role in preparing, screening, and referring employees to local businesses. A pressing need among many inner city residents is work-readiness training, which includes communication, self-development, and workplace practices. CBOs, with their intimate knowledge of the local community, are well equipped to provide this service in close collaboration with industry. The Urban League of Eastern Massachusetts, for example, has taken up the challenge in its new Employment Resource Center. The center provides workers with basic training as well as instruction on specific topics, such as customer-service and interviewing skills and written and oral communication.

CBOs can also help inner city residents by actively developing screening and referral systems. Admittedly, some inner-city-based businesses do not hire many local residents. The reasons are varied and complex but seem to revolve around a few bad experiences that owners have had with individual employees and their work attitudes, absenteeism, false injury claims, or drug use. A study of the impoverished Red Hook neighborhood in Brooklyn points to the importance of social networks—networks that are often lacking in inner cities—as informal job referral systems.[1] The study found that a local development corporation, the South Brooklyn LDC, played an important role in helping local residents get jobs by developing relationships with nearby businesses and screening and referring employees to them.

Facilitate commercial site improvement and development. Community-based organizations (especially community development corporations) can also leverage their expertise in real estate and act as a catalyst to facilitate environmental cleanup and the development of commercial and industrial property. For example, the Codman Square Neighborhood Development Corporation in Boston was part of a group including the

Boston Public Facilities Department, local merchants, and the local health center that encouraged 36 businesses to move into a depressed neighborhood. The group used its considerable community organizing talent to help merchants form an association to identify the neighborhood's needs as well as barriers to meeting them. It negotiated with the police to increase patrols in the area and pushed the mayor's office to board up abandoned buildings and to rid the area of trash and abandoned cars. After bringing together many different constituencies, it led a campaign to encourage businesses to locate in the neighborhood.

Overcoming Impediments to Progress

This economic model provides a new and comprehensive approach to reviving our nation's distressed urban communities. However, agreeing on and implementing it will not be without its challenges. The private sector, government, inner city residents, and the public at large all hold entrenched attitudes and prejudices about the inner city and its problems. These will be slow to change. Rethinking the inner city in economic rather than social terms will be uncomfortable for many who have devoted years to social causes and who view profit and business in general with suspicion. Activists accustomed to lobbying for more government resources will find it difficult to embrace a strategy for fostering wealth creation. Elected officials used to framing urban problems in social terms will be resistant to changing legislation, redirecting resources, and taking on recalcitrant bureaucracies. Government entities may find it hard to cede power and control accumulated through past programs. Local leaders who have built social service organizations and merchants who have run mom-and-pop stores could feel threatened by the creation of new initiatives and centers of power. Local politicians schooled in old-style community organizing and confrontational politics will have to tread unfamiliar ground in facilitating cooperation between business and residents.

These changes will be difficult ones for both individuals and institutions. Nonetheless, they must be made. The private sector, government, and community-based organizations all have vital new parts to play in revitalizing the economy of the inner city. Businesspeople, entrepreneurs, and investors must assume a lead role; and community activists, social service providers, and government bureaucrats must support them. The time has come to embrace a rational economic strategy and to stem the intolerable costs of outdated approaches.

NOTES

1. See Philip Kasinitz and Jan Rosenberg, "Why Enterprise Zones Will Not Work: Lessons from a Brooklyn Neighborhood," *City Journal*, Autumn 1993, pp. 63–69.

CHAPTER 12

Making Competition
in Health Care Work

Elizabeth Olmsted Teisberg

Michael E. Porter

Gregory B. Brown

HEALTH CARE REFORM in the United States is on a collision course with economic reality. Most proposals focus on measures that will produce one-time cost savings by eliminating waste and inefficiency. The question at the heart of the current political debate is whether these savings will be large enough to pay for the added costs of universal coverage. But this is the wrong question to ask if reformers are serious about achieving a lasting cure for U.S. health care.

The *right* question, and one that is conspicuously missing from the health care debate, is how to achieve dramatic and sustained cost reductions over time. What will it take to foster entirely new approaches to disease prevention and treatment, new ways to deliver services, and more cost-effective facilities?

The answer lies in the powerful lessons business has learned over the past two decades about the imperatives of competition. In industry after industry, the underlying dynamic is the same: competition compels companies to deliver increasing value to customers. The fundamental driver of this continuous quality improvement and cost reduction is innovation. Without incentives to sustain innovation in health care, short-term cost savings will soon be overwhelmed by the desire to widen access, the growing health needs of an aging population, and the

July–August 1994

unwillingness of Americans to settle for anything less than the best treatments available. Inevitably, the failure to promote innovation will lead to lower quality or more rationing of care—two equally undesirable results.

The misguided assumption underlying much of the debate about health care reform is that technology is the enemy. By assuming that technology drives up costs, reformers neglect the central importance of innovation or, worse yet, attempt to slow its pace. In fact, innovation driven by rigorous competition is the key to successful reform. Although health care is unique in some ways, in this respect, it is no different than any other industry. The United States can achieve universal access and lower costs without sacrificing quality, but only by allowing competition to work at all levels of the health care system.

What's Wrong with Competition in Health Care?

More health care competition exists in the United States than in any other industrial nation. The puzzle confounding reformers is that while competition has been enormously successful at producing quality-enhancing innovation, it appears to have failed on the crucial dimension of cost. A closer look suggests not that *competition* is failing, but that *incentives* throughout the system have been so skewed that the normal rules of competition simply do not apply. Prices remain high even when there is excess capacity. Technologies remain expensive even when they are widely used. Hospitals and physicians remain in business even when they charge higher prices for equal quality or fail to provide high-quality service. Until recently, incentives existed only for innovations that raised costs or increased quality regardless of cost.

Successful reform must begin with a clear understanding of how the current system creates incentives for unproductive competition.

Payers' Incentives Make Payers Adversaries of Patients and Providers

In most industries, the consumer makes the purchasing decision and pays for the product or service. In health care, the purchasing decision, payment, and receipt of services are separated. As a result, there are multiple tiers of customers: employers, who purchase health care coverage for their employees; third-party payers, such as insurance companies and health maintenance organizations (HMOs), which collect premiums and then pay providers for services rendered to their subscribers; patients, who ultimately receive the health care services; and doctors, who determine or advise on the tests and treatments for patients.

These customers have different interests. The employer is concerned with paying the lowest premiums while providing enough insurance to retain employees or meet contractual obligations. The third-party payer is concerned with spending less on patient care than was received in premiums. The insured patient is concerned with finding the best quality care regardless of cost. And the advising doctor often has incentives to order more services.

Since payers do not have the final legal responsibility for insured patients' bills, patients are the payers of last resort. The conflict of interest between payers and patients creates incentives for payers to compete on the basis of creative and complicated methods of denying coverage to people who might need expensive care. The payer becomes the patient's adversary, rather than advocate, denying payment on claims whenever possible. The incentives not to pay claims also set the payer in opposition to the provider by requiring the provider to assume the costs that neither payer nor patient has paid. As a result, providers expend scarce resources on bill collection and avoid patients whose insurance companies may deny claims. These skewed incentives lead to behaviors that get in the way of genuine cost reduction.

However, the conflict among payers, patients, and providers is unnecessary. Payers should be able to profit only from actually improving the quality of medical outcomes and reducing costs, not from shifting payment responsibility onto patients or providers. They should concentrate on identifying high-quality providers with good medical outcomes and negotiate lower prices for their services. Studies show that better quality care is often lower in cost due to the efficiency of experienced medical teams, fewer complications, and better long-term results.[1] For example, The Prudential Insurance Company of America estimates that it saves more than 20 percent in costs with its Institutes of Quality Program by directing bone-marrow transplant patients to high-quality providers, which are screened on the basis of the limited available data on facilities, staff, credentials, processes, and past outcomes. Recent programs like this one are productive responses to new pressures to find ways to reduce costs, not just avoid paying claims.

Patients' Incentives Discourage Cost Sensitivity

In life-threatening or urgent situations, patients and their families are rarely price sensitive. But even when it comes to receiving routine and discretionary services or choosing a health plan, most patients have had little incentive to consider cost. Patients rarely have access to relative price information; they rarely comparison shop; and they often feel uncomfortable asking about prices for fear of offending the physician on whom they rely.

In fact, most employees choose insurance plans without considering price. Sometimes employees do not pay at all for their health benefits. Other times the prices of competing plans are equalized by the employer, who pockets the difference, removing the incentive for employees to choose a lower priced plan. More efficient health plans or insurers have little incentive to reduce prices if lower prices do not help them gain market share. And once a person has insurance, the current system makes patients insensitive to price even for decisions such as where to undergo elective surgery, fill a prescription, or obtain diagnostic tests. Copayments and deductibles can compensate only to the extent that the patient can make choices about which provider to use.

Even under the current system, the patient has no choice when it comes to many types of decisions. Usually, once a patient chooses a doctor, health plan, or hospital, decisions such as which laboratory, imaging facility, or specialist to use are predetermined. This is especially true in managed care organizations and provider networks.

One choice all patients make is the frequency of visits for routine concerns. Copayments help make price a factor in these decisions. One of the results of the greater attention to health care costs in recent years has been increasing the use of copayments to reduce premiums and to discourage the overuse of primary care visits.

Fragmented Customers Have Little Negotiating Power

Well-functioning competition is characterized by demanding customers with enough clout to push providers to improve quality while at the same time reducing costs. But when customers are fragmented, as they are in health care, their power is greatly diminished.

The United States has fifteen hundred different third-party payers, such as insurance companies and HMOs, with roughly two hundred serving a given region. Typically, three to twelve payers—the number varies by region—represent significant purchase volumes to a given hospital, doctor, or other provider, while the rest of the payers and individual patients have little bargaining power. Moreover, under the current system, patients have little bargaining power with their insurance companies or other payers.

This fragmentation of patients and payers not only limits competitive pressure but also drives up transaction costs since many of the payers have different policies, procedures, and forms for provider reimbursement. The long, customized forms, different reporting requirements, and bureaucracies developed to handle the forms and requirements contribute to high administrative costs, which account for nearly 25 percent of health care expenditures.[2]

Providers, Patients, and Payers Lack Information

Health care customers also lack access to information that would improve decisions and in turn pressure providers to ameliorate medical outcomes and reduce costs. In most industries, customers can compare product performance and price with competing products. Buyers of automobiles, for example, can go on test drives, compare prices at different dealers, draw on their own and friends' past experiences, and consult publications that provide information on costs, margins, ratings of quality and reliability, and used-car values.

Health care could hardly be more different. Patients, payers, and referring physicians do not have readily available measures of quality or of the relationship between price and quality for a given physician, procedure, course of treatment, or hospital. Data from the Pennsylvania

Health Care Cost Containment Council reveal that both referring physicians and patients continue to recommend and use the services of providers that have poorer outcomes and higher costs than nearby rivals.[3] Since many health care purchases are onetime events, patients cannot draw on past personal experiences. They usually receive only the expert opinion of one doctor (or sometimes two if the patient obtains a second opinion), and they frequently have difficulty judging the quality of that advice.

Even under managed care, in which a gatekeeper physician makes supposedly informed choices about how a patient is treated, good information about the best type of care and provider for a given patient is lacking. Worse still, physicians must often refer patients within a network of approved providers, which are selected by administrators. These administrators base their selection primarily on price negotiations because they have little information about quality of care or outcomes. Without adequate quality measures and information, the dangers are that the network may either exclude high-priced providers that deliver better quality care or include substandard providers in spite of the good intentions of administrators and physicians.

This lack of relevant, comparative information based on meaningful medical outcome measures—not the complexity of medicine itself—prevents informed purchasing decisions. Customers in other complex, highly technical fields, such as aerospace and computer software, require competitive bidding on products or services and delineate precise criteria against which products are evaluated. In contrast, the poor comparative information and lack of meaningful outcome measures in health care create incentives for hospitals and physicians to compete based on *what is observed:* the hospital's pleasing physical environment, high-tech equipment, or wide array of services; the physician's comforting bedside manner; even high prices.

Measures of customers' satisfaction are inadequate quality measures. The right information concerns short- and long-term outcomes of treatments for particular diseases by specific providers, taking into consideration the patient's general health. Health care is not a monolithic service, but a myriad of types of services. Reformers must develop information and outcome measures at the level of specific conditions and treatments instead of relying on aggregate comparisons of provider networks or payment plans. Buying treatment for cancer will never be like buying a car. But incentives in the U.S. health care system will dramatically improve when payers, patients, providers, and referring doctors can base decisions on comparisons of relevant outcome measures and prices.

As health care moves increasingly toward *provider capitation* (a fixed dollar amount per patient in the plan per period of time), the need for meaningful information is more crucial than ever. Historically, the attitude of the U.S. health care system was, "If it might work, try it." Today the equally risky bias is, "If we're not sure, don't do it." This kind of thinking can only stifle innovation and erode quality. Better information is the antidote to either bias, allowing decisions to be based on expected outcomes.

Providers' Incentives Increase Costs

In a well-functioning competitive market, producers' desires to raise prices or create more demand are counterbalanced by buyers who purchase only what they need and can afford. Demand rises when prices fall or when quality at a given price increases. These simple economic laws do not apply to health care providers in the United States because the health care system skews their incentives in a number of ways.

HOSPITALS AND OUTPATIENT FACILITIES: INCENTIVES TO MAXIMIZE REIMBURSEMENT

Beginning in the post-World War II period, hospitals were reimbursed on a cost-plus basis, which in turn produced rapidly escalating hospital costs. The Medicare Prospective Payment System, implemented in 1983, granted hospitals a fixed fee based on the diagnosis that resulted in the patient's admission to the hospital. (Changes in Medicare carry particular significance because other players tend to follow Medicare and implement the same rules.) This diagnosis-related group (DRG) reimbursement created incentives to reduce hospital stays and treatment costs. In the decade following its introduction, DRG reimbursement rules reduced the average length of stay for an inpatient by half a day, and the number of inpatient hospital stays dropped by 20 percent.

Corrections needed to be made to the cost-plus system, which created incentives for providers to overtreat. But fixed-price reimbursement skews incentives in the opposite direction, pressuring providers to undertreat and to discharge patients prematurely. These incentives create the risk that undertreatment or early discharge will raise overall costs by increasing the rate of recurrent or prolonged health problems. They also encourage hospitals to admit some patients unnecessarily and then quickly discharge them.

Outpatient reimbursement has not yet changed to a DRG-like system. The cost-plus reimbursement combined with incentives for the earlier discharge of hospital patients has led hospitals and other providers to open many new outpatient facilities. Some of the resulting changes were productive. Effective outpatient treatment and surgeries are helping to reduce costs. However, there have also been unproductive results. For example, providers manipulated the DRG rules when they were first implemented by delaying admission of some patients and instead administering expensive drugs or treatments in the emergency room. While this specific practice has been forbidden, incentives for the overtreatment of outpatients remain.

PHYSICIANS: INCENTIVES TO INCREASE SERVICES

While the DRG rules encourage hospitals to undertreat, physicians currently have incentives to increase the volume of services they perform, even if those additional services do not lower costs or improve medical outcomes. Although *physician capitation* (a fixed dollar amount per primary care patient per period of time) aims to correct incentives, it may lead to undertreatment because physicians earn more by limiting care, including tests and referrals. Salary is also becoming more common, and its incentives are volume neutral. But most physicians still face an incentive structure in which they earn more by performing more tests or expensive procedures because they are paid for each service performed. The recently implemented Resource-Based Relative Value System (RBRVS) does lower reimbursement for technical procedures like surgery relative to cognitive services like office visits. But lower pay per procedure actually creates incentives for physicians to perform *more* procedures in order to maintain their incomes.

We are not arguing that doctors unscrupulously take advantage of patients and payers. Medical practice is complex and requires professional judgment. Furthermore, many legitimate efforts to care for the patient increase the use of medical services. Physicians cannot in good conscience do less for a patient or pursue less costly treatments without evidence that these decisions improve outcomes or quality of life.

But the complexity of medicine cannot explain why demand for physicians' services is higher in areas where there are more physicians. Doctors with the time and facilities can increase demand by performing more tests and procedures, seeing patients more frequently, or operating on less severely ill patients. For example, the rate of open heart surgery on residents of Manchester, New Hampshire, doubled the year a local hospital opened an open-heart-surgery service.[4] Before the local service opened, 90 percent of bypass operations on patients from the community involved three or more arteries. Three years after the local center opened, over 50 percent of the bypasses involved only one or two arteries. But an appreciable improvement in coronary-heart-disease mortality did not accompany this surgical treatment of less severe coronary disease, and it is not clear whether other measures of health outcomes were improved. Cardiologists can debate the medical merits of operating on patients with less severe coronary disease. We simply use this example to illustrate the point that doctors can increase demand for medical services without clear evidence of improving outcomes.

This tendency for supply to create demand is part of the reason that the United States has a general shortage of primary care physicians compared with the number of specialists. In a competitive system, the income potential for specialists, now higher than that of primary care physicians, would fall with oversupply. But since the availability of specialists generates demand for specialized care, the oversupply perpetuates itself. The increasing debt burden of medical school graduates, which leads them to high-paying specialties, only serves to accentuate this tendency.

PHYSICIANS: INCENTIVES TO MAKE EXPENSIVE REFERRALS

In addition to providing care, physicians also act as purchasing agents on behalf of their patients by ordering tests or making referrals. Referring physicians have traditionally had no incentive to choose a less expensive lab, ancillary service, or other provider since patients' insurance paid the bills. Instead, convenience, established relationships, perceived quality, or direct financial rewards from equity interests in labs or facilities have determined referral patterns for independent physicians.

The incentive to perform more tests and procedures is strongest when the physician has a financial interest in the facility or equipment. For example, a Florida State University study found that physician-owned laboratories in Florida performed twice as many tests per patient as independent labs. Similarly, a University of Arizona study showed that physicians with diagnostic imaging equipment in their offices ordered four times as many imaging exams as physicians who referred patients for imaging tests.

Congress passed the Stark bill, which became effective in 1992, forbidding physicians from billing Medicare patients for services performed in clinical labs in which the doctor has an equity interest. And other legislation has passed or is pending to limit self-referral further. But the more fundamental underlying problem, physicians' incentives, remains unaddressed. If physician-owned labs are more efficient, then prohibiting their existence would be a mistake. Ideally, physicians should have incentives to promote and improve *health* rather than to increase the use of health care *services*.

PHYSICIANS: INCENTIVES TO INCREASE FEES

As health care technologies evolved in the United States, high prices were placed on novel procedures, such as gastrointestinal endoscopy, because these procedures carried higher risk and were offered by relatively few, highly skilled physicians. In a competitive market, the diffusion of technology and increase in the supply of such services would drive down their prices over time. In health care, however, the fees did not decline because patients were not price sensitive and insurance payments to physicians were based on customary charges rather than on costs.

In most industries, market forces determine how much a company can charge; prices need to be high enough to cover costs but low enough to attract customers. Companies can charge higher prices only for products or services that are differentiated, that is, products and services that provide more benefit to the customer. In health care, however, the normal rules do not apply. High prices have their roots in the "usual, customary, and reasonable charges" on which insurance companies traditionally based their payments to physicians. This structure made sense in the infancy of the health insurance industry in the United States, when most patients did not have insurance, paid for their own health care, and were price sensitive. At that time, doctors faced powerful constraints in setting their customary charges.

As health insurance became more widespread, payers retained the "usual, customary, and reasonable" structure, even though a competitive market ceased to exist in physician services. With insurance the norm, doctors no longer attracted patients by setting lower prices. Indeed, patients with insurance came to view low prices as a signal of lower quality. Since any fee could become "usual, customary, and reasonable" as long as enough doctors charged it, physicians were able to boost their incomes by regularly increasing their fees so that future reimbursement calculations would be based on higher charges.

Over the past decade, changes in physician reimbursement have limited the ability of physicians to increase fees. But piecemeal regulations can be circumvented. For example, when Medicare implemented a fee freeze in 1984 that lasted for two years, physician group practices responded by setting artificially high rates for new physicians in the group. Similarly, some payers have imposed fixed-fee structures on physicians, but physicians have circumvented them with so-called balance billing: physicians simply bill patients for the difference between their "list charges" and the approved "fixed fee." This strategy reduces the payers' price sensitivity and their incentive to work for price reductions since they are no longer responsible for the entire bill. While balance billing may make patients more price sensitive, they often do not know in advance whether the bill will be significant. And when the balance is small, patients are often inclined to pay. Fortunately, an increasing number of insurance contracts now restricts doctors from balance billing patients.

PHYSICIANS: INCENTIVES TO PRACTICE DEFENSIVE MEDICINE

The threat of malpractice or the insistence of patients pushes even doctors paid by salary or capitation to practice defensive medicine by ordering more tests and procedures than are often necessary. The most widely cited study estimates the direct cost of defensive medicine to be about 1 percent of total health care expenditures.[5] But such measures understate the problem because the threat of malpractice may also indirectly affect costs by coloring physicians' judgments. Still, the popular notion that the threat of malpractice is the crux of the health care problem is oversimplified. Legal reform is essential to address the malpractice problem and help retain good physicians in fields such as obstetrics. However, malpractice reform alone will not produce the dramatic changes that U.S. health care needs.

Providers' Incentives Encourage Overinvestment

The U.S. health care system still supplies incentives for excessive capital investment by providers. Companies in a competitive market invest to enhance differentiation or to lower costs. Because they bear the costs and risks of investment, they invest only when they anticipate a reasonable return. Those that make inappropriate investments face declining profits and eventually go out of business.

This has not been the case for capital expenditures in the U.S. health care industry. Until 1992, reimbursement by Medicare for capital investments was cost-plus. Thus, providers profited by building facilities and adding new equipment without the usual market constraint of needing to be sure that the capital investments would pay off. Regulators became aware of the resulting incentive to overinvest and tried to handle it by creating review boards to determine community needs. They did not attempt to correct the incentive itself.

What's more, the excess capacity of beds or equipment, such as imaging machines or medical helicopters, did not produce lower prices. Health care defied the usual laws of gravity for three reasons. First, reimbursement was not dependent on how fully a facility was used. Second, providers were protected from failure not only by cost-plus reimbursement but also by community interests in maintaining local health care facilities. Third, once facilities existed, there was a strong tendency to create demand to fill them. Ultimately, hospitals and outpatient treatment centers had incentives to overinvest in equipment and facilities because these investments attracted both doctors and patients. Without real measures of outcomes, state-of-the-art facilities became the focus of health care competition.

In 1992, the Medicare capital reimbursement rules changed, limiting the rate at which major capital investments could be amortized. This change, coupled with increasing national attention to health care costs, substantially enhances incentives for improving the productivity of capital equipment. Cost-saving innovations in investment productivity will begin to emerge after a time lag. But the benefits of this change are unnecessarily diluted by too many loopholes allowed in the new Medicare rules. These rules include significant adjustments, such as those for geographic location (regional, as well as urban versus rural), patient population (severity of illness, or "case-mix"), and reimbursement features (percentage of uninsured or indigent patients). Together, the adjustments make the system still effectively cost-plus.

Exit Barriers Protect Substandard Payers and Providers

Incentives for cost reduction will be fully effective only if lower quality, inefficient providers and insurance companies are allowed to fail. Any healthy competitive market forces the exit of substandard players, which are displaced by efficient ones. The net result is lower costs without compromising quality.

The past two decades have witnessed dramatic reductions in the demand for hospital facilities, but relatively little capacity has been eliminated. The cost and quality penalty to the nation of too many facilities is high. Low volumes drive up costs, as fixed overhead must be spread over few patients. At the same time, quality suffers. For example, providers that perform fewer than 150 open heart procedures per year have higher death and complication rates. As a result, the American College of Surgeons has recommended that each cardiac surgery team perform at least 150 operations per year. Other studies show that hospitals that perform a higher volume of a given procedure have lower mortality rates and shorter inpatient stays.[6] It is not beneficial to have reimbursement rules that guarantee any provider the ability to offer any service even if their quality and utilization rates are low. But in U.S. health care, there has been a surprising reluctance to force substandard providers to exit either by closing entire facilities or by dropping specific services.

The idea that the closure of some hospitals and some services within hospitals would be good public policy is radical given the history of providing public incentives to open hospitals in every U.S. community. The U.S. hospital system developed at a time when the full range of medical care could be reasonably provided at a community hospital. Communities still benefit today from the ready availability of services like routine emergency care, routine obstetric care, and care for common disorders requiring hospitalization. However, for complex care such as high-risk obstetrics, trauma care, and organ transplantation, *regionalization* and *rationalization* could significantly enhance both quality and efficiency.

While traveling to a preeminent regional facility may sound expensive and inconvenient, the savings in costs and the promise of better short- and long-term medical results can easily make it worthwhile for both patients and payers. Higher volumes of specialized treatments lead to better outcomes and lower costs, not only because physicians become more skilled with more practice but also because whole teams of medical professionals learn effective routines and develop expertise in protocols and problem spotting. As a result, facilities that have high volume in a specialized service also tend to have lower costs in that service.

The current trends of consolidation into provider networks, however, could have detrimental effects on the cost and quality of specialized services. A managed care network is fine for primary care and relatively simple specialized care. However, the risks are that either high-quality providers will be excluded because they cannot conclusively prove cost-effectiveness or substandard providers of complex and highly specialized care will be hidden and protected within the networks. Although managers will not intentionally maintain clearly substandard services, measuring outcomes is difficult, and networks will be reluctant to lose their full-service status based on uncertain evidence of substandard care. The guaranteed patient flow to in-network providers, then, creates new exit barriers.

Public policy should play a critical role in fostering competition. Although some consolidation is desirable to reduce excess capacity, it is important not to relax antitrust rules to the point of undermining competition. Excessive consolidation will risk creating very powerful providers with less need to respond to their customers. It will also limit the experimentation that is critical to stimulating new procedures and treatments.

Piecemeal Solutions Treat Only the Symptoms

The skewed incentives of the U.S. health care system are not the result of inattention. A great deal of regulatory effort has focused on fixing the problems. Unfortunately, much of this effort has aimed at treating symptoms rather than the underlying causes. In fact, new regulations make the system less efficient, while failing to improve quality.

For example, when DRG reimbursement shortened hospital stays by encouraging earlier discharge, concerns surfaced that hospitals' efforts to reduce costs might diminish the quality of care. So the government added new regulations and expanded the bureaucracy to address the issues of quality and utilization. Hospitals responded to these quality regulations by creating parallel utilization review staffs. The net result was *health care* reduction, not *cost* reduction. Money previously spent on patient care was shifted to administration.

Another result of such piecemeal solutions has been a complex collection of sometimes inconsistent rules that provide rewards to those who can figure out how to manipulate the system. Billing consultants have taught doctors and hospital administrators to maximize reimbursement. For example, when fixed fees were established for a given procedure, doctors learned the practice of unbundling: billing separately for the component parts of a procedure to increase fees. The rise of fixed-fee third-party payers and the increasing burden of the uninsured encouraged cost shifting—those patients with less restrictive payment plans absorbed the costs of caring for others. Only changes in incentives can close these loopholes. Additional layers of regulation will be circumvented and will create new administrative cost burdens.

The failure to look at the health care system comprehensively and to focus on the long term has also raised systemwide costs. For example, many U.S. mothers receive little prenatal care, but the cost of universal prenatal care is almost negligible compared with the cost of intensive care for premature babies and the cost of long-term care for children with considerable health problems as a result of poor prenatal care. As improved outcome measures are developed, it is important to determine when apparently expensive care at one stage in an illness actually reduces overall costs or improves outcomes at subsequent stages.

In addition, seemingly unrelated government policies contribute to rising health care costs. The most obvious example is the subsidization of tobacco. Given the demonstrated health risks of tobacco, the subsidies drive up health care costs. The Clinton administration's suggested tax increase on tobacco products does strengthen incentives for healthful behavior by making smoking expensive. But subsidizing tobacco and then taxing it is yet another example of complicated, piecemeal regulation that could be simplified if we looked at the systemwide costs and benefits of specific policies.

Recent Progress on Cost Reduction Is Not Enough

In response to national attention to rising costs and the DRG reimbursement system, a number of cost-reducing advances began to emerge by the late 1980s. Indeed, the results of the new, albeit incomplete, incentives for cost reduction have become noticeable at the national level. Although the medical component of the consumer price index is still rising faster than inflation, the rate of increase has dropped enough to shave $15 billion off expected U.S. health care expenditures in a single year.

Specific examples of cost-reducing innovations span a wide range of treatments and procedures. Consider the antibiotic ceftriaxone. Until the mid-1980s, advances in antibiotic development tended to deliver broader spectrum antibiotics. The 1988 introduction of ceftriaxone offered a drug with essentially the same spectrum as existing drugs of the same class, but at a lower cost due to the need for only one intravenous dose every twenty-four hours instead of every three or four. Less frequent dosing means less nursing time and lower aggregate treatment costs, while providing equally good results; it also allows some patients to be discharged from the hospital and receive the injection on a daily outpatient basis. Because of these pharmacoeconomic advantages, ceftriaxone quickly became the top selling pharmaceutical product in hospitals. Other examples include new therapies and surgical techniques. Laparoscopy reduces the cost and recovery time from procedures such as cholecystectomies and appendectomies. Gene therapy is creating the potential for dramatic cost reduction by restoring normal function in congenital diseases like cystic fibrosis and ADA deficiency. Most pharmaceutical and biopharmaceutical companies are now consciously analyzing both the clinical and the economic advances of potential new products to decide which products to pursue and which research-and-development investments to make.

There are still other indications of the power of improved incentives to restore health to the U.S. health care system. Numerous private-sector initiatives have begun to ratchet down the rate of health care growth. Large employers are beginning to ask employees to pay more when choosing more expensive health care plans. Small-business coalitions are demanding and receiving greater value from insurers and providers. Employers are ferreting out information to empower their health benefit choices, and providers and insurers are learning to respond more effectively to informed buyers.

These are positive signs, but they are not enough. The current trends should not be used as an excuse to avoid the real reform of incentives. Indeed, the anticipation of reform is itself driving cost reduction. And if weak and uncoordinated incentives can encourage such innovation, a systematic introduction of clear, competitive market incentives should be able to achieve dramatic results. Innovation in response to competitive forces will bring health care costs under control without rationing care or retarding the search for cures for currently untreatable diseases.

Reform Can Cure Competition in Health Care

Competition in U.S. health care has produced a breathtaking rate of advance in state-of-the-art treatments for a wide range of diseases and injuries. People come from all over the world for treatment by U.S. doctors in U.S. hospitals with U.S.-developed technologies. Reform should preserve this excellence and expand the scope of innovation. A lasting cure for U.S. health care should incorporate four basic elements: corrected incentives to spur productive competition, universal insurance to secure economic efficiency, relevant information to ensure meaningful choice, and vigorous innovation to guarantee dynamic improvement.

INCENTIVES FOR PRODUCTIVE COMPETITION

Much of the health care debate is based on the premise that because competition has failed to control costs in the past, it will not be able to do so in the future. Paradoxically, competition, usually a powerful force for both quality enhancement and cost reduction, appears to be driving health care costs through the ceiling. But the problem, as we have seen, lies in the skewed incentives that allow providers, payers, and suppliers of drugs and equipment to prosper while costs escalate.

"Managed competition" has been offered up as a solution. It encourages patients and employers to join large purchasing cooperatives, which will contract for health plans with large payers and organize providers and physicians into integrated delivery networks. But the pooling of customers and providers could create bilateral monopolies with little incentive to innovate. More powerful payers could slow innovation by refusing to pay for new treatments in the effort to contain costs. More equal groups of customers and payers, without restructured incentives, could increase the mountains of paperwork generated by battles over who should pay the bills. Indeed, without restructured incentives, managed competition will only increase the power of the parties engaged in dysfunctional competition.

Reform must eliminate the incentives that create dysfunctional competition. Rather than managed competition, reform must foster rigorous competition among providers and among payers to deliver value to customers. Providers and their suppliers should earn higher profits only when they make cost-effective advances in medical outcomes.

Four conditions will help foster productive competition in health care:

- Avoid overconsolidation. Providers must be forced to compete with one another on the basis of quality and price for specific services.

- Maintain antitrust laws in order to ensure healthy rivalry.

- Allow exit of substandard providers when regional competition is not restricted. The opportunity to prosper must be coupled with the risk of failure. In addition, a safety net must be set up to protect subscribers if their insurance plan fails.

- Reject price caps because they will have devastating effects on innovation in new drugs and devices. Instead, competition among established products should be encouraged to push down their prices.

Payers' and patients' incentives must also be aligned. Payers should profit when they negotiate good value for their subscribers. Patients should benefit when they seek good values. It is not enough to pool patients into purchasing groups or create streamlined provider networks. Unless incentives are changed, payers will continue in their attempts to shift costs rather than identify good values, and providers will continue to manipulate the reimbursement rules without necessarily improving quality.

Four steps will help align patients' and payers' incentives and avoid the fruitless cost shifting that takes place today:

- Align interests. Payers must have the legal responsibility for paying their subscribers' bills.

- Simplify the content of health insurance to reduce disputes over claims.

- Outlaw balance billing.

- Increase patient responsibility. Patients should bear some portion of costs through a noticeable copayment up to an income-graduated cap.

INSURANCE COVERAGE FOR ECONOMIC EFFICIENCY

Universal coverage is essential for economic efficiency as well as for equity. Many of the skewed incentives and inefficiencies stem from problems created by uncompensated care.

The best way to eliminate costly practices like cost shifting and patient dumping is not by creating more reviews, audits, or penalties. Reform should make everyone a paying customer. The cost of universal coverage will not be as high as some fear because the expense of the uninsured is already largely borne by the health care system through uncompensated care assessments that providers recoup by raising average prices. Moreover, the costs now borne to serve the uninsured will be reduced because patients who lack access to primary care currently use expensive emergency-room care as a substitute.

Universal coverage is also important to ensure that competition will work in the interests of all patients. Otherwise, many providers that currently serve the poor will be forced to exit. The solution is to make the poor into paying customers who decide which providers will best serve them.

INFORMATION FOR MEANINGFUL CHOICE

Effective competition requires free choice, but choice without good information is useless. Competition will work only when decisions by providers, referring doctors, payers, and patients are based on relevant, comparable information about price and medical outcomes. That information must be at the level of specific treatments by specific providers and must include long-term outcomes and immediate results. There has been much discussion about providing consumers with information about insurance plans to help them in their purchasing decisions. It is far more critical to provide all parties with specific information about treatment outcomes and prices.

Without this kind of information, reform risks sacrificing quality to the goals of access and cost containment. Hospitals may discharge patients before they are ready for outpatient care, and physicians may skimp when ordering tests or making referrals. Medical outcome information also guards against the perils of overconsolidation. Substandard providers should not be protected from healthy competition because customers are captive within consolidated health networks.

The development of germane and accessible outcome measures should be one of the nation's highest research priorities. Admittedly, this will be no easy task. But rapid progress is already being made, and nothing will speed the development of better measures faster than the widespread dissemination of the data and measures already in use. With good information available to all parties, informed choice—not restricted choice—

will promote productive competition that raises quality and drives down costs.

INNOVATION FOR DYNAMIC IMPROVEMENT

The national debate defines technology as the enemy and focuses on how to cut fat and eliminate waste in the current system with reforms like health plan buying alliances, consolidated networks, and price caps on drugs and devices. But these reforms are essentially ways to deliver today's health care more efficiently and will not reduce costs enough. In fact, overconsolidation of networks and price restraints on or biases against new drugs and devices will undermine incentives for innovation. A real solution to our health care cost problem requires a dynamic view, one that fosters the kind of innovation that pushes down costs and enhances quality.

Pharmaceutical, biotechnological, and medical device companies are beginning to deliver cost-reducing innovations. Private companies are beginning to develop quality comparisons and outcome measures. Small businesses are beginning to form buying groups to negotiate with payers for quality care at competitive prices. As a result, the rate of health care cost increases is slowing.

Health care reform must build on this progress by creating still stronger incentives for both medical and managerial innovation. Reformers must not confuse onetime efficiencies with sustained cost improvement. Innovation, the missing principle in all the contending reform proposals, is the only true, long-term solution for high-quality, affordable health care.

NOTES

1. See, for example, J. Showstack, et al., "Association of Volume with Outcome of Coronary Artery Bypass Graft Surgery," *Journal of the American Medical Association*, vol. 257 (1987), pp. 785-89; Charles Marwick, "Using High-Quality Providers to Cope with Today's Rising Health Care Costs," *JAMA*, vol. 268 (1992), pp. 2142-45; and James W. Winkelman, et al., "Cost Savings in a Hospital Clinical Laboratory with a Pay-for-Performance Incentive Program for Supervisors," *Archives of Pathology and Laboratory Medicine*, vol. 115 (1991), pp. 38-41.

2. Steffie Woolhandler and David U. Himmelstein, "The Deteriorating Administrative Efficiency of the U.S. Health Care System," *New England Journal of Medicine,* vol. 324, no. 18 (1991), pp. 1253-58.

3. See David Wessel and Walt Bogdanich, "Closed Market: Laws of Economics Often Don't Apply in Health-Care Field," *Wall Street Journal,* January 22, 1992, p. A1.

4. Philip Caper, "Database Strategies for the Management of Clinical Decision Making," *New Perspectives in Health Care Economics* (London: Mediq Ltd., 1991), p. 65.

5. Roger A. Reynolds, John A. Rizzo, and Martin L. Gonzalez, "The Cost of Medical Professional Liability," *JAMA,* vol. 257 (1987), pp. 2776-81.

6. See V.E. Stone, et al., "The Relation Between Hospital Experience and Mortality Rates for Patients with AIDS," *JAMA,* vol. 268 (1992), pp. 2655-61; and H.S. Luft, et al., "Should Operations Be Regionalized?" *New England Journal of Medicine,* vol. 301 (1979), pp. 1364-69.

CHAPTER 13

Capital Disadvantage

America's Failing Capital Investment System

Michael E. Porter

TO COMPETE EFFECTIVELY in international markets, a nation's businesses must continuously innovate and upgrade their competitive advantages. Innovation and upgrading come from sustained investment in physical as well as intangible assets—things like employee skills and supplier relationships. Today the changing nature of competition and the increasing pressure of globalization make investment the most critical determinant of competitive advantage.

Yet the U.S. system of allocating investment capital both within and across companies is failing. This puts American companies in a range of industries at a serious disadvantage in global competition and ultimately threatens the long-term growth of the U.S. economy.

These are the principal findings of a two-year research project sponsored by the Harvard Business School and the Council on Competitive-

This article draws heavily on the research and commentary of my colleagues on the project on Capital Choices, cosponsored by the Harvard Business School and the Council on Competitiveness. Rebecca Wayland's research assistance and insights have contributed importantly to this study.

The issues discussed in this article are the subject of a large body of literature, which is extensively referenced in the project papers. Among the more broadly based studies is Michael T. Jacobs, *Short-Term America* (Harvard Business School Press, 1991). Other valuable contributions include the report of the Institutional Investor Project at the Columbia University Center for Law and Economic Studies, *Institutional Investors and Capital Markets: 1991 Update,* and the Symposium on the Structure and Governance of Enterprise, *Journal of Financial Economics,* September 1990.

September–October 1992

ness, a project that included eighteen research papers by twenty-five academic experts. This article draws on those papers and my research to offer a comprehensive analysis of the causes and recommended cures for the U.S. investment problem.

Critics of U.S. business frequently blame recent competitive shortcomings on various issues: a short time horizon, ineffective corporate governance, or a high cost of capital. In fact, these issues are symptoms of a larger problem: the operation of the entire capital investment system. The system includes shareholders, lenders, investment managers, corporate directors, managers, and employees, all of whom make investment choices in a context determined by government regulations and prevailing management practices. The American system creates a divergence of interests among shareholders, corporations, and their managers that impedes the flow of capital to those corporate investments that offer the greatest payoffs. Just as significant, it fails to align the interests of individual investors and corporations with those of the economy and the nation as a whole.

The U.S. system for allocating investment capital has many strengths: efficiency, flexibility, responsiveness, and high rates of corporate profitability. It does not, however, direct capital effectively within the economy to those companies that can deploy it most productively and within companies to the most productive investment projects. As a result, many American companies invest too little, particularly in those intangible assets and capabilities required for competitiveness—R&D, employee training and skills development, information systems, organizational development, and supplier relations. At the same time, many other companies waste capital on investments that have limited financial or social rewards—for example unrelated acquisitions.

The problems in the U.S. system are largely self-created. Through a long series of regulatory and other choices with unintended consequences, changes have occurred in areas such as the pattern of corporate ownership, the way investment choices are made, and the nature of internal capital allocation processes within companies. At the same time, the nature of competition has changed, placing a premium on investment in increasingly complex and intangible forms—the kinds of investment most penalized by the U.S. system.

Finally, the American economy has become far more exposed to global competition, making investment even more important and bringing a cross-section of U.S. companies into contact with companies based in nations with significantly different capital allocation systems. It is this comparison between the U.S. system and other nations' systems that points up the real danger of continuing current practices.

The U.S. system first and foremost advances the goals of shareholders interested in near-term appreciation of their shares—even at the expense of the long-term performance of American companies. It is flexible, capable of rapidly shifting resources among sectors—even if this is not the path to innovation, dynamism, and improved productivity. It helps the United States prosper in some industries because of the high rewards it offers—even as it pressures others toward under- or overinvestment in differing ways.

The systemic nature of the problem also suggests the need to question much of what constitutes the American system of management: its emphasis on autonomy and decentralization, its process of financial control and investment decision making, its heavy use of incentive compensation systems. Failure to change the system will simply ensure the continued competitive decline of key sectors in the U.S. economy.

Yet our analysis of the U.S. investment capital allocation system also reveals how much potential for competitive strength exists in the United States. The United States possesses an enormous pool of investment capital. The problem lies in how this capital is allocated—at what rates and into what kinds of investments. One consideration is whether there is over- or underinvestment. A second is whether an investment is complemented by associated investments—that is, whether there are linkages among different forms of investments. For example, a physical asset such as a new factory may not reach its potential level of productivity unless the company makes parallel investments in intangible assets such as employee training and product redesign. A third consideration is whether private investments also create benefits for society through spillovers or externalities. For example, a company that invests in upgrading its employees and suppliers not only enhances its own competitiveness but also creates better trained workers and stronger suppliers that may allow it to pursue entirely new strategies in the future. Nations that encourage appropriate investment across a wide variety of forms and create these social benefits can leverage their pool of capital to build a strong and competitive national economy.

Meaningful change will be difficult because the American investment problem is far more complex than the conventional wisdom suggests. Many proposals to solve America's investment problem focus on only one aspect of the system, and they ignore the critical connections that tie the system together. To work, reform must address all aspects of the American system, and address them all at once. Policymakers, institutional investors, and corporate managers must all play a role in creating systemwide change.

Evidence of an American Investment Problem

For more than a decade, anecdotal evidence from managers and academics has suggested that American companies have invested at a lower rate and with a shorter time horizon than German or Japanese competitors. There are a variety of measures of the comparative rates, patterns, and outcomes of U.S. investments and the behavior of U.S. investors that support and expand that earlier view. Among them are the following:

- The competitive position of important U.S. industries has declined relative to those of other nations, notably Japan and Germany.

- Aggregate investment in property, plant and equipment, and intangible assets, such as civilian R&D and corporate training, is lower in the United States than in Japan and Germany.

- Leading American companies in many manufacturing industries such as construction equipment, computers, and tires are out-invested by their Japanese counterparts.

- American companies appear to invest at a lower rate than both Japanese and German companies in nontraditional forms such as human resource development, relationships with suppliers, and startup losses to enter foreign markets.

- R&D portfolios of American companies include a smaller share of long-term projects than those of European and Japanese companies.

- Hurdle rates used by U.S. companies to evaluate investment projects appear to be higher than estimates of the cost of capital.

- U.S. CEOs believe their companies have shorter investment horizons than their international competitors and that market pressures have reduced long-term investment. Foreign CEOs agree.

- The average holding period of stocks has declined from more than seven years in 1960 to about two years today.

- Long-term growth has declined as an influence on U.S. stock prices.

- Many recent U.S. policy proposals such as government funding of specific industries, R&D consortia, and joint production ventures implicitly reflect a private investment problem.

These findings present a broadly consistent picture of lagging American investment. But interestingly, the research has turned up some important complexities that derail simplistic explanations of America's reduced investment levels and shorter time horizon. For example:

- The American investment problem varies by industry and even by company. A convincing explanation—and worthwhile remedies— must address these differences.

- The United States does well in funding emerging industries and high-risk startup companies that require investments of five years or more. How does a low-investing, short-horizon nation achieve such a performance?

- The average profitability of U.S. industry is higher than that in Japan and Germany, yet American shareholders have consistently achieved no better or lower returns than Japanese (and recently German) shareholders. There is thus no simple connection between average corporate returns on investment and long-term shareholder returns, as much conventional wisdom about shareholder value seems to suggest.

- U.S. industry has overinvested in some forms, such as acquisitions. How does this overinvestment square with lower average rates of investment and underinvestment in crucial forms such as intangible assets?

• There is persuasive evidence that some American companies systematically overinvest—this is documented by studies of the gains achieved from takeovers. Why is it that some companies underinvest while other companies apparently invest too much?

• The United States has the most efficient capital markets of any nation and highly sophisticated investors. How can such efficient capital markets be guilty of producing apparently suboptimal investment behavior?

• The investment problem seems to be more significant today than it was several decades ago. What accounts for this worsening situation?

Explaining these paradoxes and the differences in investment behavior across industries, companies, and forms of investment is essential to gaining a complete understanding of the American investment problem.

The Determinants of Investment

The determinants of investment can be grouped into three broad categories: the macroeconomic environment; the allocation mechanisms by which capital moves from its holders to investment projects; and the conditions surrounding specific investment projects themselves (see Figure 13.1).

The macroeconomic environment establishes the context in which investment by all companies in a nation takes place. A stable and growing economy tends to encourage investment, reassuring investors that returns will persist over the long term. In the United States, high federal budget deficits, low national savings rates, sporadic and unpredictable changes in tax policy, and a consumption-oriented tax code have dampened public and private investment over the past two decades.

Capital allocation mechanisms determine how the available pool of capital in a nation is distributed among industries, companies, and forms

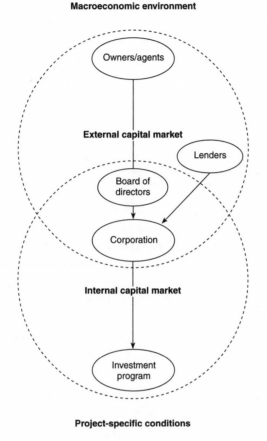

Figure 13.1   Determinants of Investment

of investment. They operate through two distinct but related markets: the external capital market through which holders of equity and debt provide capital to particular companies; and the internal capital market in which companies allocate the internally and externally generated funds at their disposal to particular investment programs. The Harvard Business School Council on Competitiveness research has focused on the operation and linkages between these dual markets and their effects on investment behavior.

Finally, some projects will yield greater payoffs than others, depending on the nature of the industry, the competitive position of the company, and the nation or region in which the investment is made. As my previous research in *The Competitive Advantage of Nations* has indicated, the capacity to invest and innovate depends on the presence of specialized skills, technology, and infrastructure; sophisticated and demanding local customers; capable local suppliers; competitive local companies in closely related industries; and a local environment that encourages vigorous competition.

The External Capital Market

Investment behavior in the external capital market is shaped by four attributes (see Figure 13.2). First is the pattern of share ownership and agency relationships—the identity of the owners, the extent of their representation by agents such as pension funds and money managers, and the size of the stakes they hold in companies. Second are owners' and agents' goals, which define the outcomes they seek to achieve through their investment choices. Goals are affected by a number of factors, including whether owners can hold debt and equity jointly and whether there is a principal-agent relationship. Third are the approaches and types of information used by owners and agents to measure and value companies. Fourth are the ways in which owners and agents can influence management behavior in the companies whose shares they own. These four attributes of the external capital market are all interrelated, and over time they will become mutually consistent.

Although exceptions may exist, each nation is characterized by a consistent system of influences that affect the majority of investors and corporations. The predominant configuration of the external capital market in the United States is strikingly different from that in Japan and Germany.

In the case of the United States, the attributes combine to create a system distinguished by fluid capital: funds supplied by external capital providers move rapidly from company to company, usually based on perceptions of opportunities for near-term appreciation. In the United States, publicly traded companies increasingly rely on a transient ownership base comprised of institutional investors, such as pension funds, mutual funds, or other money managers, who act as agents for individual

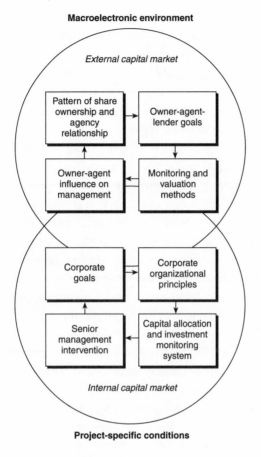

Macroelectronic environment

External capital market

Internal capital market

Project-specific conditions

Figure 13.2   Determinants of Investment Behavior

investors. In 1950, such owners accounted for 8 percent of total equity; by 1990, the figure had reached 60 percent.

These institutional agents hold highly diversified portfolios with small stakes in many—perhaps hundreds—of companies. For example, in 1990 the California Public Employees Retirement System (CalPERS) reportedly held stock in more than 2,000 U.S. companies; its single largest holding was 0.71 percent of a company's equity. This fragmented pattern of share ownership is due in part to legal constraints on concentrated ownership, fiduciary requirements that encourage extensive diversification, and investors' strong desire for liquidity.

The goals of American institutional investors are purely financial and are focused on quarterly or annual appreciation of their investment portfolio compared with stock indices. Because managers are measured on their short-term performance, their investment goals understandably focus on the near-term appreciation of shares. Mutual funds and actively managed pension funds—which represent 80 percent of pension assets—hold their shares, on average, for only 1.9 years.

Because of their fragmented stakes in so many companies, short holding periods, and lack of access to proprietary information through disclosure or board membership, institutional investors tend to base their investment choices on limited information that is oriented toward predicting near-term stock price movements. The system drives them to focus on easily measurable company attributes, such as current earnings or patent approvals, as proxies of a company's value on which to base market timing choices. The value proxies used vary among different classes of companies and can lead to underinvestment in some industries or forms of investment while allowing overinvestment in others. Given the difficulty of outperforming the market with this approach, some institutions have moved to invest as much as 70 percent to 80 percent of their equity holdings in index funds. This method of investing capital involves no company-specific information at all.

Finally, in the American system, institutional agents do not sit on corporate boards, despite their large aggregate holdings. As a consequence, they have virtually no direct influence on management behavior. Indeed, with small stakes in the company and an average holding period of two years or less, institutional agents are not viewed by management as having a legitimate right to serious attention.

The Japanese and German systems are markedly different. Overall, Japan and Germany have systems defined by dedicated capital. The dominant owners are principals rather than agents; they hold significant stakes, rather than small, fragmented positions. These owners are virtually permanent; they seek long-term appreciation of their shares, which they hold in perpetuity. Unlike the U.S. system, in which the goals are driven solely by the financial transaction, the goals in these systems are driven by relationships. Suppliers and customers own stakes in each other, not to profit from the share ownership itself but to cement their business relationship. (See Figure 13.3.)

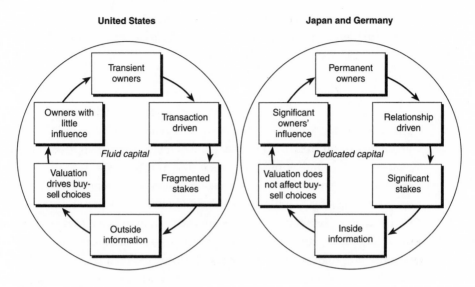

United States

Japan and Germany

Figure 13.3 External Market Overview

The pattern of ownership and the goals of owners directly affect monitoring and valuation approaches. Since owners hold significant shares for long periods of time, they have both the incentive and the ability to engage in extensive and ongoing information gathering about the companies they own. And unlike the American system, principal Japanese and German owners are driven not by the need to make quick decisions on buying or selling stock for profit-taking but by the desire to assess the ongoing prospects of the company. They therefore command the respect of management, have access to inside information concerning the company, and, particularly in Germany, can exert considerable influence on management behavior.

Interestingly, while the permanent Japanese and German owners hold their company shares for long periods of time, the nonpermanent owners in these countries arc prone to high-velocity stock churning, turning their shares over more frequently than owners do in the United States, and basing their investment decisions on even less information. While roughly 70 percent of Japanese stock is held for the long term, the remaining 30 percent is traded at such a rapid frequency that the average rate of trading in Japan is similar to the rate of trading in the United

States. Yet in both Japan and Germany, share prices and pressure from nonpermanent owners and agents have virtually no direct or indirect influence on management decisions.

The Internal Capital Market

The internal capital market, the system by which corporations allocate available capital from both internal and external sources to investment projects within and across business units, mirrors the external capital market. The four attributes that shape investment behavior in the internal capital market parallel those that shape the external market (see Figure 13.2). These four attributes are the particular goals that corporations set; the organizational principles that govern the relationship between senior management and units; the information and methods used to value and monitor internal investment options; and the nature of interventions by senior managers into investment projects.

An important aspect is highly imperfect information about future prospects and information asymmetries between capital holders—top managers—and those overseeing specific investment opportunities—business unit or functional managers. How a company organizes and manages its operations will affect the information that is available and the investments made by the company.

The U.S. internal market system is structured to maximize measurable investment returns. It is organized to stress financial returns, to motivate managers to achieve financial targets, to raise accountability for unit financial, and to base decision making and investment allocation heavily on financial criteria.

In the U.S. system, corporate goals center on earning high returns on investment and maximizing current stock prices. Management exercises the dominant influence on corporate goals, interpreting signals about desired behavior from the external capital market, influenced by compensation based on current accounting profits or unrestricted stock options that heighten stock price sensitivity.

Boards, which have come to be dominated by outside directors with no other links to the company, exert only limited influence on corporate goals. The presence of knowledgeable major owners, bankers, customers, and suppliers on corporate boards has diminished. An estimated 74 percent of the directors of the largest U.S. corporations are now outsiders, and 80 percent are CEOs of other companies. The move to outside directors arose out of calls for greater board objectivity. But the cost of objectivity has been directors who lack ties to the company and whose own companies are in unrelated businesses. As a consequence, they often lack the time or ability to absorb the vast amounts of information required to understand a company's internal operations. Moreover, most directors have limited stakes in the companies they oversee. While the median aggregate holdings of the board account for an estimated 3.6 percent of equity, many directors have no shares at all or only nominal holdings.

In terms of the organizational principles, the structure of American companies has undergone a significant change over the past two decades, with a profound impact on the internal capital market. Many American companies have embraced a form of decentralization that involves highly autonomous business units and limited information flows both vertically and horizontally. As a consequence, top management has become more distanced from the details of the business. Senior managers have little knowledge or experience in many of the company's businesses and often lack the technical background and experience to understand the substance of products or processes—partly because such knowledge is unnecessary in the typical decision-making process. Understandably, decision making in this system involves comparatively limited dialogue among functions or business units. Extensive diversification by American companies into unrelated areas has accentuated these tendencies and has further impeded the flow of information throughout the organization.

Both as a cause and an effect, capital budgeting in the U.S. system takes place largely through "by the numbers" exercises that require unit or functional managers to justify investment projects quantitatively. The system rarely treats investments such as R&D, advertising, or market entry as investments; rather they are negotiated as part of the annual budgeting process, which is primarily driven by a concern for current profitability. Intangible investments such as cross-functional training for workers may not even be tracked in the financial system—and thus may be sacrificed in the name of profitability.

Senior managers intervene infrequently, exerting central control through strict financial budgeting and control systems that focus on the unit's performance. Investment projects are placed on accelerated schedules under tight budgets, and senior managers step in only when financial measures indicate that a project is failing.

Both the Japanese and German systems are profoundly different from the American system. For both, the predominant aim is to secure the position of the corporation and ensure the company's continuity. Information flow is far more extensive, and financial criteria play less of a determining role in investment decisions than in the United States. (See Figure 13.4.)

In both systems the perpetuation of the enterprise is the dominant goal. In Japan, this goal is reinforced by the fact that most directors are members of management; moreover, lifetime or permanent employment is the norm in significant-sized companies. In Germany, the supervisory board consists of representatives of banks and other significant owners, and in large companies, 50 percent of the board comprises representatives of employees. All major constituencies thus influence corporate goals. As far as top managers' performance incentives are concerned, in both Germany and Japan, current earnings or share prices play only a modest role in promotion or compensation.

Companies practice a form of decentralization that involves much greater information flow among multiple units in the company as well

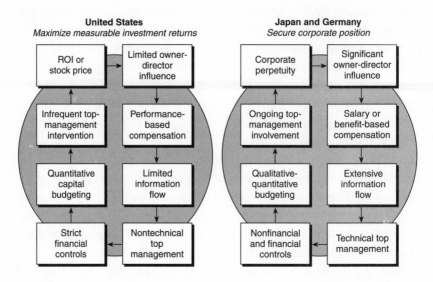

Figure 13.4 Internal Market Overview

as with suppliers and customers. Japanese and German managers tend to have engineering or technical backgrounds, spend their careers with one company, advance through tenure in one or a few units, and possess a deep knowledge of the company's important businesses. Top managers get involved in all important decisions, which are usually made after extensive face-to-face consultation and discussions aimed at building consensus. This is both an effect and a cause of the fact that companies in Japan and Germany tend to be less diversified than U.S. companies; where diversification occurs, it tends to be into closely related businesses.

Financial control and capital budgeting are part of the management process—but technical considerations and a company's desire to ensure its long-term position in the industry drive investments. German companies are particularly oriented to attaining technical leadership; Japanese companies especially value market share, new product development, technological position, and participation in businesses and technologies that will he critical in the next decade.

In comparing the U.S., Japanese, and German systems, important differences in management practices emerge. For example, American managerial innovations have resulted in less face-to-face consultation, information flow, and direct management involvement in investment choices—all in the name of responsiveness and efficiency. Many of these innovations were the American solution to the problems of size and diversity that arose in the diversification boom of the 1960s and preceded the major changes that have occurred in the external capital market.

In contrast, Japanese innovations in management, such as just-in-time manufacturing, total quality management, and greater cross-functional coordination, have resulted in more vertical and horizontal information flow and involvement by management in decisions. This comes at the expense of efficiency in the short run—but often results in greater effectiveness and efficiency over time, as knowledge and capabilities accumulate.

The extensive flow of information is perhaps the most potent strength of the Japanese and German systems. Ironically, the U.S. system, designed to boost management responsiveness to the marketplace, actually limits and constrains managers in responding effectively by limiting the information used in decisions, working against crucial forms of investment, and all but blocking the achievement of cross-unit synergies.

Comparative Systems of Capital Allocation

The external and internal capital allocation markets are linked; together they combine to form a self-reinforcing national system for allocating investment capital. The way companies allocate capital internally is influenced by their perceptions of how equity holders and lenders value companies. Conversely, the perceptions of owners and agents about how companies are managed and how they allocate their funds internally will influence the way in which investors value companies and the way in which they attempt to affect management behavior. The use of stock options in management compensation creates a direct link between stock market valuation and management behavior.

Overall, the nature of the American system of capital allocation creates tendencies and biases in investment behavior that differ greatly from those in Japan and Germany. (See Figure 13.5.) The American system:

- Is less supportive of investment overall because of its sensitivity to current returns for many established companies combined with corporate goals that stress current stock price over long-term corporate value. This explains why the average level of investment in American industry lags that in both Japan and Germany.

- Favors those forms of investment for which returns are most readily measurable—reflecting the importance of financial returns and the valuation methods used by investors and managers. This explains why the United States underinvests, on average, in intangible assets, where returns are more difficult to measure.

- Is prone to underinvest in some forms and, simultaneously, to overinvest in others. The U.S. system favors acquisitions, which involve assets that can be easily valued, over internal development projects that are more difficult to value and constitute a drag on current earnings. The greater overall rate of acquisitions in the United States is consistent with these differences.

United States

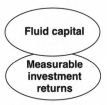

Japan and Germany

+ Quick reallocation of resources.
+ Able to capture emerging opportunities.
+ Higher private returns.
+ Pluralistic, fairer and better informed public equity markets.

− Tendency to underinvest, especially in intangibles.
− Encourages unrelated acquisitions.
− Overinvestment by profitable mature companies with few attractive investment opportunities.
− Reliance on costly takeovers as the principal form of management discipline.

+ Aggressive investment to boost productivity in existing businesses.
+ Internal diversification into closely related fields.
+ Higher social returns because externalities are better internalized.

− Tendency to overinvest.
− Slower to enter emerging fields, especially via startups.
− Inefficiencies within corporations caused by lack of individual incentives.
− Slower and more difficult redeployment of capital out of genuinely unattractive businesses.
− Public equity markets are less developed and less informed.

Figure 13.5   Comparative National Investment Systems

• Encourages investment in some sectors while limiting it in others. It is at its best with companies in obviously high-technology or emerging industries, especially those with rapid growth and high perceived upside potential. The American system also supports investment in turnarounds or other situations of clear discontinuity. In these cases, investors recognize that current earnings are irrelevant and seek other value proxies such as patents, new product announcements, research pipelines, and growth of new service locations that are more supportive of investment. This explains why the United States invests more than its competitors in some industries but less in others, why it performs well in funding emerging companies, and why it often awards high stock prices to turnarounds with current losses.

• Allows some types of companies to overinvest. For example, case studies of takeovers demonstrate a tendency by managers to continue investing (and to continue accumulating cash) as long as current earnings are satisfactory or until the company's situation so clearly deteriorates that it changes hands. This explains why some companies waste resources while American industry as a whole lags in investment.

It is important to note that there are companies and owners in the United States who operate differently from the predominant national system—who have overcome the disadvantages of the American system and achieve superior results. Examples of these are companies that have permanent and active family ownership, such as Cargill, Hallmark, Hewlett-Packard, Motorola, and others, which seem to enjoy competitive advantages in investing.

For example, two of Motorola's most important businesses, semiconductors and cellular telephones, were almost canceled in their early stages because they did not generate clearly measurable financial returns. Robert Galvin, a member of the founding family of Motorola and the company's chief executive officer, intervened in both cases and continued the investments. In the semiconductor situation, Galvin overrode the decision of his board of directors. Today semiconductors and cellular telephones form the foundation for a large part of Motorola's business, generating substantial financial returns for its shareholders.

Investors such as Warren Buffett's Berkshire Hathaway have succeeded by, in effect, becoming permanent owners of acquired companies, supporting capable managements and concentrating on building the company. Overall, however, the U.S. system as it applies to the great majority of American owners, investors, managers, directors, and employees works at cross-purposes to investment decisions that will produce competitive companies and a strong national economy.

Trade-Offs Among Systems

While the U.S. system has significant disadvantages, it would be incorrect to conclude that it lacks any advantages or that the systems of Japan and Germany are ideal. Each national system necessarily involves trade-offs; thus while the U.S. system needs reform, it also embodies important strengths that should be preserved.

The U.S. system, for example, is good at reallocating capital among sectors, funding emerging fields, and achieving high private returns each period. These benefits, of course, come at a price. The responsiveness and flexibility of the system are achieved at the expense of failing to invest enough to secure competitive positions in existing businesses, investing in the wrong forms, and overinvesting in some circumstances.

The Japanese and German systems also have strengths and weaknesses. These systems encourage continued, aggressive investment to upgrade capabilities and increase productivity in existing businesses. They also encourage internal diversification into related fields, building upon and extending corporate capabilities. These qualities, however, also exact a cost in Japan and Germany. For example, these systems create their own tendency to overinvest in capacity, to proliferate products, and to maintain unprofitable businesses indefinitely in the name of corporate perpetuity. They also exhibit a slower tendency to redeploy capital out of genuinely weak businesses and an inability to enter emerging fields rapidly, particularly through startups. Managers generally have fewer performance incentives, and companies have a harder time dismissing poor performers.

In general, the U.S. system is geared to optimize short-term private returns; the Japanese and German systems optimize long-term private and social returns. By focusing on long-term corporate position and creating an ownership structure and government process that incorporate the interests of employees, suppliers, customers, and the local community, the Japanese and German systems better capture the social benefits that private investment can create.

There is some evidence that the national systems are converging—that Japan and Germany are moving toward a more American-like system. Japanese banks may be forced to liquidate some of their equity holdings to maintain adequate cash balances; in Germany, there are proposals to limit bank ownership of equity. Yet these changes are modest—if Japanese or German owners are forced to sell some of their equity holdings, they will first sell their nonpermanent shares that are actively traded and have little influence on corporate behavior. Any major change in Japan and Germany would represent a substantial threat to those nations' economies due to their relatively uninformed traded capital markets.

Changes are also occurring in the United States, as institutional investors have discussions with management and some boards take a more active role in corporations. As in Japan and Germany, these changes appear isolated and sporadic, and the underlying causes of the U.S. investment problem remain the same. Neither small improvements in the United States nor hopes that Japan and Germany will change are substitutes for meaningful reform of the U.S. system. (See the insert "The Case of Cummins Engine: Increasing Private Ownership in a Publicly Traded Company.")

The Case of Cummins Engine: Increasing Private Ownership in a Publicly Traded Company
Rebecca Wayland

Cummins Engine Company, a $3.4 billion industrial corporation illustrates how a creative management team can structure a "privately owned, publicly traded" American company, approximating some of the advantages in the Japanese and German systems. In 1990, Cummins chairman and chief executive officer, Henry Schacht, concluded a deal that resulted in 40 percent of the company's stock being in the hands of patient investors, including three of its important business partners, company employees, and the founding Miller family. While it is still too early to evaluate the arrangement definitively, recent results indicate that Cummins' strategy may be paying off.

The Cummins story begins in 1919, when the company was founded in Columbus, Indiana. After World War II, Cummins enjoyed rapid growth into the 1970s. By 1979, Cummins Engine was the world leader in large, heavy diesel engines, with a 46 percent share of the market for over-the-road trucks. Following a succession of financings, the family stake in the company diminished; by 1980, 75 percent of the company's shares on the New York Stock Exchange were held by fragmented public investors.

In the 1980s, three factors combined to change the diesel engine market. First, the market's overall growth slowed significantly. Second, the emergence of energy efficiency and clean air as important policy issues put increased pressure on Cummins to invest in R&D—an expenditure that had already mushroomed from $22 million in 1971 to $68 million in 1980. Third, foreign competition intensified as Japanese producers prepared to enter the U.S. market armed with an estimated 30 percent cost advantage.

To respond to these challenges, Cummins embarked on a three-part strategy supported by an ambitious investment program. Cummins broadened its traditional product line within the heavy-duty markets and expanded into smaller diesel engines; entered the non-truck engine markets and developed its international operations; and initiated a full-scale restructuring program designed to reduce its costs by 30 percent, with prices scheduled to come down with costs. Cummins estimated the three measures would cost $1 billion; the company's total market value was $250 million.

By 1985, Cummins' strategy had yielded a new product line and a 5 percent reduction in costs. That year, however, Japanese producers entered the U.S. diesel market with products priced 30 percent below Cummins'. Faced with this challenge, Cummins chose to cut its prices to match the Japanese competitors, even though its costs had not yet fallen to that level—thereby sacrificing profits rather than market

share. As a consequence, Cummins suffered losses for the next three years, while reaching cost parity with the Japanese by the late 1980s.

In 1989, Cummins faced a different kind of challenge. After Hanson PLC, known for buying companies and dramatically cutting costs and investment, acquired a 9.8 percent stake in the company, Cummins' customers became alarmed at the threat of future cuts in Cummins' investment program. In July 1989, the Miller family took the unprecedented step of buying back the Hanson shares, ending the uncertainty. However, almost immediately, Hong Kong investor Industrial Equity Pacific began acquiring a large position in Cummins and demanded a seat on the board. Cummins initiated a lawsuit against IEP, which ultimately sold its stake at a loss in 1991.

These two threats convinced Schacht and other top Cummins managers that the interests of the current shareholders and the interests of customers, employees, the community, and managers were in danger of diverging—and that Cummins' strategy was potentially in jeopardy. To address this issue, Schacht sought to revise Cummins' ownership structure.

In 1990, Schacht concluded a deal with three important business partners. Ford bought a 10% stake, Tenneco-J.I. Case, a 10 percent stake, and Kubota, a 5 percent stake. In addition, Ford took an option for an additional 10 percent of Cummins' shares. Each owner paid a 25 percent premium above Cummins' then-current stock price of fifty-two dollars per share and agreed not to sell the stock for six years. The two largest shareholders, Ford and Tenneco, each received a seat on the Cummins board of directors. Financially, the deal targeted a 15 percent return on equity over a seven-year business cycle.

The Miller family retained a 4 percent stake in the company; employees held 10 percent. Together, these stable, long-term shareholders held 40 percent of the company's equity. Interestingly, other Cummins' customers applauded the move, even though it involved their competitors, citing the advantages of stable ownership and better products for all customers.

Under the new ownership structure, representatives of Ford and Tenneco participated on the board and actively supported the investment program. Senior managers worked without employment contracts, pre-venting management entrenchment and allowing strong board intervention. Accompanying the shift in ownership at Cummins were several reorganizations designed to streamline operations.

In 1990, Cummins continued to suffer reversals, this time a result of the recession and the onset of competition from a revitalized Detroit Diesel Corporation. In January 1991, Cummins stock hit a low of thirty-two dollars and fifty cents per share.

Indications, however, suggest that Cummins' nine-year effort is beginning to pay off. New product introductions have been successful; in the traditional heavy duty truck market, Cummins' market share appears to have stabilized and begun a recovery. The company's international off-highway business has continued to grow. The Japanese challengers have exited the major U.S. markets. During 1991, Cummins reached break-even and showed a profit for the first quarter of 1992. Finally, Cummins' stock rose to seventy-six dollars per share in June 1992, a 100 percent increase over its thirty-two dollar and fifty cent price of January 1991.

Proposals for Reform

Overall, the American system for capital allocation is not serving the American economy well. None of the participants in the system is satisfied, and each one blames the other for the problem. American managers complain that owners and agents do not have the company's long-term interests at heart and are seeking only high, short-term profits.

Institutional investors see managers as self-serving, overpaid, and under-performing when it comes to shareholder value. Owners are dismayed that many institutional investors underperform market averages. Small shareholders feel vulnerable and powerless. Employees fear a system that may cost them their jobs. Communities and their elected representatives worry about takeovers that threaten people's jobs, income, and the stability of the whole community.

Each group is behaving rationally—given the current circumstances. All are trapped in a system that ultimately serves the interests of no one. Each is pursuing its own narrow goals within the system—but the goals operate at cross-purposes.

Not surprisingly, there are calls for reform and regulation from all sides. Also, not surprisingly, many of the current proposals for reform would actually prove counterproductive, treating either symptoms or only a fragment of the problem and, in the process, further skewing the operation of the larger system.

One set of proposals, for example, seeks to slow down securities trading by taxing securities transactions or increasing margin require-ments. These proposals, however, merely increase the inefficiency of the equity markets without addressing the underlying problem—the lack of alignment between investors' and managers' goals. Another set of proposals seeks to reduce the rate of trading by limiting corporate disclosures—for example, doing away with quarterly financial reports. The most likely result of this reform, however, would probably be to make investors even less informed.

A third group of proposals seeks to rebalance the relative power of owners and managers, for instance, by strengthening the proxy system or increasing the number of outside directors. These proposals also fail to address the systemic nature of the problem. "Objective" outside directors, for example, are closely aligned with management, they are not as expert in the business, and they lack the detailed knowledge of the company needed for a truly objective evaluation of a business's prospects. Moreover, if the goals of owners, managers, and shareholders remain unaligned, strengthening one player at the expense of another will only tip the system in one particular direction.

A fourth set of proposals would increase the use of stock options in management compensation. Yet unless restrictions were placed on managers' ability to exercise those options, this step would only heighten current pressures toward maximizing current stock price.

Finally, there are proposals that address the investment problem indirectly while seeking to improve overall U.S. competitiveness; for example, calls for providing government subsidies to particular sectors, creating joint production ventures, and relaxing U.S. antitrust laws. These measures may allow companies to economize on investment—but they run the risk of blunting innovation and undermining competitiveness. They do not address the reasons why companies seem unable to make the investments needed for competitiveness. The only real solution to the failure of the U.S. capital allocation system is to address the system as a "system."

Directions for Systemic Reform

The aim of reform should be to create a system in which managers will make investments that maximize the long-term value of their companies. The interests of capital providers must be aligned with those of the corporation so that investors seek out high-quality information that fosters more appropriate investment choices. CEOs and top managers must organize and manage their companies in ways that encourage investment in the forms that build competitiveness. And public policymakers must craft laws and regulations designed to align private returns and the public good. Policymakers should not create protective measures to shield companies from these pressures but can exert constructive pressures on companies and managers, provided they have appropriate goals and information.

In all of this, it is essential to remember that the United States is an internally consistent system with many component parts. Reform should therefore come through a series of changes, ideally all at once. In addition, appropriate reform will require that each important constituency in the system give up some of its perceived benefits. For example, institutions should not expect to gain greater influence over management without giving up some of their current trading flexibility; management should not expect informed and committed owners without giving them a real voice in decisions.

Reform is needed in five broad areas:

1. Improve the macroeconomic environment; enlarging the pool of capital and increasing the stability of the environment will reduce risk premiums and lower the cost of capital. Public and private sector saving should be increased and a more stable macroeconomic environment created to encourage a stronger foundation for investment.

2. Expand true ownership throughout the system; the current concept of ownership in the U.S. system is too limited, involving just capital, and ownership is largely restricted to outside shareholders. Outside owners should be encouraged to hold larger stakes and to take a more active and constructive role in companies. Directors, managers, employees, and even customers and suppliers should all hold positions as important corporate owners.

3. Align the goals of capital providers, corporations, directors, managers, employees, customers, suppliers, and society. It is possible to create a system of incentives and to alter the rules in a way that helps align the goals of all these constituencies, which share an inherent long-term commonality of interest.

4. Improve the information used in decision making; even if goals are better aligned, the quality of information used to allocate capital throughout the system will affect investment choices. This means greater access to information that better reflects true corporate performance and more use of qualitative assessments of a company's performance and capabilities.

5. Foster more productive modes of interaction and influence among capital providers, corporations, and business units.

Accomplishing these reforms will require changes on the part of government, institutional investors, directors, and managers. (See the insert "The Case of Thermo Electron Corporation.")

Implications for Public Policy

Government, through policies, laws, and regulations, plays a decisive role in creating a nation's system for allocating investment capital. The current U.S. system reflects explicit regulatory choices, most of which

The Case of Thermo Electron Corporation
Rebecca Wayland

Thermo Electron Corporation, a $676 million company with products in a variety of high-technology fields, illustrates how a large company can structure itself within the U.S. capital allocation system to overcome the market's pressure toward underinvestment and to create opportunities for smaller, riskier, high-growth divisions.

Since its founding by George Hatsopoulos in 1959, Thermo Electron has grown from a startup focusing on high-technology capital equipment to a *Fortune* "500" company with products and research operations in the environmental, energy, metals processing, and biomedical fields. As Thermo Electron increased its portfolio of high-technology activities, its image in the capital markets became that of a large, mature company rather than an entrepreneurial venture. The startup losses required to develop and commercialize new technologies drained corporate earnings while the growth of emerging divisions was often lost in the company's consolidated financial results. Hatsopoulos, deeply concerned about the high effective cost of equity capital in the United States, set out to devise a way to finance the expansion of Thermo Electron that minimized the cost of funds and motivated employees. In 1983, he began

the practice of issuing minority stakes in promising high-technology divisions to the public.

One example of how the practice works—and why it is important—is the spin-off Thermo Cardiosystems, Inc. (TCI), which is currently commercializing its research on Heart-Mate, implantable cardiac-assist devices (called "ventricular assist devices" or VADs) that could ultimately offer an alternative to heart transplants. The initial research on HeartMate lasted twenty-two years and cost a total of $50 million, with grants from the National Institutes of Health providing the funding. The research was conducted at Thermo Electron and later at Thermedics, a division that was one of Hatsopoulos's early partial spin-offs. When the product reached the commercialization stage in 1988, the grant began to diminish substantially. Initial product tests for HeartMate had been promising. However, it would take at least another seven years of investment to complete the regulatory process, build manufacturing facilities, and develop the market. This need for continued investment threatened to drag down the earnings of the parent.

In 1988, the company created Thermo Cardiosystems, Inc. and

sold a 40 percent stake on the American Stock Exchange. The partial spin-off shifted TCI's ownership structure from a fragmented group of Thermo Electron and Thermedics investors to a structure in which Thermedics-Thermo Electron owned 60 percent, and a number of other investors, who were specifically interested in the long-term development of the heart technology, owned the balance. The partial spin-off also allowed TCI to raise $14.5 million in new equity at a far lower cost than its parent. TCI managers and employees received options in TCI stock, undiluted by the performance of the larger corporation.

As the controlling investor in TCI, Thermo Electron remained actively involved in its operations. Thermo Electron top managers were active members of TCI's board of directors (seven of whom were insiders), reviewed its five-year plan and quarterly financial results (often benchmarking them against other divisions), met with managers each month, and engaged in frequent brainstorming sessions to resolve divisional problems. Employees from the parent corporation's research department and from other divisions shared specialized expertise in medical-related areas and in the process of making the transition from research to manufacturing and sales. Top managers' compensation plans included options in the stock of other Thermo Electron companies to encourage this cooperation. The parent also provided cost-effective and sophisticated administrative services that TCI could not support independently.

Since 1989, TCI has continued its investment in HeartMate, receiving Food and Drug Administration approval for clinical trials, implanting the VAD in over eighty patients worldwide, and establishing sixteen FDA-approved test centers in the United States and four sites overseas. In the marketplace, TCI has benefitted from the credibility with hospitals and customers in the medical field established by other Thermo Electron products. Although the commercialization process is still underway, TCI managers believe that the partial sale strategy created by George Hatsopoulos has already been instrumental in supporting the investment and other activities needed to bring HeartMate to the medical market.

emerged in the 1930s to deal with abuses in the financial markets at that time. Yet the cumulative effects of regulation have had unintended consequences for U.S. corporations; these consequences have never been carefully examined.

The following reforms rest on principles that differ markedly from those that have defined the regulatory framework of the traditional U.S.

system. It is possible to modify incentives and eliminate unneeded regulatory guidelines to encourage more competitive investment behavior and, at the same time, avoid abuses. For example, current regulations limit the size of ownership stakes to prevent abuses by large owners. A better approach would be to broaden corporate ownership and align the goals of capital providers, corporations, managers, employees, and society. Through this approach, capital providers would become knowledgeable and constructive participants rather than adversaries.

- *Remove restrictions on investor share ownership; encourage long-term employee ownership; lower tax barriers to holding significant private ownership stakes.* It is essential to modify the structure of corporate ownership. The regulations and tax policies that artificially restrict the ability of investors to hold significant corporate stakes should be reexamined. Ownership by employees is desirable, provided that employee owners are long term rather than transient. Under this provision, the market would continue to have the strength of a wide investor base, while gaining the benefit of owners with larger stakes in particular companies. The large number of substantial U.S. institutional investors will prevent any undue concentration of economic power.

- *Create a long-term equity investment incentive.* The single most powerful tool for modifying the goals of owners and agents is a significant incentive for making long-term investments in corporate equity. This proposal aims to change the concept of ownership and the approach to valuing companies and, at the same time, to encourage the broad form of investment where the social benefits are the greatest.

Such an incentive would be carefully designed and narrowly drawn. It would apply only to investments in corporate equity of operating companies, and it would not apply to capital gains from investments in nonoperating companies holding real estate or other financial assets. Capital gains from bond appreciation, real estate appreciation, collectibles, and other sources would also be excluded. The incentive would require a minimum five-year holding period, with greater incentives provided for even longer holdings. It would be applied prospectively, limited to new investments and new gains.

The enactment of such an incentive would lead to changes throughout the entire system by changing the goals of owners and agents. Owners would begin to favor agents who deliver a greater proportion of income in the form of long-term equity gains and to penalize those who realize only short-term gains from rapid trading. Institutional investors, in turn, would modify their monitoring and valuation approaches, seeking out companies with attractive prospects five or more years in the future. A further consequence would be the development and distribution of better information, detailing the investment programs of companies and their long-term prospects, including physical and intangible assets.

If the long-term equity incentive is to have its full impact, it should be extended to currently untaxed investors, such as pension funds that account for a substantial fraction of equity capital and trading. The most practical way to do this is to pass through an equity investment incentive to pension or annuity beneficiaries. Beneficiaries would pay a rate of tax that varied depending on the source of their pension income. The effect of instituting such an incentive would be to create pressures from pension beneficiaries and trustees on their investment managers to deliver a higher and higher proportion of income from long-term equity gains. It should also be noted that extending the long-term equity incentive to pension beneficiaries extends the tax benefit to the U.S. work force, not just to Americans with high incomes.

- *Eliminate restrictions on joint ownership of debt and equity.* Financial institutions should be allowed to hold equity for investment purposes in companies to which they have provided debt financing. Debt holders who also hold equity have greater incentive to invest in information and monitoring and to provide new debt financing for worthy projects.

- *Reduce the extent of subsidies for investment in real estate.* U.S. tax policy has led to a disproportionate investment in real estate compared with other forms of investment that create greater social returns. Future investment incentives should redress this imbalance, favoring R&D, corporate equity, and training, rather than real estate.

• *Modify accounting rules so that earnings better reflect corporate performance.* Because many of the most important forms of investment must be expensed under current accounting standards, accounting earnings are a flawed measure of true earnings. The accounting profession should create new standards for accounting for intangible assets such as R&D.

• *Expand public disclosure to reduce the cost of assessing true corporate value.* Disclosure should be extended to include areas such as a company's expenditures on training, its stock of patents, or the share of sales contributed by new products, information that provides important measures of long-term corporate value.

• *Allow disclosure of "insider" information to significant long-term owners, under rules that bar trading on it.* A small group of institutions and other owners who have held a significant ownership stake for a qualifying period—1 percent or more for one year or more—should have access to more complete information about company prospects than is required to be disclosed publicly, provided they do not disclose the information to third parties. Greater disclosure would open up an avenue for significant long-term owners to have a more informed dialogue with management, and it would support more informed valuation based on long-term prospects.

• *Loosen restrictions on institutional board membership.* A direct role for significant owners on boards of directors will make boards more representative of long-term owner interest—provided, that is, that the goals of owners and managers have been realigned.

• *Encourage board representation by significant customers, suppliers, financial advisers, employees, and community representatives.* The current trend in board membership has created boards populated by busy, underinformed CEOs. A far better approach would be to create a role on boards of directors for significant customers, suppliers, investment bankers, employees, and others linked closely to the company and with a direct interest in its long-term prosperity.

• *Codify long-term shareholder value rather than current stock price as the appropriate corporate goal.* Existing corporate law identifies long-term shareholder value as the appropriate corporate goal. In practice, however, short-term stock price may take precedence as managers or directors who clearly compromise short-term shareholder returns are often subject to lawsuits. To remedy this situation, long-term shareholder value should be identified as the explicit corporate goal. The burden of proof should shift so that managers must explain any decision that is not consistent with long-term shareholder value.

• *Extend tax preferences only to those stock options and stock purchase plans with restrictions on selling.* The use of unrestricted stock options and employee stock purchase plans fails to make managers and employees true owners because managers are prone to sell shares based on short-term stock price movements. To qualify for tax benefits, such plans should be restricted in terms of holding period and percentage of shares sold at any one time.

• *Provide investment incentives for R&D and training.* Making the existing R&D tax credit permanent and creating a parallel tax credit for training investments would help stimulate private investments that become valuable national assets.

Implications for Institutional Investors

The American system of capital allocation creates perverse outcomes for institutional investors, especially for pension funds. These institutions should be the ideal long-term investors. Instead, the American system produces the paradoxical situation in which many institutions are entrusted with funds for extremely long periods, yet they trade actively. Transaction costs mean that many institutions underperform the market. Institutions are at odds with management, whom they see as misapplying corporate resources, yet they feel powerless to do anything about it. And worst of all, institutions are trapped as crucial actors in a system that undermines the long-term earning power of the American companies on which they have ultimately to depend.

Even without public policy changes, action by institutions can change this system. First and foremost, institutions must understand why managements view them as adversaries. They must understand the subtle consequences of their monitoring and valuation practices on corporate investment behavior. And they must recognize that greater influence over management will require less flexibility, slower trading, and greater knowledge of and concern for company fundamentals. Here are some specific changes institutional investors can pursue:

- *Increase the size of stakes.* Increasing the size of stakes will help align the goals of investors and companies, improve the ability of investors to conduct in-depth research on the companies whose shares they hold, and send signals that institutions are serious owners who are interested in the long-term performance of the company.

- *Reduce turnover and transaction costs.* Institutional investors underperform the market largely because of the transaction costs associated with the high turnover of investments. Reducing stock turnover will improve the return that institutions provide to their clients.

- *Select companies more carefully based on fundamental earning power.* Companies with sustained growth potential and earning power will ultimately be rewarded with higher stock prices, even in the current system. The focus of valuation models should shift in this direction. To address information costs, institutions might also form syndicates in which one institution acts as the lead owner in the relationship.

- *Encourage changes in agent measurement and evaluation systems to reflect long-term investment performance.* A new bargain between owners and institutional agents should shift the measurement and reward system toward fees tied to annual or multiyear results and ongoing reporting of fully loaded transaction costs from trading.

- *Transform interactions with management to productive, advisory discussions.* Current interactions between institutional investors and managements are too often cat-and-mouse games played around guessing next period's earnings. What is needed instead are substantive discussions about the long-run competitive position of the company.

- *Create special funds to test these new approaches.* Institutions should create special funds earmarked for long-term investing in significant corporate stakes in exchange for greater influence over management. If necessary, new agreements with owners would be drafted, modifying the funds' fiduciary responsibilities.

- *Support systemic public policy changes.* By supporting the public policy reforms outlined above, institutional investors can help balance and integrate the American system.

Some institutions will resist these changes; they involve new skills, a new definition of investment success, and reductions in liquidity and flexibility. But institutional investors will realize big direct benefits—and benefit further by the creation of stronger, more competitive U.S. companies, on which their portfolios ultimately depend.

Implications for Corporations

Managers are not simply victims of the American system; they have helped create it. Managers have not only shaped the internal market through organizational and managerial practices, but they have also defined their relationship with the external market through such things as board composition, disclosure practices, and the nature of discussions with investors. American managers can play the leadership role in redefining the U.S. capital allocation system; they are the group best positioned to make changes in the current system and to benefit most from reform.

They also may have the most to change. Stated boldly, our research suggests the need to reexamine much of what constitutes the U.S. system of management, with its extreme approach to managing decentralization, its limited flow of information, its heavy use of certain types of incentive compensation systems, and its reliance on financial control and quantitative capital budgeting processes. This system, a post-World War II innovation, carries subtle costs for investment behavior, particularly investments in intangible and nontraditional forms. Some of the most significant changes that management can initiate are the following:

- *Seek long-term owners and give them a direct voice in governance.* The most basic weakness in the American system is transient ownership. However, managers seem to underestimate their ability to do anything about this fundamental problem. As a remedy, managers should seek to have a smaller number of long-term or nearly permanent owners, thus creating a hybrid structure of a "privately held" and publicly traded company. Having fewer long-term owners would alter virtually every facet of the owner-management relationship—including governance, information sharing, measurement, and valuation.

- *Refrain from erecting artificial antitakeover defenses that insulate management.* In the absence of pressure from owners and directors on managers for long-term performance, takeovers are a necessary form of oversight. There have been, however, some inappropriate takeovers, and most takeovers occur only after a prolonged period of corporate decline. The solution is not to erect antitakeover provisions. Rather, it is to reshape the American system so that takeovers are limited to those situations where they are an appropriate response to management's failure to build a long-term competitive position for the company.

- *See management buyouts as a second-best solution.* Management buyouts are only a second-best solution to the problems of the American system. Invariably, the controlling owner in management buyouts is a transaction-driven, financial owner who seeks to realize returns on the investment over a short period of time in order to distribute them to investors.

- *Nominate significant owners, customers, suppliers, employees, and community representatives to the board of directors.* Directors from these categories are likely to have the company's long-term interests at heart and to encourage management to make investments that will improve long-term competitive position.

- *Link incentive compensation to competitive position.* The incentive compensation systems now used in much of American business are counterproductive. The incentives are simply based on the wrong things. Bonuses based on current profits obviously undermine investment, and stock options increase managers' attention to short-term share prices, particularly if there are no restrictions on selling shares. Compensation systems need to move in the direction of linking pay more closely to long-term company prosperity and to actions that improve the company's competitive position.

• *Move away from unrelated diversification.* Unrelated or loosely related diversification only wastes capital and exacerbates the current management biases against long-term investment. The only way to build competitive companies is to concentrate on a few core fields and invest heavily in them to achieve a unique position.

• *Shift from fragmented to integrated organizational structures.* The decentralized, profit center-based management structure in many American companies must be overhauled. What is needed is a system that recognizes strategically distinct businesses as the proper unit of management but manages them differently. Senior managers at the corporate level must have a substantive understanding of the core technology and the industry. Top management must be involved directly and personally in all significant decisions, particularly investment decisions. There must be extensive consultation and coordination among related business units, with opportunities for the units to share functions and expertise. Such a system would shift measurement and control away from solely financial results, raise senior management confidence in understanding complex investment choices, and better capture complementarities among discrete investment options.

• *Transform financial control systems into position-based control systems.* A new philosophy of management control must be instituted, based as much on the company's extended balance sheet as on its income statement. A company's extended balance sheet measures the assets that constitute its competitive position. Included in such a measurement would be: a broader definition of assets, such as market share, customer satisfaction, and technological capabilities; a measurement of asset quality and productivity in addition to asset quantity; and relative instead of absolute measures, tracking the company performance against significant competitors.

• *Move to universal investment budgeting.* Conventional approaches to capital budgeting were never ideal for evaluating investment choices; they fail to deal with the changing nature of investment. A new system is needed to evaluate investment programs instead of just discrete projects; to treat all forms of investment in a unified manner; and to evaluate investments in two stages—first, determining the asset positions needed for competitiveness and second, evaluating exactly how to achieve those positions.

Toward a Superior American System

The recommendations outlined above are designed to attack the weaknesses of the American system systematically, while preserving the system's considerable strengths. These changes will align the goals of American shareholders, their agents, and American corporations; improve the information used in investment decisions; better capture the externalities in investment choices; evaluate management decisions on criteria more suitable for competitive performance; and make internal management processes more consistent with the true sources of competitive advantage.

If America can make progress on these fronts, it will not only reduce the disadvantages of the U.S. system but also produce a system that is superior to Japan's or Germany's. A reformed U.S. system would be characterized by long-term rather than permanent owners, well-informed rather than speculative traders, and flexible rather than lifetime employees. A reformed U.S. system would produce more careful monitoring of management and more pressure on poor performers than what exists in Japan or Germany. The result would be less wasted investment and less internal inefficiency. Finally, a reformed U.S. system, with its higher levels of disclosure and transparency, promises to be fairer to all shareholders than the Japanese or German systems.

But altering the American system will not be easy. There is a natural tendency to limit change to tinkering at the margins, yet systemic change will be necessary to make a real difference. All of the major constituencies will have to sacrifice some of their narrow self-interests in pursuit of a system that is better overall.

Nevertheless, today there is widespread dissatisfaction with the system as it exists and concern over the direction and performance of American companies in global competition. This suggests that systemic change may be possible. If real change were to occur, the benefits would certainly accrue to investors and companies. But what is more important, the benefits would yield improved long-term productivity growth in the United States, and thus greater prosperity for the entire American economy.

Index

About the Contributors

Michael E. Porter, one of the world's leading authorities on competitive strategy and international competitiveness, is the C. Roland Christensen Professor of Business Administration at the Harvard Business School. Professor Porter was appointed to President Reagan's Commission on Industrial Competitiveness in 1983 that triggered the competitiveness debate in America. He serves as an advisor to heads of state, governors, mayors, and CEOs throughout the world. The recipient of the Wells Prize in Economics, the Adam Smith Award, three McKinsey Awards, and honorary doctorates from the Stockholm School of Economics and six other universities, Porter is the author of fifteen books, among them *Competitive Strategy* (1980), *Competitive Advantage* (1985), and *The Competitive Advantage of Nations* (1990). He lives in Brookline, Massachusetts.

Gregory B. Brown is head of health care at Adams, Harkness & Hill, Inc., a Boston-based investment bank providing services to emerging growth companies. Previously, Dr. Brown spent five years at Vector Securities International. A Fellow of the American College of Surgeons, Dr. Brown practiced thoracic and vascular surgery and served as chairman of the surgery department at St. Elizabeth Hospital in Utica, New York. Dr. Brown also founded, and was the first president of, Central New York IPA, an IPA-model HMO. Dr. Brown received an A.B. from Yale University, earned his M.D. at SUNY Upstate Medical Center, and received an M.B.A. from Harvard Business School.

Kathryn Rudie Harrigan is the Henry R. Kravis Professor of Business Leadership at Columbia University and director of three NYSE and NASDAQ companies. She is the author of *Managing Maturing Businesses: Restructuring Declining Industries and Revitalizing Troubled Operations* (1988), *Managing for Joint Venture Success* (1986), and four scholarly monographs on strategic management. She is working on her seventh book, *Strategies for Synergy.*

Formerly a partner of The Boston Consulting Group, **Thomas Hout** resided in Tokyo, London, Seoul, and Boston during his 27-year career at BCG. He is the author of *Industrial Policy of Japan,* as well as of the best-selling business book *Competing Against Time,* written with George Stalk. In addition, he has authored four *Harvard Business Review* articles and numerous op-ed pieces to the *New York Times,* the *Wall Street Journal,* and the *Boston Globe.* Currently he serves on the boards of an electric automobile company, a mutual fund, and a software producer, and serves as an advisor to BCG.

An associate at the Institute for International Management Research (FIM) of the St. Gallen Graduate School of Economics in Switzerland, **Claas van der Linde**'s research and consulting focuses on international and regional competitiveness and competition, as well as issues of international management. He is the author of the book *Deutsche Wettbewerbsvorteile* (German Competitive Advantage) and author or co-author of numerous articles in professional publications. He holds an M.B.A. from the Columbia Business School in New York and a Ph.D. in business administration from the St. Gallen Graduate School of Economics.

During his career with Arthur Andersen & Co. from 1958 to 1986, **Victor E. Millar** earned an international reputation in the management of professional services firms. He was the first in the profession to forecast the long-term growth potential of the IT services industry and to understand the correlation between investments in intellectual capital and increased profitability. Millar currently serves as chairman of The Columbus Group LLC, a consolidation of professional services firms, as well as a member of the boards of several professional services firms.

Senior vice president of communications products at Lotus Development Corporation, **Eileen Rudden** is responsible for all aspects of development, marketing, and product management for Lotus's communications products. Ms. Rudden joined Lotus in 1986 and has served in a variety of management positions in development and marketing. A graduate of Brown University and the Harvard Business School, she previously worked as a manager at the Boston Consulting Group and as a director at Wang Laboratories.

Elizabeth Olmsted Teisberg is an associate professor at the Darden Graduate School of Business Administration, University of Virginia. Professor Teisberg's research and consulting focuses on the value of innovation and analysis of strategic opportunities in high technology and health care industries. She is co-author of *The Portable MBA* (1997) and the author of numerous articles in professional publications. Prior to joining Darden, she was a professor at the Harvard Business School for eight years. She holds an M.S. and Ph.D. in engineering from Stanford University.